Hesitancy and Experimentation in Enlightenment Spain and Spanish America

Published in memory of Ivy L. McClelland, a pioneer-scholar of Spain's eighteenth century, this volume of original essays contains, besides an Introduction to her career and internationally influential writings, three previously unpublished essays by McClelland and nine studies by other scholars, all of which are focused on elucidating the Enlightenment and its characteristic manifestations in the Hispanic world.

Among the Enlightenment writers and artists, works and genres, themes and issues discussed, are: Nicolás Moratín and epic poetry, Lillo's *The London Merchant* and English and French influences on eighteenth-century Spanish drama, José Marchena and literary historiography, oppositions and misunderstandings within Spanish society as reflected in *El sí de las niñas*, Goya and the visual arts, Quintana's *Pelayo* and historical tragedy, Enlightenment discourse, the Periodical Press, theatre as propaganda, the ideology and politics of Empire, the roots of revolt in late viceregal Quito, women's experience of Enlightenment in Spain, social and cultural difference in colonial Peru, ideological debate and uncertainty during the Age of Reason, eighteenth-century Spain on the nineteenth-century stage, and public opinion in Spain on the eve of the French, and European, Revolution.

First published as a Special Double Issue of the *Bulletin of Spanish Studies* (LXXXVI [November–December 2009], Nos 7–8), this book will be of value and stimulus to all scholars concerned to investigate and interpret the culture, theatre, ideology, society and politics of the Enlightenment in Spain, Europe and Spanish America.

Ann L. Mackenzie is Ivy McClelland Research Professor of Spanish at the University of Glasgow, UK.

Jeremy Robbins is Forbes Professor of Hispanic Studies at the University of Edinburgh, UK.

I0878405

Routledge
Taylor & Francis Group
LONDON AND NEW YORK

University of Glasgow

Hesitancy and Experimentation in Enlightenment Spain and Spanish America

Studies on Culture and Theatre in Memory of I. L. McClelland

Edited, with an Introduction, by
Ann L. Mackenzie and Jeremy Robbins

Routledge
Taylor & Francis Group
LONDON AND NEW YORK

University of Glasgow

First published 2011 by Routledge

2 Park Square, Milton Park, Abingdon, Oxfordshire OX14 4RN
711 Third Avenue, New York, NY 10017

Routledge is an imprint of the Taylor & Francis Group, an informa business

First issued in paperback 2018

This book edition is a reproduction of the *Bulletin of Spanish Studies*, LXXXVI (November–December 2009), double issue 7-8. The Publisher requests that citations of this book should state, also, the bibliographical details of the special issue on which this book is based

Typeset in NewCenturySchlbk by Datapage (India) Private Limited, Chennai, India

British Library Cataloguing in Publication Data
A catalogue record for this book is available from the British Library

ISBN 13: 978-0-415-60364-5 (hbk)
ISBN 13: 978-1-138-38299-2 (pbk)

Disclaimer
The publisher would like to make readers aware that the chapters in this book are referred to in the way they were termed in the special issue. The publisher accepts responsibility for any inconsistencies that may have arisen in the course of preparing this volume for print.

CONTENTS

LIST OF ILLUSTRATIONS

Photograph of Ivy McClelland receiving from the Vice-Chancellor, Professor (now Sir) Graeme Davies, a presentation-copy of *The Eighteenth Century in Spain. Essays in Honour of I. L. McClelland*, University of Liverpool, 22 April 1991.
Reproduced by courtesy of the Archives, University of Liverpool

Preface

> Her work is in the library of every university where Spanish is taken seriously. It is and has long been essential reading for anyone working in the eighteenth-century field. Her scholarship is superb, her mind razor-sharp and her writing crisp. She dwarfed all but two or three of the British Hispanists of her generation, which was **the** generation of giants in our field.
>
> (Donald L. Shaw, Brown-Forman Professor, University of Virginia)[1]

This volume issued in memory of Ivy McClelland, which also signals the recent hundredth anniversary of her birth, is the second *Festschrift* to appear in the *Bulletin*, to honour her contributions made to Hispanic Studies. A previous volume, titled *The Eighteenth Century in Spain. Essays in Honour of I. L. McClelland*, was presented to her on 22 April 1991 in Liverpool University, her *alma mater*, at a special luncheon hosted in the University's Staff House by its then Vice-Chancellor, Professor (now Sir) Graeme Davies.[2] Of the three speeches delivered on that day (Sir Graeme gave an address, and so did I), the final one, given by Ivy McClelland herself, was by far the most witty, touching and memorable. She spoke of her studies at Liverpool University and the debt she owed to E. Allison Peers, without whose support she could never have gone on to have an academic career in a British university, where in those days, before the Second World War, it was not the normal thing for 'a mere woman' to hold a post as a lecturer and researcher.

None of us present at that celebratory luncheon in 1991 could have imagined that Ivy McClelland, then nearly eighty-three, would live for fifteen more years and on into the twenty-first century. But her small, dignified person was driven by an indomitable spirit, and was sustained, too, for many decades, by good health—a blessing for which she was quietly grateful. Her longevity, however, is not the reason why the *Bulletin* has published this second *Festschrift*; nor is it why the Introduction to it, which, understandably,

1 Extract from his letter, dated 18 May 1989, addressed to Ann L. Mackenzie, *BHS*, Liverpool University, now kept in the Ivy McClelland Papers, Archives, University of Glasgow. Donald Shaw had worked alongside Ivy McClelland for seven years at the University of Glasgow (1957–1964).

2 *The Eighteenth Century in Spain. Essays in Honour of I. L. McClelland*, ed., with an introduction, by Ann L. Mackenzie, *BHS*, LXVIII:1 (1991); also published in a hardback book edition (Liverpool: Liverpool U. P., 1991), 246 pp.

takes the form of a 'Memoir', is an article in its length. What is celebrated here is the career of one of the most original and influential scholars, of either sex, from any country and in any period, to have investigated the eighteenth century in Spain.

Like many graduates in Hispanic Studies who went on from Glasgow University to careers as Hispanists, I was taught by Ivy McClelland. For more than forty years, I had, too, the benefit and privilege of her trusted friendship. So in 2002, when Ivy, aged ninety-four, finally gave up her flat in Glasgow's Kelvinside to enter a nearby residential care home, she handed over to me all her academic books, notes and other papers, leaving me free to do with them as I judged best. Characteristically, she told me: 'do not hesitate to throw out anything that is of no worth or little interest'. In fact, her books, notes and papers were, almost without exception, of considerable value to other scholars. So, with her agreement, nearly all her books, including a few, rare eighteenth-century editions, were gifted to Glasgow University Library, where they have significantly enhanced its holdings on eighteenth-century Spain and Europe. Her undergraduate and postgraduate lecture-notes, since she was a student of Allison Peers, will, logically, be housed at Liverpool University. All her other papers, including the typescripts of several lectures and articles hitherto unavailable to other Hispanists, some handwritten poems, and her still unpublished memoirs, are being kept at the University of Glasgow.

Her poems which, with her innate modesty, she described as 'Nonsense Rhymes', reveal her fondness for animals and the influence, above all, of Lewis Carroll. To test the abilities of her Honours students in the art and techniques of prose-translation into Spanish, she liked to choose passages from *Alice's Adventures in Wonderland* or *Through the Looking Glass*, which, as those of us she taught will recall, were the very devil to render. I remember how pleased she was with one Honours student's inspired Spanish translation (not mine, I'm sorry to say!) of Humpty Dumpty's name as 'Alfondo Redondo'.[3] Since they reveal both her humour and her humanity, it seemed appropriate to make her poems available here—in an Appendix to the Introduction. Her book-length memoirs, recording her experiences as tutor and warden to women students of *The University of Glasgow's Queen Margaret Hall c.1950–60*, deserve to be published separately, as a source of valuable insights to all those interested in Glasgow University as it was more than fifty years ago.[4]

3 In this connection, see, in the 'Introduction' (p. 16), my reference to the 'Good Luck' card which, on her retirement, her Final Honours class of 1973 designed and presented to her. Among the card's handwritten illustrations (reproduced below; p. 17) is a thumb-nail sketch of Humpty Dumpty titled 'Alfondo Redondo'.

4 Until a publisher is found, this work can be consulted in typescript (Archives, University of Glasgow).

Among her Hispanic-related papers are two lectures which, after her retirement, she had been invited to deliver to undergraduates in the Department of Hispanic Studies at Glasgow. One lecture, undated but evidently delivered to Honours students in the 1980s, concerns 'The Ingenuity of Golden-Age Drama', and, as is to be expected from the author of a key monograph on Tirsian drama,[5] contains many illuminating observations. Its Golden-Age subject-matter, however, means that it is unsuitable for publication here. The other lecture, which, as noted on the folder in which she kept it, was delivered 'for Dept, Mar. 1990', does deal with an appropriately eighteenth-century topic, namely 'Goya (1746–1828) and His Times', but its principal ideas are already available to scholars, in an expanded form, in the author's final monograph.[6]

Two other unpublished contributions, both of which were on eighteenth-century Spain, would certainly have been included here had they not proved to be, for different reasons, unobtainable. After sending to press her book for Twayne on Torres Villarroel (which she did in 1975), the author found herself obliged to shorten the text substantially so as to conform to the publisher's severe restrictions on length. She did so by removing entirely the chapter she had written on Torres' 'Polemical Tactics'.[7] Unfortunately, this unpublished chapter cannot now be located, and it is presumed lost.[8] One of the last essays she wrote, on 'La contribución que hizo Gaspar Zavala y Zamora al desarrollo del Ilustrismo español', completed in or around 1995, was intended to figure in a *Festschrift* in honour of Rinaldo Froldi to which she had been invited to contribute. In this piece—for I recall reading her typescript at the

5 See I. L. McClelland, *Tirso de Molina. Studies in Dramatic Realism*, Liverpool Studies in Spanish Literature 3 (Liverpool: Institute of Hispanic Studies, 1948).

6 See I. L. McClelland, *Ideological Hesitancy in Spain 1700–1750*, Publications of the *Bulletin of Hispanic Studies*, Textual Research and Criticism (Liverpool: Liverpool U. P., 1991).

7 See I. L. McClelland, *Diego de Torres Villarroel*, Twayne's World Authors Series 395 (Boston: Twayne Publishers, 1976). 'Polemical Tactics' had been intended to form Chapter 9 (the last chapter before her Conclusion, 'Final Curtain'. Letters from Janet W. Díaz, Hispanic Editor for Twayne's World Authors Series, commiserate with the author for having to make such a substantial reduction to her monograph: 'The first, and most difficult matter is length. [...] By my count [...] you have 6990 lines, or approximately 600 too many. [...] it involves almost 10% of your total [...]. I am sorry that this shortening is necessary, because it looks quite fascinating, and I am eager to read it, but my editing it now would only delay things for you in the long run, as they would refuse it in the main office because of the length' (14 August 1975); 'Your manuscript arrived today in good order, and I have checked it for the length. It seems to fit within the limits nicely now. I am sorry that the publishers' latest regulations made this necessary' (31 October 1975) (for this correspondence, see the Ivy McClelland Papers, Archives, University of Glasgow).

8 It appears likely, however, that, fifteen years later, she utilized at least some of the contents of this now lost chapter on Torres in 'The *Vulgo*-Conception of Scientific Evidence', which is Chapter 3 of *Ideological Hesitancy in Spain 1700–1750* (see especially pp. 58–69, 76–81).

time—she analysed several of Zavala's plays, to illustrate the ideological preoccupations that developed, with the Enlightenment, in Spain. The editors of the *Festschrift* for Professor Froldi **did** receive her contribution. Eight years, or more, were to elapse, however, before this *Festschrift* was actually published. In the long interim, several contributors had withdrawn their articles, and the editors came to believe—mistakenly, as it happened—that Ivy McClelland was among them. As a result, when in 2004 this *Festschrift* did finally appear, it did not contain her article.[9] Even more regrettably, in the delay and confusion, her typescript went astray, and it has proved impossible to find any copy among her papers.[10]

Happily, Ivy McClelland's surviving documents include three important studies on appropriately eighteenth-century topics. All three of these previously unavailable studies are published here, two of which—namely, '"Impugnador de preocupaciones": *El Correo de los Ciegos de Madrid* 1787 and Public Opinion in Spain on the Eve of European Revolution' and 'A Propaganda Play of 1808: F. Enciso Castrillón's *La defensa de Valencia y castigo de traidores*'—have been edited by me. Dr Fernando Huerta Viñas, of the Universidad Autónoma, Barcelona, a close friend of Ivy McClelland and formerly her colleague at Glasgow University, has kindly edited the third contribution: '*The London Merchant* y sus relaciones con la experimentación dramática en la España del siglo XVIII'.

Besides Ivy McClelland's articles, the present Volume includes essays contributed by invitation from widely-respected scholars nationally and internationally who have major research interests in the eighteenth century in Spain, and who have welcomed 'this opportunity to honor her influence on [their] own work'.[11] It is equally fitting, however, that, alongside these, more numerous, invited studies, there are several other articles that were accepted after having been submitted to the journal, and assessed, in the usual, unsolicited, way. These articles came in, as it happens, from several women Hispanists, of a younger generation than most of the invited authors. Their unrequested but particularly welcome contributions reflect and

9 See *Un 'hombre de bien'. Saggi di lingue e letterature iberiche in onore di Rinaldo Froldi*, presentazione di Maurizio Fabbri, a cura di Patrizia Garelli e Giovanni Marchetti, e con la collaborazione di Livia Brunori, Luigi Contadini, Cristina Fiallega, Marco Presotto, Patrizio Rigobon e Roberto Vecchi (Alessandria: Edizioni dell'Orso, 2004), 2 vols.

10 My thanks are due to David Gies and to Patrizia Garelli for their efforts to locate a copy of this article in Italy and elsewhere, which proved unsuccessful. Professor Garelli recalls that, after several years, the article was returned to the author. This was apparently in response to a letter from the author expressing concern that the *Festschrift* for Rinaldo Froldi had been so long delayed. By that time, however, Ivy McClelland had entered a care home, and the returned typescript would have been sent to her previous address. Certainly she never received it.

11 See the email from Ruth Hill to the Editors, *Bulletin of Spanish Studies*, dated University of Virginia, 6 June 2007. Similar messages were received from other invited contributors.

confirm the recent and current growth of scholarly interest, in Britain and elsewhere, in the eighteenth century in Spain.

Authors of the essays collected and edited here have chosen, in the main, to study Spain itself, observing, where appropriate, its culture, ideology and society within the broader context of eighteenth-century Europe. At the same time, the New World in Spanish America is by no means neglected, and two articles explore some of the social, cultural, ideological, and other factors which in the eighteenth century operated to differentiate Spain from its colonies, so that these developed their separately national identities. Among the writers and artists, works and genres, themes and issues diversely studied are: epic poetry during the Enlightenment, Lillo's *The London Merchant* and English and French influences, direct or indirect, on eighteenth-century Spanish drama, José Marchena and literary historiography, Goya and the visual arts, Quintana's *Pelayo* and historical tragedy, Enlightenment discourse, the Periodical Press, theatre as propaganda, the ideology of Empire, the roots of revolt in late viceregal Quito, the conservatism of eighteenth-century Spanish society, political corruption and the urge to reform, women's experience of Enlightenment Spain, social and cultural difference in colonial Peru, ideological hesitancy and debate in the Age of Reason, eighteenth-century Spain on the nineteenth-century stage, and public opinion in Spain on the eve of European revolution.

Given Ivy McClelland's major interests in Spanish theatre, it seems particularly apposite that half the articles included deal, in variously enlightening ways, with Enlightenment drama. Two essays focus on *El sí de las niñas*. Though she was too much occupied with other less accomplished and less studied, but equally thought-provoking, eighteenth-century plays to write about it in detail, *El sí de las niñas* is a comic masterpiece of whose 'serious undertones' she was perceptively aware.[12] The presence of these essays dealing with Moratín *hijo*, and, indeed, of a third article which concerns Moratín *padre*, means that whatever else reviewers may say about this latest *Festschrift* for Ivy McClelland, they will have no reason to complain, as did Francisco Lafarga when he reviewed the first Volume of Essays to appear in her honour,[13] that while 'varios de los grandes autores del siglo están presentes en esta miscelánea', 'se echa en falta, sin embargo, a los Moratines, padre e hijo'. The same reviewer—it should be added—went on to express his admiration for the volume in question: 'Los dieciochistas podemos felicitarnos por ver reunidos en un solo volumen tan variados y

12 I. L. McClelland, *Spanish Drama of Pathos 1750–1808*. I. *High Tragedy*; II. *Low Tragedy*, 2 vols (Liverpool: Liverpool U. P., 1970) (simultaneously published Toronto: Univ. of Toronto Press), II, 448.

13 This first *Festschrift* was: *Studies for I. L. McClelland*, ed., with an Introduction, by David T. Gies, Special Issue of *Dieciocho: Hispanic Enlightenment, Aesthetics, and Literary Theory*, 9:1–2 (1986).

excelentes trabajos que se ofrecen en homenaje a la profesora McClelland'.[14] Indeed, this forerunner-Volume set a high standard of excellence in *Studies for I. L. McClelland* which its *Festschrift*-successors have struggled hard to reach.

Of the three hitherto unpublished essays by Ivy McClelland included here, one, placed first, effectively introduces all the other articles, while another serves aptly as their conclusion. Her contributions are illustrative of the quality and originality of the researches she conducted into Enlightenment Spain during fully two-thirds of the twentieth century. Articles from the other contributors, which collectively recall the thoroughness of her work, the breadth of her knowledge and the diversity of her approaches, serve to demonstrate how much is being done in this twenty-first century to comprehend the ideological and creative uncertainties that characterized the eighteenth century in Spain and beyond. When, early in the 1930s, Ivy McClelland began her researches, few scholars were interested in the Enlightenment as it affected Spain. Though, in her modesty, she would have been the last to realize it, it is in large measure due to the cumulative influence which her publications have exercised down the decades that at last Spain's Age of Reason, that 'once lost century',[15] is receiving from scholars internationally the attention which for so long it was deprived of, and yet so thoroughly deserves.

Ann L. Mackenzie

University of Glasgow.

14 For these quotations, see the review-article on *Studies for I. L. McClelland* by Francisco Lafarga, 'Miscelánea dieciochesca: homenaje a McClelland', *Ínsula*, 485–86 (1987), 15.

15 For David T. Gies' succinct description, quoted here, see his 'Introduction' to *Studies for I. L. McClelland*, 2.

PART I

Introduction

I. L. McClelland (1908–2006)

*Lux perpetua luceat ei**

ANN L. MACKENZIE
University of Glasgow

After an internationally influential career as a Hispanist, extending in its productivity over seven decades, Ivy Lilian McClelland, Honorary Professor and formerly Reader in Hispanic Studies at the University of Glasgow, died on 2 April 2006, only six weeks before her ninety-eighth birthday.

Born in West Derby in the county of Liverpool on 18 May 1908, she was the only daughter of William Henry McClelland, insurance-agent, and his wife, Selina (*née* Foxall). With her beloved only brother Leslie, two years her junior, she grew up in Liverpool, where she first attended a small private school run by two 'gentlewomen'. While they were less skilled in matters of academic instruction, they taught this, by her own admission, unusually silent, though thoughtful, child the principles of deportment; and the erect carriage that she learned there gave her physical presence, diminutive though it was, an unmistakable dignity which she maintained until the end. For her secondary education, she moved to Holly Lodge Girls' School in Liverpool, where expert schoolmistresses, whose lessons she remembered with gratitude throughout her life, not only nurtured her intellect, but taught her and her companions the invaluable lesson that every pupil had talents of equal worth, whether these were in the more academic subjects (English literature, Latin, mathematics and the rest) or in the more physical or creative ones, such as sports, drawing, embroidery, singing or cookery. At Holly Lodge School she acquired her abilities to communicate

* Among the expressions of sympathy and regret sent to the University of Glasgow when Ivy McClelland died was a card (dated 7.iv.06) that contained the Latin text I have repeated here. This card came from Jack Metford, Emeritus Professor of Hispanic Studies, University of Bristol (her former colleague at Glasgow), his daughter Gillian Clark, Professor of Ancient History, University of Bristol (who was Ivy's god-daughter) and his son-in-law, Stephen R. L. Clark, Professor of Philosophy, University of Liverpool.

sympathetically with others, however different from her own were their origins, talents and circumstances. It was while there, too, that she conceived a lifelong love for English literature, and the ambition to read that subject at Cambridge University. Fortunately for the development of Hispanic Studies in Britain, Providence intervened. Ivy attended classes at one of the Summer Schools of Spanish which, from the 1920s onwards, Liverpool University's inspirational Gilmour Professor of Spanish was offering to senior school pupils and adults alike, whether in Liverpool or London, in Santander or San Sebastian. These Summer schools, run so regularly by Edgar Allison Peers, won over many pupils, Ivy McClelland among them, to the undergraduate study of Spanish and of Spain.[1]

In 1927 she began to study for a BA Honours degree in Spanish, with subsidiary French, at her home-University of Liverpool, which she completed, with First Class Honours, in 1930, winning in the process, among other awards, the coveted 'Grace Brown Prize' in Romance Studies. Her undergraduate work had included a thesis on *Lyrical Poetry in the Nineteenth Century in its Relation to the Spanish Temperament*, of which any postgraduate researcher would have been proud.[2] Significantly, the thesis devoted an entire chapter to Bécquer, whose poetry became an enduring interest.[3] Peers knew a scholar in the making when he saw one, and encouraged her to write a postgraduate thesis under his supervision, for which Liverpool University awarded her the research degree of MA in 1932. Published in revised form, this thesis was to become, in 1937, her first book, in whose Preface she declared: 'Of the many debts which I have incurred during the preparation of this study, by far the greatest is to Professor Allison Peers, to whom I owe ... my entire training in research, and to whom I have never turned in vain for help and encouragement'.[4] Peers had trained her well. As one of the book's reviewers commented, '[t]he method of investigation

1 For information on Peers' Summer Schools of Spanish, see E. Allison Peers, *Redbrick University Revisited. The Autobiography of 'Bruce Truscot'*, ed., with introduction, commentary and notes, by Ann L. Mackenzie and Adrian R. Allan, E. Allison Peers Publications 1 (Liverpool: Liverpool U. P., 1996), especially pp. 127–28, 399, 401–02.

2 There are copies of this undergraduate thesis in the Sydney Jones Library, University of Liverpool and among the Ivy McClelland Papers, Archives, University of Glasgow.

3 Her first journal-article was written on 'The Poetry of Bécquer: An Appreciation', *BSS*, XII:46 (1935), 96–110 (reprinted as 'Gustavo Adolfo Bécquer', in *Liverpool Studies in Spanish Literature.* I: *From Cadalso to Rubén Darío*, ed. E. Allison Peers (Liverpool: Institute of Hispanic Studies, 1940), 220–39. Her last essay on Bécquer was written fifty years later, in 1985.

4 See I. L. McClelland, *The Origins of the Romantic Movement in Spain*, Studies in Hispanic Literatures (Liverpool: Institute of Hispanic Studies, 1937); 'Preface', vii–viii (p. viii). Her observations on 'Allison Peers as a University Teacher: Recollections of a Former Student in his Department' are included in Peers, *Redbrick University Revisited. The Autobiography of 'Bruce Truscot'*, 397–99. See also, in the same book, Audrey Lumsden-Kouvel, 'E. A. P. Remembered', 400–03.

is exhaustive. No source of information—newspapers, periodicals, pamphlets—is neglected, and the result is an analysis of an enormous amount of hitherto unused material'.[5] Chosen on Peers', for once not wholly prudent, advice, the book's title reflected his own major interests in Romanticism rather than Ivy McClelland's predominant concern with the eighteenth century.[6] *The Origins of the Romantic Movement in Spain*, was, in fact and essence, a pioneering investigation into the culture, ideology and nature of Spain during the Enlightenment, 'destined to heighten interest, provide a wealth of information, and spark debate for an entire generation of students of Hispanic Studies'.[7] From then onwards, this hitherto neglected period was to constitute Ivy McClelland's chosen principal field of research, in which she soon became, and has remained, an influential authority worldwide.

It was Peers who persuaded her to publish this first book under the name 'I. L. McClelland', so as to avoid using her Christian name, 'Ivy', which he found, so he told her, 'rather a silly name for academic use'. One might suspect that Peers' true reason for giving her this advice was to ensure that, in an academic world which, in the 1930s, was so much dominated by male scholars, her book would be received, and reviewed, seriously, with the attention it deserved. She continued to publish her work as by 'I. L. McClelland' throughout her career. As a result, since, as Donald Shaw once put it, 'she was so exaggeratedly modest and never went to conferences',[8] preferring to devote all the time she could to her researches, most Hispanists outside Britain came to assume that 'I. L. McClelland' was a man.[9] Even as recently as the 1980s and 1990s eminent specialists, when they were asked to contribute articles to volumes being prepared in her honour, were surprised to discover that the scholar whose original studies on Spain's culture and literature they had so long depended upon was a woman.[10]

---

5 See John T. Reid, review of *The Origins of the Romantic Movement in Spain*, in *Hispania* (USA), 20:3 (1937), 294–96 (p. 295).

6 The book was subsequently republished (evidence of its enduring importance) nearly forty years later (1975), at which point the author added a subtitle which specified its true focus of interest: 'A Survey of Aesthetic Uncertainties in the Age of Reason'. See the 2nd edition, and its Preface (Liverpool: Liverpool U. P./New York: Barnes & Noble, 1975).

7 See David T. Gies, 'Introduction' to *Studies for I. L. McClelland*, ed., with an Introduction, by David T. Gies, Special Issue of *Dieciocho: Hispanic Enlightenment, Aesthetics, and Literary Theory*, 9:1–2 (1986), 3–4 (p. 3).

8 Extracted from a letter written to Ann Mackenzie by Donald Shaw, University of Virginia, dated 18 May 1989, now lodged in the Ivy McClelland Papers, Archives, University of Glasgow.

9 See, for instance, the letter received by Geoffrey Ribbans, then Gilmour Professor of Spanish at Liverpool University, from Dr Antonio Castro Leal, Mexico, dated 9 June 1970. Referring to I. L. McClelland's book on Tirso, Castro Leal commented: 'Estoy en duda de si su autor es hombre o mujer. Por el estilo de algunas páginas y la vehemencia de ciertas afirmaciones me parece que se trata de una profesora, y no de un profesor' (I. L. McClelland Papers, Archives, University of Glasgow).

10 See Gies, 'Introduction' to *Studies for I. L. McClelland*, 3.

In 1930, newly graduated and aged only 22, Ivy McClelland was appointed to an assistant lectureship in Spanish at the University of Glasgow, becoming, as a result, one of the earliest women scholars to occupy a career-track post in Hispanic Studies at a British university. When the young Ivy went to live and work in Scotland she already had the highest opinions of that country and its people, instilled by her father, an Englishman but with Scottish forbears (hence the surname), who had served with a Scottish regiment in the First World War. English though she was by birth and upbringing, she immediately took the Scots to her heart. Scotland became, by adoption, her country, and Glasgow, from then onwards, her home. She spent her full-time working life of more than forty years as an academic at Glasgow University, living on or very near the University's precinct, first in digs, then in its Queen Margaret Hall of Residence, eventually, and most happily, in her own flat, part of a splendidly Victorian terraced row of greystone houses in Glasgow's Kelvinside. Her small, upright figure, familiar to colleagues and students alike, was frequently encountered in the vicinity of University Gardens, where at No. 1 students took her classes in Spanish language, history and literature, until, in 1960, Spanish moved, together with the other foreign languages, to the Garden's other end, and into the then brand-new Modern Languages Building. Even after she retired, it never occurred to her to leave Glasgow, and she maintained her regular associations with the University, particularly through the Library and the College Club. For decades she took her week-day lunches at the College Club in the University's famous Gilbert Scott Building, and she dined there regularly, too, for as long as the Club continued to serve dinner to the academic staff in the evening (with table-service, naturally!).

Only two years after Ivy McClelland had joined the staff at Glasgow, Professor William J. Entwistle moved on, to take up, in 1932, the King Alfonso XIII Chair of Spanish Studies at Oxford University. Entwistle's successor as Stevenson Professor of Spanish, later Hispanic Studies, was William C. Atkinson, then only thirty years old, who held that post, together with the permanent headship of the Department, until his retirement aged seventy.

Throughout Ivy McClelland's career, there was no such thing at Glasgow University as a 'rotating' headship of department; nor was there—except temporarily, to allow professors to take study leave—such a thing as a non-professorial departmental head. Nevertheless, for five years, throughout the Second World War, Miss McClelland (as she was then titled) **did** run Hispanic Studies at Glasgow. Under unbelievably difficult circumstances, while Professor Atkinson was seconded into service at the Foreign Office, she dealt with teaching and administration, sometimes almost single-handedly, and coped, besides, through air raids and in blackouts, with the wartime duties of fire-watching and the rest. She kept the Department going, and thereby ensured its future. In these years of war and its immediate aftermath, two recent graduates from Peers' Department at Liverpool joined her in Glasgow to give, in turn, essential, though temporary, teaching assistance. Norman Lamb taught there in 1940, but hardly had time to get used to the Scottish curriculum, and students, before he was called up for military service overseas. Then, Audrey Lumsden, later to become (on her marriage to James Kouvel, the renowned physicist) Audrey Lumsden-Kouvel, came to the Glasgow Department to teach and, fortunately, stayed for several years. Upon learning of the death of her former colleague and friend, Professor Lumsden-Kouvel was moved to recollect the times they had spent together, more than sixty years previously, in the wartime City and University of Glasgow:

> Ivy was so much a part of my life at the very beginning of my career: [. . .] though I was hired by Atkinson, he was away from Glasgow for the duration of the War and she was the effective Head. She was my guide and mentor; we spent many hours together, at the University, in her apartment, and walking in the countryside. I learned to know and love her. [. . .] [H]er intense dedication will always be an inspiration.[11]

After the War, notably in the 1950s and 1960s, there were several other terms or sessions during which, to allow Professor Atkinson to have research leave or visit Latin America, Ivy McClelland took charge of the Department. She was, by all first-hand accounts, an excellent leader—efficient, perceptive, compassionate, and always scrupulously fair. But, head of department or not, in difficult times she supported her colleagues throughout. They had much to thank her for—not least for her integrity. What they said to her privately they could be certain would never be divulged.

Her colleagues remained her friends for life, even when their career-moves took them away from Glasgow—to universities elsewhere in the UK, or to institutions overseas, or sometimes out of the academic world altogether. Audrey Lumsden(-Kouvel) went to lectureships in Liverpool and Leeds, and then on to a distinguished career as a Hispanist and Professor of Golden-Age Literature in the United States, especially in the University of Illinois at Chicago. Norman Lamb, when the War ended, went back to Liverpool University to work in the Department where, during the final years of Peers' headship, and thereafter under the leadership, in turn, of Albert Sloman and Geoffrey Ribbans, he specialized as lecturer, then senior lecturer in Portuguese Studies, in addition to maintaining his interests in nineteenth- and early twentieth-century Spanish literature. Another graduate of Peers' Department at Liverpool who became a member of staff at Glasgow was Jack Metford. In due course, he moved on, to take up

11 Letter to Ann Mackenzie from Professor Audrey Lumsden-Kouvel, Oak Park, Illinois, dated 8 April 2006 (Ivy McClelland Papers, Archives, University of Glasgow).

the Chair of Hispanic Studies at Bristol University. As lecturer in Spanish and Latin-American Studies, Donald Shaw worked alongside Ivy McClelland at Glasgow for seven years, which was, he recalls, 'a great privilege and a learning experience'.[12] He transferred, in 1964, to Edinburgh University, where he was promoted to a personal chair, then went to the United States, and he still holds the distinguished Brown-Forman Chair of Spanish American Literature at the University of Virginia. In the Glasgow Department, the vacancy left by Donald Shaw's departure was filled by Waldo Ross, who, in 1972, moved on to a professorship at the University of Montreal. Geoffrey Connell, who had come from the University of Nottingham in 1967, remained at Glasgow, as lecturer, then senior lecturer, until his early retirement in 1984. From the late 1950s until the early 1970s, Beatrice Jost was lecturer, then senior lecturer in Portuguese Studies. Even after Dr Jost left Glasgow for Switzerland she remained the firm friend of Ivy McClelland, who visited her in that country for several memorable holidays.

Conscious of the problems they inevitably had in adjusting to a university system, and to a language and way of life, foreign to them, Ivy took particular interest in the well-being of the native Spanish assistants who came to teach for a time at Glasgow. With them she nearly always conversed in Spanish, for, as Aguilar Piñal has had occasion to observe: 'El español ha sido su segunda lengua, en la que se siente tan "instalada" como en su inglés nativo'.[13] These Spanish colleagues included, in the 1950s, Arseni Pacheco who left Britain for a distinguished career in Canada, at the University of British Columbia. Antoni Turull spent two years teaching at Glasgow before returning to his native Barcelona in 1961; from there, in 1964, he went to Bristol University as *lector*, then lecturer, and finally senior lecturer. Fernando Huerta, who shared her research interests in Spain's eighteenth century, was her colleague at Glasgow, as *lector* and lecturer, between 1966 and 1972 before returning to Barcelona, where he became a professor at the Universidad Autónoma. In Barcelona, he and his family enjoyed visits from Ivy McClelland over the years, and remained her firm friends for life.

A particularly noteworthy native assistant teacher in the late 1930s and early 1940s was Luis Cernuda. Saddened by the circumstances that had brought about his exile from Spain, Cernuda was an introverted figure, temperamentally ill at ease with women. What is more, his English was extremely poor. But, with her love of Spain, her tact and her unfailing

12 See Shaw's letter to Ann Mackenzie, 18 May 1989 (Ivy McClelland Papers, Archives, University of Glasgow).

13 See Francisco Aguilar Piñal, 'Prólogo II', in I. L. McClelland, *'Pathos' dramático en el teatro español de 1750 a 1808*. I. *La alta tragedia*; II. *La tragedia menor*, traducción a cargo de Fernando Huerta Viñas y Guillermina Cenoz del Águila, con prólogos de Ann L. Mackenzie & Francisco Aguilar Piñal, Hispanic Studies TRAC (Textual Research and Criticism) 7, 2 vols (Liverpool: Liverpool U. P., 1998), I, xi–xiv (p. xii).

willingness to speak to him fluently in his native tongue, Ivy McClelland won his trust and friendship. Homesick for Spain, with its vivid landscapes and the brilliant clarity of its skies, Cernuda found the greystone buildings of Glasgow and its University, and the stone-grey Scottish weather with its relentless rains and chilling winds, intensely depressing. Yet, this gifted Spanish poet and friend of Lorca wrote some of his finest poems inspired by his walks in the University grounds and the nearby public gardens.[14]

Though administration was probably the part of her job she least enjoyed, she did her share, not only within the Department but at other levels of Glasgow University's management, serving on both Faculty and Senate, and their appropriate committees. She had plenty of opportunity, therefore, to observe the great Hector Hetherington going about his work as Principal. She had been a first-year undergraduate when Hetherington moved from his Chair of Moral Philosophy at Glasgow to become, in 1927, Liverpool's Vice-Chancellor. She never forgot the jocular 'Song of the Vice-Chancellor' which she and her student-contemporaries sang at a Freshers' Social in the Students' Union attended by the University's new chief, and which began: 'Hoots man the brainy Prof. / Hoch aye and his haggis, / He wore a sporran and a dirk / And a kilt instead of baggis'.[15] She always retained a particular admiration for Sir Hector, and was delighted, therefore, when, not many years after her own move to Glasgow, Sir Hector transferred from Liverpool back to Glasgow University, as its Principal.

Ivy McClelland was an outstanding teacher. Generations of students at Glasgow University—and by no means only the most intellectual among them—owe her an enduring debt for bringing out the best in them—not just for developing their minds, but also for imperceptibly shaping their characters. She was particularly good at drawing out the Scottish born- and educated-undergraduates (who formed the majority of those that she taught), many of whom, though bright, were inarticulate, through reserve, or perhaps from lack of confidence, coming, as frequently they did, from working-class homes and circumstances, the first in their family to obtain a university education. The group of Final Honours students whom she taught in the last session before her retirement (1973) were typical in the respect and affection they felt for 'Ivy'. For all her students knew her as 'Ivy',

14 For information on Cernuda, as teacher and poet while at Glasgow University, see Audrey Lumsden-Kouvel, 'Awaiting the Dawn: Luis Cernuda in Glasgow, 1941–1943', *BHS*, LXXVI (1999), 249–52; Hugh Matthews, ' "Ni Glasgow ni Escocia me resultaban agradables": Luis Cernuda as University Teacher', *BHS*, LXXVI (1999), 253–57; and I. L. McClelland, 'Cernuda's Local Source of Inspiration for His Poem "Los espinos" ', *BHS*, LXXVI (1999), 258–61.

15 From time to time, when she talked to friends about Hector Hetherington, and what he had accomplished, she would recite with verve some verses from this 'Song of the Vice-Chancellor (the work of A. W. Ellis). Some more lines from this 'Song' are quoted in *The Eighteenth Century in Spain. Essays in Honour of I. L. McClelland*, ed., with an introduction, by Ann L. Mackenzie, *BHS*, LXVIII:1 (1991); 'Introduction', 1–9 (p. 1).

and called her so—though never, in those more formal days, to her face. So they insisted on holding their own ceremony of farewell, at which they gave her a Celtic brooch, suitably inscribed, and a 'Good Luck' card which they had designed themselves, and on which they had written or drawn individual messages and sketches. These referred to Golden-Age authors (Cervantes, Tirso, Lope de Rueda) they had studied with her; and to English writers (Dickens, D. H. Lawrence, Lewis Carroll etc.), from whose works she had selected idiomatic, and sometimes idiosyncratic, passages for prose-translation that had given them particular difficulty, and fun, to render into Spanish. Inside, signed by them all, the card was addressed to 'Miss McClelland', 'Best wishes from your students'. But next to her name, sketched in green, there was a perfect Ivy leaf. She was not one for keeping any unnecessary papers or possessions, but that farewell card was still to be found in her study at home, among her library of books and papers, thirty-one years later when, because of her move into residential care, her house was cleared of its contents.

Given her ability to stimulate their talents and interests, it is hardly surprising that so many of the undergraduates she taught at Glasgow, following her example, went on to become university teachers and scholars, both in the United Kingdom and overseas. As one of these students in the 1960s, I took her option on Lope de Vega, in my final Honours year. I remember the hard work (we studied in detail no fewer than twelve of Lope's *comedias* in only two terms), but also the satisfaction of undertaking, under her guidance, my first efforts at research. And so my own career, as a Hispanist and specialist in Golden-Age drama, was initiated. Long after I graduated I continued to seek, and take, her advice, and generously she gave her time to commenting acutely and constructively on any work in draft I sent her. Characteristically, she would urge me to improve upon my English style, so as 'to write better than the mass of academic writers' of whom

> the majority limit [themselves] to professional or media jargon, and have a limited range of linguistic possibilities. If you use jargon, you lose the opportunity of giving force to your very good ideas. I'd like to see you becoming more literary and imaginative linguistically.[16]

And I was only one of many ex-students with whom she kept in touch: 'To the last', as Nicholas Round has said, 'she enjoyed the affection of countless former [...] pupils',[17] as well as, always, their professional respect.

James Dickie, Charles Kelley, Mervyn Lang, Annella McDermott, Giovanni Pontiero and Bernard McGuirk are only some among her former

16 Extract from her letter to Ann Mackenzie, dated 21 November 1977 (Ivy McClelland Papers, Archives, University of Glasgow).

17 See Nicholas Round, 'Professor Ivy McClelland: Scholar of 18th-Century Spain', *The Independent*, 28 April 2006, p. 46.

The 'Good Luck' card designed, signed and presented to Ivy McClellard by her Final Honours students in Hispanic Studies, on the occasion of her retirement from the University of Glasgow, June 1973.
Reproduced by courtesy of the signatories and of the Archives, University of Glasgow

students who went on to academic posts in Britain—in universities such as Lancaster, Cardiff, Salford, Bristol, Manchester and Nottingham. At Liverpool University, at the end of the 1960s, in the Department with the oldest Chair of Spanish in the country (established, as it happens, the year in which she was born),[18] there were, out of a complement of eight tenured academics, no fewer than three lecturers who had been taught by Ivy McClelland at Glasgow University (James Higgins, myself and Giovanni Pontiero). In the words of Ian Michael, she was 'such an influence for outstanding research and the highest standards of scholarship in Glasgow'.[19] More than that, as his successor in the King Alfonso XIII Chair at Oxford has observed, she 'played such an important role in the development of Hispanic Studies in the United Kingdom that we are all very much in her debt'.[20] There were others she had trained—most notably, John Walker and James Maharg—who became professors in universities overseas (in Canada, the USA and elsewhere). In fact, what this singular teacher and scholar did, from her Scottish base, was to establish a veritable 'Ivy League' of Hispanists, influential throughout the world.

Despite her heavy burden of departmental and research commitments, Ivy McClelland did not shrink from taking on teaching and examining duties beyond Glasgow University. For years, she acted as external examiner in Spanish (at the Universities of Liverpool and Leeds, to name only two). In addition, she found time to examine candidates in Spanish for the Civil Service, and to teach students enrolled at the Glasgow College of Dramatic Art (as it was then called)[21] about the characteristically performative merits of drama in Golden-Age Spain.

At the University of Glasgow's Queen Margaret Hall, she was tutor or sub-warden to its resident women-undergraduates from the late 1940s through to the early 1960s, where she had in her charge, besides those studying subjects in the Arts, many women from other faculties, who were doctors, lawyers and scientists in the making. This was a period when academic staff were by custom and tradition, if not always by personal inclination, still 'stand-offish' where undergraduates were concerned. Contacts between staff and students were largely formal or professional, only rarely social and almost never relaxed. But Ivy McClelland flouted tradition, taking an interest, in her discreet ways, in the individual well-being of the students she dealt with. As many ex-QM residents could confirm, she was generous in giving them her whole attention when they needed it,

18 The Gilmour Chair of Spanish was established in 1908, thanks to an endowment from Captain George Gilmour (see Peers, *Redbrick University Revisited. The Autobiography of 'Bruce Truscot'*, 112, n. 111).

19 Ian Michael, in an email to Ann Mackenzie, dated 3 April 2006.

20 Edwin Williamson, in an email to Ann Mackenzie, dated 3 April 2003.

21 In 1968 the Glasgow College of Dramatic Art, established in 1950, became part of the Royal Scottish Academy of Music and Drama.

tactfully giving confidential advice and practical support to resolve the matters that were preoccupying them—exam nerves, overdue essays, boyfriend-troubles, family-illnesses, financial worries, and the rest. When she finally stopped being tutor/sub-warden, her contribution was judged too valuable to lose, with the result that she was appointed to serve on Queen Margaret Hall's Board of Governors. This was a responsibility she continued to fulfil for many years after her retirement, by which time QM had become, inevitably, a residence that housed men as well as women. Let us hope that her memoirs, which deal wittily, discreetly and stylishly with her experiences in *The University of Glasgow's Queen Margaret Hall c.1950–1960*—and which at present exist only in typescript—will not be forgotten about, but will one day be published. For these memoirs reveal how life was at Glasgow University for women, both staff and students, during the critical period of development that followed after the Second World War.

Although she fulfilled all her university responsibilities, whether as teacher, colleague, hall tutor, or departmental head, with rare aptitude and commitment, it was research that was her favourite work and true vocation. Throughout her career—besides important articles, excellent editions, contributions to key encyclopaedias, and over a hundred and fifty scholarly reviews—she steadily produced a series of major monographs, admirable both for their scope and their profundity, the products of her dedicated researches in Spanish archives and libraries.

Visiting Spain, principally for research purposes, shortly before the Civil War began, Ivy witnessed at first hand the political, social and economic upheavals manifested by the frequent demonstrations in the streets, perilous to participants and bystanders alike. She was in Spain, too, going about her research-related business, when the Second World War broke out, and she had to beat a hasty retreat through France and across the Channel back to (relative) safety. Because of the Spanish Civil War, then the Second World War, for a period of almost ten years (1936–45) journeys to Spain were impossible to realize. From the late 1940s, however, she was able to resume her preferred routine, and once more spent two months of every summer in Spain for research purposes, mostly in Madrid. Perhaps her favourite library there, after the Biblioteca Nacional, was the Biblioteca Municipal, with its wealth of eighteenth-century theatre-manuscripts, altered and annotated by *autores de comedias* and carrying the *censuras* and *aprobaciones* of such official censors as Santos Díez González. Located at that time in the 'Antiguo Hospicio' in Fuencarral, this library was *en obras* for years—indeed for decades—and was officially closed to the public. But the friendship she enjoyed with such eminent Spanish scholars as Ángel Valbuena Prat and Federico Carlos Sáinz de Robles ensured her access, though, as she would amusingly recall, she had to keep the porters supplied with gifts of English cigarettes so as to encourage them to bring down from the attics where they had been stored—in conditions unlikely to assist their preservation—the manuscripts which she most needed to consult. It was in the capital's Biblioteca Municipal where most of her original researches into the drama of Spain's Age of Reason were carried out.

In Madrid, from the 1950s into the late 1970s, she stayed, while she researched, in the Calle de Fortuny at the famous Colegio Mayor de Santa Teresa de Jesús, founded by María de Maeztu. Despite its connections for most of that period with the Sección Femenina of the Falange (though these ties noticeably weakened as Franco's regime drew to its close), the Colegio, as she put appreciatively on record, was a place where she 'lived most happily during many hot summers and [was] refreshed and encouraged by the full generosity of Spanish friendliness'.[22] In later years, once she found out that women academics were at last being admitted as residents in their own right, she stayed at an even more famous university hall. This was the Residencia del Consejo, in Madrid's Calle del Pinar, now known, once again, as the 'Residencia de Estudiantes', having reverted to the name it had when it was frequented by García Lorca, Salvador Dalí and Juan Ramón Jiménez. As the years passed, Spain, with its university residences, its libraries and its theatres, as Aguilar Piñal has recorded, became 'su segunda casa, con amigos incondicionales y agradecidos'.[23] The weeks she spent there annually were a way of life, and work, that she followed well into her years of retirement, until, in the late 1980s, her stamina for foreign travel, and her eyesight, began to fail her.

She was 'one of those eminent scholars who pass easily from the eighteenth to the nineteenth century',[24] so that the many fruits of her researches have included significant publications on Spain's Romanticism. She could also write illuminatingly on twentieth-century Spanish literature, as demonstrated by her work on Cernuda.[25] Worthy of particular note, her writings on Spain's Golden Age further confirm 'her deep attachment to the richness and scope of Spanish letters'.[26] In 1948 she published a ground-breaking monograph on: *Tirso de Molina. Studies in Dramatic Realism*, which had been preceded, in the early 1940s, by three articles on 'Tirso de Molina and the Eighteenth Century', 'The Conception of the Supernatural in the Plays of Tirso de Molina', and 'The Mob Scene in Tirso de Molina's

22 See I. L. McClelland, *Spanish Drama of Pathos 1750–1808*. I. *High Tragedy*; II. *Low Tragedy*, 2 vols (Liverpool: Liverpool U. P./Toronto: Univ. of Toronto Press, 1970), I, 'Preface', vii–viii (p. viii).

23 See Aguilar Piñal, 'Prólogo II', in McClelland, *'Pathos' dramático en el teatro español de 1750 a 1808*, I, xii.

24 I quote from Geoffrey Ribbans' 'Preamble' to his unpublished 'Ivy McClelland Lecture' (1998). For details see below, note 63.

25 See her review of Cernuda's *Como quien espera el alba*, *BSS*, XXV:99 (1948), 180, which prompted the poet to write to her. See, too, her article, 'Cernuda's Local Source of Inspiration for His Poem "Los espinos"', in which Cernuda's letter is reproduced (258).

26 Quoted from Gies, 'Introduction' to *Studies for I. L. McClelland*, 3.

Antona García'.[27] Her work on Tirso came about, she once told me, because his plays were accessible to her, in printed copies, in the British Library, where she read them in depth during the Second World War, when visits to Spain, to do research into manuscripts relating to the Age of Reason, were out of the question. At a time when few others had acutely perceived Tirso's genius, she 'powerfully asserted [...] the case for Tirso's uniqueness among 17th-century playwrights',[28] and her book on Tirso stands out as '[t]he first truly analytical assessment of that playwright's individual talent'.[29]

In the 1950s, though she published important articles on eighteenth-century Spanish theatre—including 'Concerning the Dramatic Approach to the Eighteenth Century', 'The Eighteenth-Century Conception of the Stage and Histrionic Technique' and '"Comellan" Drama and the Censor'—,[30] she took precious time from her own researches in order to undertake a labour done out of the gratitude and respect she felt towards the professor who had trained her. Peers had died, in December 1952, without completing the final volume of his monumental *Studies of the Spanish Mystics*. It took his former pupil several years of painstaking scholarship, to reconstruct and finish this work, of which she was much more than editor, but in reality co-author. Yet, this was a task which she carried out anonymously. When it was published in 1960, Volume III appeared under Peers' sole name. Not even in the 'Editor's Note' did she reveal her identity.[31] The importance of this third volume of *Studies of the Spanish Mystics* was justifiably recognized by reviewers: '[T]he broad lines of the history of Spanish Golden Age mysticism are now beyond dispute', wrote Robert Pring-Mill, 'and the main lines of the development of thought within the various religious Orders emerge with stimulating clarity'.[32]

In her principal research concerns she continued to focus on eighteenth-century Spain, the role of which within Enlightenment Europe was still largely misunderstood and unresearched. One of her favourites among Spain's eighteenth-century thinkers was Benito Jerónimo Feijoo,[33] and in 1969 she published what is an 'admirable presentation of Feijoo in relation to the

27 Her book on Tirso came out, as No. 3, in the series Liverpool Studies in Spanish Literature (Liverpool: Institute of Hispanic Studies, 1948). The articles had appeared in the *Bulletin of Spanish Studies* (see *BSS*, XVIII:72 [1941], 182–204; *BSS*, XIX:75 [1942], 148–63; *BSS*, XX:80 [1943], 214–31).

28 Quoted from Round, 'Professor Ivy McClelland: Scholar of 18th-Century Spain', 46.

29 Quoted from Mackenzie, 'Introduction' to *The Eighteenth Century in Spain. Essays in Honour of I. L. McClelland*, 4.

30 These articles appeared respectively in *BHS*, XXVII:106 (1950), 72–87; *Estudios hispánicos. Homenaje a Archer M. Huntington*, ed. Ada M. Coe *et al.* (Wellesley, Mass.: Wellesley College, 1952), 393–425; *BHS*, XXX:117 (1953), 20–31.

31 Edgar Allison Peers, *Studies of the Spanish Mystics*, Vol. III (London: SPCK, 1960).

32 Robert Pring-Mill, review of *Studies of the Spanish Mystics*, Vol. III, *The Anglo-Spanish Society Quarterly Review* (April–June 1960), 33–34 (p. 34).

33 I. L. McClelland, *Benito Jerónimo Feijoo*, Twayne's World Authors Series 51 (New York: Twayne Publishers, 1969).

thinkers of his time, especially English scientists like Bacon and Boyle and Newton'. This is 'an invaluable contribution to all students of Spanish thought and more even to the historian of the conflict of ideas leading to the Enlightenment in Spain'.[34] There followed, in 1973, a similarly important book on another key eighteenth-century writer—Ignacio de Luzán.[35] In both these studies she demonstrated not only her 'profound knowledge of the eighteenth century, her keen sympathy for her subject, [and] her scrupulous scholarship',[36] but the breadth and depth of her understanding of the Enlightenment in Europe. But her *magnum opus*, the outcome of the researches she conducted in Spain during more than a decade into numerous hitherto neglected manuscripts and rare editions of plays, was the huge study that appeared in two volumes, published by Liverpool University Press, in 1970. *Spanish Drama of Pathos 1750–1808*, is justly regarded, not only in the English-speaking world but in Spain itself, as the 'definitive' work on Spain's eighteenth-century theatre. Jesús Pérez-Magallón describes it as an 'estudio absolutamente necesario para el conocimiento de la producción trágica española del siglo XVIII';[37] while Francisco Lafarga declares that the book 'debe tenerse en cuenta en cualquier estudio serio sobre el teatro español de la segunda mitad del siglo XVIII'.[38] In Francisco Aguilar Piñal's similarly authoritative view: 'Por primera vez en la historia literaria del Setecientos español se estudiaba con acierto la *Raquel* de García de la Huerta, se ponía en primer plano la parodia teatral, se dividía la tragedia para su estudio en dos novedosos capítulos y se agrupaban los textos dramáticos por temas y tesis'.[39] A measure of the book's importance is the article-length review, published in the *Bulletin of Hispanic Studies* in 1975, in which, having admired the author's 'breadth of reading that few scholars of Spanish literature possess', the reviewer finishes by proclaiming that 'at her best Miss McClelland is supreme amongst those who have written on the eighteenth-century Spanish stage; she can excite the mind'.[40] Proof of its enduring value to scholars is the Spanish translation which appeared nearly thirty years after the book's first edition. *'Pathos' dramático en el teatro español de 1750 a 1808* was the signal for a fresh evaluation, in the form of a review-article by Joaquín Álvarez Barrientos. In

34 Quoted from Edith Helman, review of McClelland, *Benito Jerónimo Feijoo*, *HR*, 40:4 (1972), 474–76 (p. 476).

35 I. L. McClelland, *Ignacio de Luzán*, Twayne's World Authors Series 221 (New York: Twayne Publishers, 1973).

36 The quotation comes from H. B. Hall's review of *Benito Jerónimo Feijoo*, *BHS*, L:4 (1973), 404–05 (p. 404).

37 See Jesús Pérez-Magallón, *El teatro neoclásico* (Madrid: Ediciones del Laberinto, 2001), 309.

38 See Francisco Lafarga, 'Miscelánea dieciochesca: homenaje a McClelland', *Ínsula*, 485–86 (1987), 15.

39 See Aguilar Piñal, 'Prólogo II', in McClelland, *'Pathos' dramático en el teatro español de 1750 a 1808*, I, xiv.

40 See the review by Robert Johnson, *BHS*, LII:4 (1975), 414–20 (pp. 417, 420).

his widely-respected judgment: 'Ivy L. McClelland ha abierto, en una época en que pocos se dedicaban a explorar el siglo XVIII, un campo inmenso, y lo hizo sin los prejuicios que habían caracterizado muchos de los trabajos anteriores de otros que siguieron la pauta interpretativa de don Marcelino'.[41]

By the 1950s her scholarship had already brought Ivy McClelland enviable international acclaim. Nevertheless, promotions were slow to come her way. She had been at Glasgow University twenty-six years when she was made a senior lecturer in 1956, and ten more years were to pass before, in 1966, she was advanced to a readership. Despite having been short-listed for chairs or headships of departments at other institutions, including Leeds University and the University of Aberdeen, she still held the title and position of Reader at Glasgow when, in 1972, Professor Atkinson finally vacated the Stevenson Chair of Hispanic Studies at the then statutory professorial retirement age of seventy. By then aged sixty-four, she hesitated long before, urged on by colleagues, she applied to succeed him. The University appointed, instead, a gifted young scholar nearly half her age. His name was Nicholas Round. Thirty-four years later, when he came to write her obituary for *The Independent*, with characteristic impartiality, he commented as follows on Glasgow's failure to promote her:

> She would have been an outstanding occupant of the Stevenson Chair, but was inexcusably passed over. She gave no hint of all that she might, legitimately, have felt about this, and the department, after her own retirement in 1973, enjoyed many more years of her help and friendship and good counsel.[42]

There is no doubt that had she been a male scholar Ivy McClelland would have been appointed to a professorship many years previously. But, in British universities, when she was in her prime, women scholars were not supposed to want, much less get, even if they richly deserved, promotion to the highest academic posts. Even in the late 1960s, Glasgow University had not yet appointed or promoted a woman to a chair, a fact which was publicized over the radio to the country at large, when a Member of Parliament complained, in the House, that the entire professoriate of Glasgow University could have moved to inhabit a monastery without causing embarrassment to the monks already in occupancy. In the 1960s, 1970s, and into the 1980s, many women academics in the United Kingdom—among them, eminent Hispanists such as Rita Hamilton, Helen Grant and Margaret Wilson—continued to be denied the career-advancement they had earned. The first woman was not appointed to an established chair in Hispanic Studies until nearly ten years after Ivy

41 See Álvarez Barrientos' review-article, *BHS*, LXXVII:2 (2000), 93–96 (p. 94).

42 See Round, 'Professor Ivy McClelland: Scholar of 18th-Century Spain', 46.

McClelland's retirement, when, in 1982, Dorothy Severin became Gilmour Professor of Spanish at the University of Liverpool.[43]

On her retirement in 1973, the Department at Liverpool University, where her studies of Spain and its literature had begun, sent a telegram of 'best wishes to Ivy on her retirement into full-time research'. These words were to prove prophetic. During the next twenty-five or more years she went on producing important books, articles and reviews, most intensively, though by no means exclusively, on Spain's Enlightenment. She also wrote on San Juan de la Cruz, and published more on Bécquer, and on Cernuda. The essay on 'G. A. Bécquer: "Porque son, niña, tus ojos ...". A Study in Green', which she contributed, in 1985, to a *Festschrift* for Geoffrey Connell,[44] so much impressed him that he wrote to her as follows:

> I loved your article on Bécquer. I don't think I've ever read anything that explored the processes of poetic creation more truly, and I just wish that the proponents of all the 'scientific' approaches to poetry I've encountered at conferences, from Stylistics in 1957 to Deconstruction in 1985, could be given your article as required reading before they open their mouths on the subject again'.[45]

In retirement, the major work she accomplished on the Spanish Age of Reason included her monograph on Torres Villarroel, which appeared in 1976, a critical edition of selected works by Feijóo, that came out in 1985, and a book elucidating *Ideological Hesitancy in Spain 1700–1750*, which was published in 1991.[46] As reviewers have observed, in her book on Torres 'McClelland combines biographical and historical criticism to survey brilliantly the writing of one of Spain's most controversial satirists of the 18th century'. This is 'Ms McClelland's third book for Twayne, and it is a good one. [...]. She has achieved her goal, which was "to present the controversial writings of Torres Villarroel in the context of their period, and

43 It is true that Jean Franco was professor at Essex University between 1968–72; but this was, I understand, a personal professorship. Thirteen years went by, after Dorothy Severin's appointment at Liverpool, before, in 1995, another woman Hispanist was appointed to an established professorship—to the Ivy McClelland Research Chair of Spanish at Glasgow University. Happily, since that time there have been many appointments of women to chairs in Hispanic Studies, personal and established, in the United Kingdom.

44 See *Readings in Spanish and Portuguese Poetry for Geoffrey Connell*, ed. Nicholas G. Round and D. Gareth Walters (Glasgow: Dept of Hispanic Studies, Univ. of Glasgow, 1985), 106–17.

45 Letter from Geoffrey Connell to Ivy McClelland, dated Lytham St Annes, 12 July 1985 (Ivy McClelland Papers, Archives, University of Glasgow).

46 *Diego de Torres Villarroel*, Twayne's World Authors Series 395 (Boston: Twayne Publishers, 1976); *Benito Jerónimo Feijóo. Obras (selección)*, estudio preliminar, edición y notas de Ivy L. McClelland, Temas de España 150 (Madrid: Taurus, 1985); *Ideological Hesitancy in Spain 1700–1750*, Publications of the *Bulletin of Hispanic Studies*, Textual Research and Criticism (Liverpool: Liverpool U. P., 1991).

to evaluate their significance"'.[47] From *Ideological Hesitancy in Spain 1700–1750*, '[w]hat emerges', as David Gies has aptly put it, 'is a new picture of the first half of the eighteenth century and a new appreciation for the intellectual rigour and seriousness of men "whose reasonable understanding of new directions of thought is partially limited by reasonably human caution"'. This is a 'study which forces us to see that things are not as simple as literary and intellectual historians would have us believe'.[48] Published twenty-one years after *Spanish Drama of Pathos 1750–1808*, *Ideological Hesitancy in Spain 1700–1750* showed her intellectual acuteness to be still undiminished. This, her final monograph, served as much as did her earlier books to ensure that the eighteenth century is now recognized as 'a period which present-day political, social and intellectual trends in Spain are bound increasingly to consider of crucial importance for the development of modern Spanish society'.[49]

With one notable exception, honours and awards, both external and internal, came to her late in life. She had been made a Corresponding Member of The Hispanic Society of America as early as 1952. Other honours, when eventually they materialized, were bestowed in abundance. It is a mark of her supremely international prestige that the first of the two homage-volumes to appear during her lifetime was instigated outside the British Isles. Conceived and realized in the United States, *Studies for I. L. McClelland* (1986) was issued from Rutgers, The State University of New Jersey, as a Double Number of the research journal *Dieciocho*, with additional financial support from the University of Virginia and the 'Program for Cultural Cooperation between Spain's Ministry of Culture and Northamerican Universities'.[50] Edited and introduced by David Gies, this Homage Volume was made up of original articles by more than twenty specialists on Spain's eighteenth century based in Spain, France, Germany, Italy, the United States and elsewhere. They had begun their 'incursions into that once lost century with her books and articles as [their] guides', and wished collectively to acknowledge their debt to her for assisting their deeper understanding of Enlightenment Spain.[51] The second *Festschrift*, on the other hand, though it also contained articles by leading Hispanists

---

47 These quotations are taken from reviews of *Diego de Torres Villarroel* by Dru Dougherty and David T. Gies respectively. For the quotation from Dougherty, see *Library Journal*, 101:17 (1.10.76), 2065; for the second quotation, from Gies, see *HR*, 45:4 (1977), 455–58 (pp. 455–57).

48 See David T. Gies, review of *Ideological Hesitancy in Spain 1700–1750*, *BHS*, LXIX:2 (1992), 200–01 (p. 200).

49 Quoted from a letter, dated 17 May 1989, from Derek Lomax, University of Birmingham, to Ann Mackenzie, Editor of the *Bulletin of Hispanic Studies* (Ivy McClelland Papers, Archives, University of Glasgow).

50 *Studies for I. L. McClelland*, ed., with an Introduction, by David T. Gies, Special Issue of *Dieciocho: Hispanic Enlightenment, Aesthetics, and Literary Theory*, 9:1–2 (1986).

51 See Gies, 'Introduction' to *Studies for I. L. McClelland*, 3.

internationally, was the outcome of a British initiative. Among the many Hispanists in the United Kingdom who took special pleasure in this tribute-volume was, it should be noted, William Atkinson. By then nearly ninety, her former Head of Department at Glasgow wrote, in his characteristically succinct fashion, to say: 'Ivy's research record leaves the rest of us standing'.[52] Supported by subventions from the British Academy and the University of Glasgow, *The Eighteenth Century in Spain. Essays in Honour of I. L. McClelland*, was edited and published in 1991—appropriately enough, as a Special Number of the *Bulletin of Hispanic Studies*.[53] For, as a distinguished former editor of the journal has testified, her 'services to the *Bulletin of Hispanic Studies* for more than 50 years'—belatedly acknowledged in 1989 through her appointment to the *Bulletin*'s Editorial Committee—

> have been absolutely outstanding—indeed exemplary [. . .]. In her most active retirement she [. . .] continued to lend *BHS* her support. I can think of no-one who has contributed so steadily, and yet so unobtrusively, to the prestige of the journal.[54]

Moreover, in the late 1990s when this journal, by then based at Glasgow University, found itself in severe financial difficulties as a consequence of the protracted legal dispute with the University of Liverpool over the ownership of its title, Ivy McClelland was one of four individuals, three of whom were Hispanists, who, it may now be revealed, privately contributed substantial sums (amounting, in total, to some £30,000) to assist with the legal costs incurred, thereby ensuring the journal's survival.

It was fortunate that she lived long enough to receive personally the internal honours which the University of Glasgow bestowed upon her in the 1980s and 1990s, for she prized them above all others. In 1981 The Ivy McClelland Lecture in Hispanic Studies was established in her name, which since then has been delivered by many distinguished scholars both from the United Kingdom and abroad. Regularly she graced each lecture by her presence until she became too frail to attend. In 1989 Glasgow University recognized both her decades of committed service and her worldwide

---

52 See his letter addressed to Ann Mackenzie, dated 28 March 1991 (Ivy McClelland Papers, Archives, University of Glasgow). For extracts from letters welcoming this British *Festschrift*, sent by other Hispanists (including Albert Sloman, Victor Dixon, Derek Lomax, Donald Shaw, Brian Tate, Arthur Terry, Geoffrey Ribbans and Nicholas Round), see Mackenzie, 'Introduction' to *The Eighteenth Century in Spain. Essays in Honour of I. L. McClelland*, 6–7.

53 *The Eighteenth Century in Spain. Essays in Honour of I. L. McClelland*, ed., with an introduction, by Ann L. Mackenzie, *BHS*, LXVIII:1 (1991).

54 Letter from Geoffrey Ribbans to Ann Mackenzie, Editor, *Bulletin of Hispanic Studies*, dated Brown University, Providence, May 1989 (Ivy McClelland Papers, Archives, University of Glasgow).

reputation as a scholar by awarding her the honorary degree of Doctor of Letters. Responding to this news, Geoffrey Ribbans surely spoke for many of his fellow Hispanists when he wrote:

> I am delighted [. . .] that Glasgow is recognizing Ivy McClelland's devoted and outstanding scholarship by offering her an honorary degree. It is some small compensation for having failed to take a splendid opportunity to give her a personal chair—the result, I suspect, of her sex. I always feel it is such a pity when true dedication is not properly rewarded, usually as a result, not of any bad intentions but simply of nonchalance or unconscious prejudice. At any rate, the degree is great news.[55]

Having retired without ever having held a university chair,[56] this pioneer woman scholar received a further rare distinction when, in 1995, Glasgow University established the 'Ivy McClelland Research Chair of Spanish'. In his letter seeking her prior agreement to its name, the then Principal of the University, Sir William Kerr Fraser, declared that, in founding such a chair in her honour,

> the University would bring credit on itself by recognising in this way your pre-eminence in the field of Hispanic Studies.[57]

The recipient no doubt found equally gratifying another letter that came to her, a month later. This was from Professor Gareth Walters, writing, as Head of Hispanic Studies, to express 'the immense pleasure' her fellow Hispanists at Glasgow

> derived from the decision to establish a Chair in this department that bears your name. [. . .] [Y]our immense contribution to the department, [. . .] and your continued support and encouragement over the years have been properly recognised. That you should have taught the first holder of the new Chair is also most fitting.[58]

At long last, in 1997 the University of Glasgow made Ivy McClelland herself an Honorary Professor in Hispanic Studies. This was for the usual five-year

55 Letter to Ann Mackenzie, dated Brown University, Providence, 26 January 1989 (Ivy McClelland Papers, Archives, University of Glasgow).

56 It should be noted, however, that, after her retirement, she was invited to take up a visiting professorship at University College, Galway. Eager to dedicate herself entirely to research, she regretfully declined. Clearly she valued the invitation, for she preserved the telegram from Galway, dated 22 August 1977, offering her this appointment (Ivy McClelland Papers, Archives, University of Glasgow).

57 Letter to Ivy McClelland from Sir William Kerr Fraser, Principal, dated University of Glasgow, 6 February 1995 (Ivy McClelland Papers, Archives, University of Glasgow).

58 Letter to Ivy McClelland from Professor D. Gareth Walters, dated University of Glasgow, 5 March 1995 (Ivy McClelland Papers, Archives, University of Glasgow).

term, which was not normally extended. But in 2002, in a letter sent on the University's behalf, Dugald Mackie, Secretary of the University Court, informed her that her tenure was being extended for a further five years, citing, in explanation, her 'exceptional contributions to University life, both as teacher and as an internationally renowned scholar in Hispanic Studies during what is now nearly three quarters of a century'.[59] Hispanists everywhere rejoiced in her elevation, even though, as Geoffrey Ribbans commented when he delivered the Ivy McClelland Lecture at Glasgow University on the exact occasion of her ninetieth birthday (18 May 1998), her professorship had come 'about fifty years late'.

Ribbans' 'Ivy McClelland Lecture' on 'The Attitude to Women, and Women Poets, in Spanish Romantic Poetry',[60] attended by many former colleagues and students,[61] was delivered in her presence, following which she was presented with a leatherbound copy of *'Pathos' dramático en el teatro español de 1750 a 1808*, published just in time to mark her four score years and ten. Making the definitive book on *Spanish Drama of Pathos 1750–1808* available for the first time to non-English-speaking Hispanists in Spain and elsewhere, this translation represented, in effect, a further 'Homage' to Ivy McClelland—this time from Spain. For the translation was the work of Fernando Huerta Viñas, her former colleague, now at the Universidad Autónoma, Barcelona, and of his wife, Guillermina Cenoz del Águila. And it was co-introduced by a leading Spanish scholar on the eighteenth century and senior member of Spain's Consejo Superior de Investigaciones Científicas. In his Prologue, Francisco Aguilar Piñal testified that the author of *'Pathos' dramático en el teatro español de 1750 a 1808* had 'los méritos necesarios para ser considerada, no solamente la Decana del hispanismo femenino, sino también una de las más importantes figuras del hispanismo mundial en nuestros días'.[62]

Of all that was spoken and done at Glasgow University on that ninetieth birthday, what touched Ivy McClelland most deeply, as she confessed afterwards, was what Geoffrey Ribbans said in the 'Preamble' to his 'Ivy McClelland Lecture'. That 'Preamble', addressed, for the most part, personally to her, summed up the significance of her career in the following terms:

---

59 Letter to Ivy McClelland from Dugald Mackie, Secretary of the University Court, dated University of Glasgow, 22 August 2002 (Ivy McClelland Papers, Archives, University of Glasgow).

60 This lecture remains unpublished, but its typescript is preserved in the Ivy McClelland Papers, Archives, University of Glasgow.

61 The audience included, most notably, Professor Audrey Lumsden-Kouvel, her colleague at Glasgow during World War II, who had travelled from Chicago especially to attend these ninetieth-birthday celebrations.

62 Aguilar Piñal, 'Prólogo II', in McClelland, *'Pathos' dramático en el teatro español de 1750 a 1808*, I, xi.

> [T]he title of 'Honorary Professor' in the University of Glasgow is a most welcome, if belated, testimony to your distinction, and no less welcome for being about fifty years late. Your record of service, from 1930 till the present day, must be unrivalled anywhere. [...] [T]his annual lecture, which I am privileged to give on this very special day, [...] signals a birthday and a lifetime of achievement it is almost impossible to emulate (I can think only of Don Ramón Menéndez Pidal in terms of scholarship and longevity). As much as to your eminent scholarship [...], I should like to allude to your status as an exemplary role model for university scholars and teachers, especially for women, over this last half-century: to generation upon generation of undergraduates at this university, as tutor as well as teacher, to graduate students who have become teachers and professors, to women scholars in other disciplines in the British Isles and elsewhere, to Hispanists in Spain and all over the world [...] [A] pioneer woman scholar in our discipline, [you have been] the first among a dedicated group who have not had full justice done to them [...]. Professor Ivy McClelland, *prima inter pares*, can and does represent not only her own outstanding achievements but the largely unsung successes among female contemporaries and near contemporaries.[63]

Following Geoffrey Ribbans' lecture, a ninetieth-birthday dinner for her was hosted in style by the University at the Principal's Lodging. On that occasion, the then Principal, Sir Graeme Davies undertook, on the University's behalf, to mark her hundredth year, when it came, in similar fashion. Always the soul of modesty, she is doubtless relieved that she did not quite live long enough to qualify for any centenary celebrations.

Ivy McClelland never married and outlived the members of her immediate family. But, at home in Glasgow, she was blessed with the companionship of her devoted family of close friends. It was thanks to their support—and, above all, to that of Dr Gillian Rodger, a former colleague and trusted friend for nearly sixty years—that she was, even in her nineties, still living in her own flat. A devout Anglo-Catholic, she attended church services twice a week, even when her failing eyesight made the short walk between her home and St Bride's, nearby in Hyndland Road, a perilous excursion. Her favourite indoor relaxations were choral-singing and dress-making. Out of doors, walking was always the activity she most enjoyed. She particularly loved walking in the countryside. Horse-riding was another pleasurable exercise. Astonishingly, she was sixty when she first learned to ride a horse, but, unflustered, she took to it naturally, and into her eighties she continued to go out riding in the countryside near Loch Lomond. She loved all animals, wild or domestic. Written in her later years, her poetry usually dealt with

63 See the 'Preamble' to his lecture on 'The Attitude to Women, and Women Poets, in Spanish Romantic Poetry', 18 May 1998 (Ivy McClelland Papers, Archives, University of Glasgow).

animals, though she sometimes creatively worked in references to universities or Spain. Rich in wit and humour, these 'Nonsense Rhymes', as she called them, are reminiscent of such favourite authors as Lewis Carroll and Edward Lear.

In her nineties, as she confessed privately to her closest friends, she really felt herself to be no different essentially than she had ever been. Her mind still clear and acute, she remained, in the words of her favourite hymn, 'Just as I am' until the end.[64] This came, from a heart attack, some four years after her frailty and deteriorating eyesight had obliged her to enter a nursing home. The short poem that she wrote when country excursions had become too difficult to undertake, revealing, as it does, not only her love of her adopted Scottish countryside but something of her contemplative self, serves fittingly to be her epitaph:

It would be nice
To see the grouse and all the grice,
To hear the birds and bumble-bees
Practise their part songs in the trees.

Then I, beside a heather heap,
Could comfortably fall asleep
Among the sleeping moles and mice
In country air.

It would be nice.

64 She asked for this hymn, by Charlotte Elliott, to be sung at her funeral.

Appendix

Ivy L. McClelland†

Nonsense Rhymes

A Birthday Party*

A birthday party at the Zoo[1]
In honour of a kangaroo,
Was held for him and seven guests
(Invited at their own requests).

A seal leapt from the Zoo-side lake
Holding his gift of an eccles cake.
A bear and lion, paw in paw,
Brought each a carrot, rich and raw.

A tiger, wolf, and chimpanzee
Brought each a pot of birthday-tea.
An elephant arrived in state
With eight iced biscuits on a plate.

Then, afterwards, as soon as each
Had made his lengthy birthday speech,
They changed their seats, to set in place
Two groups, one tenor, and one bass.

They sang about the earth, and seas,
The Ides of March, and apple trees,
Things round about, and things afar,
Etcetera ... etcetera ...

In fact the truth should now transpire:
This was the Zoo's official choir.[2]

---

* Written, the handwriting suggests, in the late 1990s.

1 Ivy enjoyed visits to the zoo in her more active years, observing animals such as elephants and bears that she would not otherwise have met in the flesh. She was particularly fond of elephants. I recall visiting London Zoo with her, at her invitation, in the 1970s.

2 Ivy was for many years a member of the University of Glasgow's Choral Society, and loved singing in this 'official choir', made up not only of members of the University's staff but also of its students.

Letter from a Cat*

Dear Dog,

I wish you wouldn't yap
And thrash around, and leap.
It doesn't get *you* anywhere,
But it disturbs my sleep.

The way you throw your weight about
Is neither right nor nice.
You merely put your foot in things
And it disturbs the mice.

I wish you wouldn't bark and boast.
And that dear hound is that!
With kind regards, I shall remain
Yours faithfully,
a Cat.

Ballad of the Travelling Cats**

There was a row of travelling cats,
Fourteen of them, folk say,
Who started out to see the world
One autumn Saturday.

They crossed a pleasant turnip field
In tidy single file
And disappeared from turnip view
Across a wooden stile.

The first of them was white as snow,
The second black as sloes,
The third, was grey and dignified
And walked upon his toes.

---

* The handwriting indicates that this poem was written no later than the 1980s.

** The handwriting suggests that this was a late poem written, perhaps, in the late 1990s.

The fourth was like a tortoiseshell
With patterns on his back,
The fifth was black with bits of white,
The sixth was white with black.

A ginger cat with tiger stripes
Came next in the parade,
And then a cat of darker fur
Like orange marmalade.

A Persian and a moleskin cat
Then entered into view.
A creamy feline followed them,
Of buttermilky hue.

A Manx cat and a Cheshire cat
Were next ones to appear.
And finally a Siamese
Brought neatly up the rear.

A little later they were seen
Still in a tidy row
Hiring a boat to carry them
As far as it would go.

It sailed away to Eastern lands,
And when they went ashore
They examined the nature of mice and men
And of everything else they saw.

The Shah of Persia, we are told,
On each of seven nights
Invited them to dine with him
And see the Persian lights.

The Persian lights were powerful
And brightened all the air.
The cats put on sun-spectacles
They couldn't stand the glare.

The local bird-choirs in all lands
Through which the travellers passed
Gave concerts for their benefit
And left them all aghast.

A life of such publicity
Left them a little tired.[1]
So they decided to return
And find the boat they'd hired.

It took them back into the West,
They landed where they'd started.
The turnips watched them filing back.
They'd missed the long departure.

The black, the white, the black and white,
The white and black as well,
The ginger cat, the Siamese,
The grey, the tortoiseshell,

The moleskin and the Persian cat —
—Now in a different order—
Went pawing back across the field
Towards the fartherest border.

The orange, Manx and creamy cats
Were next cats to appear,
And smilingly the Cheshire cat
Brought neatly up the rear.

The Haddock*

Oh tell me, have you seen my friend,
My finny friend, the Haddock?
I left him singing chanties
In a corner of the paddock.

1 Ivy McClelland herself, as has been noted, shunned the limelight, rarely, for instance, attending conferences (see 'Introduction', 11).

* Undated, but the writing reveals she composed it before her eyesight began to deteriorate—therefore before 1995, and possibly as early as the 1970s. In verse 2 she reveals her particular fondness for, and high opinion of, horses. She had taken up riding at aged 60.

I told him it was dangerous —
I told him he would rue it.
I warned him time and time again,
And begged him not to do it.

I've asked the frogs and sparrows
And the busybody hen.
I've searched the bank, the watertank,
The whortlepecker's pen.
I even asked a passing horse
Who rushed by in a hurry.
He shouted something kind at me,
Telling me not to worry.

Oh tell me, have you seen my friend
My special friend, the Haddock?
Didn't you hear him singing
At the bottom of the paddock?
I always knew he oughtn't to
Especially in September.
Didn't you hear the words he sang?
I wish I could remember.

His skin is smooth, his eyes are bright,
He moves with rhythmic paces.
He wears a clinging bathing suit
Held up by clinging braces.
He usually waits to sing
Until he starts to swim.
But this time he was indiscreet,
Unnaturally so, for him.

Oh tell him, if you should see my friend,
My finny friend the Haddock,
That I have been searching here for hours
Around and about the paddock.
Tell him I want his company.
I want to hear his news,
I want to know the ins and outs
Of all this subterfuge.

The Polar Bear's Umbrella/The White Umbrella*

It was light when they stole it, as light as day
When they stole his best umbrella away.
If only they'd carried it off at night
—his best umbrella, so sleek and white—[1]
He wouldn't have worried so much, he said.
He never did worry when once in bed.

They carried if off in a little boat.[2]
To all his relations he wrote and he wrote,
And told them the story, with crossings and blots,[3]
Of his beautiful brolly with cinnamon spots,
His best umbrella with cinnamon fringes
And cinnamon handle and cinnamon hinges.

They rowed it away to a rocky cave,
And left it alone, all white and brave!
Alone with the gloomy wuroops and their cousins,
A hundred wuroopans who sauntered in dozens,
And slithered all over the cavernous cobbles
Along with some neighbouring dribbledidrobbles.[4]

---

* There are two versions of this poem, one called 'The White Umbrella', while the other, shorter and unfinished (apparently an earlier attempt), is titled 'The Polar Bear's Umbrella'. The completed version, the handwriting indicates, belongs to the later 1990s, while the first draft dates probably from the 1980s.

1 In the other version this line reads: 'His best umbrella, so clean, so white'.

2 Original version: 'They carried it off in a rowing boat'.

3 Original version: 'And told them the story, with dashes and dots'.

4 In the original draft, this is the poem's final stanza, reads differently and is left unfinished, as follows:

They rowed it away to an island cave,
And left it alone, so white, so brave,
Alone with the gloomy cahoots and their cousins,
The flibberty gibbets, who came in their dozens,
To stare and to wonder as they sauntered [. . .]

But when others forgot about brolly the brave,
The robbers returned to the cavernous cave
And rowed it away to a region of Spain,
Where a don rushed to buy it, though not for the rain.
So now the brave brolly, its rainy work done,
Is happy to shield that rich don from the sun.[5]

Boss-Dog Sweep*

I know a tiny boss-dog.
His Christian name is Sweep.
His barked commands are loud and shrill,
His interests wide and deep.

He keeps two women servants,
Elizabeth and Ann,
And shows them as much courtesy
As any boss-dog can.

His men-friends, Charles and Logan, like
To hear him air his views.
Agnes, his part-time help, is given
The whole of his canine news.

He's courteous too to visitors.
He lets them sit and talk.
He sometimes joins in games with them,
Or takes them for a walk.

He only barks protestingly,
Or registers displeasure,
If staff or guests distort his plans
Or interrupt his leisure.

5 A not surprising happy end, then, to the adventures of the polar bear's umbrella, when it fetches up in Spanish hands in the country the poet-narrator so much loved.

* A poem written *c.* 1990 by Ivy in humorous and appreciative tribute to our family's Yorkshire terrier, Sweep (1982–1997), whose friendship she enjoyed his entire life. The 'Elizabeth and Ann' referred to in verse 2 are myself and my late sister. My brother Charles and late Uncle Logan (d. 2008), with our friend Agnes, get a mention in verse 3—a verse which Ivy, somewhat reluctantly, inserted at my sister's request! AM.

In fact it is an honour, then,
To meet this boss-dog lord.
And if you bow to his commands
A lick is your reward.

Anon.

Terrier Dialogue*

"I'm glad", said Ollie to her terrier-mate,
"That we agreed to come to this estate.
"The grounds are big enough for outside sport,
"The house has inside rooms of every sort.

"Our human staff, Elizabeth and Ann,
"Do everything for us as best they can.
"They seek our favour. They observe our wishes
"In preparation of our dinner-dishes."

"The only thing", said Roly, "that I hate
"Is that they bring our meals some minutes late.
"These human animals depend on clocks
"And do not hear when nature calls and knocks."

"Talking of food", said Ollie, in her turn,
"There is a problem which gives me concern.
"That human animal who brings us meat
"Does not know how to make it fit to eat.

"It's either overcooked without a taste
"Or underdone like bits of meaty-waste.
"Shall we get someone to write her a letter
"Telling her firmly she must cook meat better?"[1]

* This poem and its companion-piece were written *c.*1999. They may reflect, to an extent, Burns' poem 'The Twa Dogs', or Cervantes' *El coloquio de los perros*, an exemplary novel for which Ivy had a particular fondness. By then, at my sister Elizabeth's insistence, our family had acquired, to replace Sweep, two Yorkshire terriers, called Roly and Ollie, with whom Ivy established, as she had with Sweep, an excellent rapport. Roly died by misadventure in late July 2009. Ollie, now aged 12, lives on.

1 A self-mocking reference. On her regular visits to our family home, usually on a Sunday, Ivy would bring the dogs the leftovers from her Sunday roast. She had a low opinion of her own culinary abilities, reflected here.

"Oh, no", said Roly, "she would take offence
"And that would make the atmosphere so tense."
"All right", said Ollie, "leave this for a session.
"Humans are cautious about self-expression.

"Meanwhile let's teach them how to bark and growl,
"How to release all tension with a howl.
"We can prepare such teaching here and now.
"Bow Wow, Bow Wow, Bow Wow Wow, Wow, Wow, Wow."

Anon.

Terrier Dialogue Part II

Increasing notice of the human mind
Was causing the two terriers to find
That dogs — and cats — have sharper brains than those
Which any human beings can disclose.

"We understand all languages", said Roly.
"We have instinctive genius", said Ollie.
"But since all language now is taught by rules,
"Our language must", they said, "be taught in schools."

"All Universities should now prepare
"Extra Departments for Dog Language there."
"All University Vice-Chancellors
"Ought now to study this idea of ours."

It Would Be Nice*

It would be nice
To see the grouse and all the grice,
To hear the birds and bumble-bees
Practise their part songs in the trees.

Then I, beside a heather heap,
Could comfortably fall asleep
Among the sleeping moles and mice
In country air.

It would be nice.

---

* Indications are that this was one of the last poems Ivy wrote.

I. L. McClelland (1908–2006) Bibliography (1930–1999)

CERI BYRNE

University of Glasgow

Note

This bibliography is an updated and expanded version of Ann L. Mackenzie, 'I. L. McClelland: A Bibliography of Her Publications', in *The Eighteenth Century in Spain. Essays in Honour of I. L. McClelland*, edited, with an introduction, by Ann L. Mackenzie, *BHS*, LXVIII:1 (1991), 10–11, which served me as an invaluable starting point. Under each heading, entries have been ordered chronologically. I have included Ivy McClelland's publications that have appeared since 1991 and to these I have added the previously unpublished writings that form part of the present memorial volume. I have listed several other items which either are still only available in typescript, or appear no longer to be obtainable in any form. I have recorded as many of her reviews as I have been able to locate. I have given details, in the notes provided, of some of the most noteworthy reviews by other scholars of her own books. I have also recorded Ivy McClelland's non-Hispanic writings, some of which are still unpublished. I am indebted to Ann Mackenzie for making accessible to me writings which exist only in manuscript or typescript. Items currently in her keeping, will, I understand, be lodged in due course in the Archives of the University of Glasgow.

Theses

Lyrical Poetry in the Nineteenth Century in its Relation to the Spanish Temperament, thesis submitted for the degree of BA Honours (Spanish) (Liverpool University, 1930). (Unpublished; copies held in the Sydney Jones Library, University of Liverpool; Ivy McClelland Papers, Archives, University of Glasgow).

The Native Origins of the Nineteenth-Century Romantic Movement in Spain, MA thesis (Liverpool University, 1932). (An abstract and list of contents are held in the Ivy McClelland Papers, Archives, University of Glasgow). (Revised, enlarged and published as *The Origins of the Romantic Movement in Spain* [1937; see below]).

Books

Antología castellana, Publications of the Institute of Hispanic Studies, Plain Text Series 9 (Liverpool: Institute of Hispanic Studies, 1935), vi+60 pp.[1]

The Origins of the Romantic Movement in Spain. (A Survey of Aesthetic Uncertainties in the Age of Reason), Studies in Hispanic Literatures (Liverpool: Institute of Hispanic Studies, 1937; 2nd ed., with a new Preface, Liverpool: Liverpool U. P., 1975), xiv+402 pp. (2nd ed. simultaneously published New York: Barnes & Noble, 1975).[2]

Tirso de Molina. Studies in Dramatic Realism, Liverpool Studies in Spanish Literature 3 (Liverpool: Institute of Hispanic Studies, 1948), vii+256 pp.[3]

[Anon. Editor], E. Allison Peers, *Studies of the Spanish Mystics*, Vol. III (London: SPCK, 1960), xxiv+338 pp.[4]

Benito Jerónimo Feijoo. Twayne's World Authors Series 51 (New York: Twayne Publishers, 1969), x+172 pp.[5]

Spanish Drama of Pathos 1750–1808. I. *High Tragedy*; II. *Low Tragedy*, 2 vols (Liverpool: Liverpool U. P., 1970), 641 pp. (simultaneously published Toronto: Univ. of Toronto Press), I, xiv+346 pp.; II, xi+295 pp.[6]

1 Reviewed by A.L.S. [?'A Liverpool Scholar'; ?pseudonym of Edgar Allison Peers], *BSS*, XII:47 (1935), 169.

2 First edition reviewed by Nicholson B. Adams, *HR*, 6:1 (1938), 80–82; Anon., 'Romantic and Academic in Spain. A Study of Influences', *TLS*, 5 June 1937, n.p.; Aubrey F. G. Bell, *BSS*, XIV:55 (1937), 156–57; Georges Cirot, *Bulletin Hispanique*, XXXIX:4 (1937), 418–20; Joseph E. Gillet, *MLN*, 53:5 (1938), 371–76; R. Hilton, *MLR*, 32:4 (1937), 643–45; Abelardo Lulio, 'El romanticismo en España', *The Linguists' Review* (1938?), n.p.; John T. Reid, *Hispania* (USA), 20:3 (1937), 294–96; Sterling A. Stoudemire, *The Romanic Review*, 28:4 (1937), 360–61; W. J. E. [William J. Entwistle], *The Oxford Magazine*, 28 October 1937, pp. 100–01. Second edition reviewed by H. B. Hall, *BHS*, LIV:1 (1977), 86.

3 Reviewed by Aubrey F. G. Bell, *BSS*, XXV:100 (1948), 285–86; Courtney Bruerton, *HR*, 17:4 (1949), 343–47.

4 Reviewed by Anon., *Church Times*, 26 February 1960, n.p.; Anon., *Mothers' Union Official Workers Paper* (May 1960), n.p.; Anon., 'The Road to Heaven', *TLS*, 15 April 1960, n.p.; Denis Brass, *The Tablet*, 25 June 1960, pp. 606–07; F. L. Cross, 'Held in Veneration' (review-article), *The Guardian*, 2 March 1960, p. 7; H. D., *Revue d'Histoire Ecclesiastique*, LV:4 (1960), 1152; C. S. Mann, *Church Quarterly Review* 161:341(October–December 1960), 528–29; Margaret, O.H.P, Prioress of Whitby, *View-Review* (May 1960), 10; Robert Pring-Mill, *The Anglo-Spanish Society Quarterly Review* (April–June 1960), 33–34; E. J. Tinsley, *The York Quarterly* (May 1960), n.p.

5 Reviewed by A. Owen Aldridge, *MLR*, 67:3 (1972), 676–78; Anon., *Choice* (March 1970), 180; H. B. Hall, *BHS*, L:4 (1973), 404–05; Edith Helman, *HR*, 40:4 (1972), 474–76; Guido E. Mazzeo, *Hispania* (USA), 53:2 (1970), 336.

6 Reviewed by Anon., *Choice* (March 1971), 142–43; R. Merritt Cox, *Philological Quarterly*, 51:3 (1972), 620–21; John Dowling, *MLN*, 87:2 (1972) [Hispanic Issue], 367–71; Robert Johnson, *BHS*, LII:4 (1975), 414–20; Guido E. Mazzeo, *Hispania* (USA), 55:1 (1972), 178–79; P. P. Rogers, *Romanic Review*, 65:1 (1974), 72–75.

Ignacio de Luzán, Twayne's World Authors Series 221 (New York: Twayne Publishers, 1973), 198 pp.[7]

Diego de Torres Villarroel, Twayne's World Authors Series 395 (Boston: Twayne Publishers, 1976), 162 pp.[8]

Benito Jerónimo Feijoo, *Obras (selección)*, estudio preliminar, edición y notas, Temas de España 150 (Madrid: Taurus, 1985), 216 pp.[9]

Ideological Hesitancy in Spain 1700–1750, Publications of the *Bulletin of Hispanic Studies*, Textual Research and Criticism (Liverpool: Liverpool U. P., 1991), viii+152 pp.[10]

'Pathos' dramático en el teatro español de 1750 a 1808. I. *La alta tragedia*; II. *La tragedia menor*, traducción a cargo de Fernando Huerta Viñas & Guillermina Cenoz del Águila, con prólogos de Ann L. Mackenzie & Francisco Aguilar Piñal, Hispanic Studies TRAC (Textual Research and Criticism) 7, 2 vols (Liverpool: Liverpool U. P., 1998), I, xxvi+422 pp.; II, vii+344 pp. (Spanish translation of *Spanish Drama of Pathos 1750–1808*).[11]

Articles

'The Poetry of Bécquer: An Appreciation', *BSS*, XII:46 (1935), 96–110. (Reprinted in *Liverpool Studies in Spanish Literature*. I: *From Cadalso to Rubén Darío* [see entry below]).

'Bécquer, Rubén Darío, and Rosalía Castro', *BSS*, XVI:62 (1939), 63–83. (Reprinted in *Liverpool Studies in Spanish Literature*. I: *From Cadalso to Rubén Darío* [see entry below]).

'Gustavo Adolfo Bécquer' and 'Bécquer, Rubén Darío and Rosalía Castro', in *Liverpool Studies in Spanish Literature*. I: *From Cadalso to Rubén Darío*, ed. E. Allison Peers (Liverpool: Institute of Hispanic Studies, 1940), 220–39, 240–64.[12]

'Tirso de Molina and the Eighteenth Century', *BSS*, XVIII:72 (1941), 182–204.

'The Conception of the Supernatural in the Plays of Tirso de Molina', *BSS*, XIX:76 (1942), 148–63.

---

7 Reviewed by Anon., *Choice* (April 1974), 265.

8 Reviewed by Anon., *Choice* (April 1977), 228–29; Dru Dougherty, *Library Journal*, 101:17 (1.10.76), 2065; David T. Gies, *HR*, 45:4 (1977), 455–58.

9 Reviewed by Philip Deacon, *BHS*, LXV:2 (1988), 187–88.

10 Reviewed by Anon., *The British Bulletin of Publications on Latin America, the Caribbean, Portugal and Spain*, 91 (October 1994), 70; David T. Gies, *BHS*, LXIX:2 (1992), 200–01; Paul Ilie, *HR*, 60:4 (1992), 489–91; Sally-Ann Kitts, *MLR*, 87:4 (1992), 1011–12.

11 Review-article by Joaquín Álvarez Barrientos, *BHS*, LXXVII:2 (2000), 93–96.

12 Reviewed by Nicholson B. Adams, *HR*, 10:2 (1942), 168–71; A. F. G. Bell, *BSS*, XVIII:70 (1941), 98–100.

'New Interpretations of Spanish Poetry: V.—Bécquer, "Rima XV"', *BSS*, XIX:75 (1942), 135–36.

'The Mob Scene in Tirso de Molina's *Antona García*', *BSS*, XX:80 (1943), 214–31.

'Biblioteca de Autores Españoles, 1846–1946' (review-article), *BSS*, XXIII:92 (1946), 240–48.

'The New St Teresa' (review-article on *The Complete Works of St Teresa de Jesús*, trans. & ed. E. Allison Peers), *BSS*, XXIV:93 (1947), 55–57.

'Concerning the Dramatic Approach to the Eighteenth Century', *BHS*, XXVII:106 (1950), 72–87.

'The Eighteenth-Century Conception of the Stage and Histrionic Technique', in *Estudios hispánicos. Homenaje a Archer M. Huntington*, ed. Ada M. Coe, Jorge Guillén, Anita Oyarzaba and Justina Ruiz de Conde (Wellesley, Mass.: Wellesley College, 1952), 393–425.

'"Comellan" Drama and the Censor', *BHS*, XXX:117 (1953), 20–31.

'Comentario sobre *La disputa del teatro*. Sainete anónimo de 1776', in *Homenaje a J. A. van Praag*, ed. G. F. Pijper *et al*. (Amsterdam: L. J. Veen, 1956), 81–88.

'The Significance of Feijoo's Regard for Francis Bacon', *Studium Ovetense. Revista del Instituto Superior de Estudios Teológicos del Seminario Metropolitano de Oviedo*, 4 (1976), 249–74.

'Prólogo en inglés y castellano', in *30 sonetos* [translations from Shakespeare], traducción y selección de J. F. Elvira-Hernández (Piedrahita [Ávila]: Sexifirmo, 1977), 10–19.

'*Raquel*, drama histórico racional', in *Historia y crítica de la literatura española*, coord. por Francisco Rico, vol. IV, tomo 1: *Ilustración y Neoclasicismo*, coord. por José Miguel Caso González (Barcelona: Editorial Crítica, 1983), 281–87.

'G. A. Bécquer: "Porque son, niña, tus ojos ...". A Study in Green', in *Readings in Spanish and Portuguese Poetry for Geoffrey Connell*, ed. Nicholas G. Round and D. Gareth Walters (Glasgow: Dept of Hispanic Studies, Univ. of Glasgow, 1985), 106–17.

'El estilo humano de Feijoo', in *Historia y crítica de la literatura española*, coord. por Francisco Rico, vol. IV, tomo 2: *Ilustración y Neoclasicismo: primer suplemento*, coord. por David T. Gies (Barcelona: Editorial Crítica, 1992), 92–95.

'The Comellan Conception of Stage-Realism', *Dieciocho*, 16:1–2 (1993), 111–17.

'Allison Peers as a University Teacher: Recollections of a Former Student in his Department', in E. Allison Peers, *Redbrick University Revisited. The Autobiography of 'Bruce Truscot'*, ed., with intro., commentary and notes, by Ann L. Mackenzie and Adrian R. Allan, E. Allison Peers Publications 1 (Liverpool: Liverpool U. P., 1996), 397–99.

'En los alrededores del "Ilustrismo": Cándido María Trigueros y Antonio Valladares', in *El siglo que llaman ilustrado. Homenaje a Francisco Aguilar Piñal*, coord. por José Checa Beltrán y Joaquín Álvarez Barrientos (Madrid: CSIC, 1996), 629–34.

'The Mystical "Dark Night" of San Juan de la Cruz as Interpreted in Poetic Summary', in *Spain and its Literature. Essays in Memory of E. Allison Peers*, ed., with an Introduction, by Ann L. Mackenzie, Hispanic Studies TRAC (Textual Research and Criticism) 15 (Liverpool: Liverpool U. P./ London: MHRA, 1997), 103–08.

'La personalidad literaria de Torres Villarroel', in *Revisión de Torres Villarroel*, coord. por Manuel María Pérez López y Emilio Martínez Mata, Acta Salmanticensia 270 (Salamanca: Univ. de Salamanca, 1998), 61–65.

'Cernuda's Local Source of Inspiration for His Poem "Los espinos"', *BHS*, LXXVI:2 (1999), 258–61.

'"Impugnador de preocupaciones": *El Correo de los ciegos de Madrid* 1787 and Public Opinion in Spain on the Eve of European Revolution', ed. Ann L. Mackenzie, in *Hesitancy and Experimentation in Enlightenment Spain and Spanish America. Studies on Culture and Theatre in Memory of I. L. McClelland*, ed., with an Introduction, by Ann L. Mackenzie and Jeremy Robbins, *BSS*, LXXXVI:7–8 (2009), 60–81. (Previously unpublished article).

'*The London Merchant* y sus relaciones con la experimentación dramática en la España del siglo XVIII', ed. Fernando Huerta Viñas, in *Hesitancy and Experimentation in Enlightenment Spain and Spanish America. Studies on Culture and Theatre in Memory of I. L. McClelland*, ed., with an Introduction, by Ann L. Mackenzie and Jeremy Robbins, *BSS*, LXXXVI:7–8 (2009), 170–79. (Lecture, previously unpublished, delivered at the Universidad Autónoma de Barcelona, 7 June 1982).

'A Propaganda Play of 1808: F. Enciso Castrillón's *La defensa de Valencia y castigo de traidores*', ed. Ann L. Mackenzie, in *Hesitancy and Experimentation in Enlightenment Spain and Spanish America. Studies on Culture and Theatre in Memory of I. L. McClelland*, ed., with an Introduction, by Ann L. Mackenzie and Jeremy Robbins, *BSS*, LXXXVI:7–8 (2009), 238–57. (Previously unpublished article).

'Polemical Tactics [of Torres Villarroel]'. (Chapter written 1975; unpublished and now lost).[13]

13 This was intended to be the third chapter in Ivy McClelland's monograph on Torres Villarroel (1976) for Twayne. But she found herself obliged to withdraw this chapter, so as to shorten the book sufficiently, to adhere to the strict limits of length imposed by the publishers. As a result, this chapter on Torres' 'Polemical Tactics' was never published, and evidently no longer exists.

'La contribución que hizo Gaspar Zavala y Zamora al desarrollo del Ilustrismo español'. (Unpublished and now lost).[14]

Numerous articles on Spanish authors and subjects published in key-works of reference, which essays include the following:

'Juan Ruiz de Alarcón'; 'Guillén de Castro'; 'Benito Feijoo'; 'José Francisco de Isla'; 'Leandro Fernández de Moratín'; 'José Manuel Quintana'; 'Tirso de Molina; Galicia (in part); Madrid (in part) (*Chambers Encyclopaedia*).

'José Martínez Ruiz (Azorín)'; 'Ramón de Campoamor y Campoosorio'; 'Alonso de Castillo Solórzano'; 'Antonio de Capmany y Montpalau'; 'Emilio Cotarelo y Mori'; 'Ramón de la Cruz'; 'Bernal Díaz del Castillo'; 'Don Juan'; 'Pedro Espinosa'; 'Juan Pablo Forner'; 'V. A. García de la Huerta y Muñoz'; 'Tirso de Molina' (*Encyclopaedia Britannica*).

Book Reviews

Innumerable book reviews published, *inter alia*, in *Modern Language Review, Theatre Research / Recherches Théâtrales* (*later Theatre Research International*), *Review of English Studies, the British Journal for Eighteenth-Century Studies*, but, above all, in the *Bulletin of Spanish / Hispanic Studies* (1930–1999), for which she wrote more than 135 reviews of books mostly on aspects of the eighteenth century in Spain, but also on a wide range of other topics and periods, including the mystics, Golden-Age drama, the Age of Romanticism, Spanish history, Spanish America and modern Spanish poetry.

Juan Cano, *La 'Poética' de Luzán*, *BSS*, VII:25 (1930), 41–42.

Alfonso de Valdés, *Diálogo de Mercurio y Carón*, ed. José F. Montesinos, *BSS*, VII:27 (1930), 148–49.

Charles Wickestead Armstrong, *Life in Spain Today*, *BSS*, VIII:29 (1931), 55.

Azorín [José Martínez Ruiz], *An Hour of Spain*, trans. Alice Raleigh, with an intro. by Salvador de Madariaga, *BSS*, VIII:29 (1931), 54.

Ronald M. Macandrew, *Naturalism in Spanish Poetry*, *BSS*, VIII:31 (1931), 163–65.

14 This invited article was written and accepted in the mid 1990s for publication in *Un 'hombre de bien'. Saggi di lingue e letterature iberiche in onore di Rinaldo Froldi*, presentazione di Maurizio Fabbri, a cura di Patrizia Garelli e Giovanni Marchetti, e con la collaborazione di Livia Brunori, Luigi Contadini, Cristina Fiallega, Marco Presotto, Patrizio Rigobon e Roberto Vecchi. However, publication of this *Festschrift* (Alessandria: Edizioni dell'Orso, 2004), 2 vols, was so long delayed that several articles originally intended to appear in it were withdrawn or went astray—among them the contribution by Ivy McClelland. Regrettably, it has proved impossible to locate any copy of this essay.

Cecilia Hill, *Moorish Towns in Spain*, *BSS*, IX:33 (1932), 59–60.

Fr Bruno de J. M., *Saint John of the Cross*, ed. Fr Benedict Zimmerman, with an intro. by Jacques Maritain, *BSS*, X:38 (1933), 93–95.

William J. Entwistle, *The Scope of Spanish Studies*, *BSS*, X:37 (1933), 50–51.

Edith Fishtine, *Don Juan Valera: The Critic*, *BSS*, XI:43 (1934), 182.

Cuentecitos, ed. Lawrence A. Wilkins & Ana L. de Oller, *BSS*, XII:47 (1935), 170.

María F. de Laguna, *Outlines of Spanish Pronunciation and Intonation, BSS*, XII:47 (1935), 171.

Salvador de Madariaga, *Don Quixote: An Introductory Essay in Psychology, BSS*, XIII:49 (1936), 42–44.

Aubrey F. G. Bell, *Castilian Literature*, *BSS*, XV:59 (1938), 158–60.

J. R. Spell, *Rousseau in the Spanish World before 1833, BSS*, XVI:62 (1939), 114–15.

Rubén Darío, *Escritos inéditos*, ed. Erwin K. Mapes, *BSS*, XVII:68 (1940), 236–38.

Handbook of Latin American Studies, IV, ed. Lewis Hanke, *BSS*, XVIII:69 (1941), 46–47.

E. Allison Peers, *A History of the Romantic Movement in Spain, Review of English Studies*, 17:65 (1941), 116–17.

Julio Jiménez Rueda, *Juan Ruiz de Alarcón y su tiempo*, *BSS*, XX:80 (1943), 250–51.

E. Allison Peers, *Spain in Eclipse, 1937–43*, *BSS*, XXI:82 (1944), 97–98.

James F. Shearer, *The 'Poética' and 'Apéndices' of Martínez de la Rosa: Their Genesis, Sources and Significance for Spanish Literary History and Criticism, BSS*, XXI:82 (1944), 108.

Rachel Bérendt, *Sarah Bernhardt en mi recuerdo*, *BSS*, XXIII:91 (1946), 231.

Emilio A. Coni, *El gaucho*, *BSS*, XXIII:90 (1946), 141–43.

Alfonso Junco, *El Milagro de las Rosas*, *BSS*, XXIII:92 (1946), 295.

Moisés Ochoa Campos, *Juan Ignacio María de Castorena Ursúa y Goyeneche (1668–1733): primer periodista mexicano, BSS*, XXIII:91 (1946), 230–31.

Jesús Pabón, *Las ideas y el sistema napoleónicos*, *BSS*, XXIII:92 (1946), 288–89.

Fernán Pérez de Oliva, *Diálogo de la dignidad del hombre*, *BSS*, XXIII:92 (1946), 295–96.

Luis C. Pinto, *El gaucho rioplatense frente a los malos historiadores, BSS*, XXIII:90 (1946), 141–43.

José Roberto del Río, *Vida de José Hernández*, *BSS*, XXIII:90 (1946), 141–43.

José Torre Revello, *La orfebrería colonial en Hispanoamérica y particularmente en Buenos Aires, BSS*, XXIII:91 (1946), 230–31.

Carmelo V. Zingoni, *Formación universitaria del maestro*, *BSS*, XXIII:92 (1946), 295.

Joaquín Casalduero, *Jorge Guillén: 'Cántico'*, *BSS*, XXIV:96 (1947), 291–92.

Fernando Díaz-Plaja, *La vida española en el siglo XVIII*, *BSS*, XXIV:95 (1947), 219.

Arturo Farinelli, *Don Giovanni*, *BSS*, XXIV:95 (1947), 202.

Ángel Ganivet, *Spain: An Interpretation*, trans. J. R. Carey, *BSS*, XXIV:95 (1947), 206–07.

Philip Hendy, *Spanish Painting*, *BSS*, XXIV:95 (1947), 204–05.

María Jiménez Salas, *Vida y obras de D. Juan Pablo Forner y Segarra, BSS*, XXIV:95 (1947), 217–18.

Salvador de Madariaga, *The Rise of the Spanish-American Empire*, *BSS*, XXIV:96 (1947), 279–81.

E. Allison Peers, *'New' Tongues*, *BSS*, XXIV:93 (1947), 70.

Tirso de Molina [extracts from his plays], rev. ed., *BSS*, XXIV:95 (1947), 219.

Duke of Berwick and Alba, *The Great Duke of Alba As a Public Servant*, *BSS*, XXV:97 (1948), 84.

Luis Cernuda, *Como quien espera el alba*, *BSS*, XXV:99 (1948), 180.

Mariano Darenas, *El periodismo, profesión social*, *BSS*, XXV:97 (1948), 85.

Myra Caldwalader Hole, *Bartolomé Mitre: A Poet in Action*, *BSS*, XXV:99 (1948), 183–84.

Fernando José de Larra, *La sociedad española a través del teatro del siglo XIX*, *BSS*, XXV:97 (1948), 85–86.

Rafael Maya, *Alabanzas del hombre y de la tierra*, *BSS*, XXV:97 (1948), 75–76.

Rafael Maya, *Poesía*, *BSS*, XXV:97 (1948), 75–76.

Poetas en el destierro, ed. José Ricardo Morales, *BHS*, XXVI:103 (1949), 192.

Fernando Lázaro Carreter, *Las ideas lingüísticas en España durante el siglo XVIII*, *BHS*, XXVII:105 (1950), 54–55.

Tirso de Molina, *Por el sótano y el torno*, ed., pról. & notas de Alonso Zamora Vicente, *BHS*, XXVII:106 (1950), 119.

Tirso de Molina, *La prudencia en la mujer*, ed., with intro. & notes, by Alice Huntington Bushee & Lorna Lavery Stafford, *BHS*, XXVII:106 (1950), 117–18.

Juan Pablo Forner, *Cotejo de las églogas que ha premiado la Real Academia de la Lengua*, ed. Fernando Lázaro Carreter, *BHS*, XXIX:113 (1952), 71.

Kate O'Brien, *Teresa of Ávila*, *BHS*, XXIX:113 (1952), 70–71.

E. Allison Peers, *The Mystics of Spain*, *BHS*, XXIX:114 (1952), 118–19.

Ada M. Coe, *Carteleras madrileñas*, *BHS*, XXX:118 (1953), 123.

Tomás de Iriarte, *Poesías*, ed., with intro. & notes, by Alberto Navarro González, *BHS*, XXXI:4 (1954), 249.

Tirso de Molina, *Obras dramáticas completas*, II, ed. Blanca de los Ríos, *BHS*, XXXI:1 (1954), 56–57.

María Carmen de Artigas-Sanz, *El libro romántico en España*, *BHS*, XXXIV:1 (1957), 56–57.

Manuel Bretón de los Herreros, *El pelo de la dehesa*, ed. Joseph Manson, *BHS*, XXXIV:1 (1957), 58.

Tirso de Molina, *Antona García*, ed., with an intro., by Margaret Wilson, *BHS*, XXXV:2 (1958), 101–02.

José de Cañizares, *Angélica y Medoro*, ed. Julius A. Molinaro & Warren T. McCready, *BHS*, XXXVII:1 (1960), 65–66.

John A. Cook, *Neo-classic Drama in Spain. Theory and Practice, BHS*, XXXVII:2 (1960), 120–21.

Fr Crisógono de Jesús Sacramentado, *The Life of St John of the Cross*, trans. Kathleen Pond, *BHS*, XXXVII:1 (1960), 65.

Jean-François Gilmont, *Les Écrits spirituels des premiers jésuites*, *BHS*, XL:1 (1963), 56–57.

Ignacio Iparraguirre, *Répertoire de spiritualité ignatienne*, *BHS*, XL:1 (1963), 56–57.

María Jiménez Salas, *Santa Teresa de Jesús: bibliografía fundamental, BHS*, XL:3 (1963), 202.

San Juan de la Cruz, *Avisos para después de profesos. Nuevo escrito del santo doctor*, ed. Simeón de la S. Familia & Tomás de la Cruz, *BHS*, XL:1 (1963), 57–59.

Russell P. Sebold, *Tomás de Iriarte: poeta de 'rapto racional', BHS*, XL:2 (1963), 120–21.

Mario di Pinto, *Studi su la cultura spagnola nel settecento, BHS*, XLIII:1 (1966), 64–65.

Francisco Aguilar Piñal, *La Real Academia Sevillana de Buenas Letras en el siglo XVIII, BHS*, XLV:3 (1968), 237–39.

Rinaldo Froldi, *Un poeta iluminista: Meléndez Valdés*, *BHS*, XLV:4 (1968), 314–16.

Frank P. Casa, *The Dramatic Craftsmanship of Moreto, Theatre Research / Recherches Théâtrales*, X:1 (1969), 55–56.

Francisco Aguilar Piñal, *Cartelera prerromántica sevillana. Años 1800–1836, BHS*, XLVII:1 (1970), 83–84.

Nicasio Álvarez de Cienfuegos, *Poesías*, ed. José Luis Cano, *BHS*, XLVII:3 (1970), 260–61.

Félix María de Samaniego, *Fábulas*, ed. Ernesto Jareño, *BHS*, XLVII:3 (1970), 260–61.

Austin Clarke, *Two Interludes. 'El viejo celoso' and 'La cueva de Salamanca' Adapted from Cervantes, Theatre Research / Recherches Théâtrales*, XI:1 (1971), 54–55.

J. P. Wickersham Crawford, *Spanish Drama before Lope de Vega*. Reprinted (1967) with corrections and Bibliographical Supplement by W. T. McCready, *Theatre Research / Recherches Théâtrales*, XI:1 (1971), 59.

René Andioc, *Sur la Querelle du théâtre au temps de Leandro Fernández de Moratín, BHS*, XLIX:4 (1972), 408–10.

Juan Pablo Forner y Segarra, *Los Gramáticos, Historia chinesca*, ed. John H. R. Polt, *MLR*, 67:1 (1972), 199–200.

Juan Vélez de Guevara, *Los celos hacen estrellas*, dramatic text edited by J. E. Varey and N. D. Shergold, musical texts edited by J. Sage, *Theatre Research/Recherches Théâtrales*, XII:2 (1972), 196–97.

Javier Herrero, *Los orígenes del pensamiento reaccionario español*, *MLR*, 68:2 (1973), 429–30.

John R. Polt, *Gaspar Melchor de Jovellanos*, *MLR*, 68:4 (1973), 915–16.

Nigel Glendinning, *A Literary History of Spain. The Eighteenth Century*, BHS, LI:2 (1974), 177–79.

Ignacio López de Ayala, *Numancia destruida*, ed. Russell P. Sebold, *BHS*, LI:1 (1974), 98–99.

J. E. Varey y N. D. Shergold, *Teatros y comedias en Madrid: 1651–1665. Estudio y documentos, Theatre Research/Recherches Théatrales*, 13:2 (1974), 202.

Fernando Wagner, *Teoría y técnica teatral, Theatre Research/Recherches Théâtrales*, 13:2 (1974), 217.

Diego de Torres Villarroel, *Vida*, ed. Guy Mercadier, *BHS*, LII:4 (1975), 413–14.

J. E. Varey, *Los títeres y otras diversiones populares de Madrid, 1758–1840, BHS*, LII:1 (1975), 99–100.

R. Merritt Cox, *Juan Meléndez Valdés*, *MLR*, 71:3 (1976), 706–07.

Gabriela Makowiecka, *Luzán y su 'Poética'*, *BHS*, LIII:2 (1976), 155–56.

Gustavo Umpierre, *Songs in the Plays of Lope de Vega: A Study of Their Dramatic Function, Theatre Research International*, II:1 (1976), 68–69.

Francisco Aguilar Piñal, *Impresos sevillanos del siglo XVIII, BHS*, LIV:1 (1977), 64.

_____ *Sevilla y el teatro en el siglo XVIII, BHS*, LIV:1 (1977), 64–65.

M. Fabbri, P. Garelli, & P. Menarini, *Finalità ideologiche e problematica letteraria in Salazar, Iriarte, Jovellanos, BHS*, LIV:1 (1977), 65–66.

Ignacio de Luzán, *La Poética*, ed. Isabel M. Cid de Sirgado, *BHS*, LIV:1 (1977), 63–64.

Guy Mercadier, *Diego de Torres Villarroel: masques et miroirs, BHS*, LV:3 (1978), 268–69.

Ramón del Valle-Inclán, *Luces de Bohemia/Bohemian Lights*, trans. A. N. Zahareas and G. Gillespie, *Theatre Research International*, 3:3 (1978), 218–19.

Louise Fothergill-Payne, *La alegoría en los autos y farsas anteriores a Calderón, Theatre Research International*, 4:2 (1979), 150–51.

Nigel Glendinning, *Goya and His Critics*, *BHS*, LVI:1 (1979), 69–70.

Francisco Aguilar Piñal, *La prensa española en el siglo XVIII*, *BHS*, LVII:1 (1980), 90.

An Annotated Analytical Bibliography of Tirso de Molina Studies, 1627–1977, ed. Vern G. Williamson and compiled by Walter T. Poesse, *Theatre Research International*, 6:1 (1980), 74–75.

Tomás de Iriarte, *El señorito mimado. La señorita malcriada*, ed. Russell P. Sebold, *MLR*, 75:1 (1980), 221–22.

Joan Lynne Pataky Kosove, *The 'Comedia lacrimosa' and Spanish Romantic Drama (1773–1865), MLR*, 75:1 (1980), 222–23.

José de Cadalso, *Escritos autobiográficos y epistolario*, ed. Nigel Glendinning & Nicole Harrison, *BHS*, LVIII:3 (1981), 268–69.

R. Merritt Cox, *Eighteenth-Century Spanish Literature*, *MLR*, 76:1 (1981), 222–24.

David T. Gies, *Nicolás Fernández de Moratín*, *BHS*, LVIII:3 (1981), 267–68.

N. D. Shergold & J. E. Varey, *Teatros y comedias en Madrid: 1687–1699. Estudio y documentos, Theatre Research International*, 6:2 (1981), 149–50.

Diego de Torres Villarroel, *Vida*, ed. Dámaso Chicharro, *BHS*, LIX:4 (1982), 344.

Francisco Aguilar Piñal, *Bibliografía de autores españoles del siglo XVIII*, I, *BHS*, LX:2 (1983), 154–55.

_____ *Índice de las poesías publicadas en los periódicos españoles del siglo XVIII, BHS*, LX:2 (1983), 154–55.

La época de Fernando VI. Ponencias leídas en el Coloquio Conmemorativo de los 25 años de la fundación de la Cátedra Feijoo, BHS, LX:4 (1983), 343–44.

II Simposio sobre el Padre Feijoo y su siglo: ponencias y comunicaciones, *BHS*, LX:4 (1983), 342–43.

Fray Benito Jerónimo Feijoo, *Obras completas*. I. *Bibliografía*, ed. José Miguel Caso González & S. Cerra Suárez, *BHS*, LXI:4 (1984), 525.

Juan Meléndez Valdés, *Obras en verso*. I, ed. John H. R. Polt & Georges Demerson, *BHS*, LXI:4 (1984), 526.

Ramón de la Cruz, *Sainetes*, ed. John Dowling, *BHS*, LXII:4 (1985), 408–09.

José de Cañizares, *El anillo de Giges*, ed. Joaquín Álvarez Barrientos, *BHS*, LXIII:4 (1986), 388–89.

Paul Mérimée, *L'Art dramatique en Espagne dans la première moitié du XVIIIe siècle, BHS*, LXIII:3 (1986), 291–92.

La biblioteca de Jovellanos (1778), ed. Francisco Aguilar Piñal, *BHS*, LXIV:2 (1987), 164.

Guillermo Carnero, *La cara oscura del Siglo de las Luces*, *BHS*, LXIV:2 (1987), 166–67.

Tony Cross, *Joseph Blanco White. Don José María Blanco y Crespo, BHS*, LXIV:3 (1987), 263.

Ramón de la Cruz, *Marta abandonada y carnaval de París*, ed. Felisa Martín Larrauri, pref. de Ermanno Caldera, *BHS*, LXIV:2 (1987), 166.

Maurizio Fabbri, *Vagabondi, visionari, eroi: apunti su testi in minore del Settecento spagnolo, BHS*, LXIV:2 (1987), 163–64.

Gaspar Melchor de Jovellanos, *Obras completas.* I. *Obras literarias*, ed. José Miguel Caso González, *BHS*, LXIV:3 (1987), 262–63.

_____ *Obras completas.* II. *Correspondencia.* I *(1767–1794)*, ed. José Miguel Caso González, *BHS*, LXIV:4 (1987), 377–78.

Francisco Lafarga, *Las traducciones españolas del teatro francés (1700–1835). I: Bibliografía de impresos, BHS*, LXIV:3 (1987), 262.

_____ *Voltaire en España (1734–1835), BHS*, LXIV:3 (1987), 262.

José López de Sedano, *Marta aparente*, ed. Antonietta Calderone, *BHS*, LXIV:2 (1987), 166.

Brancanelo el Herrero, ed. Joaquín Álvarez Barrientos, *British Journal for Eighteenth-Century Studies*, XIII:2 (1990), 275–76.

Juan de Grimaldi, *La pata de cabra*, ed. David T. Gies, *BHS*, LXV:3 (1988), 306–07.

Manuel Pardo de Andrade, *'La Conversione de Sant'Agostino', tragi-commedia*, ed. María Rosa Saurín de la Iglesia, *BHS*, LXV:2 (1988), 188–89.

Russell P. Sebold, *Descubrimiento y fronteras del neoclasicismo español, BHS*, LXV:3 (1988), 306.

Diego de Torres Villarroel, *Vida*, ed. Russell P. Sebold, *BHS*, LXV:2 (1988), 186–87.

Francisco Aguilar Piñal, *Bibliografía de autores españoles del siglo XVIII,* II–IV, *BHS*, LXVI:2 (1989), 204.

_____ *Un escritor ilustrado: Cándido María Trigueros, BHS*, LXVI:4 (1989), 382–83.

Diario de los literatos de España, ed. & intro. by J. M. Ruiz Veintemilla, *BHS*, LXVI:4 (1989), 382.

Iris M. Zavala, *Lecturas y lectores del discurso narrativo dieciochesco, BHS*, LXVI:3 (1989), 285–86.

Francisco Aguilar Piñal, *Bibliografía de estudios sobre Carlos III y su época, BHS*, LXVIII :2 (1991), 335.

José Antonio de Armona y Murga, *Memorias cronológicas sobre el teatro en España (1785)*, ed. Emilio Palacios Fernández, Joaquín Álvarez Barrientos & María Carmen Sánchez, *BHS*, LXVIII:3 (1991), 424.

Edward V. Coughlin, *Nicasio Álvarez de Cienfuegos, BHS*, LXVIII:4 (1991), 542.

Gaspar Melchor de Jovellanos, *Obras completas.* IV. *Correspondencia (1801–1808)*, ed. José Miguel Caso González, *BHS*, LXVIII:3 (1991), 425–26.

Manuel Pardo de Andrade, *Los artículos del 'Diario de Madrid' (1794–1800)*, ed. María Rosa Saurín de la Iglesia, *BHS*, LXVIII:4 (1991), 541–42.

Francisco Aguilar Piñal, *Bibliografía de autores españoles del siglo XVIII*, V, *BHS*, LXIX:2 (1992), 200.

Gaspar Melchor de Jovellanos, *Obras completas. V. Correspondencia (1808–1811)*, ed. José Miguel Caso González, *BHS*, LXIX:4 (1992), 282.

Francisco Aguilar Piñal, *Bibliografía de autores españoles del siglo XVIII*, VI, *BHS*, LXX:3 (1993), 378.

_____ *Introducción al siglo XVIII, Historia de la literatura española*, XXV, *BHS*, LXX:3 (1993), 378.

Jesús Pérez-Magallón, *En torno a las ideas literarias de Mayans*, *BHS*, LXX:4 (1993), 469–70.

Emilio Martínez Mata, *Los 'sueños' de Torres Villarroel*, *HR*, 61:2 (1993), 286–87.

Joaquín Álvarez Barrientos, *La novela del siglo XVIII*, *BHS*, LXXI:2 (1994), 273–74.

José Francisco de Isla, *Historia del famoso predicador Fray Gerundio de Campazas, alias Zotes*, ed. José Jurado, *BHS*, LXXI:3 (1994), 404.

Pen and Peruke: Spanish Literature of the Eighteenth Century, ed. Monroe Z. Hafter, *BHS*, LXXI:3 (1994), 403–04.

Ignacio de Luzán, *La virtud coronada*, ed. Francisco Jarque Andrés, *BHS*, LXXII:2 (1995), 233–34.

Francisco Aguilar Piñal, *Bibliografía de autores españoles del siglo XVIII*, VII–VIII, *BHS* (Glasgow), LXXIV:4 (1997), 478–79.

Gaspar Melchor de Jovellanos, *Obras completas*. VI. *Diario, Cuadernos 1790–94*, *BHS* (Glasgow), LXXIV:2 (1997), 228–29.

Joaquín Álvarez Barrientos, François López & Inmaculada Urzainqui, *La República de las Letras en la España del siglo XVIII*, *BHS* (Glasgow), LXXV:2 (1998), 267–68.

Historia literaria de España en el siglo XVIII, ed. Francisco Aguilar Piñal, *BHS* (Glasgow), LXXV:4 (1998), 553–54.

Negotiating Past and Present: Studies in Spanish Literature for Javier Herrero, ed. David T. Gies, *BHS* (Glasgow), LXXVI:2 (1999), 305–06.

Gabriel Sánchez Espinosa, *La biblioteca de José Nicolás de Azara*, *BHS* (Glasgow), LXXVI:5 (1999), 711.

Cándido María Trigueros, *Los menestrales*, ed. Francisco Aguilar Piñal, *BHS* (Glasgow), LXXVI:4 (1999), 577–78.

Lectures

'Goya (1746–1828) and His Times'. (Unpublished lecture, delivered in the Department of Hispanic Studies, University of Glasgow, March 1990; original handwritten version is located in the Archives, University of Glasgow).

'The Ingenuity of Golden-Age Drama'. (Unpublished lecture probably delivered [?1980s] to Honours students in the Department of Hispanic Studies, University of Glasgow; original handwritten version is located in the Archives, University of Glasgow).

Homage Volumes in Honour of Ivy McClelland

Studies for I. L. McClelland, ed., with an Introduction, by David T. Gies, Special Issue of *Dieciocho: Hispanic Enlightenment, Aesthetics, and Literary Theory*, 9:1–2 (1986), 297 pp.[15] Published with funding support from Rutgers, The State University of New Jersey, the University of Virginia and the 'Program for Cultural Cooperation between Spain's Ministry of Culture and Northamerican Universities'.

The Eighteenth Century in Spain. Essays in Honour of I. L. McClelland, ed., with an introduction, by Ann L. Mackenzie, *BHS*, LXVIII:1 (1991), 246 pp. Published with funding support from the British Academy and the University of Glasgow. Also published as a book: Liverpool: Liverpool U. P., 1991.[16]

Hesitancy and Experimentation in Enlightenment Spain and Spanish America. Studies on Culture and Theatre in Memory of I. L. McClelland, ed., with an Introduction, by Ann L. Mackenzie and Jeremy Robbins, *BSS*, LXXXVI:7–8 (2009), 269 pp. Also published as a book: Abingdon: Routledge, Taylor & Francis Group).[17]

Obituaries and Memoirs

Nicholas Round, 'Professor Ivy McClelland: Scholar of 18th-Century Spain', *The Independent*, 28 April 2006, p. 46.

Ann L. Mackenzie, 'Ivy McClelland: Academic, Honorary Professor, Renowned Hispanist and Poet', *The Herald*, 2 May 2006, p. 14.

Anon., 'Ivy McClelland', *The Times*, 29 May 2006, 43.

Kevin Gopal, *Northwest Enquirer*, Issue No. 7, 9 June 2006, p. 28.

Unattributed [David T. Gies], 'I. L. McClelland', *Dieciocho*, 29:2 (Fall 2006), 309.

Ann L. Mackenzie, 'Introduction: I. L. McClelland (1908–2006)', in *Hesitancy and Experimentation in Enlightenment Spain and Spanish America. Studies on Culture and Theatre in Memory of I. L. McClelland*, ed., with an Introduction, by Ann L. Mackenzie and Jeremy Robbins, *BSS*, LXXXVI:7–8 (2009), 9–30.

---

15 Reviewed by Francisco Lafarga, 'Miscelánea dieciochesca: homenaje a McClelland' (review-article), *Ínsula*, 485–86 (1987), 15; Carmen Chaves McClendon, *South Atlantic Review*, 53:2 (1988), 154–56.

16 Reviewed by Peter B. Goldman, *BHS*, LXIX:4 (1992), 380–81.

17 The book edition is forthcoming in 2011.

Ann L. Mackenzie, 'McClelland, Ivy Lilian (1908–2006), Scholar of Spanish Literature', *Oxford Dictionary of National Biography* (Oxford: Oxford U. P., 2010), Article ID 97189.

Creative and Non-Hispanic Writings

The University of Glasgow's Queen Margaret Hall c.1950–60. (Unpublished memoirs which she discreetly disguised, deliberately left unattributed, and titled only as *Women's Hall of Residence circa 1960*. These memoirs, in fact, concern Ivy McClelland's experiences as tutor and sub-warden of Queen Margaret Hall of Residence for Women Students at Glasgow University. The typescript is located in the Ivy McClelland Papers, Archives, University of Glasgow.)

Nonsense Rhymes[18]

'A Birthday Party'
'Letter from a Cat'
'Ballad of the Travelling Cats'
'The Haddock'
'The Polar Bear's Umbrella/The White Umbrella'
'Boss-Dog Sweep'
'Terrier Dialogue'
'Terrier Dialogue. Part II'
'It Would Be Nice'

18 This is the author's own title for her poems, which were found, handwritten, in a separate folder among her papers (see Ivy McClelland Papers, Archives, University of Glasgow). These poems are published in this Memorial Volume (see Appendix to the Introduction, pp. 31–42).

PART II

‘Impugnador de preocupaciones’ *El Correo de los ciegos de Madrid* 1787 and Public Opinion in Spain on the Eve of European Revolution

I. L. McCLELLAND†
University of Glasgow

ed. Ann L. Mackenzie
University of Glasgow

Introductory Note to I. L. McClelland†, 'Impugnador de preocupaciones' *El Correo de los ciegos de Madrid* 1787 and Public Opinion in Spain on the Eve of European Revolution

In *The Origins of the Romantic Movement in Spain* (1937) Ivy McClelland refers as follows to the *Correo de los ciegos*, which,

> primarily a reporter of general news, and only in a secondary degree literary, sustained throughout its course a sturdily independent attitude towards all topics. Its bi-weekly publications, because of their varied matter, reached a wider public than the monthly ones of the *Memorial Literario*, and in every respect it is more truly a journal of the people. Yet it is not be despised. [...] It is a mine of information on the social and literary life of Madrid. Its pages were open to all shades of literary opinion, and its literary correspondents, if frequently of popular tastes and not given to academic preciseness, seldom passed unreasonable judgments or praised extravagances. Indeed, they had a knack, as good popular journalists often have, of hitting the mark exactly.[1]

Apparently written around 1981,[2] this hitherto unpublished article, in which she discusses the periodical in much greater detail than in any of her other writings,[3] exemplifies, characteristically, the profundity of Ivy McClelland's thinking on Spain's profoundly complex eighteenth century, to which she devoted so many researches. The article sheds light on that

1 See I. L. McClelland, *The Origins of the Romantic Movement in Spain* (*A Survey of Aesthetic Uncertainties in the Age of Reason*) (Liverpool: Institute of Hispanic Studies, 1937; 2nd ed. Liverpool: Liverpool U. P., 1975), 147–48.

2 The used brown envelope in which she kept this piece is postmarked '29.5.81'. Besides the article's title, the envelope carries, in her handwriting, a brief message to herself: 'Alter'. Clearly she **did** indeed alter her original draft. For, as well as the final version, the envelope contains an earlier typed draft with her handwritten alterations added throughout.

3 Nevertheless, as indicated, there are valuable comments on this periodical in McClelland, *The Origins of the Romantic Movement in Spain*, especially pp. 147–51.

century's vital shifts in mentality, to the exploration of which, some ten years later, she was to devote her final monograph—*Ideological Hesitancy in Spain*.[4] Written with the breadth of knowledge, fresh insights and elegant precision in style for which she was renowned, this essay could not be more suited to serve as an introduction to the other studies, which, in her memory, scholars internationally have contributed here, to deepen further our understanding of the eighteenth century in Spain and in its colonies.[5]

Ann L. Mackenzie

University of Glasgow.

4 See *Ideological Hesitancy in Spain 1700–1750*, Publications of the *Bulletin of Hispanic Studies*, Textual Research and Criticism (Liverpool: Liverpool U. P., 1991).

5 In editing this article, I have expanded Ivy McClelland's original short title 'Impugnador de preocupaciones' to give a fuller indication of its concerns. To assist readers, I have also added some notes. The author's own notes, which were only three in number, have had, in consequence, to be renumbered, but carry asterisks, so as to be readily differentiated from my additions. I have not otherwise altered the article which the author herself had so carefully revised.

‘Impugnador de preocupaciones’ *El Correo de los ciegos de Madrid* 1787 and Public Opinion in Spain on the Eve of European Revolution

I. L. McCLELLAND†
University of Glasgow

ed. Ann L. Mackenzie
University of Glasgow

The correspondent who, in April 1787, applied the description ‘impugnador de preocupaciones’ to the *Correo de los ciegos de Madrid* was presumably unaware either of the whole significance of his phrase to journalism, or of the fact that European ‘preoccupations’ were becoming involved in a revolutionary movement. But, like many of his compatriots, he was sufficiently affected by ideological disturbance to recognize the potential force of a relatively new instrument of expression, the Periodical Press, and perhaps to perceive direction in the currents of troubled opinion. ‘Preoccupation’, in Spanish eighteenth-century terminology, meant ignorance, prejudice, superstition, the unventilated, the obscure, the perplexed; and by the spring of 1787 the Periodical Press had begun to regard itself as an informed exponent of and commentator on public opinion.

El Correo de los ciegos de Madrid,[1] appearing first in October, 1786, and continuing publication until 1791, is one of the longer-lived eighteenth-century periodicals of the capital,[2*] with a more general appeal than the *Memorial literario* which considerably outlived it, and perhaps with a more consciously spacious outlook than the news-minded *Diario de Madrid* which began in 1758 and continued well into the next century. The *Correo* is,

1 *Correo de los ciegos de Madrid*, later called *Correo de Madrid y de los ciegos* (Madrid: Imprenta Real, later J. Herrera, 1786–91). The author consulted, and quotes from, the copies of this periodical housed in the Hemeroteca, Madrid.

2* See Eugenio Hartzenbusch, *Apuntes para un catálogo de periódicos madrileños desde el año 1661 al 1870* (Madrid: Sucesores de Rivadeneyra, 1894), 12–13. Cotarelo (Emilio Cotarelo y Mori, *Iriarte y su época* [Madrid: Sucesores de Rivadeneyra, 1897], 320–21, n. 5) attributes the editorship of the *Correo de los ciegos de Madrid* to Nipho (‘redactado por el infatigable Nifo’), though he offers no proof to support this attribution.

therefore, as suitable a periodical as any from which to observe the shifts of Spanish public opinion on the eve of a European revolution that carried the confuting of 'preoccupations' to extremes. Also, as this journal, within the first six months or so of publication, shows not only a marked development in social awareness but in the conception of its own modern function, it serves economically to illustrate, on the popular level, Spain's agony of transition.

A few decades earlier the Periodical Press—very young and unsteady—had been struggling to find a form of expression free from the aridity of the announcement-and-advertisement sheet and the constrictions of the polemical pamphlet. Most periodicals of the 'sixties were primarily critics, with a specialized and partisan appeal, though the wide interests of Nipho frequently indicated lines along which more general development might be possible.[3] But Spain of the 'sixties was still easily shocked by non-Peninsular standards of values, and few there were in a midway position between the small company of the scandalizing and the large body of the scandalized to suggest that Spain's future might be linked exclusively neither with foreign innovation nor with a mere prolonging of tradition. Consequently journalists, bent on proving theses, were usually more compelling than receptive, and their work was an exacting assertion of their captious personalities. By the 'eighties more foreign ideas had had time, and, at certain slackening periods of censorship, opportunity to circulate. It was under this wider stimulus of foreign, objective self-questioning and analysis that Spain's periodicals learnt to trace an independent course for themselves and to grow in maturity. Once alive to the newer spirit of editorial 'chairmanship', as opposed to editorial dogmatism, their growth was rapid, so rapid that it can be startlingly illustrated within the first half year of this new bi-weekly, *El Correo de los ciegos*.

Theoretically and originally the *Correo*'s manner was unashamedly pedagogic. Its tone was self-righteously moral. Its utilitarian aim was to improve the reader's mind by fomenting a 'taste for reading' on the broad basis of what would nowadays be called general knowledge or current topics:

> La idea pues se reduce a presentar alternativamente algunos rasgos particulares de Historia, de Economía, de Política y de Moral, y a reproducir *bajo diverso aspecto* las novedades y cosas *más útiles* y curiosas que anunciaren todos los papeles públicos de España, y las que pudiéramos recoger por nosotros mismos, no sólo de España, sino también de las naciones extranjeras. Extractaremos igualmente, y copiaremos todo lo que nos parezca oportuno, aprovechándonos de las lecciones de la experiencia, y

3 Francisco Mariano Nipho (Nifo) (1719–1803), the presumed editor of the *Correo de los ciegos*, engaged in numerous periodical-related projects. 'Su labor periodística', as has been noted, 'le otorga el carácter de primer periodista español' (see Jerónimo Herrera Navarro, *Catálogo de autores teatrales del siglo XVIII* [Madrid: Fundación Universitaria Española, 1993], 336). For a useful study, see L. Enciso Recio, *Nipho y el periodismo español del siglo XVIII* (Valladolid: Univ. de Valladolid, 1956).

> de los sugetos juiciosos, y amigos de la patria que tuvieren la bondad de advertirnos, corregirnos y aconsejarnos; [. . .] (Tuesday, Oct. 10th)[4]

So far, probably, no European periodical addressed to the general public had completely rid itself of a preceptive aim deriving from the superiority of the lettered over the unlettered, and to some extent determining the selection of news or instruction to be included for the good of the less discriminating reader. In the days of reforms from above readers expected instruction, and that it would be given in tutorial tones unacceptable to more modern generations. Consequently the periodical, predisposed to a pedagogic approach, automatically assumed the *rôle* of teacher rather than that of shaper or organizer of public opinion. Moreover in an epoch which revered utility of ends it seemed natural to the journalist to direct himself paternally to the public's moral welfare. The tone suggesting that one member of the public is addressing his mental equals and fellow citizens is modern and depends on the assertiveness of an educated middle class. Even at the outset, however, the *Correo* did its best to mingle with the crowd. Its sale was in the hands of the blind poor, always conspicuous citizens of Madrid, who, as receptively-minded beggars, or as leisured vendors of songs or pamphlets, or, nowadays, lottery tickets, have always been near to the Villa's pulse of opinion. Further, the public was informed that signed or unsigned articles of correspondence might be handed to the blind vendors if authors preferred this alternative to forwarding manuscripts directly to the editor. Such arrangements would not be unusual. What is notable is the emphasis given to all this democratic and popular transaction in the title of the periodical itself. When in 1787 it changed its name to *Correo de Madrid* to identify itself more urgently with its locality, it did not dissociate itself from the popular and retained its original name as a sub-title.

In the long run it was not so much the *Correo*'s all-too-obvious modes of instruction, its educational information, that constituted its enlightenment. Its teaching of history or ethics by anecdote, its reports of scientific and social achievement in themselves do not progress beyond the didactic. The significant element in its journalistic growth over the first six months is its increasing ventilation of topical problems as problems, rather than as object lessons, and so its increasing exercise in social self-analysis and ultimately in scientific objectivity. While letters from the provinces and reports from the capital have their news value, news, on the whole, is made of less account than assessment and discussion. After publishing the opposed views of two correspondents the editor sometimes allows a general debate to develop by impartially printing letters with a range of opinions on the same theme, so as to constitute, spiritually, if not formally, something like the correspondence page of a modern newspaper where opinions, shouted with individual feeling,

4 An extract taken from the 'Advertencia' in the first issue of the *Correo*, of 10 October 1786, explaining the periodical's aim.

acquire their combined or relative meaning by being recorded side by side. Admittedly many correspondents were incoherent, fatuous, and carried away by the desire to see themselves in print. They have their counterparts to-day. Many, however, factual, analytical, deeply serious, or humorously tolerant, produced views of length and breadth and depth which gave to numerous popular problems a three-dimensional aspect, enabling readers to move round those problems for themselves and make up their own minds about them from almost any angle. It is a method which registers for posterity the whole process in the public mind of its assimilation of any new idea. Growth of this nature was not, of course, envisaged in the editorial aims of October. Any suggestion at that stage that the paper might provide a means of pooling popular doubts, perplexities and criticisms of social conditions instead of pooling useful information, would presumably have been unacceptable to the didactic editor. The *Correo*, then, is didactic in theory, and is receptive, impartial and progressive only incidentally and through practical experience.

A reference in the first issue to the infamous article '¿Qué se debe a España?' published in the *Encyclopédie méthodique*, indicates one source of exterior stimulus to Peninsular stocktaking and comparative analysis.[5] This wounding French article had the excellent effect of provoking Spanish critical activity throughout the 'eighties and 'nineties. The *Correo* echoes Franco-Spanish controversy on the subject and contributes constructively to defence-morale by instancing the technical *Examen marítimo* as a fresh example of Spanish scholarship. But in these later 'eighties external stimuli were hardly necessary. The *Correo*, with its colleagues and rivals, reflects a busy process of stocktaking already set in motion, and an experience of teeming new ideas, as painful or confusing as they were invigorating. Puzzling its way through the last years of this critical decade the *Correo* is probably, despite its relative cautiousness of expression, as intelligent and as sensitive to European atmosphere as any good popular periodical abroad.

Not a few of the articles published in the first quarter are of a kind to predispose the reader, albeit unwittingly, to healthy controversy. But as if to emphasize its position on the side of tradition and conventional respectability the *Correo*, in its 'Rasgos morales', primly discourses at frequent intervals on orthodox morality and religion, generally with relation to relaxed discipline abroad: for instance, on belief in God as author of all life, in face of 'impious philosophers' who attribute life to 'chance' (Nov. 14th); on the dangers of the primrose path of self-interest (Nov. 21st); on the need to subordinate passions to higher interest (Dec. 15th); on the sin of hopelessness; on the wrongness of

5 This was the article in the *Encyclopédie méthodique. Géographie moderne*, ed. Didier Robert de Vaugondy and Nicolas Masson de Morvilliers, 3 vols (Paris: Panckoucke, 1783 [1782]–1788); see Vol. I, 565–66. The article was 'written by a certain M. Masson de Morvilliers, who, in the bluntest and most insulting terms, denied that Spain had made any contribution to any branch of European civilization' (McClelland, *The Origins of the Romantic Movement in Spain*, 100–01).

suicide (Nov. 7th): a moral consideration which had often troubled Spanish lovers of classical tragedy attracted to refinements of ordered logic and proportion but half-repelled by pagan criteria. Nevertheless even in these partly dogmatic, partly self-defensive assertions of orthodoxy the threat of disturbance is present. An article of November 14th on fundamental principles of Moral Philosophy is notable for its fervent emphasis of fundamentals, like scholastic proofs for the existence of God, and for the fact that in devout Spain it seemed necessary to the author to argue on a popular level for the existence of God at all. For, behind the determined implication of Faith, was the recognition that, somewhere, it was being questioned, and the tone of the article, unlike the serene tone of *a priori* reasoning in catechismic question and answer, or the tone of intellectual zest in scholastic exercises, is slightly excited, with the excitement of one who supports a life-size motion against life-size opposition. It anticipates potential danger.

This does mean, however, that the *Correo* in deploring the attitude of the impious on revealed religion is instinctively in favour of negative methods of obscurantism. Like most liberal Englishmen, and most thoughtful Spaniards, the *Correo*'s Editor sought a middle way: progress without heresy. There is a difference, it is implied, between religion and superstition. Certainly the 'Rasgo moral' of December 29th as determinedly defends the cause of knowledge and enlightenment as the existence of God had been defended the month before, and with a similar tone of excitement as if, this time, it were anticipating life-size protest from the opposite direction. The words excuse, emphasize, constructively argue:

> Si los pueblos que cultivan las ciencias no se ven exentos de ciertos desastres, es porque las ciencias no están aún bien extendidas; porque la parte que gobierna, no está bastante ilustrada, y conserva todavía la marca de los siglos bárbaros [...] Delante de las luces esparcidas en una nación, se ve desaparecer la crueldad y la autoridad más fiera calla cuando está destituida de razón. El pueblo más ignorante y más supersticioso es también el más perverso y más cruel.

On more concrete levels the *Correo* early and eagerly displays interest in the kinds of social projects, news, or grievances, capable of acting for the public as social talking points; in the practical Caroline reforms that encouraged reformist orientation of mind. In one way or another the attention of all classes had been directed to possibilities of material betterment. The *Correo* acts as popular guide, reporter and commentator. All sorts of practical topics are passed under review: building developments in Toledo; a new inn there with all modern comforts, and a fine new episcopal palace (Oct. 20th, Nov. 10th, etc.); dramatic performances, the physical state of the theatres, acting and actors, provide obvious food for debate;[6*] experiments in agriculture, possible dangers, likely to be of general interest, of continuing the experiment of producing sugar from maize (Oct. 24th); the peasants' need of small holdings (Nov. 17th); the problem of their low standard of living, the disadvantages of their public bakeries, with incidental reference to the democratic view of Henri IV: 'No he de parar hasta que cada uno de mis vasallos coma gallina en el puchero todos los días' (Dec. 26th); problems of infant mortality (Oct. 20th), freak illnesses (Oct. 20th); and many other topics in the discussions from which we can learn about the epoch's applications to everyday life of the movements occurring within the practical sciences.

More significant, however, is the treatment of controversial topics neither dangerously theological nor limitedly concrete: topics on which, at least until Floridablanca began to erect his barriers against the alarming incursion of French Liberalism in 1789,[7] discussion could freely develop in new directions, and topics, which, of themselves, could promote discussion to infinity. The *Correo* zestfully catches at what is vital in the mental life of the times. At a period when a self-conscious *costumbrismo*—invariably popular in Spain at all social levels—might have turned this periodical into a chatty *Spectator* of Cruz-like modes and manners,[8] it displayed a less literary and more progressive desire to act as promoter, sometimes as Chairman, of social debates.

Its most progressive instinct of the first quarter was its valiant, conscious attempt to re-adjust public attitudes to conform to more objective principles, at least in selected spheres. Perhaps the most positive lesson which the destructive, disillusioned century had to teach was that truth is many-sided and that serious thinkers could not afford to study it from one side only. In pursuit of complex truth the age had begun clumsily to remove unproved assumptions cluttering its field of reason, and was prepared, or was preparing to re-consider cause and effect in everyday experience as a means of obtaining new evidence. On its humble level the *Correo* imitates this bid for empiric judgment. A new mental orientation is illustrated, for instance, in papers appearing at intervals under the title 'Rasgos históricos'.

The subject of historical truth is introduced with notable force of sincerity by the publication on November 21st of a letter criticizing historical method. Historians, thought the correspondent, had been reprehensively content

6* As I have discussed theatres in other contexts, I have omitted the *Correo*'s references to them in the present survey.

7 'Before the growing menace of the French Revolution, Charles IV's chief minister, Floridablanca, tightened all censorship' (I. L. McClelland, *Spanish Drama of Pathos 1750–1808*. I. *High Tragedy*; II. *Low Tragedy*, 2 vols [Liverpool: Liverpool U. P., 1970] [simultaneously published Toronto: Univ. of Toronto Press], I, 188).

8 A wittily indirect reference to Addison's *Spectator*, and, of course, to the social 'modes and manners' portrayed in Cruz's *sainetes*.

when reporting on celebrated figures of the past—on the successful conquerors and lawgivers with their military prowess or heroic pronouncements—and had failed to keep them in perspective by neglecting their defects, their private characteristics, and, in fact, all qualities falling short of exterior brilliance. The correspondent therefore proposes for the *Correo* a historical sketch impartially drawn; and, as a first essay, in perspective, considers the character of Alexander the Great with due reference to his vindictive cruelty. (See Nov. 24th and succeeding issues.) And if in this and other portraits of great men appearing frequently in the *Correo* from this time onwards,[9] a tendency can be discerned towards political innuendo, or to advance the moral thesis that the sword is less glorious than pastoral staff or rod of Justice; if, increasingly through the series, the 'historical' method turns anecdotal under the European influence of anecdotal reporting on, in particular, the private life of Frederick the Great of Prussia, that does not destroy the initial force of significance of this passionate plea in this letter, in this popular periodical, for a more realistic standard of values:

> Semejante infidelidad es ciertamente muy perniciosa. Contra ella no tenemos otro antídoto que el de la crítica. Al favor de ella descubrimos los motivos que pudieron obligar al historiador a callar lo malo, publicando sólo lo bueno, castigando de este modo su parcialidad, o negligencia. La contemporaneidad a su héroe, cierto respeto, o deferencia hacia su memoria, cuando aún está reciente su muerte, un interés mal entendido, que toma el autor en su asunto por ser tratado por su pluma, y algunas veces una tímida política, ve aquí las miserables pasiones, que no le dejan llevar su pluma con la libertad y desinterés, que exigen el honor de la verdad, y más que todo el provechoso modelo o escarmiento que sacaría la posteridad de una exacta y verídica narración. (Nov. 21st)

Historical notes in ensuing weeks (Nov. 28th, Dec. 5th, Dec. 8th, Dec. 12th) are still busily occupied with the remote Alexander, but by January 1787 the death of Frederick the Great had released a flood of royal anecdotes and inspired the *Correo*'s historian with modern matter for the examination of heroes of flesh and blood. Frederick the Great himself comes under scrutiny in an anecdotal 'Rasgo de Virtud' of December 29th, and is followed, in later numbers, by a whole band of modern monarchs: Charles XII of Sweden (Jan. 5th), Peter the Great of Russia (Jan. 12th, Jan. 16th), the sixteenth-century Czar Ivan who, according to tradition, went about in disguise to discover what his people really thought of him (Mar. 9th), his contemporary the great Duke of Alba (May 2nd)—all of whom illustrate the century's scientific interest in what

9 For comment on these 'portraits', see McClelland, *Spanish Drama of Pathos 1750–1808*, II, 510–15.

in monarchs is ordinary, and incidentally present embodiments of real-life virtues and defects for the experimenting theatres. Collectively, as popular illustrations of the period's lack of confidence in inherited estimates of 'greatness' these articles are more important than intrinsically and individually they might seem. Concentrating on human means rather than on god-like ends, they strike a mental attitude which is part of the authentic life of the times.

In the same way tentative articles of this first quarter on social institutions or on problems raised by reforms roughly indicate the extent to which social questions were occupying the mind of the general public. A set of articles (Oct. 13th and later issues) on ancient Roman economics seems, by implication, to be identifying itself with criticism of Spain's uneasy economic conditions, and to be suggesting modern remedies disguised as ancient Roman policy. For instance these articles pointedly hint at the need for freedom in the choice of a trade or profession, perhaps with the idea of showing that the Caroline policy of raising guild-restrictions was as yet insufficiently radical (Nov. 10th); they stress the dangers of under-population and the value to the community of marriage and family life especially in places where celibacy is unduly widespread and where sexual intercourse outside wedlock is undermining the family's importance. Not only do these articles, in their indirect way, urge particular solutions like the restriction of celibacy to those for whom marriage is incompatible with their office, with the implication that the number of official celibates might be kept within reasonable bounds, but in general they help to prepare the ground for open discussion on eighteenth-century problems like the financial complications created by undertaking marriage responsibilities, or the strain of regular planning on slender means, or the need to save for education, widowhood, and other hazards of the kind (see Oct. 13th, Oct. 17th, Nov. 24th, Dec. 12th).

One is hardly surprised, when, even in the first quarter, two of the most notorious of Spain's age-old 'preoccupations' are calculatedly brought out for review. One is the almost Oriental obsession with *hidalgo*-caste, a disproportionate indulgence, at whatever cost or sacrifice and against all practical principles, in leisurely living and freedom from manual or mercenary enterprise. The other is the extreme Spanish version of the European gentleman's code of honour which tacitly assumed that the law courts, certainly cumbersome and corrupt, were not proper repositories for a gentleman's private affairs and could not, by cowardly reasoning, relieve him of his sense of outrage, or take away his traditional privilege of clearing his own name in his own direct way.

Now that the state, with money, prizes, moral support and other forms of encouragement, was endeavouring to increase the working population and to coax indigent gentlepeople into considering commerce as a more honourable occupation than ruinous idleness, now that the private enterprise of an intellectual minority had obtained royal recognition for technical colleges of the societies of the Amigos del País, the conservative public, even if cynical of the government's intentions, talked about them; and as subjects of conversation they circulated through the Press, gradually and indirectly disturbing over-fixed ideas.

'In London, Paris and Rome', states a correspondent on October 17th, 'men of status are treated with respect', and he invites the public which tends to despise the servant-class, to consider how much better it is to serve and work in a servant-capacity than to do no work at all. On October 20th the writer of the *Correo*'s Moral Notes describes a dream in which he had been translated to a lofty social plane where he had full opportunities for 'commanding' and 'despising', and here, having acquired a belief in the natural superiority of the upper classes, he was affronted to hear that nobility ought to be founded solely upon personal virtue:

> Habiéndole ocurrido a uno decir en mi mesa que los hombres no tienen más que una estirpe, y que la nobleza debería fundarse sobre virtudes personales, le sostuve, que para ser algo en este mundo, era preciso haber nacido hidalgo [. . .]

This idea stirred up considerable feeling in subsequent weeks after a correspondent of November 7th had passionately revived the subject. The new writer took the conservative view that those of noble birth who can demonstrate their nobility in their actions are, and always have been, more rightly respected than commoners endowed with equal virtues, and that class-distinction has always been necessary for good government. So heated did this correspondent become that the editor felt obliged to explain that the Moral Dream criticized only non-virtuous nobility, and was not an attack on social hierarchies. At the same time he felt impelled stubbornly to add in the cause of common sense, as opposed to traditional illusion, that reason will only grant natural superiority to the man of rank so long as he is equal in merit to the commoner, and emphatically not if he is inferior in that respect:

> Prefiérase en hora buena un hidalgo a un plebeyo en igualidad de mérito; pero que sobrepujando el de éste, se haga más aprecio del noble sólo por ser noble, ni lo sufre la razón, ni puede ser buena máxima política, ni creemos haya gobierno ilustrado que lo practique [. . .]

The same subject was brought up again in an outspoken letter (Dec. 1st) from a young *extremeño* who commented on the innate vanity of the nobly born and asserted that since any virtue of our forefathers was virtue in them and not in us, there can be no pride so ill-founded as that which is founded on birth:

> Es tan difícil el apartar de la nobleza la vanidad como sacar plata de las minas sin mezcla de tierra . . . en vano las mejores plumas de todos los siglos . . . se empeñaron en persuadir que no hay orgullo más mal fundado que el que se arregla por el nacimiento . . .

Closely connected with this research into preoccupation with birth is a whole series of pronouncements on man's inherited conception of personal honour and the relation of his *pundonor* to what had come to be recognized in Europe as one of the evils of society: the duel of honour, or the usurpation of objective judicial authority of the state by the impassioned individual. The duel had long offended the reasonable century in that it was incompatible with the conception of collective justice embodied in that ideal state which towered over the imagination of famous thinkers. In eighteenth-century Utopia, where government was directed by a disinterested council of the wise few for the benefit of the less gifted, average citizen, there could be no question of the illegality of a citizen's taking the law into his own interested hands. A sense of humour might undermine visionary states bookishly advocated by those who did not know themselves or their fellow men, but the man in the street, as well as the intellectual citizen of the world, was in favour of some kind of social reform, and, in one way or another, in books or through the Press, became familiar with certain political ideologies too perfect to exist in their entirety, but capable of being imitated in part.

Justice and the crying need for judicial reforms were to become favourite subjects of debate in the periodical's next quarter. Meanwhile the topical problem of private vengeance against which the Spanish state, like others, had been trying to legislate, is introduced by way of an anecdote from a foreign newspaper. This tells of an offended Frenchman who, in anger, struck a Scots Captain 'Douglas', and instead of being challenged to a duel for the blow, was courteously forgiven. The story sounds so like the incident recorded by Boswell while on the Grand Tour in 1764, about himself and a French Captain Durand,[10*] that the two anecdotes may be related. The Boswell-incident had doubtless been re-told frequently. At all events, since more is known about the working of Boswell's mind than about that of Captain Douglas, one may assume that, mingled with Scots magnanimity and practical common sense in these Northerners, there went a certain alarm at having landed themselves in a nasty predicament before witnesses and on foreign soil. The *Correo*'s Captain sounds more equal to an international trial of swordmanship than the dilettante Boswell, whose alarm is all too evident. But, fortunately for the latter, the question of what constituted true or false points of honour had already been ventilated so thoroughly that he was able to take advantage of the publicity it had received and avoid a duel without damage to his reputation. This question, though not new in 1786 to proud, touchy, individualistic Spaniards, had been less thoroughly ventilated than in France or England and was less susceptible to reason. So that had 'Captain Douglas' eased himself out of a duel in Madrid his story might have been sung—especially by street ballad-mongers—to a different tune; unless, of course, as a foreigner he could have

10* See *The Yale Editions of the Private Papers of James Boswell*, ed. Frederick A. Pottle, 13 vols (New York: McGraw 1950–1981), IX, *Boswell on the Grand Tour, 1764*.

passed for a man of eccentric reactions like the notorious archtype Frederick II of Prussia, and could seem to be striking an individualistic attitude on a heroic plane. There is always the chance that the Spaniard may admire eccentric persons where he cannot admire logical systems.

> Estoy [Douglas is speaking] seguro que en este momento siente él [the Frenchman] penas mil veces más crueles que las que podría causarle mi espada. Voy a abrazarle y a procurar reconciliarle consigo mismo; pero me batiré con el primero de Vms que se atreva a ofender mi honor.

For its part the *Correo* is at pains to support the case for reason. 'Nobody', it therefore adds wishfully and firmly, 'would fail to agree that had Douglas fought out of a false sense of honour he would have behaved less honourably'.

This story had fairly caught the interest of the *Correo* which, in a note on November 3rd, again took up the case for civilized behaviour by vigorously reminding readers that the duel, unlike the single combat, was a modern tradition founded on a poor conception of honour which nobody had been able properly to explain or define, and which, converting man into a savage egoist, allowed him to defy the claims of reason and the majesty of the law. If Spain were to be converted to the ways of reason, as these were understood abroad, the work of journalists in popularizing rational arguments was at least as compelling as state decrees, especially if the journal had no obvious connection with the government. Yet a publicity-campaign organized from above but conducted as matter of topical discussion on the mental level of the average citizen, and in journals of a sufficiently popular standard to dispel his distrust, is not necessarily, at this popular stage, a conscious, missionary enterprise. The journals largely presented a state of awareness. In the eighteenth century our modern Press methods were beginning to take shape, and the changing mind of that transitional period must have been more generally affected by this dramatic new instrument of awareness than by an academic climate of abstracts. So the *Correo*, if originally didactic in intention, was in these instances indulging no more and no less in deliberate propaganda than modern counterparts independent of government opinion. It was primarily reviewing problems in the light of modern experience, and giving publicity to them by the mere fact that they were common to all men sufficiently high on the social scale to be able to read.

Another burning question of those days when technical demands of competitive commerce and industry revealed the lack of technical education, and when reforms in education involved thinking to some extent in terms of Locke, Rousseau and the Encyclopaedists, was the advantage or otherwise of empiric method. Liberally educated by foreign informants, yet mindful of national values, the *Correo* takes an enlightened attitude on all questions of educational development, and early in 1787 breaks out into observations on empiric techniques. A much earlier issue (Oct. 20th, 1786) contains a letter on

Spain's need of more free schools, and refers to the enlightened work undertaken by the Sociedades Económicas de Amigos del País, and by the Minister Campomanes.[11] On October 31st further correspondence on the same subject discusses the need for aid over and above that supplied by Sociedades Económicas, and, on November 14th, another letter makes the point that the provision of statistics has been imperfectly organized in some places, so that Spain's pressing need of more free schools, particularly in small communities, is not yet fully realized. The whole question of education becomes, in the next quarter, a regular subject of discussion.

A similar development in interest is shown in articles on the mental potentialities of women. The Spaniard travelling abroad, as the *Correo* did, soon discovered that Spain for various reasons—good reasons to some minds, bad to others—had been neglecting the less obvious aspects of womankind, notably her intellect. While few Spanish men could instinctively approve of woman in a position as dominating as that of an English Blue Stocking or the presiding genius of a French salon, and probably none would have been prepared to ask, for example, renowned actresses to meet his wife and children, some were beginning to understand that for industrial and commercial reasons the daughter of a working-class family needed to know more than her catechism, more even than to read and write; while a gentlewoman could no longer be considered cultured by international standards on the basis of her achievements in embroidering, music, and, perhaps, spelling. Cautiously, but inevitably since foreign ideas still had relatively free circulation, the educated Spaniard was obliged to revise his views about what every woman should know and how and by whom she should be taught; while the *Correo* and its fellow journals, automatically registered the moods, reactions, the half comprehension, and the dawning perceptions of this process in the popular mind.

In early numbers of the *Correo* women's topics are conducted in the half fatherly, half gallant tone of a Spanish *Spectator*: their looks, their characters (Nov. 10th), their mania for following fashions, even fashion in medicines (Nov. 17th), their extravagance and frivolity that frighten suitors away, and—by implication—constitute therefore a potential danger to a modern state (Nov. 28th): all these traditional thoughts about the sex came out in the traditional way. It was easy and popular to blame women who had little chance of retaliating. But on December 8th an energetically worded letter took cognisance of this fact and fell to distributing praise and blame according to a brutally realistic—that is empiric—criterion. What about the harsh and unnatural demands made on women who still are virtually 'sold' in the marriage-market without their own consent?, it wants to know. Persons who blame women for the evils of society, it asserts,

11 It will be recalled that Campomanes was the founder of the Sociedades Económicas de Amigos del País.

would be more fairly occupied in praising those who, against all their natural inclinations, have respected their forced marriage vows and their unwanted state:

> Se clama contra la corrupción de las costumbres y no se ve que es preciso que el hombre tenga una bondad natural, superior a todas las malas instituciones, puesto que el orden existe aun después de tantos insultos. Se censura a las mujeres, y sólo se debería alabar a aquéllas, que contra la elección de su corazón respetan sus enlaces, y son fieles al juramento, que les hizo pronunciar un poder irresistible.

In the same number a notice on the death of an English actor is extended into an account of the respect paid to actors in England, and includes a comment on Mrs Siddons, 'probably the most famous tragic actress in Europe', as one of a group of actresses notable for their culture, virtue and modesty who are accepted in society and deemed worthy of performing before the very Queen. Such comparisons were impressive and attracted public attention, which is the first step towards making the public change its mind.

During its first quarter the *Correo* had been sounding public interest and experimenting in the presentation of subjects for discussion. There is a tentative and leisurely air about some of the articles, suggesting that their authors, like amiable and slightly condescending Addisons, still half conceived of journals as collections of relatively polite essays. This is specially true of the *Rasgos*, moral, historical and philosophical, designed for readers' improvement and inevitably adopting an attitude, if not of superiority, at least of authority.

Comfortably established in the new year, the *Correo*, without changing the type of its contents, shows a certain inclination to change its tone and attitude, to behave according to more modern conceptions of the function of the Periodical Press. It seems to cast about less for instructive matter for debate and to confine attention to directing discussion already under way. Rather than lecture from the rostrum the editor tends to take the Chair. Presumably, topical opinions and problems introduced in the first three months had been vital enough to promote debates capable of developing under their own power and requiring the editor's presence largely for purposes of procedure. Indeed this editor goes out of his way to encourage criticism even of editorial views—letters of protest to the editor duly figure among the correspondence—and sometimes, abandoning the Chair, he joins unassumingly in the discussion. The explanation for such a change lies in the fact that most of the subjects selected by the *Correo* for review had been of practical and even urgent importance not only to the average citizen but to the editor himself in his capacity as an ordinary member of the community.

While it is true that moral, philosophical or religious sermons continue to be preached on traditionally prescribed texts, they are now seldom unaffected by immediate social pressures. An allegorical dream, this time about covetousness—the reformist century, partly for political reasons, partly for didactic ones, found allegory a convenient medium—, is really directed against the mercenary mind of modern civilization. This was an apposite theme, for the Spaniard, who temperamentally had not tended to err in mercenary directions, was being drawn inevitably into the unfamiliar vortex of commercial competition (Jan. 19th). Another kind of disturbing unfamiliarity lurks behind articles for example on Descartes; on the modern conception of the body as a piece of mechanism with no will of its own (Feb. 23rd); on the 'infallible existence of God' and the inability of 'impious Philosophers' to appreciate the self-evident proof of the savage's instinctive fear of an unknown deity (Mar. 20th); on the nature of biblical resurrections: for while the debate on whether the resurrected one, after having once rendered his account to God, had then acquired a new life with free will to sin again, or whether, in such cases, death was merely a trance-extension of life, has an air of collegiate and theological exercise, it suits the prevailing interest in rationalized cause and effect (Mar. 16th). Moral articles in anecdotal dress even more vividly represent the mind of the time. The European emphasis on social welfare had produced a social self-consciousness which the public, turning the general into the particular and breaking it up into easily comprehensible units of individual acts and model individuals, converted easily into tales of 'doing good' or, as a later century would think of it, of 'slumming': tales which, for all their real value in helping to stimulate awareness of social inequalities, went to intensify an unreal atmosphere in literature, where condescensions on the one hand and maudlin gratitude on the other produced artificial contrasts. In the *Correo*, as in most up-to-date journals of the period, we find humanitarian anecdotes about the condescensions of great men and the gratitude of the humble poor; the pity of kings, or of famous foreign commoners like M. de Montesquieu who, incognito, presented a poor young man with the means of rescuing his father from captivity. There are also reformist tales of a wider international range, like those turning on the social evil of gaming, a subject which in England and France had found a powerful outlet in drama. In the *Correo* on April 18th this theme is presented in the guise of a letter from a parish priest to a supposed gamester and not only points out destructively that gaming is a sin, but enumerates positively the good works, of which a list is provided, that could be accomplished with money wasted on gambling.

An interesting characteristic of this quarter is the increasing attention given to local topics: another feature bringing the *Correo* into line with modern newspapers. Correspondents, whether in approval or protest, now took to commenting more and more on the material state of the capital, not as writers detachedly interested in *costumbrismo* but as citizens moved to discuss conditions intimately affecting themselves. Their letters are consequently valuable documents on common points of view and ordinary circumstances.

The voice of Lucas Alemán, a journalist given to writing a species of 'Fourth Leader',[12] is heard on February 6th protesting with rather less facetiousness than usual about the mismanagement of the transport system (of chairs). Other correspondents complain about Madrid's shop-closing hours; its mud, and the need for determining whose business it should be to water and clean the pavements; its bad smells; the speeding of drivers to the danger of pedestrians, with an example of a coach which failed to stop after knocking a woman down; the traffic congestion within the Villa's gates, which, in view of the narrowness of unpaved streets, must have produced a problem as acute then as a different kind of traffic congestion produces today (see Feb. 23rd, Mar. 2nd, Mar. 16th). It is also fascinating to learn from such a popular source of information as the *Correo*, that the new monuments erected in Madrid, which we might have expected to dazzle a less world-weary generation than our own, were not always accepted uncritically. A letter of February 23rd takes exception to the imposing statue of Neptune. Other topical notes explain to *madrileños* what Neptune, or Cibeles, represents (Feb. 23rd, Mar. 13th). The effect of such constant, direct expression on ordinary local affairs is to produce, as in modern newspapers, a kind of club-atmosphere in which local inhabitants feel that they are equal sharers in local experience.

Some of the most progressive articles of 1787 are directed against prejudiced thinking and unsupported suppositions on a variety of subjects, and continue in their various ways the quest for objective truth advocated earlier as the goal of historical research. 'Judgments will always be false', states an article of April 28th, 'when not supported by evidence'. The good parish priest, it is argued in the same issue, will help teach the ignorant to destroy popular fanaticism and superstition, whereas the bad parish priest, a correspondent had already said on February 6th, is like the one who, knowing nothing of the matter, preached against a publication on civil economy which had been accredited by the most informed authorities on that subject. Unfortunately, this writer had gone on to say, the unlettered public would be impervious to written refutations of such ignorant judgment, and would remember only the uninformed denunciations made to them orally. Illiteracy, which affected so large a part of the European community—for Spain was not alone in having an illiterate peasantry, beyond the reach even of the Popular Press—must have presented reformers of any kind with their most frustrating stumbling block:

12 In McClelland, *The Origins of the Romantic Movement in Spain* Lucas Alemán is commented upon as follows: 'Among the *Correo*'s permanent contributors was one Lucas Alemán,[1] who rejoiced in a not unmerited reputation as a wit, and who, from time to time, tossed off sprightly philosophy in verse or prose'. She reminds us that 'Hartzenbusch gives this name [Lucas Alemán] as a pseudonym for Manuel Casal y Aguado, a medical doctor of Madrid (see "Maxiriath" [J. E. Hartzenbusch], *Unos cuantos seudónimos de escritores españoles* ..., Madrid, 1904, p. 5)' (p. 148, and note 1).

> ¿Quién nos liberta de la ignorancia, o de los errores de los que suben a los púlpitos y son mirados como oráculos de la verdad? (Feb. 6th)

An article of April 21st, speaking of the individual freedom of expression that should characterize the writing community, assumes, rather optimistically, that the general company of writers represents enlightenment and ought to be revered for its search for what is true and good. But, the author, acutely departing from the commoner advocacy of collective endeavour among intellectuals, asserts that one philosopher thinking by himself is more likely to reach truth than a body of men debating together. His main point, however, is that a writer divinely discontent with his country's defects has a right to speak out against them:

> Es preciso que un escritor tenga la desgracia de vivir descontento de todo lo malo que se hace en su patria, a fin de que sus escritos no carezcan de aquellos rasgos varoniles, que despiertan la atención, y estos rasgos han de pronunciarse con vehemencia cuando se dirigen a los oídos soberbios, y endurecidos.

By 1787, too, Justice, or the lack of it, was a favourite subject of debate even in a country as far removed as Spain was from centres of revolutionary Liberalism. Starting in a letter on the troubles of litigants (Feb. 20th) the subject recurs under various heads: the suitability of talionic punishment (Feb. 27th); the tragic consequences of ignorance in magistrates, and the need for Judges to depend neither on emotion nor innate talent but to base their judgment on a careful study of the law; the social wrongs committed by men of wealth and position who, dominated by their passions and representing as virtue that which is cruelty and vice, use their power to override the weak (May 2nd). Talk of justice also revives the topic of private vengeance, and in April and May contributors express themselves strongly against the false sense of honour attendant on duelling, and even against the much more generally accepted principle of international war.

Other aspects of social unfairness are sometimes discussed in relation to the arts, social politics, or economics. A frank article on the right value to the state of the wealthy, appearing on March 13th, comments that although this theme has already come up for discussion it is one which will bear repeating. Here the charge of social unfairness is levelled against wealthy and powerful Spanish landowners who, instead of promoting the public good, as they are in a position to do, neglect their social duties. 'They do not foment patriotism who alone are in a position to do so':

> El artesano, el soldado, u otro cualquiera que se mantenga de su trabajo u oficio ¿cómo ha de dar pruebas reales de buen patriota, como puede darlas un rico poseedor de mayorazgos, tierras pingües, y lugares fuertes, cuyas posesiones le contribuyen con rentas excesivas, que malgasta o

> desaprovecha: bienes que únicamente le ha cedido la suerte, y que por tanto deben brillar más las muestras de agradecido?

Equally frank is an article of April 25th on abuses practised in seigniorial towns and villages—a theme which presumably would have met with sympathy from Spain's centralizing government. But this observer finds himself marvelling not merely at seigniorial tyrants, but at the ignorance and stupidity with which seigniorial towns have accepted the feudal conditions they inherited:

> [...] no se decidirá [the observer] a dónde aplicar su admiración con preferencia, si a la nisensibilidad [*sic*] o ignorancia de los pueblos, que contentos con su heredado abatimiento, arrastran la cadena feudal que les pusieron los Señores [...] o si a la industria con que sostienen un sistema tan cruel los que en él interesan a pesar de los conocimientos del siglo actual, y la feliz situación en que las benéficas miras de nuestro Soberano se ven apoyadas de Ministros que desean la dicha y los adelantamientos de la Nación.

After which burst of divine discontent, not to mention many other indications of liberal interest in *égalité* and *fraternité*, it seems strange to read, in the same issue, a repressive letter against the iniquity of apeing one's betters and of undermining the traditional class-distinctions which prevent an artisan from looking like a man of means. It seems strange, that is, until we remember that in liberal England class-distinction was, in practice, as strongly marked as in Spain, much as theory may have misrepresented it there, and that the *Correo* of 1787 reports, not an experience or knowledge of *égalité*, but confused inconsistent, preliminary suppositions as to how the social change in the air might be expected to materialize.

The eighteenth century, like the twentieth, and as a result of a similar scientific revolution to that which has changed our own direction of thought, was predisposed to change even in places where change was unwelcome, partly because the Popular Press, a new instrument of publicity, had an ideological influence in quality not unlike that of the powerful Press of modern times. To condition the mind of the general reading public to change, it suffices for change to be publicly discussed. Activity in the average mind is largely a motion of familiarizations. But talk of change in one direction is enough to cause discontent, divine or petulant, to find scope for activity in others. To criticize what is new abroad involves taking stock of what is national; and discussion on the tangible effects of new ideas involves comparisons of institutions and customs, which, in a practical era, distrustful of idealistic enthusiasm, provoke in their turn comparative surveys of material benefits and disadvantages. By means of comparisons, therefore, the Spanish mind, ranging from one sphere to another, took new stock of the general state of affairs at home, and was duly reflected in the popular mirror of the *Correo*. With increasing ease contributors move there from one piece of stocktaking to another. Some continue to write on economics, debating, for example, the waste of productive manpower exemplified in the large servant-population (May 25th), or the relative rightness or wrongness of luxury and the sumptuary laws, and examining the passive state of Spanish commerce, since luxury, one writer realizes, can mean different things at different times (Mar. 6th). Some comment on experiments in agriculture (Jan. 2nd, Feb. 13th), some on current medical problems, for instance venereal diseases (Feb. 13th); some excitedly discuss newly discovered forces like electricity (Apr. 28th), or the eclipse, and methods of viewing it (June 16th)—this last being a subject which seems to have enjoyed considerable publicity especially, perhaps, when the authorities' calculations slightly miscarried. Also, recurring persistently among more casual observations on bread-making, or books, or theatres, along with defences of Spain, or topical tales of the Orient as idealized in its remoteness by Montesquieu and Goldsmith (Jan. 9th, Jan. 12th), are sober contributions on male and female education.

Some explanation for the renewal of pedagogic topics is undoubtedly to be found in the report of an examining body at Salamanca on an abnormally advanced child who had been taught by his father by methods described in a discreetly unnamed book on education (Mar. 30th). But this particular instance led to a general discussion on teaching methods, and the editor commented on August 25th that so many letters on the subject had been received that he was unable to publish them all. In a related field a projected reform of monastic studies raised the question as to whether wider theological and philosophical studies would be as suitable for religious as for secular clergy (Mar. 27th, 30th). But one of the most vehement articles of that period is on the need for the better education of gentlewomen in order to give them greater resources in conversation and provide men with a more intelligent means of addressing themselves to women than through gallantry, scandalmongering, or talk on fashions:

> Que las mujeres sean admiradas es indiferente; pero importa mucho que sean respetadas. Esto se consiguiría si tuviesen más conocimientos, y por consiguiente más recursos en la conversación. Los hombres que las tratan, no se verían en la alternativa de hablarlas continuamente de modas, de galantería, o de murmuración.
>
> (Feb. 16th. See also Mar. 9th, Aug. 1st)

Nor is the *Correo* lacking in the popular facetiousness common in modern periodicals. Much of it was supplied by Lucas Alemán in articles or verses intended to do little more than raise a chuckle or otherwise supply light relief, where needed, to the news, views and announcements that occupy more space.

But perhaps it is as well to remember that Spaniards, like the English, may be at their most serious when they speak in jest, and that their silliness even in the silly season may represent more than one layer of mood or thought. With this in mind it might be worth investigating the blatant nonsense of such as Lucas Alemán who bespatter the adolescent newspaper with their sometimes irritating inanities. That, however, is matter for a separate study. More important for the present purpose is the general impression conveyed by the *Correo* of 1787 as, for the period, an up-to-date newspaper dealing with up-to-date topics. By the summer of that year it could take for granted its popular acceptance, could cater determinedly and easily for the developing social criticism of its readers. In June it is advocating subscription libraries, and demanding trained architects for new buildings. In August it is discussing Rousseau-esque theories of breast-feeding by mothers instead of by wet nurses, criticizing a wrong use of leisure, and rousing a woman contributor to demand whose fault it is if women are ignorant. In September it is attempting to define a politician as ideally he ought to be. And, significantly, now that autumn symbolizes another end, and the year of crisis of 1789 is round only one more corner, readers are reminded that 'old systems should not be advocated for new times'; that changed times bring changed problems. The *Correo de los ciegos* was not without inner vision.

Rewriting Spanish Epic Poetry in the Enlightenment Period: Two Competing Interpretations of *Las naves de Cortés destruidas*

CIARA O'HAGAN

Trinity College, Dublin

The wholesale neglect of eighteenth-century Spanish epic poetry in current Hispanic scholarship stands in dichotomous relation to the pre-eminence enjoyed by the genre during the eighteenth century. Jovellanos' description of the genre as 'el más noble de todo'[1] is reinforced by Francisco Sánchez Barbero's claim that it was 'el poema por excelencia; la obra más grande del genio'.[2] Similarly, Manuel José Quintana in his essay *Sobre la poesía épica castellana* (1833) holds the genre up as 'el blasón principal de su literatura', and champions it as a 'joya de tan inestimable precio'.[3] It was precisely this celebration of the sublime status of the epic which led to the proliferation of national and public poems during the eighteenth century: 'se ponen de moda y consiguen una gran popularidad en toda Europa'.[4] The epic genre, both practised and discussed, became the source of intense interest and debate in Enlightenment Europe. Frank Pierce regards the eighteenth century as signalling the beginning of a more systematic treatment of the epic genre. He cites Voltaire's *Essai sur la poésie épique* (1726) as instrumental in this process, describing it as the impetus behind subsequent Spanish studies of

1 Gaspar Melchor de Jovellanos, '*Lecciones de Retórica y Poética*', in *Obras*, BAE XLVI (Madrid: Rivadeneyra, 1858), 114–46 (p. 142).

2 Francisco Sánchez Barbero, *Principios de Retórica y Poética* (Madrid: Imprenta de la Administración del Real Arbitrio de Beneficencia, 1805), 203.

3 Manuel José Quintana, '*Sobre la poesía épica castellana*', in *Obras completas*, ed. Antonio Ferrer del Río, BAE XIX (Madrid: Rivadeneyra, 1852), 158–73 (p. 158). Frank Pierce describes Quintana's essay as 'the most comprehensive study of the Spanish literary epic' (see *The Heroic Poem of the Spanish Golden Age: Selections* [Oxford: Dolphin Book Co., 1947], ix).

4 Santiago García-Sáez, 'La visión del indio en *La Conquista del Mégico por Hernán Cortés: Poema épico* de don Pedro Montengón y Paret', *Dieciocho*, 4 (1981), 135–54 (p. 137).

the genre,[5] most notably Ignacio de Luzán's analysis of the epic form in Book IV of his *Poética* (1737).[6] In fact, it was Voltaire's study of Alonso de Ercilla's *La Araucana* (1589) which did much to promote eighteenth-century interest in Ercilla's poem;[7] Frank Pierce draws attention to two well-known Spanish editions of Ercilla's poem that were made in 1733 and 1776.[8]

Spanish poets who took up epic in the eighteenth century typically drew on native historical and literary traditions from sixteenth- and seventeenth-century Spanish history. Their emphasis on translating national missions and expeditions into epic dimensions was very much in keeping with the traditional subject-matter of epic poetry. The epics they wrote were of military action, and were peopled with idealized national heroes who embodied the chivalric ideal. In light of this, it is not surprising that those about Hernán Cortés should emerge as a distinctive subdivision of the genre during this period. The heroism and grandeur exemplified by Cortés, together with the perilous nature of the conquest, the real but remote events, and the opportunities created for a clash of civilizations, collectively made Cortés and his conquest of Mexico ideal subjects for epic treatment. William Prescott in *History of the Conquest of Mexico* (1843) underscores the heroic capacity of Cortés's New World conquest:

> Among the remarkable achievements of the Spaniards in the sixteenth century, there is not one more striking to the imagination than the conquest of Mexico. The subversion of a great empire by a handful of adventurers, taken with all its strange and picturesque accompaniments, had the air of romance rather than of sober history.[9]

The importance of Hernán Cortés as a rhetorical focus of epic poetry during the eighteenth century is particularly evident given the choice of Cortés's destruction of his ships as the subject of a literary competition on epic poetry,

5 Frank Pierce, *La poesía épica del Siglo de Oro* (Madrid: Gredos, 1961), 41.

6 See Ignacio de Luzán, *La Poética, o reglas de la poesía en general, y de sus principales especies*, ed. Russell P. Sebold (Barcelona: Labor, 1977). All references are to this edition. Luzán's *Poética* was first published in 1737 and later revised in a posthumous edition in 1789.

7 In his *Essai sur la poésie épique*, Ercilla is studied alongside other prominent epic poets such as Homer, Virgil, Camões, Lucan and Trissino. Voltaire's comments on *La Araucana* are amplified throughout the eighteenth century in numerous works of writers who responded to his ambivalent treatment. These included Luzán, *Poética* (Zaragoza, 1737), L. J. Velázquez, *Orígenes de la poesía castellana* (Málaga, 1754), G. Conti, *Colección de poesías castellanas* (Madrid, 1782–1790), J. F. Masdeu, *Poesie di ventidue Autori spagnuoli del cinquecento* (Rome, 1786), J. P. Forner, *Exequias de la lengua castellana* (1780) and L. Fernández de Moratín, *Reflexiones críticas, de la edición de 1785, que se atribuyen a Moratín, el hijo* (1785).

8 See Alonso de Ercilla, *La Araucana* (Madrid: Francisco Martinez Abad, 1733); and *La Araucana* (Madrid: Antonio de Sancha, 1776). (Pierce, *La poesía épica*, 375).

9 William H. Prescott, *History of the Conquest of Mexico*, ed. John Foster Kirk (London: Bickers & Son, 1885), vii.

organized by the Real Academia Española in 1777.[10] Further evidence is found in the epic poetry of Francisco Ruiz de León (1685–1765), who published his *Hernandia* in twelve cantos in 1755.[11] In 1797, Juan de Escoiquiz wrote *México conquistado*, an epic in twenty-six books,[12] while Pedro Montengón wrote his final work, the epic poem *La conquista del Megico* in 1820.[13]

It is somewhat ironic, however, that despite the marked outflow of national epics during the eighteenth century not one 'merece ser llamado épico'.[14] While the status of the genre as the highest literary form is undisputed, Quintana reveals that no great epic poems were written during this period and points to the difficulty of cultivating the genre successfully as one of the chief reasons for this:

> Y como los prodigios son raros, los poemas verdaderamente épicos no lo son menos. Así es que el desenfado de algunos rigoristas llega a decir que no se ha escrito más que uno y medio en el mundo; no siendo, en su concepto, los otros más que imperfectos bosquejos o débiles y frías imitaciones.[15]

Juan Pablo Forner in his *Exequias de la lengua castellana* (1782) also underlines the failure of Spanish poets to make any significant contribution to the genre and concludes that 'no nos falta poesía épica, sino poema épico'.[16] None the less, the failure of Spanish writers to produce a successful epic poem was more an indication of the restrictive rules governing the genre than any comment on their literary competence. Their situation was an unenviable one: adherence to the conventions of traditional epic poetry resulted in formulaic and verbose posturing which called into question the literary merit of the poems they produced. Quintana, for example, claims that 'de todos modos resulta que son muy pocas las obras de esta clase dignas de atención y de memoria'.[17] Adherence, however, to such conventions was essential if readers' demands for traditional, epic poetry were to be satisfied.

---

10 A total of forty-five poems were submitted to the contest by some of the most prominent literary figures of the time, notably José Iglesias de la Casa and Cándido María Trigueros. For further details of the competition, see Emilio Cotarelo y Mori, *Iriarte y su época* (Madrid: Rivadeneyra, 1897), 213–17.

11 See Francisco Ruiz de León, *Hernandia* (Madrid, 1775; repr. México: Frente de Afirmación Hispanista, 1989).

12 See Juan de Escoiquiz, *México conquistado* (Madrid: Imprenta Real, 1798).

13 See Pedro Montengón, *La conquista del Megico por Hernan Cortés. Poema epico* (Naples: Battista Settembre, 1820).

14 Sánchez Barbero, *Principios de Retórica y Poética*, 210–11.

15 Quintana, *Sobre la poesía épica castellana*, 158.

16 Juan Pablo Forner, *Exequias de la lengua castellana: sátira menipea*, ed. José Jurado (Madrid: CSIC, 2000), 306.

17 Quintana, *Sobre la poesía épica castellana*, 158.

If the literary merit of eighteenth-century epic poetry is questionable—a viewpoint which would seem to be endorsed by the almost total neglect of the genre today—what, it may be asked, is the value of submitting it to detailed critical analysis? Such an objection may be countered, however, by highlighting the morally didactic purpose which underpins all epic poetry. Quoting Pablo Benio's comments on Aristotle's teaching on the genre, Ignacio de Luzán, in Book IV of his *Poética*, advises that:

> 'instruya a los que mandan y gobiernan en lo que conduce para las buenas costumbres para vivir una vida feliz, y los anime y estimule a las más excelentes virtudes y esclarecidas hazañas'.[18]

Epic poetry with its emphasis on renewal and transformation is, therefore, an important index of the political and cultural health of a nation. The aesthetic merit of epic poetry may be debatable, but it is, nevertheless, of undoubted political and historical interest in view of the insight it provides into the Spanish consciousness of the eighteenth century. Moreover, the centrality of the Horatian maxim, *utile dulci* to all literary activity during the eighteenth century places greater emphasis on its social utility: 'destaca el cultivo de la poesía como expresión de los polémicos habituales por entonces'.[19] If epic poetry is to be fully understood by the modern reader it is imperative that it is read in the political and cultural context in which it was first written.

* * * * *

In order to illustrate the contribution that studies of epic poetry can make to scholarly understanding of eighteenth-century Hispanic culture and society, this analysis will focus on two neglected epic poems considered as representative examples of the genre. The poems, both identically titled *Las naves de Cortés destruidas*, were submitted by José María Vaca de Guzmán (1744–1803) and Nicolás Fernández de Moratín (1737–1780) to the poetry competition organized by the Real Academia Española in 1778 and were awarded first and second place respectively.[20] Although the expressed

18 Luzán, *La Poética*, 556.

19 Enrique Rull Fernández, *La poesía y el teatro en el siglo XVIII* (Madrid: Taurus, 1987), 19.

20 See José María Vaca de Guzmán, '*Las naves de Cortés destruidas*', in Cayetano Rosell, *Poemas épicos*, BAE XXIX (Madrid: Rivadeneyra 1864), 499–502. All references to Vaca de Guzmán's poem here are taken from the editon of Cayetano Rosell. For Nicolás Fernández de Moratín, '*Las naves de Cortés destruidas*', see John Dowling, 'El texto primitivo de *Las naves de Cortés destruidas* de Nicolás Fernández de Moratín', *BRAE*, 57 (1977), 431–83 (pp. 451–83). It is important to note that Moratín's poem was published posthumously, in a somewhat revised form, by his son Leandro Fernández de Moratín, in 1785, and again in 1821. It is the revised versions of Moratín's poem which are included in volumes II and XXIX of the Biblioteca de Autores Españoles. All references to Moratín's poem here are taken from the edition of John Dowling.

intention of the Real Academia Española behind the competition was to 'promover el estudio de la elocuencia y de la poesía',[21] Maurizio Fabbri, underlining the highly politicized nature of Hernán Cortés's and Spain's American conquest, which 'se había[n] convertido en aquellos años en objeto de violentas polémicas', suggests that:

> no podemos pensar que la Real Academia pretendiera únicamente promover, tal como dice el anuncio que apareció el 7 de octubre de 1777 en la *Gaceta de Madrid*, el 'estudio de la poesía'.[22]

Fabbri identifies 'un esfuerzo ideológico y patriótico' as informing the 1778 competition, and views the choice of Hernán Cortés and the destruction of his ships as a means of inspiring patriotism and restoring pride in the Spanish nation:

> una aportación fundamental a la obra de restauración de la imagen de España tan deteriorada por tantas incisivas críticas, válida tanto para los extranjeros menos prevenidos cuanto para los españoles mismos quienes además habían manifestado desde siempre una especial admiración por el héroe extremeño.[23]

Assessing the social penetration achieved by the epic poems of Vaca de Guzmán and Moratín more than two centuries ago is difficult, but some insight has been provided by María José Rodríguez Sánchez de León, who remarks on the 'significante interés' that both poems awoke. Her comments on their post-publication history reveal their positive reception and popular appeal.[24] Although Vaca de Guzmán and Nicolás Fernández de Moratín are establishment authors who wrote constrained by the demands of institutional patronage, their works should not for this reason be considered as any

21 Dowling, 'El texto primitivo de *Las naves de Cortés destruidas*', 443. This comment is taken from the announcement that appeared in the *Gaceta de Madrid* launching the competition on 7 October 1777.

22 Maurizio Fabbri, '*Las naves de Cortés destruidas* en la épica española del siglo XVIII', *Revista de Literatura*, 84 (1980), 53–74 (p. 60).

23 Fabbri, '*Las naves de Cortés destruidas* en la épica española del siglo XVIII', 60.

24 She notes: 'A la edición individual de los trabajos premiados, se sumaron dos ediciones conjuntas, en 1782 la primera, y la segunda en 1799, bajo el título de *Colección de las obras de elocuencia y poesía premiadas por la Real Academia Española*' (María José Rodríguez Sánchez de León, 'Los premios de la Academia Española en el siglo XVIII y la estética de la época', *BRAE*, 67 [1987], 395–425 [p. 401]). Ángel Palencia González records the favourable treatment given to Vaca de Guzmán's epic, which was translated almost immediately into French, in the *Journal de Paris* on 4 January 1779: 'Cet ouvrage nous a paru plein de mouvements, d'imagination et de veritable enthousiasme [...]. Si l'Espagne nourrit dans son sein beaucoup de pareils Poètes, nous croyons qu'elle pourra bientôt le dispute aux Nations qui se sont le plus distingués en ce genre parmis les anciens et les modernes' (Ángel González Palencia, 'Don José María Vaca de Guzmán, el primer poeta premiado por la Academia Española', *BRAE*, 18 [1931], 293–347 [p. 314]).

the less valuable. Both these officially approved texts are important expressions of the dominant political and cultural currents of eighteenth-century Spain.

Before turning to analyse both poems in detail, something should be said about the socio-political and cultural context in which they were written. The marked decline of the Spanish-American empire is particularly noteworthy. Although still the largest colonial power in the eighteenth-century world, Enlightenment Spain was by then a country severely disillusioned with her diminished colonial status, and one haunted by 'borrados recuerdos de [...] antiguo esplendor'.[25] At the same time, Spain's 'colonial' anxieties were heightened by Enlightenment debates elsewhere in Europe over the legitimacy of the New World conquest. Prominent Enlightenment thinkers such as Montesquieu, Voltaire, Raynal and De Pauw speculated over whether it would have been better if the New World had never been discovered at all. Spain's colonial record was central to their calumnious attacks which culminated in Masson de Morvilliers' highly provocative and injurious question over the contribution Spain had made to Europe. In his entry 'Espagne', in the *Encyclopédie méthodique* in 1782, he asked: 'Después de dos siglos, después de cuatro, después de diez, ¿qué ha aportado a Europa?'[26] The Spanish response to European criticism was one of righteous and aggressive indignation: 'clamarosa y violentísima diatriba'.[27] Spanish writers abandoned previous attempts to reform the flagging Spanish empire in favour of defending Spain's New World conquest against anti-Hispanic criticism. In doing so, they frequently referred to Hernán Cortés as a national hero capable of restoring pride in a ruined Spain:

> Hernán Cortés se convirtió en punto constante de referencia para poetas, dramaturgos, eruditos, historiadores, políticos y polemistas que se preocupaban por la defensa del prestigio nacional y de la cultura española.[28]

25 José María Blanco White, *Bosquejo del comercio de esclavos y reflexiones sobre este tráfico, considerado moral, política y cristianamente*, ed. Manuel Moreno Alonso (Sevilla: Ediciones Alfar, 1999), 18.

26 See Nicolas Masson de Morvilliers, 'Espagne', in *Encyclopédie méthodique. Géographie moderne*, ed. Didier Robert de Vaugondy and Nicolas Masson de Morvilliers, 3 vols (Paris: Panckoucke, 1783–1788), I, 554-68. The original quote in French reads: 'Mais que doit-on à l'Espagne? Et depuis deux siècles, depuis quatre, depuis dix, qu'a-t-elle fait pour l'Europe? Elle ressemble aujourd'hui à ces colonies foibles et malheureuses, qui ont besoin sans cesse du bras protecteur de la métropole', 565. The *Encyclopédie méthodique* circulated legally in Spain and a translation of it was permitted by Antonio de Sancha. However, it was promptly banned following Masson's calumnious attack on Spain in 1782.

27 Giovanni Rossi, 'España en la *Notizie* de José de Osuna', in *Estudios sobre las letras en el siglo XVIII* (Madrid: Gredos, 1967), 222–47 (p. 234).

28 Fabbri, '*Las naves de Cortés destruidas* en la épica española del siglo XVIII', 68.

Vaca de Guzmán and Nicolás Fernández de Moratín, as Fabbri's earlier comments make clear, were no doubt aware of their place within the Enlightenment dispute over the legitimacy of Spain's American conquest when they wrote their poems. Vaca de Guzmán even makes self-conscious reference to the two centuries of 'Black Legend' rhetoric which characterized European attitudes to Spain's New World endeavours: 'La fama de dos siglos contradice / De la envidia los bárbaros agravios' (vv. 419–20).

The reading of both poems which follows will demonstrate that, although they are written on an identical epic subject, Hernán Cortés is differently represented in each work. While Nicólas Fernández de Moratín's epic poem, with its emphasis on military heroism and its strict observance of epic conventions, may be held up as the epitome of the conservative epic, a reading of Vaca de Guzmán's epic through the comparative lens of Moratín's reveals an author with anxieties over the suitability of the epic genre in an age of rational and scientific zeal. Both poems, in general, have been critically overlooked, and, to the extent they have been taken account of, have been traditionally viewed as the simple products and reflections of official propaganda and as providing enthusiastic endorsements of the dominant imperial ideology. However, there is a rhetoric of distance and displacement that underpins Vaca de Guzmán's poetics, in studying which I shall disclose the subversive charge that characterizes Vaca de Guzmán's poetics; and, in doing so, I shall uncover his attempts to redefine the genre in terms relevant to the eighteenth century.[29]

Though it was awarded second place in the 1778 literary contest, Nicolás Fernández de Moratín's entry has received little favourable commentary. Fabbri in particular is highly critical of Moratín's poem, comparing it unfavourably to Vaca de Guzmán's entry, which he claims 'en las 60 octavas de su canto consiguió lo que Moratín no había conseguido en doble número de estrofas'.[30] Fabbri singles out for criticism Moratín's hackneyed and schematic treatment of Cortés, judging it:

> Bastante débil, especialmente si se relaciona con la amplitud del canto y con la consiguiente posibilidad de profundizar en su personalidad. Pero es, sobre todo, una imagen fatigada, calcada de los más repetidos estereotipos de la iconografía cortesiana.[31]

Throughout the poem's 122 stanzas, Moratín everywhere complies punctiliously with the conventions of traditional epic poetry. Opening his poem in the manner of Virgil, Moratín follows his initial statement of intent:

29 Something of the subversion and revisionism of Vaca de Guzmán's epic is evident in the poem's endorsement of the Republican poetics of Lucan rather than the military imperialism of Virgil: 'renazcan sus Lucanos y Marciales' (v. 440).

30 Fabbri, '*Las naves de Cortés destruidas* en la épica española del siglo XVIII', 61.

31 Fabbri, '*Las naves de Cortés destruidas* en la épica española del siglo XVIII', 63.

'Canto el valor del capitán hispano' (v. 1) with an invocation to Apollo and the muse, Clío: '¡Divina Clío, / Tu alto influxo mi espíritu levante!' (vv. 337–38).[32] This conventional invocatory address sets the mythological context of the poem and places it squarely within the boundaries established by classical tradition. Nowhere is this more evident than in Moratín's foregrounding of 'valor' as the aspect of Cortés to be championed in the poem. In doing so, Moratín endorses the military heroism and martial courage typical of the genre. In subsequent stanzas, Moratín's grandiose vision of Cortés and his celebration of his courage is supported by a series of references to his heroic exploits: he speaks of Cortés's capacity to inspire singlehandedly patriotic self-sacrifice in his troops (vv. 2–4); his victory in the face of insurmountable odds (vv. 18–19); the suppression of a barbaric native monarchy (vv. 19–21); and the spiritual salvation won for the natives as a result.

Further evidence of Moratín's use of the genre's conventional machinery is visible in the abundant catalogue of descriptions of Cortés's soldiers, their arms, and their armour. From stanzas IV to XVII, Moratín introduces a whole series of soldiers by name, placing the emphasis squarely in each case on their heroic achievements in battle. For Moratín it is difficult to conceive military plunder as anything other than glorious. Indeed, he depicts warfare as the highest kind of outlet and expression for male strength and valour, as his description of Argüello makes clear:[33]

> Aquel membrudo de mirar sangriento
> Que cinco lirios por empresa tiene,
> Arguello el de Leon es que violento
> Vive en quietud; y asi â la Guerra viene:
> Mirarle que terrible y corpulento,
> Como cruge la lanza y se sostiene
> Con la ancha cota de dobleces once,
> Y el escudo con làminas de bronce. (vv. 233–40)

Such detailed militaristic descriptions culminate in the representation of Cortés himself in stanzas XLIII to L, where the image Moratín creates of an armoured figure on horseback holds Cortés up for our admiration as the equivalent of a medieval chivalric knight. While it is certainly to be acknowledged that 'la prioridad concedida a la descripción' weakens the poem somewhat,[34] the visual impact of the pageantry created produces an intoxicating militarism which arrests the reader's senses from the outset.

32 In citations from both poems, I have used the original spelling and punctuation throughout.

33 Argüello is just one of twenty-three soldiers each of whom Moratín deals with in turn and delineates in great detail in the opening stanzas of the poem.

34 Rodríguez Sánchez de León, 'Los premios de la Academia Española en el siglo XVIII', 404.

The inescapable martial overtones of the poem are further heightened by the emphasis placed on the sound of bugles and gunfire: 'resonando / Gentil descarga de arcabuceria' (vv. 30–31). The introduction of Doña Marina and Gerónimo Aguilar in stanzas XX and XXV—Indians who served as interpreters for Cortés and therefore who are historical rather than fictional figures—is indicative of Moratín's attempts to satisfy the demands of epic theorists for historical authenticity. Doña Marina's favourable, though victim-eyed, view of the Mexican conquest serves not only to exalt Cortés's heroic exploits, but also to legitimize them. Doña Marina 'admira tan lucida cavalgada / Y espectaculo' (vv. 170–71), while Aguilar apotheosizes Cortés: 'Oh que valor obstenta! y que nobleza / O quanta heroycidad y gentileza!' (vv. 343–44), granting him almost omnipotent status: 'Siendo por ademan y por acciones / A cosa mas que humana semejante' (vv. 403–04).

The shift from third person narration to direct speech in the appeal made by Cortés to his troops in stanza LI is a dynamic and enthusiastic reinforcement of the military heroism which Cortés is made to exemplify. The poem's support for the conquest of Mexico as a heroic and noble enterprise is undiminished. Cortés praises the 'heroyco brio' (v. 412) and 'heroycos pensamientos' (v. 423) of the Spanish, and, describing it as an 'accion tan señalada' (v. 418), questions whether the immense courage needed successfully to execute the conquest is even quantifiable:

> ¿Qual organo mortal será bastante
> A cantar tanta hazaña celebrada
> Que debo yo al valor de
> vuestra espada? (vv. 406–08)

Eager to ensure that the conquest is seen as a thoroughly noble enterprise, Cortés denies any exploitative basis for Spain's imperial endeavours and interprets these exclusively in terms of expansion and settlement, seeing them as patriotic rather than mercenary, as he tells his troops: '... como tiene ya por vuestra mano / Su España en tierra y nombre duplicada' (vv. 419–20). Moratín describes the Spanish as divine agents, sent as 'los Campeones que la Cruz alista' (v. 438), in order to deliver the natives from the tyranny and human sacrifice of Montezuma's rule. Cortés is shown to justify the conquest as a religious war, upholding it as a morally righteous mission:

> Marchamos à vedar el horroroso
> Holocausto que al Ydolo perfuma
> Con victimas humanas, anhelantes,
> Corazones y entrañas palpitantes. (vv. 453–56)

Moratín successfully confers yet further legitimacy on Spain's conquest of the New World by his consistently negative portrayal of the New World inhabitants. Throughout the poem his descriptions of their savagery is unrelenting. Descriptions of them as 'brutos' (v. 28) and references to the 'terror' of these 'gentes fieras y remotas' (v. 23) serve conveniently to transform Spain's New World conquest into a heroic moral rescue.

The episodical account of Montejo and Portocarrero's agreement to bring news of the Mexican conquest back to Spain in stanzas LIX to LXIII is used to reinforce further the heroic virtues exemplified by Cortés: obedience, service, self-sacrifice and duty. And Montejo's and Portocarrero's pledge of commitment to Cortés confirms Cortés's capacity to inspire others through his own military heroism. Moratín is clearly confident of the inspirational and regenerative potential in the patriotic and sacrificial militarism exemplified by Cortés, a potential which is exemplified at the outset of the poem, where the impression made on the indigenous population by the sight of Cortés's soldiers is being described: 'Asombra la feroz Caballeria, / Tal es el fuego que en los brutos arde: / La robusta española infanteria / Haliento infunde al pecho mas cobarde' (vv. 27–30). In stanza LXV, the ability of 'el brio español' to inspire is once again affirmed when the veteran Torres comments:

No está el brio español tan apagado,
Ni aun en tal clima y tan distante suelo,
Quando aun se admira entre fieras gentes
Tal esfuerzo de Jovenes valientes. (vv. 517–20)

The diabolical intervention of Satan in stanzas LXXII to LXXXII is a further example of the clichéd nature of Moratín's epic. Satan's role confirms the poem's theological vision of the Spanish conquest, which Moratín carefully presents as a divinely-ordained mission. In keeping with the poem's earlier emphasis on duty and obedience, Spain's American conquest is seen as a fulfilment of God's divine purpose. Satan, however, since he is representative of Montezuma and the New World inhabitants, is seen angrily to reject this purpose:

Que la gente española vencedora
Al Catolico yugo humillaria
Los climas de el Ocaso y de la Aurora:
El Principe infernal que ya veia
Cumplirse los pronosticos ahora,
Concilio horrendo de la negra gente
Llama, y hablò con colera impaciente. (vv. 578–84)

In his reactions Satan unintentionally reveals Spain to be the champion of true religion and civilization:

Yà alli los sacrificios [España] no consiente,
En que yo, contra el hombre vengativo

> Victima le hago â un tiempo y delinquente
> De vida eterna y temporal le privo?
> Y ya templo consagra reverente
> A esa Madre del hijo de Dios vivo,
> A esa Muger, que lo es, aun que divina,
> Y à quien mi frente à mi pesar se inclina? (vv. 601–08)

Through Satan's descriptions, Moratín shows Spain's imperial endeavours to be inseparable from the religious and moral imperative of the Spanish, '¿Porque sin ella [the Mother Church] España que seria?' (v. 612), and therefore, confers further legitimacy on their exploits, explicitly reinforcing the dignity, chastity and integrity of Spanish imperialism. As noted previously, Moratín makes no attempt to condemn the violence and warfare which is needed to sustain imperial ambition. On the contrary, the poem endorses the ethos of the classical epic by presenting the violence endemic within conquest as justified by the higher moral intent of the Spanish.

Escudero's mutinous address to Cortés's troops to rebel against Cortés in stanzas LXXXVII to XCVIII is the only instance in the poem where epic heroism is challenged. Urging them to rise up against Cortés, and possessed by the same infernal spirits as Montezuma was earlier, Escudero declares to the troops that they have been deceived by the 'temeraria altaneria / De ese imprudente' (vv. 691–92). He rejects Cortés's claims that their displays of courage and sacrifice are heroic or glorious and seeks to expose the hollowness of their military triumphs: 'No es valor la frenetica osadia / Ni el ir â un Mundo entero contrastando / Con tan corto esquadron' (vv. 693–94). For Escudero, it is absurd that Spain should invest so much effort in battles fought against 'ignoradas gentes' in distant territories while neglecting the very real threat that she faces on her own shores:

> [. . .] Los Moros Africanos,
> Ricos, Vecinos, Moros y valientes,
> Ynfestan nuestras costas [. . .]. (vv. 745–47)

Addressing his soldiers as 'compañeros fieles', (v. 809), Cortés's response to Escudero's attempted insurrection reveals precisely the qualities which have made him such a powerful national hero. He demonstrates his concern for their well-being, a concern which is based on personal experience and knowledge of the sacrifice that is being demanded of them. The martial codes celebrated earlier in the poem are endorsed as Cortés reminds his soldiers of the positive benefits their heroic exploits will achieve. He emphasizes that order and good government have replaced the tyranny and irrationality of Montezuma's regime. And he reminds them of their role as divine agents in a unique religious mission:

¡[. . .] que altas hazañas
Dignas de vuestro ardor habrà algun dia.
No estimais cosas leves y tamañas?
Que propio en la Española valentia!
Ya me dareis albricias por estrañas
Empresas que ollarà vuestra osadia,
La Fama con excelso y nuevo canto
Pondrà en el Mundo admiracion y espanto. (vv. 793–800)

Nevertheless, recognizing that the soldiers, unconvinced by his claims, are eager to return to Cuba ('Mas viendo que eran sus esfuerzos vanos' [v. 825]), Cortés dramatically orders all his ships to be burned and urges each of his soldiers either to conquer or die: 'O venza ô muera: su unica esperanza / Cayga deshecha al tiro de mi lanza' (vv. 831–32). Cortés's action is a telling reminder of his unswerving loyalty and dedication to Spain. Yet this is a loyalty which does not prevent him from sharing in the self-sacrifice of his soldiers and in the hardships he makes them endure.

The destruction of Cortés's ships takes place while the resplendent image of the Holy Spirit descends upon them, and Cortés makes his open-armed declaration of his total submission to God's will:

Ya entiendo, Espiritu divino,
Que no de mi fervor te desagradas,
Sigo pronto tu nuncio y mi destino. (vv. 944–46)

Cortés is unequivocal about the redemptive and evangelizing role of the Spanish. He is adamant that they will not stray from God's plan until His will is done, that is until the evangelization of the New World is complete. As a result, his men:

Juran no desistir del gran camino
Hasta ensalzar en vez del Dios horrendo
La cruz que tremolada van siguiendo. (vv. 948–50)

Thus the action of the epic concludes on a religiously-imperial note that reaffirms the Christian military imperialism which has informed Cortés's New World exploits throughout.

What is clear from Moratín's highly conventional representation of Cortés is how valuable the epic genre was as a means, for those wishing to do so, of reinforcing official colonial discourse. For Moratín, the genre's reliance on heroic and patriotic rhetoric makes it an effective propagandistic vehicle for regenerating pride and strength in Spain. By recreating through his epic the noble, heroic and selfless virtues embodied by Cortés, Moratín provides his readers with source-material with which to defend Spain's standing in the eighteenth century. Furthermore, as a genre which does not tolerate ideological divisions well, the epic enables Moratín to use its eulogistic thrust to emphasize his protagonist's heroic achievements and to suppress the more negative and contradictory aspects of Cortés's conquest. Ultimately, the vision of conquest which Moratín's epic creates is thoroughly optimistic and positive.

In contrast to Moratín, a well-established and renowned writer in eighteenth-century Spain, José María Vaca de Guzmán, rector of the Colegio de Santiago de los Caballeros at the University of Alcalá de Henares, was relatively unknown. As Leopoldo de Cueto shows, it was the success of Vaca de Guzmán's epic poems which 'sacaron su nombre de la obscuridad en que probablemente habrá permanecido'.[35] Although Vaca de Guzmán described himself as a novice to the genre of epic poetry, 'no habiendo formado en mi vida un rasgo épico',[36] his poem was much more favourably received than was, by comparison, that of Moratín:

> En la obra de Vaca de Guzmán, que es casi la mitad de la de Moratín, hay más proporción entre sus partes y es más briosa en su estilo, y a esto quizá hay que atribuir el que sea más agradable la lectura de este canto que el de su contrario.[37]

Although, as I commented earlier, Vaca de Guzmán's epic engages in generic subversion, there is still much in his poem which is conventional. For instance, he invokes the muse, Clío, in much the same way as Moratín does. Nowhere are the conventional aspects of Vaca de Guzmán's epic more apparent than in the opening stanza in which the speaker, making clear that he applauds Cortés's heroic destruction of his ships and the expansion of the Spanish empire which he brought about as a result, draws on the codes and expressions of the epic and on the militaristic heroism characteristic of the genre:

> Oigan la hazaña que cantar intento,
> Con que á su gente y bravos campeones
> Supo empeñar al último ardimiento
> El héroe grande, que enlazó al hispano
> El opulento imperio mejicano. (vv. 4–8)

Subsequent verses celebrate the global reach of the Spanish empire—'¡Dichoso suelo! ¡Célebres umbrales / Ocupacion de siglos inmortales!' (vv. 38–40)—, and, exulting in the union of two nations under a common sovereign—'Tejiendo lazos de cristal profundos / Al augusto monarca de dos mundos' (vv. 22–24)—, not only reveal but are meant to evoke a patriotic fervour no less ardent than

35 Leopoldo Augusto de Cueto, *Poetas líricos del siglo XVIII*, BAE LXI, LXIII, LXVII, 3 vols (Madrid: Rivadeneyra, 1869–75), I (BAE LXI, 1869), 277.

36 González Palencia, 'Don José María Vaca de Guzmán, el primer poeta premiado por la Academia Española', 336–37.

37 Cotarelo y Mori, *Iriarte y su época*, 217.

that found in Moratín. Frequent references such as to the 'marciales genios' (v. 64) and 'espíritu brioso' (v. 45) of Spain's 'héroes invencibles' (v. 44), reinforce the militarism of Vaca de Guzmán's epic. The poem's militaristic overtones are also present in the highly stylized, epic reference to the Spanish *conquistadores* as lions, and in the classical allusion made to the Roman God of War, Mars—allusions which are used to generate enthusiasm for the animal courage and warlike heroism displayed by Cortés and his men:

> Héroes que de tu espíritu brioso
> En tus mismas entrañas alimentas
> Y de la guerra intrépidos leones
> A rugidos asombran las regiones.
> Cuna de Marte, que mostrarnos puedes
> Triunfos, conquistas, bélicos afanes. (vv. 45–50)

While Vaca de Guzmán was no doubt aware of the classical epic tradition in which he wrote, he actually represents Cortés as an epic hero, who, although constructed in the classical mould, outdoes and surpasses the heroism exemplified by traditional Roman war heroes: 'Tú á Roma afrentas, á Cartago excedes' (v. 51).

What is notably absent in Vaca de Guzmán's epic is the inflated and tediously detailed series of descriptions of Cortés's troops that Moratín provides in his pursuit of realism. Vaca de Guzmán, by contrast, employs a much more subtle type of realism—as in his initial scene-setting, when he describes the Manzanares river in Madrid, 'Pisaba yo del claro Manzanares / Una tarde las márgenes amenas' (vv. 17–18), which is indicative of the plain style he could utilize when he chose to do so. However, this initially concrete spatial setting is soon transformed. For in a scene reminiscent of the Annunciation, America, personified as a 'matrona', appears to the speaker in a dream:

> En un deliquio tal, en tanto abismo
> Voz imperiosa á mi ilusion resuena,
> Que de la esfera sacra desprendida,
> Ocupa el viento y mi atencion convida.
> "Alza los ojos", dijo; y yo humillado
> El celestial decreto obedeciendo,
> Cada vez mas absorto y trasportado
> Juzgué que una matrona estaba viendo. (vv. 69–76)

Significantly, it was Vaca de Guzmán's use of such supernatural machinery that his contemporaries frequently singled out for criticism: 'quita algo de espontaneidad a la obra la forma alegórica, por la visión de América; recurso poético que ridiculizó Moratín, hijo'.[38] The appearance of

38 Cotarelo y Mori, *Iriarte y su época*, 217.

America sent by God, and identified with the Olympian goddess, Juno, is, of course, another example of the poem's recourse to traditional epic conventions. Relying on classical tradition Vaca de Guzmán endows his female personification of America with the classical ideals of beauty and perfection. Her decorative appearance is suggested by picturesque descriptions of her feathered cincture, gold sandals, and fine pearls and jewels, while references to her bow and arrow underline her bellicose nature. Successfully cast in the role of the quintessential Roman heroine, America echoes previous references (stanzas VI to VII) made to the grandeur and heroism embodied by ancient Roman war heroes. Her victorious appearance is accompanied by celebrations of her military triumph, and hymns which sing of her extensive colonial possessions underline Vaca de Guzmán's desire to represent America primarily in terms of conquest and expansion. So unmistakably pro-colonialist rhetoric and patriotic imperialism underpin the poem. The rivalry between the Spanish and Roman empires hinted at earlier reaches a climax with the image of America triumphantly presiding over the pillars of Hercules and exemplifying Spain's old motto of *non plus ultra*:

> Y en dos columnas, que á sus piés humilla,
> Los caractéres de Hércules burlaba,
> Dando á entender que á fuerzas españolas
> Fijar no pueden limite las olas. (vv. 93–96)

In this way, the unchallengeable superiority of the Spanish empire is dramatically affirmed to exceed even the greatness of the Roman empire.

Integral to the poem's rhetoric of distancing and displacement is the shifting narrative perspective, of which the change from the first-person narration of the opening stanzas to the speaker's interiorized vision of America in stanza IX is a good illustration. In the poem, the speaker is first of all displaced by America: '. . . yo humillado / El celestial decreto obedeciendo' (vv. 73–74), then America is, in her turn, displaced by God: 'los cielos quieren que tu norte sea' (v. 116). Ultimately, it is God who is held accountable for the vision of Cortés which is acclaimed in the poem, not the speaker or America. Moreover, references to the speaker as 'trasportado' (v. 75) by his vision of America, which, he claims, 'dulcemente me enajena' (v. 66), are further indications of the poem's distancing rhetoric. It is significant, too, that it is not the speaker who applauds the heroic conquest of America in the poem, but a vague and indeterminate 'they': 'en himnos cantan su dominio extenso' (v. 97). The impression, and illusion, of impartiality which this sets up is further heightened when America herself applauds Cortés's conquest of Mexico. By having America herself, the supposed 'victim' of the Spanish conquest, celebrate it with patriotic platitudes—Cortés is described as being 'adorado' by the New World (v. 194), and is 'el ánimo valiente' (v. 153) whom America 'veneró triunfante' (v. 184)—, Vaca de Guzmán lays further emphasis on the heroism and integrity of Cortés's exploits. The poem's rhetoric of displacement is also observable in the way that America distances herself from the enthusiastic portrayal of Cortés that is given in the poem, disclaiming, it seems, any direct responsibility for creating it. For America reveals to the speaker that the account she will give of the general will be based on a pre-existing painting, 'un lienzo', that 'el arrojo mio [de América] / Arrebató del templo de la Fama' (vv. 161–62). Yet, if America disassociates herself in this way from the poem's portrayal of Cortés, so, too, does the speaker himself, for he is cast in the passive role of a third-person observer. It is, therefore, neither America nor the speaker who is represented to be the author responsible for the poem's portrayal of Cortés, but the very glory and fame that the latter has gained by his exploits: 'saben sus laureles / Comunicar su gloria á los pinceles' (vv. 175–76). Interestingly, America is explicit about the partisan poetics and colonial arrogance which colour the epic's treatment of Cortés: '[...] ese trasunto / Que trabajó el pincel con arrogancia' (vv. 209–10). And, her self-conscious use of 'lienzo', 'retrato vivo' and 'arte' to refer to the account of Cortés provided reveals the extent to which fabrication and fiction are integral to its composition.

Having made clear that partisan glory and nostalgia will inform the poem's account of Cortés, America, placing Cortés in metonymic relation to Spain, then celebrates him as the embodiment of Spanish military heroism:

> Los blasones de España el mundo vea [...]
> Ellos ilustran de Belona el templo;
> De ellos Hernan Cortés será el ejemplo. (vv. 117–20)

Seeing him as a 'modelo ... / De la region guerrera en que naciste' (vv. 443–44), the poem recounts Cortés's heroic defeats of Grijalva, Narváez and Cualpopoca and provides an inventory of the *conquistador*'s spectacular martial exploits from Tabasco to Cholula. Depicted as an intrepid, sagacious and valiant general, Cortés is extolled as the quintessential epic hero:

> Si quieres ver el ánimo valiente,
> Que tanta gloria á tu nacion ha dado,
> Prevenido en los riesgos y prudente,
> Resuelto en las empresas y arrestado,
> Un general de la española gente,
> Cuyo valor el mundo ha respetado,
> En el grande Cortés lo verás todo,
> En el grande Cortés, mas de este modo. (vv. 153–60)

Admired as a key element of Spain's heroic national past, Cortés is shown to exemplify the magnitude of Spanish valour. He is seen as the fulfilment of Spanish destiny, the 'nuevo Cid, el español Aquiles' (v. 201) who epitomizes the courage and invincibility of the Numantians and Saguntians (vv. 213–14).

In a further narrative shift, America's account of Cortés's enterprise is followed by the general's direct address to his troops prior to the destruction of his ships. Rejoicing in an old-style sacrificial patriotism which calls men to abandon their homeland and to fight and die for Spain's greatness overseas, Cortés is unequivocal about the glory to be won through conquest. Blood is the price of empire and immortal glory its reward: 'Si el eco de la sangre es halagüeño / Es glorioso también' (vv. 273–74). Seeking to encourage his troops in their commitment to empire, Cortés, like America, delivers an address that is within the Spanish heroic tradition, in that he stresses the kinship between the enterpise his men have taken on and the heroic deeds of Pelayo and the achievements of the Reyes Católicos. Drawing parallels between the Christian Reconquest of Spain and the Spanish conquest of the New World, Cortés stimulates his men's patriotic zeal for an enterprise that he presents as the inevitable fulfilment of Spain's historical destiny: 'Así venzamos los que así nacimos / Nuestro es ya su valor, nuestro su acero' (vv. 289–90). Cortés's display of duty and obedience is central to the poem, with its self-justifying rhetoric, which later draws on nature, royalty and religion as proof of the legitimacy of Spain's American conquest. Cortés, indeed, is frequently equated with the Reyes Católicos as the author of this conquest. And portentous and favourable descriptions of nature, depicting clear skies, still waters and helpful winds, are used to indicate how Nature cooperates ('En anda fija, el mar sin movimiento / El cielo claro, sosegado el viento' [vv. 231–32]) with Cortés and his captain, 'Alaminos, diestro Palinuro' (v. 226), to facilitate Spain's imperial ambitions.

The poem provides the most compelling justification for the Spanish American conquest and the ideology of empire by insisting that Cortés is an instrument chosen by Providence to carry out a peaceful and benevolent mission to the New World: 'Pues la causa que siguen [his troops] es del cielo' (v. 328). Cortés himself insists on the divine designs that underpin their exploits by claiming that God is on Spain's side in the conquest: 'ya á favor nuestro se explicó en cometas' (v. 329). Like Moratín, Vaca de Guzmán has little doubt in his mind as to the superiority of the Spanish. He, too, draws on contemptuous stereotypes of New World natives which accentuate the old Aztec system of blood sacrifice, in order to set up a binary opposition between the barbarism of the indigenous societies and the racial superiority of the Spanish. Subsequently he exploits this opposition to present the Spanish destruction of paganism as a further justification of their New World conquest.

Until this point in Vaca de Guzmán's poem, there is little difference between the epic heroism which he extols and that celebrated by Moratín. Nevertheless, what sets Vaca de Guzmán's treatment of Cortés apart from that of Moratín is his awareness of how incongruous it is in the eighteenth century for him to depict Cortés as a conventional epic hero. Fabbri, notably, criticizes Moratín for drawing on conventions more typical of Baroque than Enlightenment poetry: in fact for 'una formación [...] influida considerablemente además por esquemas y estilemas barrocas que pueden parecer más propios, éstos últimos, de un poeta épico del Siglo de Oro que de un poeta correspondiente al "siglo de luces"'.[39] In contrast to Moratín, Vaca de Guzmán attempts in his poem to reinvent Cortés as a more 'enlightened', epic hero by drawing attention to his humanity, sensibility and mercy. He is, for instance, compared to the Roman Emperor Constantine (vv. 195–96), while diverse references throughout the poem to his 'corazón' (v. 165) and 'alma' (v. 175) emphasize his sensibility. Cortés is the people's warrior, 'un general de la española gente' (v. 157). Military fame and the merits of sacrificial patriotism are no less marked in Vaca de Guzmán's heroic epic than they are in that of Moratín. Cortés's charge to his troops is a familiar one: 'Morir famosos, ó vencer valientes; / Pompa triunfal ó decorosa pira / Solo os aguarda' (vv. 409–11). But greater emphasis is placed by Vaca de Guzmán on the positive effects of Spanish colonialism by highlighting the enlightened virtues of peace, liberty and justice which are the promised effects of Cortés's conquest. The Cortés of Vaca de Guzmán projects an image of an ideal post-conquest society of idyllic perfection, rooted firmly in the Enlightenment values of 'la justicia, la paz y la abundancia':

> Cesarán los prodigios, los obscuros
> Visos del sol envuelto en arreboles;
> Verá el gran lago sus reflejos puros:
> Serán los indios nuevos-españoles;
> [...] Y el Nuevo-Mundo admirará en su infancia
> La justicia, la paz y la abundancia. (vv. 361–68)

Peace and justice, this Cortés predicts, will triumph over cruel barbarism. He envisages the peaceful surrender of the New World natives, 'con mitotes en públicos festines / Brindará esta region al europeo' (vv. 371–72), who, living under the 'sabias leyes' (v. 387) of the enlightened despot Carlos III, will co-operate willingly with the Spanish. Aztec riches will be offered, not plundered: 'Nos traerá de sus mas remotos fines / Nácar y perlas, [...] / Las piezas de oro y láminas de plata' (vv. 372–76). In this way Vaca de Guzmán successfully uses the epic genre in order to project a vision of Spanish imperialism which is paternalistic, mutually beneficial, and benign.

None the less, America's final address to the speaker in stanza LVII provides a reminder that the speaker has not yet endorsed the portrayal of Cortés offered in the poem. From stanza IX onwards the speaker has been a

39 Fabbri, '*Las naves de Cortés destruidas* en la épica española del siglo XVIII', 56.

silent listener to America's account of Cortés. Yet, while America is confident of Cortés's ability to inspire others and achieve great things, it is not yet clear to her whether her confidence is shared by the speaker:

> Y tú, jóven, que errante y discursivo
> Los lauros de tu patria recorriste,
> Y un modelo buscabas expresivo
> De la región guerrera en que naciste,
> Ya has visto bien aquel retrato vivo,
> Y su accion valerosa atento oiste,
> Ya la grandeza adviertes de esta hazaña:
> Este es Hernán Cortés; esta es España. (441–48)

When America departs in stanza LXVIII, the narrative perspective shifts back to the speaker, a figure presented in sharp contrast to her. America's departure is a lofty spectacle, which he describes as follows: 'en una nube densa, que formaron / Exhalados los húmedos vapores, / Los pavones de Juno arrebataron / De mi vista sus bellos resplandores' (451–54). Yet, the speaker himself is left disorientated, and gropes desperately amid the darkness of the Guadarrama hills in an attempt to find his way. The nightmarish image created here is a menacing one and foreshadows the anxiety which the speaker expresses in the final stanza: 'Así el portento, que aun dudoso admiro / Confuso me dejó, ciego y cobarde' (vv. 465–66).

In this work, then, Vaca de Guzmán falls short of the positive ending usually recommended for an epic poem. Indeed Luzán goes so far as to say: 'El final de la tragedia suele ser infeliz, mientras que en la epopeya siempre deberá ser feliz'.[40] Unsettled by his vision of America, the speaker expresses a sense of confusion and other feelings, wavering between admiration and cowardliness which contrast with the mood of enthusiasm and optimism which have pervaded earlier sections of the poem. These contradictory feelings and uncertainties stand in direct opposition to the consummate confidence in Spanish imperialism expressed at the end of Moratín's epic. That the speaker should choose to qualify his sense of 'admiración' with adjectives like 'dudoso' is significant, granted that 'admiration' was the very emotion which, as Luzán comments, the genre sought to cultivate: 'la admiración que debe excitar'.[41] Vaca de Guzmán seems to struggle to use the old militaristic rhetoric of patriotic self-sacrifice and the cult of the Christian, military hero with sufficient conviction to inspire his readers and renew their optimism. Conquest and expansion might be avowed by the

40 Luzán, *La Poética*, 613. However, it is significant that Lucan, who Vaca de Guzmán cites as a model, also ended his epic *Pharsalia* on a tragic note.

41 Luzán, *La Poética*, 613.

poem's protagonists but this orthodox position is not wholly sustained, for there is also a self-conscious and distancing rhetoric operating in places to remind the reader of the fictionality of the poem's treatment of Cortés. The rhetorical devices which the poem deploys—supernatural machinery, metonymy and allegory, prophecy and prediction—reinforce our impression of fantasy and superficiality, even as do the speaker's self-conscious references to the artifice used in composing the work: 'según me le *pintó mi fantasia*' (v. 111). Indeed, the entire epic is revealed as one long hallucination: 'un deliquio' (v. 69), 'un éxtasis dentro de mí mismo' (v. 65). As a consequence the epic heroism of Cortés it describes is exposed by Vaca de Guzmán as a largely fictionalized creation, the product of panegyric and heroic hyperbole.

Vaca de Guzmán's epic poem clearly does much more than simply reproduce official propaganda. The despair and uncertainty which the speaker expresses, most notably in the final stanza, are indicative of Vaca's anxieties over the suitability of the epic genre as a means of artistic and ideological expression in and for the eighteenth century. The epic's concern to describe and exalt martial and jingoistic heroism, and its emphasis on sacrificial patriotism and chivalric adventure, expressed and elaborated within a tightly-knit religious framework, made it a particularly anachronistic genre for and in an age of scientific and rational zeal.

Although both epic poems are written on identical subjects, the different ways in which Hernán Cortés is interpreted in each of them shows that in the eighteenth century there was a lack of consensus over what constituted a truly epic poem. Interestingly, unlike Moratín, Vaca de Guzmán suggests that by the eighteenth century the traditional epic genre is an exhausted medium whose familiar and time-worn motifs can no longer adequately inspire the reader. Yet he fails to identify and make the kinds of revisions needed to reconstitute the genre so that it can continue to serve valid political and patriotic as well as artistic and generic functions. By reconfiguring Hernán Cortés as a more enlightened, heroic figure, Vaca de Guzmán attempts to reinvent Spain's heroic tradition for the eighteenth century. Nevertheless, the 'abismo' and 'obscuridad' which affect and unsettle the speaker in the final stanzas underline the failure of Vaca de Guzmán's attempts to resolve the problems of adapting the traditional epic to the artistic and ideological demands of the eighteenth century. In the end, he produces no new epic and no new myth. He may struggle to give form and expression to a new Enlightenment ideology of empire, but, ultimately, he fails. In many ways, however, his task was an impossible one: the traditional epic genre *was* the imperial mode and Vaca de Guzmán was bound by its intrinsically patriotic and conservative conventions. It is therefore to Vaca de Guzmán's contemporaries, using different genres, that the reader must turn for proposals for a new, 'enlightened', legitimizing ideology of empire that would replace the 'intransigencia heroica' of the epic genre and more adequately defend Spain against the strident criticism of Spain's colonial record emanating from much of the rest of Enlightenment Europe.[42]

42 José A. Valero, 'Manuel José Quintana y el sublime moral', *HR,* 71:4 (2003), 585–611 (p. 608).

José Marchena y Menéndez Pelayo
La invención de un personaje

JOAQUÍN ÁLVAREZ BARRIENTOS

Consejo Superior de Investigaciones Científicas, Madrid

Marcelino Menéndez Pelayo era un gran escritor. Como muchos contemporáneos suyos y como otros historiadores que ejercieron su profesión antes que él, entendía su actividad como cercana o casi como una variante de la actividad del artista o de la del escritor, de manera que el resultado final debía tener, además de solidez y rigor intelectual, una textura estética hermosa. De hecho, escribió sobre esta cuestión en distintas ocasiones y en su juvenil discurso de ingreso en la Real Academia de la Historia (1883), al considerar esta disciplina como una 'arte bella'.[1] Aunque el modo de escribir historia literariamente fue desapareciendo a medida que se profesionalizó en los años del cambio de siglo el trabajo del historiador y el del filólogo, Menéndez Pelayo nunca abandonó su fidelidad a un estilo limpio, cada vez menos adjetivado, y a una frase que estaban al servicio de los valores culturales que defendía. Aspiraba a que la historia que contaba trascendiera el caso individual (el de Marchena, por ejemplo) y contribuyera a asegurar los ideales colectivos a cuyo servicio estaba su pluma. Para ello utilizó una retórica eficaz, que sostenía sus grandes narrativas historiográficas y las pequeñas, a base de componer retratos de los personajes que trataba—como mostró principalmente en los *Heterodoxos*

---

1 *Discursos leídos ante la Real Academia de la Historia en la recepción pública del doctor D. Marcelino Menéndez Pelayo el 13 de mayo de 1883* (Madrid: Imprenta Central, 1883). Incluye la contestación de Aureliano Fernández-Guerra. 'Voy a hablar [...] de la historia considerada como arte bella, de la noción estética de la historia' (11). Para un análisis de este discurso, véase últimamente, Kurt Spang, 'La Historia como arte bella', *Boletín de la Biblioteca de Menéndez Pelayo*, 82 (2006), 453–73, y la bibliografía allí citada. Una visión general, en Antonio Santoveña Setién, *Marcelino Menéndez Pelayo. Revisión crítico-biográfica de un pensador católico* (Santander: Univ. de Cantabria/Asamblea Regional de Cantabria, 1994), y José Alberto Vallejo del Campo, *Menéndez Pelayo, historiador. Su formación y su concepción de la disciplina* (Santander: Fundación Marcelino Botín/Asamblea Regional de Cantabria, 1998).

españoles—;[2] todo ello destinado a desarmar los puntos de vista que amenazaban la ortodoxia.

Menéndez Pelayo se encuentra con José Marchena. Cómo se gestó la edición de las *Obras literarias*

Desde el punto de vista de la publicidad, José Marchena tuvo suerte de que Menéndez Pelayo se encontrara con él, porque, aunque otros se habían ocupado ya de su figura, quien le dio el espaldarazo como personaje importante—aunque pretendidamente atípico—de nuestra historia fue él. Se puede estar o no de acuerdo con su interpretación, puede decir (como ocurre) cosas que ya antes indicaron Bono Serrano, Latour y Cueto,[3] pero él consigue que lleguen al gran público y que los que después se acerquen a la figura del sevillano, para bien o para mal, deban partir de la interpretación que formuló. Y esto no sólo vale para la figura del abate.

Hasta llegar a la edición de las *Obras literarias* de José Marchena, que Menéndez Pelayo realiza en dos tomos en 1892 y 1896,[4] el erudito investigador recorrió un largo camino de unos veinte años que, en parte, puede recomponerse gracias a su epistolario. Gracias a él se conoce la intrahistoria del libro y cómo se construyó la imagen del *personaje*, o la interpretación histórica, abate Marchena, con el que mantuvo una relación de amor y odio, ya señalada por la crítica.[5]

Plasmación de su interés por él es el retrato que realiza en la serie de los heterodoxos españoles, publicada entre 1880 y 1882; pero, con el paso del tiempo, ese retrato lleno de adjetivos se convirtió en otra cosa. La primera noticia que localizo en su epistolario, relativa a Marchena, por entonces poco conocido, es del 25 de enero de 1876, en carta dirigida a Damián Menéndez Rayón, en la que le dice que ha descubierto que es el autor de la traducción de *De rerum natura*, por las iniciales que figuran—D[on] J[osé] M[archena] R[uiz] C[ueto]—y porque el trabajo 'es muy propio de su gusto poético e ideas materialistas'.[6] Este testimonio señala que llevaba ya tiempo suficiente

2 Marcelino Menéndez Pelayo, *Historia de los heterodoxos*, en *Obras completas*, edición definitiva, revisada por el autor, 21 vols (Madrid: Suárez, 1911–33; 2ª ed. refundida, 7 vols, Madrid: Suárez, 1911–32]); o, entre las ediciones más modernas y asequibles de esta obra: *Historia de los heterodoxos*, con estudio final sobre Menéndez Pelayo y su *Historia de los heterodoxos* por Rafael García y García de Castro, 2 vols (Madrid: Biblioteca de Autores Cristianos, 1986–87).

3 Me refiero a Gaspar Bono Serrano, Antoine de Latour y Leopoldo Augusto de Cueto (marqués de Valmar) (ver nota 14).

4 *Obras literarias de D. José Marchena (el abate Marchena)*: ver nota 12.

5 Juan Francisco Fuentes, *José Marchena. Biografía política e intelectual* (Barcelona: Crítica, 1989).

6 Marcelino Menéndez Pelayo, *Epistolario*, ed. Manuel Revuelta Sañudo, 23 vols (Madrid: FUE, 1982–1989), XXII, 288. A partir de ahora, citaré sólo por el tomo y la página correspondiente.

trabajando sobre él como para haberse hecho una idea de su estilo y pensamiento o de que, al menos, conocía, como se verá luego, las interpretaciones previas. El siguiente es del 21 de junio de 1876. Como otras en las que pide o comenta la información que recibe de los diferentes corresponsales a los que les ha solicitado ayuda para redactar los *Heterodoxos*, en ésta dirigida a su amigo Gumersindo Laverde cuenta que trabaja sobre su traducción de los poemas de Ossian, publicada en 1804 en el periódico dirigido por Quintana, *Variedades de Ciencia, Literatura y Artes*. Ya le adelanta que no cree que el autor de la versión sea Juan Maury, como se pensaba, sino el abate (II, 77). En sucesivas cartas irá perfilando más su figura—panteísta, enciclopedista, espinosista (II, 202)—; mientras al año siguiente se interesa por su *Fragmentum Petronii* y por sus traducciones de Safo, Catulo, Lucrecio y otros autores, que quiere incluir en la *Biblioteca de traductores españoles*.[7] Su opinión de esos fragmentos y de otras obras traducidas, como son varias comedias de Molière, es que todo eso es digno de conservarse, 'porque son buenas y raras versiones' (II, 555), en lo que sólo repite lo ya señalado por otros antes que él.

En estas primeras referencias presenta ya la dicotomía en que se va a mover su apreciación del escritor, deudora de anteriores formulaciones: por un lado, valorar sus cualidades literarias y eruditas; por otro, desaprobar sus tendencias religiosas y filosóficas. Desde pronto se interesa por editar parte de la obra del abate, en concreto aquella que no desafiaba la ortodoxia, era desconocida para la comunidad científica y con la que podía sentirse más cómodo. Así, ya en 1878, a pesar del materialismo del texto, quiere editar la traducción del *De rerum natura* de Lucrecio, de la que se ocuparía el impresor Navarro. No había decidido aún si hacer uno o dos tomos, todo dependería de si se anotaba o no la obra. También desea sacar un tomo de opúsculos, prescindiendo de los impíos (III, 62), porque considera que sería un buen negocio, ya que 'lo estrafalario y singular del personaje' llamaría la atención de los curiosos (III, 506).

Aun no había publicado el tomo III de los *Heterodoxos*, en el que aparece la información recogida hasta el momento—lo fue en 1881—, pero es claro el interés que la figura ha despertado en él. Interés que no se enfría cuando Morel-Fatio le informa de que en París han encontrado un manuscrito con poesías de Marchena y que el profesor al que se debe el hallazgo quiere dar a conocer las inéditas (III, 435). A lo largo de esos años, sigue trabajando, recopila información, persigue el paradero de los papeles del autor, averigua que algunos fueron a parar a las manos de Martínez de la Rosa y otros a las de Pedro José Pidal (IV, 30), pero no consigue ir más allá en su localización, mientras sigue empeñado, 1882, en editar 'el Lucrecio'.

7 Véase José Marchena, *Fragmentum Petronii*, ed. Joaquín Álvarez Barrientos (Sevilla: Renacimiento, 2007).

Enfrascado en otros trabajos, y a la espera de la edición de los inéditos, parece olvidarse de Marchena, aunque no es así, pues sus amigos le envían informaciones cada vez que se les cruza en el camino. Así Wentworth Webster, que en 1885 le pasa 'portraits [. . .] evidently taken *de visu*' de él, Martínez de Ballesteros y otros (VII, 191). Sin embargo, el impulso más fuerte llega cuando, en febrero de 1887, Morel-Fatio le refiere que, tras cuatro años de guardar el manuscrito con los poemas, el profesor no ha hecho nada y lo ha devuelto a la biblioteca (VII, 268–69). Es entonces cuando le pide que elija un buen pendolista y le mande copia. Él correrá con los gastos, pues piensa, otra vez, hacer un tomito con las poesías, en el que refundirá y aumentará lo que escribió en los *Heterodoxos* (VIII, 272); quiere también localizar los opúsculos franceses escritos en tiempos de la Revolución y dedicar el verano de ese año a terminar el libro (VIII, 402). Fue, finalmente, el mismo Morel-Fatio quien realizó la copia, al no fiarse de nadie, en lo que se demoró varios meses, pues hasta julio no tuvo Menéndez Pelayo en su poder el total del manuscrito copiado:

> Las nuevas poesías son muy curiosas para la vida de Marchena, dan razón de algunos amigos suyos literatos y de algunas vicisitudes de su vida, nos informan de su modo de pensar sobre acontecimientos políticos de que fue testigo, y nos permiten juzgar exactamente sobre sus cualidades poéticas, que brillan más en las traducciones y en las imitaciones que en las obras propias. (VIII, 502)

Mientras prepara ese trabajo, Alfred Morel-Fatio, que le ha cedido la propiedad y uso de los poemas, publica un artículo en la *Revue Historique*, de gran importancia porque no sigue en él el tono de cuantos se habían ocupado de Marchena hasta el momento, y porque aporta documentación sobre los años revolucionarios, que tanto interesaban al santanderino.[8] Poco después, el 21 de diciembre de 1890, le manda copia del 'aviso' *A la nación española* de Marchena y de parte de la segunda edición del mismo, que tiene bastantes variantes (X, 548). Pero, para ese momento, se había producido un hecho determinante que decidió la suerte de la edición de las obras de José Marchena. José Mª Asensio, admirador de Menéndez Pelayo, fundador de la Sociedad de Bibliófilos Andaluces en 1869, cervantista reconocido que había dado a conocer numerosos documentos sobre el autor del *Quijote*, y más tarde académico de la Española y de la Historia, le informa el 29 de octubre de 1890 de que los 'utreranos' han sabido que existe 'el Lucrecio' y se ofrecen a publicarlo, ya que el autor era natural de allí. 'Todos los gastos serán

8 Alfred Morel-Fatio, 'José Marchena et la propagande révolutionnaire en Espagne en 1792 et 1793', *Revue Historique*, 44 (Sept-Oct. 1890), 72–87. Adolfo de Castro se escapa también del tono habitual en el artículo que publicó en 1889 en *La España Moderna*, citado en nota 14.

satisfechos por hijos de Utrera' y dejan a Menéndez Pelayo como director de la edición (X, 503).[9]

A partir de ese momento, Asensio se convierte en el intermediario entre el impresor Enrique Rasco, los financieros y el editor; le envía y reclama pruebas y galeradas, que don Marcelino no siempre manda con la rapidez deseada por el impresor, y le importuna con numerosas peticiones: que reseñe el trabajo que, coincidiendo con la celebración del Descubrimiento, ha escrito sobre Cristóbal Colón, cosa que tampoco hace a tiempo, mientras él insiste una y otra vez; puesto que se rumorea que va ser ministro de Fomento (mayo de 1891), que se acuerde de él y de su hijo, etc. La insistencia de Asensio, por otra parte, ofrece datos interesantes sobre las incidencias del proceso de impresión (14 de septiembre de 1891), pues primero se retrasa el inicio de los trabajos porque no hay papel, luego eligen 'uno superior-catalán de primera', y más tarde discuten sobre la tirada recomendable: él considera que deben hacerse doscientas cincuenta copias; cien para vender y el resto para regalar. ¿Qué opina el maestro? (XI, 219).[10]

Las múltiples ocupaciones del maestro retrasan la corrección y el envío de las pruebas, por lo que Rasco se queja de que no tiene trabajo. Por su parte, Asensio le recuerda que debe hacer la biografía de Marchena (XI, 340), le pregunta dónde deben ir la traducción de Lucrecio y la biografía, ¿en el primero o en el segundo tomo? (XI, 393). El mes de enero de 1892 es especialmente angustioso—en realidad, todo ese año y el siguiente—, ya que don Marcelino no contesta o tarda mucho en hacerlo, no responde a las preguntas, no devuelve las pruebas, con lo cual están parados. Y de nuevo, ¿dónde se coloca la biografía? (XI, 526). Ahora sabemos que Menéndez Pelayo ganaba tiempo, pues no tenía redactado el ensayo crítico, para el que seguía buscando información, que acabó colocado en el segundo tomo, publicado cuatro años después, en 1896, junto con 'el Lucrecio'. Además de continuar la investigación, en 1892 y después estaba embarcado en la edición de las obras de Lope de Vega que la Academia le había encomendado unos años antes, lo cual le ocupaba mucho tiempo; a esa y a otras ocupaciones, se sumó en septiembre de ese año el encargo, por parte de la misma Corporación, de la *Antología de poetas hispano-americanos*, para conmemorar el Descubrimiento de América (XII, 64).[11]

Durante ese año y el siguiente las cartas de Asensio menudean recriminándole que 'les haya olvidado'. La biografía debería ir al final del segundo tomo, para cerrar la obra 'con llave de oro' (24 de julio de 1892; XII, 19); no envía las pruebas de 'Lucrecio', o, por el contrario, van ya por las

9 En las cartas no queda muy claro, pero parece inferirse que Asensio fue quien estableció el contacto.

10 Así fue finalmente, según la 'Comprobación de la tirada' que figura detrás del colofón del segundo tomo.

11 Marcelino Menéndez Pelayo, *Antología de poetas hispano-americanos*, prólogo y selección, 4 vols (Madrid: RAE, 1893–95).

terceras de la traducción (el 25 de enero de 1893); que termine 'el juicio crítico' pronto para que el libro esté antes de la Feria de ese año (XII, 148). Pero Menéndez Pelayo sigue recopilando materiales para la biografía de Marchena, a pesar de las expectativas de Asensio y 'los utreranos' de tener el trabajo terminado ese año, y así Carmelo de Echegaray, en carta del 23 de abril de 1894, que es respuesta a una consulta suya, le asegura que el abate no perteneció a la Sociedad Bascongada, pero, por el contrario, le proporciona información sobre Vicente María Santibáñez, que luego aprovecha (XII, 520–21).

Finalmente, es el propio Rasco, dueño del establecimiento tipográfico donde se imprime el libro, quien el 18 de septiembre de 1896 le envía desde Sevilla terceras pruebas de la biografía, ya que en las segundas había añadido muchas novedades, y le pide que dé su 'conforme' en pormenores relativos a la portada, anteportada, titulillos y otros detalles (XIV, 53–54). El colofón de este segundo tomo indica que se terminó de imprimir el jueves 31 de diciembre. Las obras literarias del heterodoxo ya estaban en la calle, debidamente expurgadas para que no ofendieran a ningún bienpensante:

> Ni el señor Cuadra [marqués de San Marcial, que ya había muerto], al proyectar esta edición, ni yo, al aceptar el encargo de dirigirla, insertando en ella todos los materiales inéditos que sobre Marchena poseo, tuvimos otro propósito que el de hacer un libro de pura erudición y destinado a correr en manos de muy pocas personas; advertencia que no considero inútil para prevenir escrúpulos y justos recelos que el nombre de Marchena trae fatalmente consigo.[12]

La corta tirada aseguraba la difusión entre eruditos y clase dominante, preparada, en teoría, para interpretar correctamente lo que iba a leer, aunque el 'Estudio crítico-biográfico' ya orientaba debidamente la lectura. Pasado el tiempo, no debió pensarse del mismo modo, pues en 1900, y formando parte de la edición de las obras completas de don Marcelino, se publicó junto con su trabajo sobre Torres Naharro y con el título de 'El abate Marchena', dentro de los *Estudios de crítica literaria*, luego recogido en el tomo IV de *Estudios y discursos de crítica histórica y literaria*, 1942, y en 1946, con prólogo de José Mª de Cossío, lo editó de nuevo la editorial Espasa-Calpe, sin que haya vuelto a ser impreso.[13] En 1900 le añade un 'Apéndice a la biografía', resultado de las pesquisas de Manuel Gómez Imaz, que le envía

12 *Obras literarias de D. José Marchena (el abate Marchena) recogidas de manuscritos y raros impresos con un estudio crítico-biográfico del doctor D. Marcelino Menéndez y Pelayo, de la Real Academia Española*, 2 vols (Sevilla: Imprenta de Enrique Rasco, 1892–1896), I, vi.

13 'El abate Marchena', en *Obras completas. Estudios de crítica literaria. Tercera serie. Bartolomé Torres Naharro y su 'Propalladia'. El abate Marchena* (Madrid: Suc. de Rivadeneyra, 1900), 185–388; *Estudios y discursos de crítica histórica y literaria*, IV (Madrid: CSIC, 1942), 107–221, y *El abate Marchena*, con prólogo de José Mª de Cossío (Madrid: Espasa-Calpe, 1946). En la actualidad preparo una edición de este texto.

en septiembre de ese año un opúsculo anónimo que cree obra de Marchena (XV, 450–51). Se trata de la 'Carta de un oficial retirado a uno de sus antiguos compañeros', fechada en Toledo el 23 de abril de 1808, que corrió anónima por Madrid y muchos pensaron que había sido impresa en el palacio de Murat.

La invención de un sentido

Pero, antes de que Menéndez Pelayo invirtiera unos veinte años de su vida en trabajar sobre Marchena (y en otras cosas a la vez), hubo investigadores que se ocuparon de él y orientaron la interpretación que había que dar de su trabajo y personalidad. De esos primeros estudios es deudor el erudito santanderino, porque asumió su construcción en lo ideológico, no tanto en lo literario. Me refiero a las aportaciones de Gaspar Bono Serrano, Antoine de Latour y Leopoldo Augusto de Cueto. El primero es autor de unas páginas que aparecieron en el periódico madrileño *Escenas Contemporáneas*, 1866, reelaboradas en 1870 al publicar la semblanza del autor en su *Miscelánea religiosa, política y literaria*. Tuvo entonces a la vista el artículo de Antoine de Latour, impreso primero en el periódico *Le Correspondant*, del 25 de febrero de 1867, y luego en 1869 en *Espagne. Traditions, moeurs et littérature*, donde, a su vez, recogía la aportación de Bono.[14]

El trabajo que realiza Gaspar Bono va dirigido a ensalzar la religión católica y a defender una forma de ser. De este modo, utiliza a sus 'objetos de estudio'—Quintana, Marchena—para mostrar el triunfo de la fe sobre los ataques de la incredulidad, del ateísmo y de la heterodoxia, todo ello enfermedades y deformaciones de la cultura. Si finalmente, porque fue empeño suyo, consigue que Quintana abjure de sus creencias (o de sus no

14 La secuencia cronológica es ésta: Gaspar Bono Serrano, 'El abate Marchena', *Escenas Contemporáneas*, X:2 (1865–1866), 169–80; Antoine de Latour, *Le Correspondant*, 25 de febrero de 1867; Antoine de Latour, 'L'Abbé Marchèna', en *Espagne. Traditions, moeurs et littérature. Nouvelles études* (Paris: Didier et cie., 1869), 51–76; Leopoldo Augusto de Cueto, marqués de Valmar, 'Bosquejo histórico crítico de la poesía castellana en el siglo XVIII', en *Poetas líricos del siglo XVIII*, BAE LXI, LXIII, LXVII, 3 vols (Madrid: Rivadeneyra, 1869–75), I (BAE LXI, 1869). En el tomo III (BAE LXVII, 1875) de estos *Poetas* también incorporaba nuevas noticias. Gaspar Bono Serrano, 'El abate Marchena', en *Miscelánea religiosa, política y literaria en prosa y verso* (Madrid: Imprenta de la viuda de Aguado e hijo, 1870), 308–22. De esta línea de interpretación escapa Adolfo de Castro, quien en el prólogo a *Obras escogidas de filósofos*, BAE LXV (Madrid: Rivadeneyra, 1873), cxxxii–cxxxviii, estudia a Marchena de un modo bastante neutral y valora sus aportaciones. Posterior a la primera versión de la biografía de Marchena en los *Heterodoxos* es Adolfo de Castro, 'Un girondino español: el abate Marchena', *La España Moderna*, I (enero 1889), 37–71, que, en la línea del trabajo anterior, valora las traducciones y el discurso de las *Lecciones* [*Lecciones de filosofía moral y elocuencia: o colección de los trozos mas selectos de poesía, elocuencia, historia, religión y filosofía morales de los mejores autores castellanos*, puestas en orden por D. José Marchena], 2 vols (Bordeaux: Beanne, 1820). Ver también José Marchena, 'Documento curioso: carta inédita del abate Marchena, sacada de la colección del Excmo. Sr. D. Antonio Cánovas del Castillo', *La España Moderna*, I (feb. 1889), 147–60.

creencias, más bien) y termine aceptando de buena fe, como nos dice, recibir los santos sacramentos en los momentos finales de su vida—demostrando así cuál es el carácter de los verdaderos españoles—, con Marchena, que no se convierte, nos encontramos ante el devenir vital, necesariamente atropellado e insatisfactorio, de alguien que termina mal sus días porque es incrédulo, crítico y ateo. Su final es 'justo castigo del satánico orgullo que le dominaba', lógico desenlace a su forma de vivir y a las creencias que observaba:

> Es una desgracia bien lamentable para este escritor y aun para la España que le dio el ser, que en lugar de venerar con humilde respeto y conservar constantemente la católica fe de sus buenos y piadosos padres, renunciase a las consoladoras creencias religiosas, entregándose al escepticismo desde muy joven, y cayendo por fin como era natural en el abismo insondable de la incredulidad y del ateísmo.[15]

Esta interpretación de su vida, así como de su obra poética, no debe extrañar, si se tiene en cuenta que, para estos historiadores y críticos, ser católico era un rasgo de identidad nacional y que seguían los preceptos dictados por Pío IX en su *Syllabus de Errores* incluido en la encíclica *Quanta Cura*, de 1864. Por tanto, y del mismo modo que Chateaubriand explicó que Voltaire no llegó a ser el primer historiador de Francia porque no era cristiano, Bono resuelve que Marchena 'no pertenece al reducido número de nuestros poetas de primer orden' por haber sido incrédulo.[16]

Gaspar Bono Serrano deja establecidos unos principios de interpretación que, con matizaciones, serán los que continúe Menéndez Pelayo. Por su parte, Antoine de Latour insiste en ellos, motivado por un afán didáctico, porque piensa que los jóvenes españoles están tentados por peligrosas novedades seculares, que les pueden llevar a tener el mismo desgraciado destino de 'ce douloureux avortement', que es el abate:

> Je me suis proposé un autre but, en écrivant à mon tour cette biographie; c'est de montrer comment le talent le plus heureux peut se trouver frappé de stérilité finale, lorsque se laissant égarer par ses passions ou par de vaines théories, il perd avec la foi cette sérenité de l'âme si nécessaire à son libre et complet développement.[17]

Esta perspectiva, que utiliza la literatura y el pensamiento para hacer historia moral y de las creencias religiosas en la época, es la que siguió Cueto,

15 Bono Serrano, 'El abate Marchena', en *Miscelánea religiosa*, 309. La mayor parte de las informaciones de este trabajo está tomada del artículo que René Alby escribió sobre Marchena, en J. Fr. Michaud, *Biographie universelle ancienne et moderne*, 26 (Graz: Akademische Druck-u. Verlagsanstalt, 1968), 489–91, originariamente publicado en 1854.

16 Bono Serrano, 'El abate Marchena', en *Miscelánea religiosa*, 310.

17 Latour, 'L'Abbé Marchèna', 76.

al escribir sobre Marchena en su 'Bosquejo crítico'. Bajo la excusa de intentar conocer a la persona, se hace apología de una creencia y se analizan los textos del autor, pero para conocer su incredulidad y condición levantisca, no para dilucidar sus cualidades estéticas; desde ahí se ofrece un modelo vital que debe ser rechazado, y otro que es el ejemplar. Así, en la línea de Latour, a quien cita, escribe: 'Su índole desmandada y su condición impetuosa le impedían comprender la terrible responsabilidad que implica el desquiciamiento repentino del asiento moral en que descansa toda sociedad organizada'.[18] Por lo tanto, destaca sus errores de fe, su protestantismo, cuenta anécdotas que en sí mismas suponen ya el desprestigio del autor y de su obra, para destacar que, a pesar de todo, siempre fue sincero en sus opiniones.[19] Quizá por eso murió 'en el gremio de la fe católica',[20] cosa que negaba Bono. Valora, como hará Menéndez Pelayo, sus traducciones y la prosa del 'Discurso preliminar' a las *Lecciones de filosofía moral y elocuencia*, para terminar:

> No es dable negar que Dios depositó en el alma de Marchena la acción, la luz y el temple que constituyen la inspiración de cierto linaje. El soplo del encono político torció el rumbo natural del alma y agostó las flores de aquella inspiración. El infortunio consumó la obra destructora, y probablemente ni un solo afecto puro y sereno llegó a iluminar con un rayo de dicha verdadera aquella trabajosa y trabajada vida.[21]

De estas interpretaciones, de esta estructura retórica y de pensamiento, adolece el trabajo de don Marcelino, de que el objetivo de los historiadores fuera contribuir a determinar la identidad de la nación desde la moral religiosa y de estar al servicio de un proyecto cultural determinado, trascendente, que incluía la salvación de los españoles. Pero también se resiente de algo que es rasgo común a otros y, aparentemente, podía ser considerado hecho positivo. Me refiero a que, al trabajar sobre autores cercanos en el tiempo, de los que aún quedaban amigos, familiares o testigos, pueden servirse de fuentes orales, más o menos directas, para construir su narración. Sin embargo, el uso de estas fuentes fue sumamente peligroso, pues dieron a anécdotas (reales o no) y a recuerdos, el valor de autoridad y autenticidad histórica que tal vez no tenían y, desde ellos, elaboraron teorías o los utilizaron para validar interpretaciones. Así, por ejemplo, Bono reproduce una anécdota que le contó el librero Salvador Faulí, relativa a la admiración que Marchena sentía por Fray Luis de Granada—'lo oí en Valencia de boca del mismo Faulí en 1827'—, y para dar

18 Cueto, 'Bosquejo histórico crítico', cciv.

19 Con frecuencia, los historiadores y biógrafos entendieron esa sinceridad como manifestación del carácter utópico o iluso del personaje.

20 Cueto, 'Bosquejo histórico crítico', ccvii.

21 Cueto, 'Bosquejo histórico crítico', ccviii.

mayor valor a la fuente oral, añade: 'Años después me hizo referencia del mismo suceso el Sr. D. Juan Nicasio Gallego, que lo había sabido por un amigo del abate, a quien éste se lo había contado'.[22] Antes había aludido a unos 'informes que he recibido últimamente de un primo suyo anciano octogenario y respetable, que lo trató muy de cerca'. La adjetivación y la venerable edad autorizan y dan credibilidad a los testimonios.

Pero, dejando a un lado el aire de patio de vecinos que adquiere de este modo la redacción de la historia, y sin desmerecer de la cercanía narrativa que tales manifestaciones consiguen sobre el lector, fiar en la vacilación de la memoria, en la manipulación posible de los recuerdos, en la inseguridad de las tradiciones orales, no parece el modo más seguro de construir los relatos historiográficos. Sin embargo, fue moneda corriente en la época entre historiadores y novelistas, mostrando la tenue barrera que había entre unos y otros. Cueto, Menéndez Pelayo, Pérez Galdós se valieron de esos testimonios que, dependiendo de quien los enunciara—por lo general alguien ilustre en la República de las Letras—, daban autoridad al recuerdo, al rumor, a la anécdota. La repetición del 'dato' y la condición de quien lo transmitía, otorgaban valor.

Hay que tener presente que, en esos años del siglo XIX, aún no estaba suficientemente definida ni la labor del historiador, ni su metodología, de manera que, por lo general, lo que hacían era contar una historia, interesarse por el hombre, por conocer al personaje, y servirse de él para otras cosas, más que hacer el estudio de su producción literaria o artística, como se indicó. Se mezclaba o se confundía el género 'historiográfico' con el 'memorialístico', al historiador con el literato. Algunos, como Emilio Cotarelo y Mori, criticaron esta forma de hacer, que confundía novela, leyenda, biografía e historia, y reclamaron una metodología más fidedigna y rigurosa. Pero los grandes cambios llegarían de la mano de los miembros de la Junta para la Ampliación de Estudios.[23]

Ahora bien, mientras ese momento llega, Menéndez Pelayo, que tenía buena pluma y no dudaba en utilizar a los personajes que historiaba para reflejar la interpretación de la historia de España que tenía por correcta, insiste en el uso de las tradiciones orales—tan valiosas como la documentación inédita, con la que se equiparan—, y en contar historias. La suya es una narración que, a menudo y en consonancia con su idea de la Historia como 'arte bella', se ajusta a los parámetros y requisitos externos de la narrativa de ficción, si bien trabaja sobre materiales históricos, aunque se permita manipular la información, o utilizar juicios de valor, sumarios y prejuicios, para llegar a las conclusiones que desea, como sucede con casi todos los retratos

22 Bono Serrano, 'El abate Marchena', en *Miscelánea religiosa*, 318.

23 Véase mi introducción a la edición de Emilio Cotarelo y Mori, *Isidoro Máiquez y el teatro de su tiempo* (Madrid: Asociación de Directores de Escena de España, 2009 [1 ed. Madrid: Imprenta de José Perales y Martínez, 1902]).

que hace de quienes pasan por su galería de heréticos españoles,[24] tal y como habían hecho sus predecesores. Ya se han señalado ejemplos en Bono Serrano y en Cueto. Todos eran herederos de una idea romántica de la Historia y todos sufrieron en esa segunda mitad del siglo la presión del *Syllabus de Errores* incluido en la encíclica *Quanta Cura* (1864) de Pío IX, según el cual cuanto se alejara de la visión integrista de la doctrina era pecado y contrario a la Iglesia. Marchena y los heterodoxos de los que se encargó Menéndez entraban de lleno en lo que el *Syllabus* rechazaba.[25] Al asumir esos presupuestos como líneas de actuación, los trabajos históricos de estos estudiosos no podían sino acabar siendo historias eclesiásticas y doctrinales, como la de los heterodoxos españoles. En el texto de Pío IX aparecía condenado el siglo XVIII por regalista, por la Revolución Francesa y por todas aquellas actitudes que llevaban a secularizar la vida y a hacer que el individuo pensara por sí mismo: es decir, se anatematizaba cuanto iba dirigido a liberalizar y modernizar la sociedad, y, de manera muy especial, lo referente a la ciencia y al pensamiento: el naturalismo, el materialismo, el sensualismo. A ninguna de estas 'desviaciones' escapaba o era ajeno el abate Marchena.

A la vista de estos testimonios y de otros, comprobado el uso reiterado, por eficaz, de una retórica concreta, está claro que su objetivo era contribuir a la pintura ideológica de España y que el mejor modo de hacerlo era a contrario, pues, al caracterizar a algún heterodoxo, en este caso a Marchena, creaba la imagen negativa de toda una parte de la historia española, y proponía la modélica. De este 'método' que consiste en hacer 'retratos', y es técnica literaria propia del costumbrismo, participaron muchos.[26] En el caso de don Marcelino, su uso ha tenido extraordinaria influencia en la conformación de un sentido, de modo que se esté o no de acuerdo con él, ha habido que partir de su versión, lo cual, desde luego, influía en el desarrollo del pensamiento.

Como los que escribieron antes que él sobre Marchena, se valió de juicios de valor, de la descripción o enumeración de rasgos de carácter que, por su condición, servían para legitimar o ridiculizar opciones vitales. Menéndez Pelayo escribe con sobreentendidos porque lo hace para un público de ya convencidos que comparten un mismo sistema moral, el único verdadero. Todo aquello que se aparta de ese registro es erróneo y heterodoxo; ejemplo de lo que no hay que hacer y de lo que no es español. Le interesa conocer al individuo (de ahí la importancia de las anécdotas, por lo que contribuyen a

24 Sobre el modo de construir su relato, Fernando Durán López, 'Ideas que imprimen carácter: narración, retrato y otras maniobras de distracción en la *Historia de los Heterodoxos*', *Boletín de la Biblioteca de Menéndez Pelayo*, 82 (2006), 353–91.

25 Un estudio de los cambios de interpretación que tuvo respecto del siglo XVIII, en Joaquín Álvarez Barrientos, 'El siglo XVIII, según Menéndez Pelayo', *Boletín de la Biblioteca de Menéndez Pelayo*, 82 (2006), 297–329.

26 'Para completar el retrato de tal personaje', escribe, consciente, Menéndez Pelayo en el 'Estudio crítico' de las *Obras literarias de D. José Marchena*, II, clvi.

acercarlo y hacerlo más real), para describirlo, desacreditar sus ideas y proponer, por el método inverso, el modelo válido.

Sin embargo, al dedicarse tantos años al abate, además de mostrar admiración por aquella parte de su vida y obra que podía aceptar—lo referido al humanismo y al mundo clásico—, se perciben matices respecto del objeto de estudio; tensiones entre lo que publicó en los *Heterodoxos* en 1881 y lo que escribió en 1896, cuando tiene más información y conoce mejor al personaje. Salva en ambos casos su cultura clásica y sus cualidades de erudito, rechazando las aventuras ideológicas, pero en el estudio crítico de la edición (que se resiente de ser una amplificación y no haber sido formulado de nuevo) hay más comprensión e incluso a veces algo de identificación y proyección. Sus biógrafos han señalado de qué manera, a partir de un momento, Menéndez Pelayo se siente desencantado y preso de aquellas ideas y proyectos político-religiosos que había contribuido a levantar (o en los que se apoyó para conseguir sus objetivos), y cómo se alejó de ellos y se moderó en un regreso a cierto liberalismo católico juvenil. Envuelto en esas tensiones, aunque las rechazara y ridiculizara, no dejaría de comprender las huidas de personajes como José Marchena, a la búsqueda de otras posibilidades vitales que le permitieran desarrollarse, o las de Blanco Crespo/Blanco White y Olavarrieta/Clararrosa, por ejemplo.[27]

Pero lo que parece claro es la admiración hacia individuos que no dudan en desafiar lo establecido, aunque su discurso desautorice esos desafíos a la ortodoxia y los entienda como parte de la historia de la decadencia española, moral, pero sobre todo política; como formas de enfermedad de la cultura nacional. El trabajo sobre Marchena ejemplifica el conflicto entre el bien y el mal, entre los buenos y los malos españoles, el debate entre mantener y ajustarse a un conjunto de valores eternos y esenciales o, por el contrario, permitir que los individuos los cambien y creen sus nuevas guías. En esta batalla vence la tradición y Menéndez le gana para la causa católica, civil y moral, pues, aunque no puede asegurar (como sí había hecho Cueto) su conversión, él la encuentra 'verosímil', ya que le dieron sepultura eclesiástica. 'Por otra parte, la impenitencia final es rarísima entre los españoles, y en tiempo de Marchena lo era mucho más', para concluir con un retrato que pretende ser templado y equilibrado, muestra seguramente intencionada de que la historiografía conservadora podía tratar a los 'otros' españoles con rigor y generosidad, con tolerancia, pues la estrategia, al final, es hacer que casi sea o acabe siendo 'uno de los nuestros', a pesar de sus excesos:

27 Especulando quizá demasiado se puede entender que, ante la imposibilidad de cambiar o desaparecer, o ante la falta de valor para ello, el trabajo se convierta en el territorio de la libertad, aquel espacio donde se es como realmente se es. Y del mismo modo el que pasara cada vez más tiempo en Santander.

> Marchena fue toda su vida un estudiantón perdulario y medio loco, con mucha ciencia y mucha gracia, pero sin seriedad ni reposo en nada. Y con todo había en su alma cualidades nobles y generosas. Su valor rayaba en la temeridad, y le tuvo de todos los géneros, no sólo audaz y pendenciero, sino, lo que vale más, estoico y sereno. En sus amistades fue constante y fervoroso hasta el sacrificio [...]. En materias de dinero era incorruptible y cumplía al pie de la letra con la austeridad republicana.[28]

Por la distancia ideológica existente entre uno y otro, resulta atractivo señalar que Menéndez Pelayo y Karl Marx tenían, como hijos de su época, una noción similar del arte de hacer historia. Han sido varios los críticos que se han acercado al *Manifiesto comunista*, pero sobre todo a *El Capital*, y no sólo han encontrado numerosísimas referencias literarias en ambas, en especial en la última, cuya edición se inicia en 1867, sino que han descubierto que puede asociarse a diferentes registros literarios. En parte es lo que le sucede a la *Historia de los heterodoxos españoles*, que se puede leer como una novela gótica, cuyos protagonistas están esclavizados y cegados por sus errores de pensamiento; como un melodrama, pues las vidas se presentan como oportunidades perdidas, e incluso, apurando, como una comedia negra o una tragedia griega, en clave ejemplarizante. Por otra parte, tanto Marx como Menéndez Pelayo emplearon la ironía constantemente para desmontar argumentos y desautorizar supuestos; en el caso del primero para deshacer la lógica del capitalismo, en el del segundo para hacer obvias las deficiencias de personajes como Marchena.[29] De modo que se podría pensar en *El Capital* como una sátira de los escritos sobre economía, y en los *Heterodoxos* como la burla de los trabajos sobre historia eclesiástica (si esto último no fuera desconocer la realidad en la que se escribió y la personalidad de su autor).

Karl Marx era consciente de que su libro, al menos la parte que él pudo ver impresa, no era un alarde de estilo, pero siempre mostró su interés por la forma literaria y por escribir una obra de arte, como comenta en varias cartas a Engels, y como sí consiguió hacer el gran escritor que era Menéndez Pelayo. Tanto uno como otro son herederos y cultores de la fórmula aristotélica, que consideraba forma máxima de verdad la que aunaba historia y poesía, es decir, la que contaba las cosas como fueron pero también como deberían haber sido o ser. Y si leemos la obra de Marx y la de Menéndez, en este caso, su Marchena, veremos que nos cuentan cómo fueron las cosas (las vidas) y, por rechazo o ironía, cómo deberían ser, o haber sido.

---

28 Menéndez Pelayo, 'Estudio crítico', *Obras literarias de D. José Marchena*, II, clvii-clviii.

29 Fue Edmund Wilson, en *Hacia la estación de Finlandia. Ensayo sobre la forma de escribir y hacer historia* (Madrid: Alianza, 1972), publicado originalmente en 1940, quien reparó en la dimensión irónica del texto de Marx. Véase también Francis Whenn, *Marx's 'Das Capital'* (London: Atlantic Books, 2006).

An Eighteenth-Century Visual Representation of the Black Population in Trujillo del Perú: Picturing Cultural and Social Difference

MARISELLE MELÉNDEZ

University of Illinois at Urbana-Champaign

In 1785, the Bishop of Trujillo, Baltasar Martínez Compañón decided to record a complete history of the province of Trujillo del Perú based on his observations about the inhabitants, cultural practices, customs, architecture, indigenous antiquities and natural history of the provinces. The result was a nine-volume manuscript composed only of watercolour illustrations, entitled *Truxillo del Perú*. An index that listed the titles and specific number of each illustration accompanied each volume. The illustrations were based on the observations he had made while serving as a bishop in Trujillo since 1779. Martínez Compañón decided to send the manuscript, which he referred to as an 'obra gráfica', to the king and not necessarily to the Council of Indies or to church authorities. What is most fascinating about this *historia* is the fact that it did not include any narrative about what was depicted. *Truxillo del Perú* was strictly a visual text considered by Martínez Compañón himself to be a type of 'Museo Histórico, Ficico, Político y Moral del Obpdo. De Truxillo del Perú'.[1]

This article examines Martínez Compañón's manuscript exactly as the author envisioned it: as a type of 'museum', in order to explore the particular cultural history that he recreates of the African population in this province. First, I focus on the metaphorical and literal dimensions of the word 'museum' at the time, to better understand the implications of its use and, therefore, how the work is to be studied and understood. I then discuss the importance of the visual image as a powerful rhetorical tool. For my case study, I will focus on his

1 See his letter of 1785 in Baltasar Martínez Compañón, *Trujillo del Perú*, ed. Manuel Ballesteros Gaibrois, facsimile reproduction in 9 vols (Madrid: Ediciones de Cultura Hispánica, 1998 etc.); see *Apéndice III* (1994), 32. All references are to this edition.

visual representations of the black population in the territories comprising the archbishopric of Trujillo del Perú. I discuss the crucial role that these visual images had in the construction of the particular cultural identities concerned, and especially in how they were visually represented in portrayals of the human body within the political, religious and cultural context of that colonial time. For Martínez Compañón, class, social economy and cultural habits became signifying factors to categorize social groups and to illustrate the concomitant contradictions whenever other social groups were also represented. I contend that visual images of the human body aimed to record and encode a particular notion of cultural history within this particular province of Peru, and that the human body itself functions as an object of display, desire, utility, commodity and consumption.

1 History as 'Museum'

In the eighteenth century the word 'museum' referred to 'El lugar destinado para el estudio de las Ciencias, letras humanas y artes liberales'.[2] It also referred to 'El lugar en que se guardan varias curiosidades, pertenecientes à las ciencias: como algunos artificios matemáticos, pinturas extraordinarias, medallas antiguas'. It came, of course, from the Latin word 'museum' which meant 'of the muses', the Greek divinities who protected a specific art or activity and provided inspiration. More importantly, these divinities also controlled their own 'sphere over learning and the arts'.[3] Given the different connotations of the word 'museum' at the time, one can justifiably underline its intrinsic association with the act of observing, studying and learning. The museum constituted a repository of knowledge and of valuable information and objects that were to be kept, displayed and studied. To a certain extent we can associate this notion of 'museum' with the one which is offered by Pierre Bourdieu when he describes the modern museum as 'an institution for recording, preserving and analyzing works' that ultimately aim to 'conserve the capital of symbolic goods'.[4] In the eighteenth century, the role of the visual in the process of learning and disseminating knowledge was crucial to discerning the value of what was displayed and observed. Within this context, one can view the act of reordering things in a museum, as Tony Bennett suggests, 'as an event that was simultaneously epistemic and governmental'.[5] The isolation and ordering of cumulative

2 *Diccionario de Autoridades* [1726–37], edición facsímil, 3 vols (Madrid: Editorial Gredos, 1990), II, 636.

3 James Hall, *Dictionary of Subjects & Symbols in Art* (New York: Harper Collins Publishers, 1979), 217.

4 Pierre Bourdieu, *The Field of Cultural Production. Essays on Art and Literature* (New York: Columbia U. P., 1993), 110, 121.

5 Tony Bennett, *The Birth of the Museum. History, Theory, Politics* (New York/London: Routledge, 2005), 33.

material emerged from the desire to observe, to study, and determine what was exhibited and/or collected. In contrast to the notion of 'archive', which Antony Higgins explains is 'the materialization of a sphere of knowledge production', that served the educated *criollo* population as a means to position themselves 'as a discrete identity' within colonial society,[6] the notion of the 'museum' works for Martínez Compañón as a way scientifically to categorize the population of Trujillo as objects of knowledge for the sake of greater colonial investment.

When Baltasar Martínez Compañón referred to his work *Truxillo del Perú* as a kind of 'Historical, Physical, Political and Moral Museum', he stressed the importance of his visual representation of Trujillo del Perú in disseminating knowledge about these territories. He perceived his work as a spatial depository for information which, when displayed, would generate a desire to learn about the province. The eye was to be the vehicle to capture the natural, human and moral history of Trujillo del Perú. The visual images of these Peruvian provinces were to be read as texts and interpreted as historical artifacts. The act of seeing was to improve upon the omitted word in functioning as the intermediary of knowledge. As with any particular object viewed in a museum, the act of seeing, as Pierre Bourdieu reminds us, takes place within a space marked by 'silence and methodical inspection according to a fixed arrangement and constraint'.[7] What Martínez Compañón did not envision, however, was the degree to which the gaze of the observer would be conditioned by cultural beliefs that affected the manner in which objects were seen. This was the case with Martínez Compañón himself, whose visual re-creation of the history of Trujillo was certainly influenced by his own cultural values. He envisioned a particular way of seeing, observing and interpreting history. One cannot deny, as Rolena Adorno says, the importance of visual representation as an instrument of ideological expression and rhetorical persuasion.[8] However, what one must question is the value and role that the bishop's visual representation of Trujillo del Perú had in his re-creation of the natural, physical, moral and political history of the province. There was after all a specific image he wished to portray and disseminate in his graphic rendition of Trujillo.

6 Antony Higgins, *Constructing the Criollo Archive. Subjects of Knowledge in the 'Bibliotheca Mexicana' and the 'Rusticatio Mexicana'* (West Lafayette: Purdue U. P., 2000), 13.

7 Bourdieu, *The Field of Cultural Production*, 298.

8 Rolena Adorno, 'Retórica y resistencia pictóricas. El grabado y la polémica en los escritos sobre el Perú en los siglos XVI y XVII', in *Las imágenes de resistencia indígena y esclava*, ed. Roger Zapata (Peru: Editorial Wari, 1990), 13–32 (p. 47).

2 Baltasar Martínez Compañón: A Man of the Enlightenment

Baltasar Martínez Compañón was born in Cabedro, Spain between 1735–1738.[9] He studied canon law at the University of Huesca and became an ordained priest in 1761. He worked as a doctoral canon for different cathedrals in Santo Domingo and Santander, Spain until 1766. It was in 1767 that Charles III offered him the position of cantor of the Metropolitan Cathedral of Lima. From 1767 to 1777 Martínez Compañón occupied different ecclesiastical positions including, in 1773, general secretary and moderator of the First Provincial Council of Lima. In 1778, Charles III named him Bishop of Trujillo del Perú as a result of the respect he had gained from his peers in Lima. At the time, Trujillo was considered one of the largest dioceses in Peru, extending 1,300 kilometres long and 500 kilometres wide, from the coast to the highlands. As a bishop, he built a successful career by locating priests in parishes that had previously lacked guidance, and by repairing the fragile state of the cathedral which had been damaged by different earthquakes. He had a pivotal role in improving the working conditions and curriculum of the Seminaries of San Carlos and San Marcelo, where he increased the salary of the professors and offered scholarships to those who were unable to afford tuition. He also founded twenty towns and fifty-four schools, erected thirty-nine churches and rebuilt many others. He fomented agriculture in the new towns and created vocational and art schools for indigenous children. In addition, he made a great effort to visit all parishes, convents and churches that were under the jurisdiction of Trujillo del Perú, despite the large distances involved and the difficult terrain. These pastoral visits were crucial in providing source-material for the creation of his graphic representation of Trujillo del Perú.

The visits made by Martínez Compañón began in 1782 and lasted until 1785. As Matilde López Serrano has observed, the bishop took with him on his journeys topographers to draw detailed plans and maps of the territories, along with other artists and painters who were to capture the appearance of the people and their cultural habits.[10] A royal decree issued by Charles III in 1775 relating to the Americas also motivated his visits. The decree asked for a collection to be made of curious objects illustrative of natural and human history which were to be sent to Spain for the newly founded Gabinete de Ciencias Naturales in Madrid.[11] As Juan Marchena reminds us, in order for the reforms proposed by the Bourbon regime to be successful, it was crucial to

9 Most of this synopsis of the biography of Martínez Compañón derives from the works of Matilde López Serrano, *Trujillo del Perú en el siglo XVIII* (Madrid: Editorial Patrimonio Nacional, 1976) and Manuel Ballesteros Gabrois, 'Un manuscrito colonial del siglo XVIII, su interés etnográfico', *Journal de la Société des Américanistes*, 27 (1935), 145–73.

10 López Serrano, *Trujillo del Perú en el siglo XVIII*, 52.

11 The task of collecting these materials was given by the king to the Regimen de Intendencias in the urban centres of the viceroyalties. The *intendentes* were supposed to visit specific territories to gather information and send it back, in the case of Peru, from Lima to

collect true, exact and exhaustive information about a vast number of matters pertaining to the colonial order.[12] In fact, between 1788 and 1790, Martínez Compañón sent approximately six hundred items of indigenous pottery he had collected during visits he had made, along with one hundred and ninety-five clay artifacts and a box containing parts of objects made of gold and silver.[13] The bishop's passion for natural sciences and history can certainly be noted in his nine-volume, monumental work, *Truxillo del Perú*. This work can be considered an outcome of the dynamic productivity that characterized the intellectual and scientific environment of the eighteenth century, one deeply influenced by the ideology of the Enlightenment and its utilitarian search for knowledge. Within this tradition, 'observation and speculation' became two vital means of acquiring knowledge.[14]

Martínez Compañón's illustrated manuscript in nine volumes was composed of watercolours done on linen paper, with various types of watermarks and colour. The use of watercolours made his task more viable as it was considered at the time as a portable and convenient method of painting when travelling in difficult territories.[15] It was also considered very practical as the artists themselves were able to produce the colours they needed on the spot. It was indeed the method preferred by topographers and botanists to produce their maps and illustrations of natural and human history. In the Andean territories, minerals such as azurite, malachite, vermilion and red ochre, used to produce the colours they required, were in abundance. As Gabriela Sirucasano observes, these pigments were already

---

Madrid. Among the materials requested were maps, censuses, and detailed and statistical information pertaining to the population, geography, climate and economic production of the territories. According to Juan Marchena, Peru had a total of twenty-four *intendentes* in forty years. Their task was so overwhelming that in many cases these officials were unable to gather all the information requested by the king. In other instances, the *intendentes* sent thousands of documents that were not always consulted by the Crown. The *intendentes* had to enlist the help of priests to carry out the necessary visits. Priests and other clergy served as primary providers of information due to their familiarity with the region and the trust they had earned from the people who inhabited it. It was an extremely expensive enterprise due to the number of people required to conduct the census, to take notes, to prepare maps, and to draw visual representations of what was observed. Sometimes it took years for this information to arrive in Spain (see Juan Marchena, 'Su Magestad quiere saber. Información oficial y reformismo borbónico en la América de la Ilustración', in *Recepción y difusión de textos ilustrados*, ed. Diana Soto Arango *et al.* [Madrid: Colección Actas Tavara, 2003], 151–85 [pp. 160–65]).

12 Marchena, 'Su Magestad quiere saber. Información oficial y reformismo borbónico en la América de la Ilustración', 152.

13 Those items are to be found today in the Museo Arqueológico de Madrid and the Museo de América.

14 Diana Soto Arango and Jorge Tomás Uribe, 'Textos ilustrados en la enseñanza y tertulias literarias en Santa Fe de Bogotá en el siglo XVIII', in *Recepción y difusión de textos ilustrados*, 59–75 (p. 67).

15 Christopher Finch, *19th Century Watercolors* (New York: Abbeville Press, 1991), 8–10.

used as an influential part of many of the rituals and religious ceremonies practised by the native Andeans before the arrival of the Europeans.[16] In his manuscript illustrations Baltasar Martínez Compañón used blue pigments such as were produced when fabrics were dyed in that colour, as well as using extracts from plants such as 'brasil' and 'sangre de drago' for his illustrations of these plants to recreate their red hues.

A table of contents is found at the end at the end of each volume, and statistical information, city maps and plans, and musical compositions accompany some of them. The volumes are made up of the following subjects:

- **Volume I**: maps of Trujillo del Perú and its provinces, statistical charts, portraits of Charles III and Charles IV, and of all the bishops that preceded Martínez Compañón, as well as drawings of the uniforms and attire worn by military, religious and civil authorities, of the Spanish coat of arms, and of Gualcayoc Hill.
- **Volume II**: another illustration of the Spanish coat of arms, portraits of the king and queen, various illustrations of the habits of dress and the racial/ethnic characteristics of Trujillo's population, drawings of job-related tasks, as well as of cultural practices, including dances, festivals, music, games, and other celebrations. This volume also includes drawings illustrating various diseases suffered by the indigenous people.
- **Volume III**: the flora of Trujillo
- **Volume IV**: the flora of Trujillo
- **Volume V**: 138 illustrations of medicinal plants
- **Volume VI**: 104 illustrations of quadrupeds, reptiles, and insects
- **Volume VII**: 159 illustrations of birds
- **Volume VIII**: 178 illustrations of marine fauna
- **Volume IX**: pre-Hispanic antiquities of the Chimu, Moche and Inca culture

According to Martínez Compañón himself, in a letter sent in 1785 to the Viceroy of Peru after his return from Trujillo, the purpose of the illustrations concerned with geography, metallurgy, mineralogy and botany was 'no por servir de una vana curiosidad, sino en cuanto puedan ser material de

16 Gabriela Siracusano, *El poder de los colores. De lo material simbólico en las prácticas culturales andinas. Siglos XVI–XVIII* (Buenos Aires: Fondo de Cultura Económica, 2005), 29–33.

industria y comercio'.[17] Natural resources played a major part in his illustrative descriptions of Trujillo because these were viewed as economic incentives to bring people over from Spain. Indeed, in the 1780s the mining sector in the Viceroyalty of Mexico as well as that in Peru enjoyed so great an economic development that local mine-owners and business-owners joined together to create powerful and influential corporations with their own tribunals etc.[18] The fact that many of these business-owners were Creoles represented an ongoing threat that the Crown had to contain. After all, it was the Spanish Crown which was supposed to have total control of every financial aspect of its own territories. Although six volumes are devoted to natural history, the two volumes which deal with human nature and cultural practices form an important part of the bishop's depiction of Trujillo. The manner in which Martínez Compañón's eye has ordered and illustrated its population provides us with his particular interpretation and representation of the racial groups that occupied those territories.

In a letter sent to D. Antonio Polier in 1790 announcing the existence of *Truxillo del Perú*, Martínez Compañón insists on the authenticity of the illustrations he includes, underlining the fact that he was present and saw them composed with his own eyes (*Apéndice III*, 52).[19] To prove his point, he sent to Spain a box that included indigenous artifacts and pottery which he meant to be compared with the ninth volume of his manuscript. According to him, the comparison was to prove 'la conformidad y perfecta semejanza entre unas y otras, y por ellas pueda congeturarse o creerse y comprenderse ser igual la correspondencia de las estampas de los ocho restantes tomos y sus originales' (*Apéndice III*, 54). Martínez Compañón considered his work a significant contribution to the study and knowledge of the Peruvian territories concerned which, viewed from his own perspective, possessed such a variety of fauna, flora, minerals and people, that they deserved to be the beneficiaries of investments from royal resources in the future.

In this 1790 letter, the bishop urged the colonial authorities in Lima to send his work immediately to the king, who he believed would certainly understand its value. His manuscript, according to Compañón himself, had already been examined and had received all the necessary permits from the *intendente* of Trujillo, the ministers of the Royal Treasury, the ecclesiastic authorities, and the Viceroy of Peru, D. Francisco Gil y Lemos. He added that each volume had been approved with 'unique praises'. He was aware of the

17 This letter and the one sent to D. Antonio Polier in 1790 were reproduced in *Apéndice III* (1994) of the facsimile reproduction of *Trujillo del Perú* edited by Ballesteros Gaibrois, 52 etc. (see note 1 for the full reference to this edition). All references made to *Apéndice III* relate to this edition.

18 Juan José Saldaña, 'Ilustración, ciencia y técnica en América', in *La Ilustración en la América colonial*, ed. Diana Soto Arango *et al.* (Madrid: CSIC, 1995), 19–53 (p. 21).

19 This letter was, in fact, sent from Cartagena de Indias where he held the post of Archbishop of Santa Fe.

singularity of his work acknowledging that in terms of 'su extension, distribucion de partes y methodo, sea poco vulgar y común'. He argued that, despite its lack of refinement, 'podría a lo menos servir de estímulo para que otras personas de las muchas que hay de mayor instrucción y robustes, y menos cuidadas al oficio que yo en las Americas se dedicasen a escribir una historia general cumplida y perfecta de estas bastas regiones' (*Apéndice III*, 54–55). Notwithstanding his eagerness to send the manuscript to the king, the nine volumes were not actually sent to Spain until 1803, six years after his death in Santa Fe de Bogotá in 1797, where he had taken up the position of archbishop in 1791.[20] The nine volumes were sent to Spain, already bound in a typical eighteenth-century Peruvian sheepskin binding protected by a fine layer of wax.[21]

The most fascinating aspect of Martínez Compañón's manuscript is the fact that he evidently never envisaged it as accompanied by any written text. In the letters he sent to the Spanish authorities in Spain, or the ones he sent to the Viceroy of Peru, he made no mention of any intention to include any written explanations in the volumes. In a dedication written to the King of Spain in 1786, which he wrote to accompany a detailed map he had drawn of Trujillo del Perú and which he published in the *Mercurio Peruano* in 1794, Martínez Compañón does mention that while travelling through the territories concerned to compose his illustrative manuscript, he also took notes that could have served him as a basis for writing a general history of Trujillo: '[. . .] tengo hechos algunos apuntes para formar una historia general de este Obispado, ò unas memorias à lo menos que puedan servir para ella'.[22] Although this mention of his notes and memoirs exists, his letter of 1790 never suggests that the illustrations gathered were meant to form part of any general history of the region. In fact, as noted above, the author declares that he has neither the good health nor the time to write such a history. The fact that there are no words to guide them through 'reading' and interpreting the visual history he provides, no doubt presented then (and still presents) challenges to non-specialist readers. Indeed, Raúl Porras Barrenechea, writing in 1978, considered the format the bishop chose to be a deficiency in the work: 'Es ya un defecto el hecho de que no se acompañe a las láminas una descripción o explicación del dibujo respectivo'.[23]

20 Martínez Compañón was named Archbishop of Santa Fe in 1788; however, he did not arrive there until 1791. He was buried in the cathedral of that city in 1797.

21 López Serrano, *Trujillo del Perú en el siglo XVIII*, 36.

22 'Copia de la dedicatoria con que ofrecio a S.M. un cunplido Mapa de la Intendencia y Obispado de Truxillo su Dignisimo Prelado el Illmo. Señor Don Baltasar Jayme Martínez Compañón [1786]', in *Mercurio Peruano*, 11:347 (1794) (Lima: Biblioteca Nacional del Perú, 1966), 4.

23 Raúl Porras Barrenechea, 'Informe de Raúl Porras Barrenechea respecto de la obra del Obispo Martínez Compañón sobre Trujillo del Perú en el siglo XVIII', in *La obra del Obispo Martínez Compañón sobre Trujillo del Perú en el siglo XVIII* (Madrid: Ediciones Cultura Hispánica, 1978), 25–33 (p. 32).

Other critics have considered these particular drawings of the inhabitants to be lacking in expression and differentiation, to the extent that the only aspects which are altered are the faces and the representative clothing of the people portrayed.[24] Judging by the 'quality' of the drawings, López Serrano argues that the work was the product of different artists, and she points to the fact that some illustrations, such as the ones depicting architecture, flora and birds were technically more sophisticated than others in the volumes.[25] Technicalities aside, what I believe to be most fascinating are the reasons behind the illustrative history in nine volumes which Martínez Compañón put together of these regions, and what the illustrations he provides tell us about the people concerned, their cultural and work habits as well as their customary celebrations. Can we consider this type of inventory as another example of the Enlightenment's characteristic efforts to categorize and rank people and territories? To what extent do visual images of this kind offer the 'reader' a more complete view of Trujillo del Perú? What kind of significances do these images convey? How does the author visualize social differences? Does this manuscript oblige the reader, to some extent, to see the population and natural history of a province in a certain manner? What challenges did/does this graphic rendition of Trujillo present not only for the visual reader of the time, but for contemporary readers as well, by the fact of having to be 'read' without any actual words provided? In considering this manuscript in terms of the Enlightenment and its culture in Peru, we must take account of these questions, to better understand the role that 'visuality' had in determining how the culture, society and bodies of colonial inhabitants were represented and construed.[26] This visual text which I propose to examine offers us central insight into how a specific colonial locality was viewed at a time of profound social, political, economic and cultural changes. Furthermore, the bishop's watercolour illustrations become, as in the case of *casta* paintings, portrayals of 'the social economy of bodies and spaces that constituted late-colonial culture'.[27]

3 Illustrations and the Production of Cultural Meaning

Visual representations have historically been used by many societies as forms of expression and reconstructions of reality. They have been exploited

24 On this issue see López Serrano, *Trujillo del Perú en el siglo XVIII*, and Ballesteros Gaibrois, *Trujillo del Perú, Apéndice III*.

25 López Serrano, *Trujillo del Perú en el siglo XVIII*, 12.

26 Gillian Rose, drawing on an H. Foster definition, summarizes 'visuality' as the 'way in which vision is constructed in various ways', specifically what we see or we are allowed or able to see in a specific object (Gillian Rose, *Visual Methodologies* [London: SAGE Publications, 2001], 6).

27 Magali M. Carrera. *Imagining Identity in New Spain. Race, Lineage and the Colonial Body in Portraiture and Casta Paintings* (Austin: Univ. of Texas Press, 2003), xvi.

to capture and explain the world and the perceptions which human beings have of their own surroundings. They have helped to preserve memories of the past and, therefore, the cultural history of humankind. The interest shown in the visual in current approaches to history, culture, literature and popular media is nothing new, for images have always been used as discursive and persuasive tools, in order to generate specific versions of reality. When studying such visual representations, one must pay close attention to the objects and subjects being produced or reproduced, and must question by whom and for whom these images were produced. As Gillian Rose argues, 'all visual representations are made in one way or another, and the circumstances of their productions may contribute towards the effect they have'.[28] Visuality is extremely important in Martínez Compañón's volumes, since the illustrations he includes were envisaged as part of a 'museum', and were specifically addressed to the Spanish king. For the bishop, the bodies of the inhabitants were symbols of the cultural reality of Trujillo del Perú and were to be portrayed and, therefore, documented as examples of social and cultural history. Through the visual reconstructions of their bodies provided, the observer would be able to form an impression of the history of Trujillo and its provinces. The museum, in the words of Tony Bennett, is 'a technology of memory' through which the body is conceived as 'a storage and retrieval device' and through which the past is to be remembered,[29] and Martínez's visual collection, if anything, makes an even more lasting impression. By recording the present for the benefit of the authorities in the Spain of his time, the bishop was simultaneously preserving history. In this sense, the material he offers serves figuratively as a 'museum', in which the captured bodies recount for us a specific social and cultural history. By representing past realities, these bodies have come to embody knowledge. However, as tended to happen in the eighteenth century, through the ways they were visually represented, these bodies were 'assessed, classified, and inscribed within a hierarchy of social meanings and values'.[30]

Truxillo del Perú can also be regarded as a visual encyclopedia, bearing in mind that an encyclopedia can and has been defined as a 'general system of instruction or knowledge' and 'a work in which the various branches of knowledge ... are discussed separately'.[31] For the bishop, it was important to organize and manage knowledge. Martínez Compañón's work also reflects what was common practice in the seventeenth and eighteenth centuries in

28 Rose, *Visual Methodologies*, 17.

29 Tony Bennett, 'Stored Virtue: Memory, the Body and the Evolutionary Museum', in *Regimes of Memory*, ed. Susannah Radstone and Katharine Hodgkin (London/New York: 2003), 40–54 (pp. 42–46).

30 Carrera. *Imagining Identity in New Spain*, 4.

31 *Webster's Universal Dictionary of the English Language*, comp. by Joseph Devlin (Cleveland: The World Publishing Company, 1940), 557.

that it seeks to 'use visual reproduction as a critical aid to the study and ordering of nature'.[32] The process of ordering nature implies an attempt to clarify ambiguities as well as to offer a comprehensible, even transparent representation of the object or subject in question. Nevertheless, one must bear in mind the cultural context that led to such a process of reconstruction, because, as Beth Fowkes Tobin argues, images do not merely reflect, they also mediate.[33]

Martínez, Compañón's work can be considered as an example of eighteenth-century historiography, which, according to Jorge Cañizares-Esguerra, aimed to write a new history of America on the basis of 'new critical techniques for creating and validating knowledge'.[34] The Royal Academy of History, founded by the Spanish Bourbons in the eighteenth century, functioned as a cultural institution that requested and promoted books of this type. New natural and civil histories of the New World were in demand, especially so if they defended the record of Spanish colonization of the Americas. The Council of Indies established a series of guidelines that members of the Academy were required to follow when writing such histories. Cañizares-Esguerra notes that the Council 'also asked the Academy to assemble a compendium of facts that would allow anyone to put together different narratives by an almost mechanical permutation of information'.[35]

Although Martínez Compañón did not write his nine volumes intending to send them to the Royal Academy of History, his work was in accord with what the Council of Indies believed works like his should achieve. His nine-volume compilation offered visual information that could be considered useful to assist the writing of future histories. At the time it was written, his work also aimed to persuade the Spanish authorities that there was still a need to further 'discover' and colonize the territories portrayed. Each illustration was meant to be seen as a means to draw attention to the relevance of these territories and their people, and to evoke thoughts about the possibility of further colonial expansion. The message, or so the bishop thought, needed to be conveyed clearly through illustrations, so as to be free of equivocal meanings. At the time visual representations were thought to be the very sort of unequivocal material that would lead to the creation of reliable histories. Scholars in the eighteenth century looked keenly for ways to eliminate the potential for ambiguity that a written text could produce. As

---

32 David Freedberg, *The Eye of the Lynx. Galileo, His Friends, and the Beginning of Modern Natural History* (Chicago: Univ. of Chicago Press, 2004), 55.

33 Beth Fowkes Tobin, *Picturing Imperial Power: Colonial Subjects in Eighteenth-Century British Painting* (Durham, NC: Duke U. P., 1999), 13.

34 Jorge Cañizares-Esguerra, *How to Write the History of the New World: Historiographies, Epistemologies, and Identities in the Eighteenth-Century Atlantic World* (Stanford: Stanford U. P., 2001), 1.

35 Cañizares-Esguerra, *How to Write the History of the New World*, 165.

a result, illustrations were utilized in the interests of 'capturing an unambiguous, undistorted reality'.[36]

However, visual representation is a risky route to follow in pursuit of transparency. For, as mentioned earlier, visual images always have the potential for being interpreted in different ways, depending on who is creating the image, why it is being created, who is viewing it, where it is to be found and to whom it is being directed. One must take into account, in particular, that the person who chooses or creates the image always influences the manner in which an object is represented, simply because of his/her specific views and intentions. As W. J. T. Mitchell argues, images 'are not stable, static, or permanent' because they 'involve multisensory apprehension and interpretation'.[37] In the case of *Truxillo del Perú*, what we have are specific visual interpretations of peoples, cultures, animals, plants, and other things. My aim is to determine what kind of view or interpretation Martínez Compañón was attempting to convey of Trujillo del Perú, in particular when it came to his portrayal of cultural differences and social relationships. I shall focus particularly on his representation of the black population in the archbishopric of Trujillo. His representation of this black population is important because before the bishop set about compiling his work in the 1780s, the most authoritative work on Trujillo del Perú was Miguel Feijoo's *Relación descriptiva de la ciudad y provincia de Truxillo del Perú*. Published in 1763 by the Supremo Consejo de Indias, this book failed to deal with the black sector of the population despite acknowledging that this was indeed one of the groups that inhabited the province.[38] What exactly Martínez Compañón's intentions were in devoting a special part of his work to the black population of Trujillo is a subject worthy of study in itself.

4 A Visual Representation of Trujillo del Perú

Martínez Compañón's second volume offers one of the most fascinating portrayals of a cross-section of the people of Peru, using class, race and cultural habits as signifying factors to categorize the different social groups. It offers a hierarchically structured pictorial representation of the groups, starting with the Spaniards, followed by the Indians, *quarterones*, *mestizos*, blacks, mulattos, *sambos* and *cholos*. The impression of a rigid social order is clearly conveyed from the outset. For at the beginning of the volume Martínez Compañón inserts a chart listing the number of inhabitants in the provinces that make up Trujillo and dividing them into their different *castas* (**Figure 1**). The title states: 'Estado que demuestra el numero de Abitantes del Obpdo. de Truxillo del Perù con distincion de castas formado [por] su actual Obpo'. This

36 Cañizares-Esguerra, *How to Write the History of the New World*, 17.

37 W. J. T. Mitchell, *Picture Theory* (Chicago/London: Univ. of Chicago Press, 1999), 14.

38 Miguel Feijoo de Sosa, *Relación descriptiva de la ciudad y provincia de Truxillo del Perú* (Madrid: Imprenta del Real y Supremo Consejo de Indias, 1763).

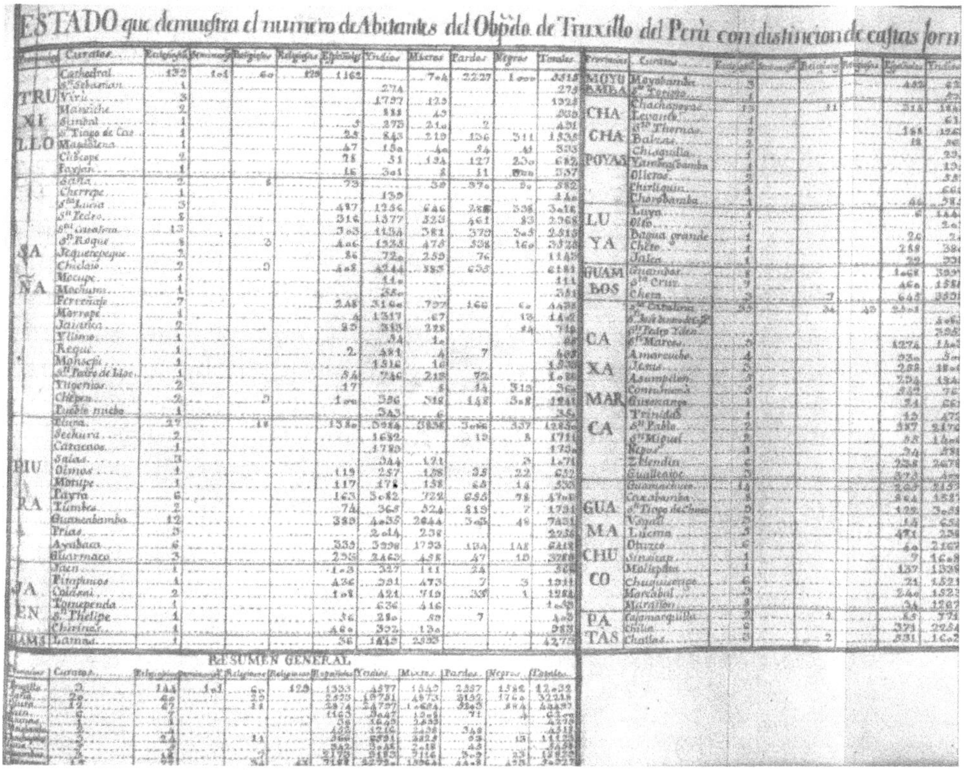

Figure 1
'Estado que demuestra el numero de Abitantes del Obpdo. de Truxillo'.
Courtesy of the Biblioteca del Palacio Real, Madrid.
Copyright © Patrimonio Nacional

statistical chart is extremely important because, aside from some maps and musical compositions which also include written information, it provides the only written data incorporated into the manuscript.

This table therefore served him as a point of reference from which to contextualize the population that he was to depict in his 'historical, physical, political and moral museum'. It lists the different groups in the following order: Spaniards, Indians, Mixed, *Pardos* and Blacks. According to the bishop, Trujillo had 241,740 inhabitants; of which 980 were Spaniards, 118,324 were Indians, 79,043 were of mixed race (*mestizos*), 16,630 were *pardos* and 4,846 blacks. The majority of the inhabitants were therefore Indians and *mestizos*, followed by the *pardos*, blacks and Spaniards. This information coincides with that given by Miguel Feijoo, who, writing in 1763, also mentioned that the majority of inhabitants in the Trujillo province were Indians.[39]

39 Feijoo, *Relación descriptiva de la ciudad y provincia de Truxillo del Perú*, 28–31.

For the visual illustrations, the order remained the same, although some groups were further subdivided depending upon the region to which they belonged (this is so in the case of the Indians in particular) (**Figure 2**). The number of visual illustrations the bishop devoted to each group also depended on the size of each group within the population; that is, he included more illustrations of the more numerous groups, namely the Indians and the *mestizos*. Some of these groups are depicted dressed for different occasions or according to their social status. As is the case with *casta* paintings, these images offer a 'visual index' of human genealogy.[40] Images in which inhabitants are portrayed performing different agricultural and other manual tasks, from weaving to dyeing wool, come after the first group of watercolour paintings. Another group then follows in which are represented various cultural practices, such as dancing, games and other cultural celebrations particular to Indians, *mestizos* and blacks. The bishop concludes

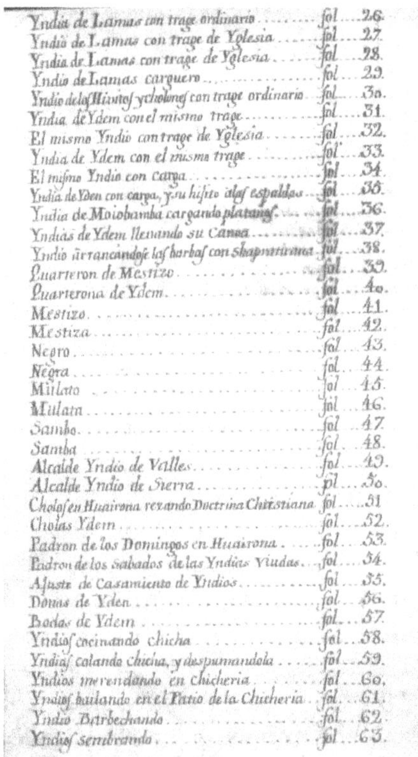

Yndia de Lamas con trage ordinario .... fol ...26.
Yndio de Lamas con trage de Yglesia ...... fol ...27.
Yndia de Lamas con trage de Yglesia ...... fol ...28.
Yndio de Lamas carguero .... fol ...29.
Yndio delos Hivitos ycholones con trage ordinario .. fol ...30.
Yndia de Ydem con el mismo trage .... fol ...31.
El mismo Yndio con trage de Yglesia ...... fol ...32.
Yndia de Ydem con el mismo trage .... fol ...33.
El mismo Yndio con carga .... fol ...34.
Yndia de Yden con carga, y su hijito alas espaldas .. fol ...35.
Yndia de Moiobamba cargando platanos ...... fol ...36.
Yndias de Ydem llevando su Canoa .... fol ...37.
Yndio arrancandose las barbas con shapnatirana . fol ...38.
Quarteron de Mestizo .... fol ...39.
Quarterona de Ydem .... fol ...40.
Mestizo .... fol ...41.
Mestiza .... fol ...42.
Negro .... fol ...43.
Negra .... fol ...44.
Mulato .... fol ...45.
Mulata .... fol ...46.
Sambo .... fol ...47.
Samba .... fol ...48.
Alcalde Yndio de Valles .... fol ...49.
Alcalde Yndio de Sierra .... fol ...50.
Cholos en Huairona rezando Doctrina Christiana fol ...51
Cholas Ydem .... fol ...52.
Padron de los Domingos en Huairona ...... fol ...53.
Padron de los Sabados de las Yndias Viudas .. fol ...54.
Ajuste de Casamiento de Yndios .... fol ...55.
Donas de Yden .... fol ...56.
Bodas de Ydem .... fol ...57.
Yndios cocinando chicha .... fol ...58.
Yndias colando chicha, y despumandola ...... fol ...59.
Yndios merendando en chicheria .... fol ...60.
Yndios bailando en el Patio de la Chicheria .. fol ...61.
Yndio Barbechando .... fol ...62.
Yndios sembrando .... fol ...63.

Figure 2
'Estado que demuestra el numero de Abitantes del Obpdo. de Truxillo'.
Courtesy of the Biblioteca del Palacio Real, Madrid.

40 Ilona Katzew, *Casta Painting: Images of Race in Eighteenth-Century Mexico* (New Haven/London: Yale U. P., 2004), 5.

his volume with a set of illustrations that depict the pain and suffering associated with the different illnesses that afflicted Indians.

Aside from a descriptive list indicating what each illustration is about, located at the end of the volume, no captions accompany the individual illustrations. However, in the ordering of his illustrations Martínez Compañón follows the social hierarchy as this was established and maintained by the colonial authorities; so he includes the images showing the Spaniards first, and those depicting the blacks and other groups of African descent are located at the end. We perceive in the tasks and cultural practices depicted that clear social and racial divisions are made, so that Indians, blacks and other *casta* groups are found among members of their own kind, and rarely interact with others that are racially different. This dynamic is observable in illustrations 'E104 Mestizas de Chachapoyas cosiendo rengos' (**Figure 3**) and 'E 141 Ydem [Danza] de Negros' (**Figure 4**). In these illustrations, as in many others, racial groups seem to be frozen within their own social spaces, and are kept neatly separated from other groups.

Figure 3
'Mestizas de Chachapoyas cosiendo rengos'.
Courtesy of the Biblioteca del Palacio Real, Madrid.
Copyright © Patrimonio Nacional

Figure 4
'Ydem [Danza] de Negros'.
Courtesy of the Biblioteca del Palacio Real, Madrid.
Copyright © Patrimonio Nacional

This social order is also obvious in the few watercolour illustrations included in which we can observe a certain amount of interaction among groups of different races. In these cases, the Indians, blacks and other *casta* groups are invariably portrayed in positions of servitude and are shown to be under the supervision of those white persons that are their superiors in the social hierarchy. The clothes of the non-white groups serve as symbols of their lower social status as distinct from those in power, and their physical location in the illustration underlines their subordinate status. The illustration 'E 195 Negro sacando piques' (**Figure 5**) is a case in point, in which we can observe the subordinate status of the African slave reflected in three significantly symbolic ways: (1) there is the physical position which he occupies; (2) there is his particular attire; and (3) there is the profound contrast portrayed between the colour of his skin and that of his master. Despite the fact that both men are on the ground, the author positions the slave so that he is carrying out his task in an inferior physical space. The

Figure 5
'Negro sacando piques'.
Courtesy of the Biblioteca del Palacio Real, Madrid.

difference in their clothing also emphasizes the difference in their social status, as the slave is barefoot and wearing a simple cotton shirt, while his master's attire is much more elaborate and features fashion components typically used by individuals of the upper class. Examples of these items are: a lace shirt, a long jacket, buttoned pants worn to the knees, white embroidered socks, and shoes with buckles. Finally, the contrast between the black servant's skin and the master's white skin is emphasized by the intense use of black colour, to such an extent that it is quite difficult to make out the slave's actual facial features. The tiny whites of his eyes seem to be lost in the accentuated blackness of his skin.

Two other illustrations which Martínez Compañón considered truly representative of Trujillo's black population also convey the impression that that population had a characteristic lack of distinctive facial features and expression (**Figure 6**, 'E43 Negro' and **Figure 7**, 'E44 Negra'). The faces of the black people depicted are noticeably blurred, and are memorable only because of their profound blackness. The observer can barely locate their

Figure 6
'Negro'.
Courtesy of the Biblioteca del Palacio Real, Madrid.
Copyright © Patrimonio Nacional

Figure 7
'Negra'.
Courtesy of the Biblioteca del Palacio Real, Madrid.
Copyright © Patrimonio Nacional

eyes while their lips, noses, eyebrows and ears seem to disappear into their overall facial blackness. In contrast, their attire and the work tools they are holding become symbolic indicators of their racial and social identities. They are recognizable by what they wear and the type of work they perform. As portrayed by Martínez Compañón, the attire typical of the black male denotes primitiveness when compared to the clothing worn by other sections of the population, such as the Spaniards, the *mestizos*, or even the mulattos. Moreover, the black female wears the clothing typically worn by black women slaves at the time: a simple white cotton shirt and a pleated cotton skirt covering a white underskirt. In this connection, it is important to remember that, as had been stipulated in the 'Real Cédula de su Majestad sobre la Educación, trato y ocupaciones de los esclavos en todos sus dominios de Indias e Islas Filipinas', drawn up in 1789, the material and style of such clothes were imposed by the slave owners who, as part of their obligation, needed to provide their black slaves with clothing.[41] On the other hand, the work tools of the slaves typically consist of a type of spade, a machete, and a stick, all of which underscore their social occupation and role in this society. As the aforementioned 'Real Cédula' also makes clear, 'la primera y principal ocupación de los Esclavos debe ser la Agricultura y demás labores de campo'.[42]

Although the bishop visually includes blacks as well as Indians, *mestizos* and other *casta* groups as part of Trujillo's population, they are clearly perceived as occupying specific, subordinate positions within the social strata. The illustrations function as graphic discourse, reproducing the ideology of their time. In other words, they function collectively as a 'symbolic system of meaning-making' that emphasizes the ideology of those in power.[43] These images also reinforce the idea of total social immobility, since they show the blacks and other disadvantaged groups constrained to occupy spaces predetermined by specific tasks or cultural practices solely associated with their subordinate social status within colonial society. These illustrations also reflect and support the view of the ruling classes that keeping these subordinate groups circumscribed and under control within determinate social spaces was a reasonable and acceptable way of maintaining good order in the colonies. In fact, these illustrations, as did *casta* paintings, used such a rigid classification of the different social groups,

---

41 'Real Cédula de su Majestad sobre la Educación, trato y ocupaciones de los esclavos en todos sus dominios de Indias e Islas Filipinas, bajo las reglas que se expresan, (1789)', in Carlos Aguirre, *Breve historia de la esclavitud en el Perú. Una herida que no deja de sangrar* (Lima: Fondo Editorial del Congreso del Perú, 2005), 226–35 (p. 228).

42 'Real Cédula de su Majestad sobre la Educación, trato y ocupaciones de los esclavos', 228.

43 Fowkes Tobin, *Picturing Imperial Power,* 13.

their dress and their activities as 'a way of rendering visible and stable [what was in reality] an increasingly fluid society'.[44]

Another illustration, which emphasizes the subordinate status of the black population in the territories subject to the archbishopric of Trujillo (and, indeed, elsewhere in Peru), is 'E140 Danza de bailanegritos' (**Figure 8**). This dance encapsulates the dynamics of class distinction and of racial hierarchy as established as the norm by the Spanish authorities. Within this system, 'the statutory and customary status of blacks was far inferior to that held by whites, regardless of their class and corporate identity', due to the association of the blacks with a state of slavery.[45] In this illustration, the colour of the skin of the individuals portrayed and their attire again play a crucial role in the manner in which the social status of each person depicted

Figure 8
'Danza de bailanegritos'.
Courtesy of the Biblioteca del Palacio Real, Madrid.

44 Katzew, *Casta Painting*, 151.

45 Mark A. Burkholder and Lyman L. Johnson, *Colonial Latin America* (Oxford/New York: Oxford U. P., 2001), 201.

is recognized. Though the dance is performed only by blacks, this picture includes also the figure of a white master who is differentiated from the rest especially strikingly because of the use of a white mask. Shown in stark contrast to the black dancers, this mask draws special attention to the colour of the master's skin. The fact that he is wearing shoes, and white socks, also distinguishes him from the servants who surround him. His other attire is also greatly differentiated from the clothing worn by the servants: he wears the typical hat that Spanish masters wore at the time; and his pants are also different from those of the rest, corresponding indeed to his much higher social status.

Ironically, although the petite servant who, significantly, is located at the bottom of this illustration, wears similar pants, he nevertheless lacks shoes, white socks, and the black hat his master wears, highlighting the fact that he will never be able to achieve the position that his Spanish master occupies in the social hierarchy. The big umbrella takes up a large part of the visual space available, because it is a symbol of the master's social status and prosperity. The umbrella, as such, is located near the top of the illustration, in marked contrast, therefore, to the small figure of the black musician at the bottom, and his tiny African drum. The spatial location of the individuals portrayed here reiterates the class differences which prevailed in that colonial time and place. Still more fascinating is the fact that, according to Martínez Compañón, even when they were engaging in their own cultural practices, as they are doing in this dance, the blacks themselves had learned to internalize their subordinate position in Peruvian colonial society: they acknowledged the superiority of their white master, and their own inferiority.

In the illustrations he included in the manuscript Martínez Compañón portrays the population in Trujillo del Perú according to how they contributed, through their various occupations, to its economy as a whole. As regards the black population, its members are certainly depicted as devoted workers. For example, illustration 'E112 Saca y beneficio de la brea del mineral amotape' (**Figure 9**) shows the blacks intensely focused on their tasks and aware of their individual roles in the collective production of tar. They seem to be so much focused on their jobs that they are unaware of those others who are working around them. This watercolour illustration certainly portrays members of the black population as industrious workers in producing the commodity concerned, and, as such, they would serve as incentives to the Crown to invest further resources into developing the potentiality of those lands. The African population is presented by Martínez Compañón as being made up of peaceful and manageable citizens who are to be trusted to execute their tasks with almost no supervision. This representation was certainly intended to persuade the king and his representatives, the Spanish authorities in Lima and Spain, that the territories of Trujillo del Perú, along with their inhabitants, were worthy

Figure 9
'Saca y beneficio de la brea del mineral amotape'.
Courtesy of the Biblioteca del Palacio Real, Madrid.
Copyright © Patrimonio Nacional

of substantial investment from the Crown. As Martínez Compañón made clear in his letter to the Viceroy of Peru in 1785, all his observations that he recorded by means of such illustrations were aimed at serving the interests of industry and commerce: '[e]n quanto puedan ser material de industria, y de comercio' (*Apéndice III*, 352). Given that in the eighteenth century 'idleness was fiercely condemned',[46] it was essential for Martínez Compañón to emphasize that hard work and not idleness was what characterized the way of life of the population of Trujillo del Perú. Since the 'Recopilación de las Leyes de Indias', colonial legislation had been greatly preoccupied with the need to keep blacks, even those who were free and not slaves, under total control, but this preoccupation seems not to be in evidence in these images of Martínez Compañón. Legislation demanded, for example, 'que al Negro, o Negra ausente de el servicio de su amo quatro dias, le sea dado en el rollo

46 Katzew, *Casta Painting*, 112.

cincuenta azotes', and called for other severe punishments when blacks did not report to work.[47] But there seemed to be no need for implementing laws like these where the population of Trujillo del Perú was concerned. The way that blacks are represented by Martínez de Compañón underlines the fact that they were industrious and peaceful citizens.

A letter he addressed to the Spanish king in 1786 reveals how much importance the bishop placed on the utilitarian nature of his enterprise. He is extremely eager to stress how much, economically speaking, the territories and population of Trujillo have to offer the Spanish Crown:

> Lo que unicamente necesita es aumentar y hacer mas util su población, y para conseguirlo reducir á sus habitantes á sociedad, dar crianza a la niñez de ambos sexos, impulso a la agricultura y mineria, movimiento y accion á su comercio interior y exterior, y que se fomenten asi mismo aquellos ramos de industria que siendo útiles á su provincias, no traigan perjuicio á las demas del Reyno, ni á esa Peninsula: cuyos objetos he procurado promover con todas mis fuerzas en mi Visita, y ántes y después de ella, como Prelado, como Vasallo del mejor Soberano de la tierra, y como miembro de la sociedad, y hermano de los demas hombres.
>
> (*Apéndice III*, 6–7)

The illustrations discussed above—as well as many others about which I do not have room to comment on within this article—, not only demonstrate the bishop's personal conviction of the value to the Spanish Crown of developing the archbishopric of Trujillo del Perú but also reveal his powers in persuading others that these were territories worthy of figuring both in the immediate and in the future plans of Spain for colonial investment and exploitation. The bishop's illustrations served as rhetorical messages to the king, and as powerful reminders that the Spanish presence in and control and utilization of these peripheral territories of the Viceroyalty of Peru needed to continue and indeed to be strengthened. The visuality of these illustrations emphasized vividly the case for the urgent development of the abundant natural and human resources and benefits available to Spain in Trujillo del Perú. Within the bishop's manuscript, images are used as visually functioning principles, to make clear the social and cultural differences within the population that inhabited this region, and what the region and its people had to offer Spain as the colonizing power. These regions and people are colonial bodies that are portrayed as material and symbolic objects visually presented as readily available for utilitarian purposes. In *Truxillo del Perú*, as in many works deeply influenced by the philosophy and scientific writings of the Enlightenment, the body, of a place and its people, constituted an object of material knowledge which needed to

47 *Recopilación de las Leyes de los Reynos de las Indias* (1680), Libro VI, ley xxi, in <http://www.congreso.gob.pe/ntley/LeyIndiaP.htm>.

be organized, controlled and ordered. Figuratively, this body functioned as Rebecca Haidt suggests, as 'the location where beliefs, practices, laws and institutions ... collide'.[48] So the establishment and maintenance of control and organization were essential.

5 Final Remarks: Speaking to the Eyes

John Berger reminds us of the fact that 'we only see what we look at. To look is an act of choice. As a result of this act, what we see is brought within our reach'.[49] Martínez Compañón's choice of visual images involves an act of selection remarkably similar to that which Berger describes. In creating his work, *Trujillo del Perú*, the bishop ordered a world in keeping with his own personal agenda. This agenda was that of a religious figure and representative of the Crown, and of one who still believed in the need for Spanish religious and political guidance in specific territories of the Viceroyalty. For Martínez Compañón, the image of the museum embodied the idea of a material space that could contain and order knowledge. In his case, that museum of knowledge was the nine volumes which constituted his manuscript. Visual images, he implicitly believed, would facilitate the process of observing and learning that would eventually guide individuals to the creation of pragmatic ways to take advantage of the cultural accumulation which was Trujillo del Perú. The body of this colonial subject-territory was to serve as a vehicle to comprehend and make sense of its world, to observe it and organize it. In this regard, the bishop viewed the body politic—in this case of Trujillo del Perú—as it was mainly viewed in the eighteenth century; as 'a form of political representation and a scientific scale of knowledge'.[50] As Barbara Stafford suggests, in this age, too, 'the human body represented the ultimate visual compendium, the comprehensive method of methods, the organizing structure of structures'.[51] It was indeed the social body of humanity which occupied the centre of the type of museum that the bishop was concerned illustratively to create, one that would communicate visually the cultural history of Trujillo del Perú. In this sense, for the bishop, and for other writers and thinkers of his time, as Ilona Katzew observes, 'image production' served to codify meaning.[52] Visuality, therefore, offered what the bishop thought to be the most efficient, direct and uninterrupted manner in which to characterize the

48 Rebecca Haidt, *Embodying Enlightenment. Knowing the Body in Eighteenth-Century Spanish Literature and Culture* (New York: St Martin's Press, 1998), 10.

49 John Berger, *Ways of Seeing* (New York: The Viking Press, 1972), 8.

50 Antoine de Bacque, *The Body Politic: Corporeal Metaphor in Revolutionary France, 1770–1800* (Stanford: Stanford U. P., 1997), 7.

51 Barbara Stafford, *Body Criticism: Imagining the Unseen in Enlightenment Art and Medicine* (Massachusetts: Massachusetts Institute of Technology, 1997), 12.

52 Katzew, *Casta Painting*, 9.

world of Trujillo del Perú. Martínez Compañón would have agreed with Alexander Cruden's 1738 commentary on the power of the visual image: 'All agree that it is an admirable invention: To paint speech, and speak to the eyes, and by tracing out characters in different forms to give colour and body to thoughts'.[53]

53 Alexander Cruden, *Concordance to the Old and New Testament* (1738); as quoted in Mitchell, *Picture Theory*, 111.

The Roots of Revolt in Late Viceregal Quito: Eugenio de Espejo between Adam Smith and St Rose

RUTH HILL

University of Virginia

Francisco Javier Eugenio de Santa Cruz y Espejo (1747–95) was the son of a *quechua* surgeon and a Spanish woman from Riobamba. Known as Eugenio de Espejo, he practised law and medicine and enjoyed the life of a middle-income *criollo* in the Spanish Kingdom of Quito.[1] Scholars have discussed how Espejo's dual emphasis on education and politics defined his literary production, and his life: he was imprisoned several times for his satires of political and religious figures.[2] He suffered his first imprisonment in 1785, after an aristocratic *criolla* sued him for defamation of character.[3] He was arrested again in 1795 for plotting to overthrow the Crown, and died from mistreatment in December of that same year. While literary historians have concentrated almost exclusively on Espejo's satires, discounting his treatises and sermons,[4] historian Martin Minchom's analysis of revolutionary activity in late viceregal Quito focuses our attention on the priest Juan Pablo Espejo,

1 Martin Minchom, *The People of Quito, 1690–1810: Change and Unrest in the Underclass* (Boulder/San Francisco/Oxford: Westview Press, 1994), 191–97.

2 Julie Greer Johnson, *Satire in Colonial Spanish America: Turning the New World Upside Down* (Austin: Univ. of Texas Press, 1993); Philip L. Astuto, *Eugenio Espejo (1747–1795), reformador ecuatoriano de la Ilustración* (México: Fondo de Cultura Económica, 1969); Luis Hachim Lara, *Tres estudios sobre el pensamiento crítico de la ilustración americana*, prólogo de Nelson Osorio (Murcia: Univ. de Alicante/Univ. de Santiago de Chile, 2000); Max Ontaneda Pólit, *Eugenio de Santa Cruz y Espejo: examen de su obra* (Quito: n.p., 1986).

3 Minchom, *The People of Quito, 1690–1810*, 192, 235.

4 Previously, I have analysed the nexus of epistemology, rhetoric, and identity in Espejo's fiction (Ruth Hill, 'The Problem of Conceit and the Politics of the Imagination in Satires by Eugenio de Santa Cruz y Espejo', *Hispanic Journal*, 20:2 [Fall 1999], 277–90), and the neo-classical footing of Espejo's sacred oratory (Ruth Hill, 'Local, Regional, and Mediterranean Sources for Espejo's *Sermones panegíricos de Santa Rosa de Lima* [1793–94]'. *Revista Interamericana de Bibliografía*, 14:2 [Fall 1999], 101–16). The most provocative study of Espejo's satires is Johnson's *Satire in Colonial Spanish America*.

Eugenio's brother, and his rather fluffy ideology.[5] Minchom overlooks the decades-long continental reach of Eugenio's economic and political thought by ignoring his writings altogether. In what follows I focus on two panegyrical sermons on St Rose of Lima penned by Eugenio and delivered by Juan Pablo in 1793–94. The stated proposition of Espejo's sermons is the exemplary life of St Rose of Lima. However, Rose of Lima becomes equal parts wise virgin and model *paisana* as Espejo develops through his headings the unstated proposition of Spanish-American unity and revolt against the Spanish Crown and Church. I approach these sermons as logical extensions of Espejo's treatises from the 1780s, which balance a fiery condemnation of moral and political corruption with a sophisticated economic analysis of the Kingdom of Quito.

Until the establishment of the Viceroyalty of New Granada in 1719, Quito was a kingdom whose high court (*real audiencia*) deferred to the high court in Lima and whose bishropic was a suffragate of the archdiocese of Lima. After the dissolution of the Viceroyalty of New Granada in November 1723, Quito again fell under the civil and religious jurisdiction of the Viceroyalty of Peru. This situation continued until the Viceroyalty of New Granada was re-established in August 1739 and the new Viceroy assumed his duties in April 1740.[6] Trade through Guayaquil in the Kingdom of Quito linked the Viceroyalties of Peru (including Chile and the Riverplate), New Granada (including Panama, Nicaragua, Costa Rica) and New Spain (including Guatemala).[7] Religious jurisdiction over Quito was held by the Archbishop of Lima, even after Quito was placed under the civil jurisdiction of the Viceroyalty of New Granada. With Lima, Quito shared church leaders, artists and patron saints. Retables of Saint Rose were built in the cathedral

---

5 Minchom sees in Juan Pablo Espejo's declarations after his own imprisonment in 1795 a 'Creole utopia, with a strong strain of French Enlightenment radicalism' (*The People of Quito, 1690–1810,* 240), but it appears from the passages quoted by Minchom (239–41) that the intellectual concerns of Juan Pablo were limited and his political clarity far removed from the sort of profound economic analysis shown by Eugenio.

6 The Count de la Cueva, Jorge de Villalonga, was named Viceroy of New Granada in 1717 and assumed his duties when the Viceroyalty was officially established in November 1719. His tenure lasted four years, the duration of the first incarnation of the Viceroyalty. A member of the Orden de Santiago, Lieutenant-General Sebastián de Eslava governed from April 1740 until 1749, and unlike his predecessor and subsequent viceroys, his base was in Cartagena de Indias rather than Santa Fe de Bogotá. On the political and religious history of the Viceroyalty, see the first chapter of Abel Romeo Castillo, *Los gobernadores de Guayaquil del siglo XVIII. Notas para la historia de la Ciudad durante los años de 1763 a 1803* (Guayaquil: Publicaciones del Archivo Histórico del Guayas, 1978); José Manuel Groot, *Historia eclesiástica y civil de Nueva Granada*, 4 vols., 2nd rev. ed. (Bogotá: Casa Editorial de M. Rivas & Ca., 1889-90), II; on communications and economics, see Dionisio Alcedo y Herrera, *Descripción geográfica de la Real Audiencia de Quito*, prólogo y ed. de C. A. González Palencia (New York: Hispanic Society of America, 1915). Further references are to González Palencia's edition. Alcedo y Herrera's work dates from 1766.

7 Alcedo y Herrera, *Descripción geográfica, passim.*

of Quito, and the spiritual daughter of the Jesuits, the ascetic and mystic Mariana de Jesús, imitated her.[8] Ties between the Viceroyalties of Peru and New Granada were also tightened by the rotation of Church officials from North to South and by the rotation of Crown officials between Spain and Spanish America.[9] Espejo's panegyrical sermons seek to link the Viceroyalties in a third way, on an affective level, through the figure of St Rose of Lima.[10]

In the exordium of *Primer sermón panegírico de Santa Rosa de Lima*,[11] Eugenio de Espejo joins Church and Crown on the authority of St Augustine's distinction between the city of man and the city of God:

> Pero, señores, permitidme que sin salir de mi texto, me limite á estas últimas palabras, y que, acomodándome como orador cristiano á las circunstancias presentes de un siglo calamitoso, os muestre á Rosa, dentro del precioso cautiverio de la Iglesia, obligada á seguir el sistema de la vida cristiana, atada á las inestimables cadenas de su vocación, encerrada en el interior misterioso de la santidad: *Et clausa est janua.* Metodicemos, Señores, el discurso, y reduzcámosle para nuestra edificación, á sólo estas dos reflexiones: Rosa, ligada á la unidad de la Iglesia por la infinita misericordia del Todopoderoso; Rosa, ligada á la grandeza del Estado, por la eterna Providencia [. . .]. (II, 545)

Here we see how Espejo's arrangement and style exemplify the neo-classical retrofitting of Augustine for the rationalist milieu of 'method' and 'system'. And yet, the figure of St Rose will not be pressed into the service of Enlightened despotism in the Spanish Bourbon mode (as Espejo's allusion to the 'Grandeur of the State' here might suggest); it will aspire to an altogether different ideology: that of continental revolution and independence from the Spanish Crown.

Espejo truly wants to talk about the wise and the foolish residents of Spanish America, and he quickly moves to the unstated proposition of his

---

8 José María Vargas, *Historia de la Iglesia en el Ecuador durante el patronato* (Quito: Editorial 'Santo Domingo', 1962), 253–66, 335.

9 Groot, *Historia eclesiástica y civil de Nueva Granada*, II, *passim.*

10 Juan de Espinosa Medrano (d. 1688) had glorified Rose as a *peruana* and a *criolla* destined to become the patron saint of the New World. See his *Oración panegírica*, in *Apologético*, ed. Augusto Tamayo Vargas (Caracas: Biblioteca Ayacucho, 1982), especially pp. 199, 201, 205. Also see the uncontrollably baroque panegyric in French by Anonymous, *Panegyrique de la bienheureuse Rose de Sainte Marie de Lima du Pérou pronounce en l'Eglise des RR. Dominicains de la Rue S. Honoré* (Paris: Imprimerie d'Edme Martin, 1669).

11 Francisco Javier Eugenio de Santa Cruz y Espejo, *Primer sermón panegírico de Santa Rosa de Lima predicado en la Catedral de Quito el día 30 de agosto de 1793,* in *Escritos del Doctor Francisco Javier Eugenio Santa Cruz y Espejo*, pról. y notas de Federico González Suárez, ed. Jacinto Jijón y Caamaño y Homero Viteri Lafonte, 3 vols (Quito: Imprenta Municipal, 1912–1923), II, 543–64 (hereafter, *Primer sermón panegírico*; further references, which will be included in my main text, are to this edition.

sermon: continental unity. After praising St Rose to the heavens (II, 546–51), Espejo makes her human once again: Rose is their *paisana*. Rose is, indeed, a saint, but, more importantly, for Espejo's purposes, she is their model citizen, their model patriot:

> [. . .] Rosa es una niña nacida bajo de un cielo que nos comprende y encierra, producida al calor de un clima que nos estrecha y abraza; dada a luz sobre un mismo suelo que nos sustenta y reúne. [. . .] Rosa es nuestra paisana, es hija de Lima, de esta ciudad magnífica, brillante y opulenta [. . .]; el teatro de la grandeza americana [. . .].
>
> (*Primer sermón panegírico*, II, 552)

Lima, as Espejo invents it, is always torn between its divine blessings and its punishments; between brilliance and dissipation; between eloquence and loquaciousness; between talent and flights of fancy; between a thirst for wisdom and pedanticism; between, finally, what is sound of mind and what is superficial (553). This contrasting of opposites is a common means of amplification—of extending the discourse while moving the emotions of listeners or readers. Another rhetorical figure for moving the passions in order to amplify, the *interrogatio* (rhetorical question) serves the ends of argumentation also: '¿Mas, á qué conduce, me diréis, la descripción, moral, física y política de la primera ciudad de la América y de esta famosa capital del Perú?' Espejo answers that St Rose of Lima is the homegrown example for patriotic parishioners: 'Todos los fieles estamos obligados á imitarla en las capitales abandonadas y en las cortes corrompidas [. . .]' (II, 553). 'Abandoned capitals' and 'corrupt courts' and St Rose? What compelled Espejo in 1793 to write of abandonment and corruption?

A distressing description of the Province of Quito during Pedro Messía de la Cerda's tenure as Viceroy of New Granada (1761–1773) was written by the Jesuit Mario Cicala. Theft and Quito Province were synonymous, according to Cicala, who had spent over twenty years there before he was exiled to Italy in 1767. Armed robbery and church and residential burglaries were rampant.[12] Still, the most widespread of vices, the one that had reduced Quito to 'pobreza y miseria' (Cicala, 220), was gambling. Its deleterious effects on economics and demographics in the capital startled the Jesuit: 'Cuando yo llegué a la ciudad de Quito, oí decir que el número de todos sus habitantes subía a más de 60 mil, y que el año 1730 había cerca de 80 mil almas, ya que entonces sólo los indios eran en la ciudad 18 mil. Pero al presente [1771] apenas llega a 30 mil, y aun de este número dudo mucho, toda vez que por la decadencia del comercio mucha gente se ha ido a otras

12 Mario Cicala, *Descripción histórico-topográfica de la Provincia de Quito de la Compañía de Jesús* (Quito: Biblioteca Ecuatoriana 'Aurelio Espinosa Pólit', 1994), 216. Cicala finished writing his account in 1771. Further references to Cicala's work are to this edition, and will be given in my main text.

partes' (Cicala, 223–24). 'Abandoned capitals' were not merely products of Espejo's rhetorical invention in 1793–94; they, like revolutionaries, are not made overnight.

During Espejo's early adult years, the Crown's monopoly of alcohol distilled from sugar-cane, the Estanco de Aguardiente, cast a long shadow over the spheres of physical and moral health in the Kingdom. 'Comenzó a disminuir el número de indios', Cicala observes, 'pues morían en gran cantidad: de los 18.000 indios existentes y habitantes en la ciudad, hoy apenas si hay 6000; también el gran número de mestizos ha disminuido notablemente, ya que, según las autopsias hechas innumerables veces por los médicos y cirujanos en el Hospital, se ha visto y observado con evidencia que todos mueren con las vísceras quemadas e inflamadas por el aguardiente de caña de azúcar, pues lo beben como si fuera agua [. . .]' (Cicala, 218). As a surgeon, Espejo's father certainly would have known first-hand such patterns of mortality, which were by no means confined to the lower orders and castes. Spanish residents were especially fond of the rum punch brought into Portobelo, Cartagena, Panama, Guayaquil, Quito and Lima by the French and British merchant ships and their American and Peninsular Spanish agents on the ground. Noblemen and noblewomen, friars and priests, monks and nuns, all succumbed to it (Cicala, 219). Venerable politicians became the butt of children's rhymed ripostes. Wealthy widows and mothers abandoned their maternal responsibilities to embrace '*gentilísimamente* (término usado por ellas) [. . .] la nueva moda' (Cicala, 220). Men and women squandered family fortunes, and children were left homeless, their once respectable mothers and fathers engaged in prostitution and other crimes (Cicala, 220).

In May 1766, *pasquines* appeared in the capital city that were veritable calls-to-arms. The offices of the Estanco de Aguardiente and Customs were looted and burned to the ground. Judges on the court called on the Jesuits to defuse the rebellion. An amnesty was issued and a tax on alcohol was cut. In June 1766 there was another uprising, and the Viceroy of New Granada called in troops from Maracaibo, Panama and Lima to restore order. Three years before the circulation of Espejo's most famous satire, *El nuevo Luciano de Quito* (1779), Viceroy Amat of Peru painted a still life of Quito, 'en circunstancias de haverse ya serenado el tumulto, manteniendose la Pleve en la más profunda sumision [. . .]'.[13] One suspects, after reading Espejo's works from the 1780s, that Crown ministers often elected to paint people and events as they should have been, rather than to record them as they were.

---

13 Francisco Javier Eugenio de Santa Cruz y Espejo, *El Nuevo Luciano de Quito o Despertador de los ingenios quiteños en nueve conversaciones eruditas para el estímulo de la literatura*, intro. Isaac J. Barrera, ed. Aurelio Espinosa Pólit (Quito: Imprenta del Ministerio de Gobierno, 1943). I quote from Manuel de Amat y Junient, *Memoria de gobierno*, ed. Vicente Rodríguez Casado and Florention Pérez Embid (Sevilla: Escuela de Estudios Hispano-Americanos, 1947), pt. 2, ch. 17 ('Tumulto de la Pleve de Quito'), 289–90.

In *Reflexiones [...] acerca de un método seguro para preservar a los pueblos de las viruelas* (1785),[14] Espejo observed that Quito's agricultural bounty notwithstanding, the poor did not benefit:

> La gente de alguna comodidad, come con abundancia: la [gente] rica puede presentar en su mesa sin mucha diligencia, afán ni costo, manjares muy exquisitos y capaces de lisonjear la gula de los mismos que se jactan de haber comido con esplendidez en Europa. Pero la gentalla, esta que parece tener alma de lodo por inopia, no se atreve á gastar el infeliz medio real que coge en pan, sino por hacer más durable su socorro, le expende en harina de cebada. De esta desigualdad de condiciones resultan estas monstruosidades de parecer una tierra fértil, y al mismo paso estéril.
> (*Reflexiones*, II, 430)

It is likely that Espejo's status on a par with that of a middle-income *criollo*, and his consistent interest in economic planning, caused him to consider inequalities among different cultural or ethnic groups (*castas*) as a species of the genus 'desigualdad de condiciones'. Whatever his motivations, it is clear that Espejo saw a chasm between the lower and the higher orders. Wherever one looks, where Espejo writes of the Kingdom of Quito, there are egoists whose cruel design is to accumulate riches, chasing after accolades and the finer things in life, at the expense of public welfare. Such men seek to be the only repository of happiness, forgetting entirely that of the Republic (*Reflexiones*, II, 357).

In *Defensa de los curas de Riobamba* (1786),[15] Espejo again catalogued the Kingdom of Quito's woes and possible remedies. Economic reform, inseparable from the political interests of the Crown, was predicated on investment in mining, incentives for businessmen to invest their capital in the Kingdom, and the diversification of agriculture. Hard currency in Quito was scarce, and the Kingdom could not keep pace with its trading partners in the Viceroyalty of Peru (*Defensa*, III, 178–80; 191). Agriculture suffered from an abundance of fallow fields and a poverty of planning (*Defensa*, III, 158–63). Commerce—well, there is nothing that goes by that name here, so Espejo flatly states. The owners of manufacturing centres were themselves so impoverished that they borrowed money from the Church to stay open (*Defensa*, III, 170–72). 'Esta infeliz constitución de este Reino, y de su

14 Francisco Javier Eugenio de Santa Cruz y Espejo, *Reflexiones sobre la virtud, importancia y conveniencias que propone Don Francisco Gil, Cirujano del Real Monasterio de San Lorenzo y su sitio, é individuo de la Real Academia Médica de Madrid, en su disertación físico-médica, acerca de un método seguro para preservar á los pueblos de las viruelas*, in *Escritos del Doctor Francisco Javier Eugenio Santa Cruz y Espejo*, II, 341–522. Further references to this work are to this edition, and will be given in my main text.

15 Francisco Javier Eugenio de Santa Cruz y Espejo, *Defensa de los curas de Riobamba*, in *Escritos del Doctor Francisco Javier Eugenio Santa Cruz y Espejo*, III, 1–234. All references to this work, hereafter given in my main text, are to this edition.

comercio provinciano, fácilmente la puede delinear, por sus principios y origen, un genio verdaderamente político', remarks Espejo (*Defensa*, III, 180).

The Viceroys of New Granada did not fail to acknowledge that corruption and mismanagement of the Kingdom of Quito's resources were a drag on development and put a financial squeeze on the lower orders. Manuel de Guirior, marqués de Guirior, served as Viceroy of New Granada for three years (1773–1776) before he became the Viceroy of Peru (1776–1780). In his *Relación* (written in 1780),[16] Guirior applauded the Crown proposal that would transfer royal officials (European and American Spaniards alike) who had served in America to Spain, 'sirviendo este premio de estimulo para el mejor desempeño, y que no contraigan apego ni perjudiciales enlaces de parentesco que tanto impide el fiel manejo de la Justicia' (*Relación*, t. II, f.125). He lamented the grave difficulty 'que se encuentra en hallar sujetos de la fidelidad que requiere el delicado encargo de manejar la Real hacienda por el envejecido vicio de defraudarla aun los mismos encargados de su Administración, prescindiendo de las omisiones e inacción en el cumplimiento de su ministerio' (*Relación*, t. II, f.133). The Viceroy complained of the disorder and decline in revenues at Quito's office of the Royal Treasury's coffers [*las Cajas*], due to 'el descuido o poca fidelidad de los que las han administrado...' (*Relación*, t. II, f. 143). He grumbled that old titles and the Church's incorporation of farmland were impeding agricultural development and commerce (*Relación*, t. II, ff. 115–16). Guirior's successor, the Spanish Archbishop Antonio Caballero y Góngora, blamed the *hacendados* for the Kingdom of Quito's economic malaise in his *Relación* (1789).[17] He compared these estate-owners to feudal lords and enumerated social inequities[18] that Espejo had already detailed in his treatises from the 1780s and would hint at in his two sermons on St Rose.

16 Manuel Guirior, Marqués de Guirior, *Relación que en el año de 1776 dio el Excelentísimo Señor Virrey del Nuevo Reino de Granada D. Manuel de Guirior a su sucesor D. Manuel de Flores del estado en que dejaba aquel Gobierno*, Colección Ayala, t. II, MS. 2842, ff. 92–165, Biblioteca del Palacio Real, Madrid. Further references to this work are given in my main text.

17 Antonio Caballero y Góngora, *Relación del Estado del Nuevo Reino de Granada, que hace el Arzobispo Obispo de Córdoba a su succesor el excelentísimo señor Don Francisco Gil y Lemos* (1789), in José Manuel Pérez Ayala, *Antonio Caballero y Góngora, Virrey y Arzobispo de Santa Fe 1723–1796* (Bogotá: Imprenta Municipal, 1951), 297–392. Further references to this work are to this edition. Alcedo y Herrera lodged a similar complaint in 1766 about the laziness and lack of initiative among Quito's residents: 'Por lo cual dicen los del Perú y los del Nuevo Reino que no hay en las Indias provincias más ricas y más pobres que las de Quito, porque como poseen las mayores riquezas de aquella parte del Nuevo Mundo en sus montes y en sus ríos, manteniendo las unas encerradas en sus veneros, y dejando perder las otras, llevadas de las corrientes al mar por la flojedad, ocio y pereza de sus habitantes que no las labran y cultivan porque no las necesitan para mantenerse, contentándose con la bondad de los climas, benignidad de los temples, fertilidad de las tierras y fecundidad de los frutos' (*Descripción geográfica*, 61).

18 'Los hombres medianamente acomodados, se llaman aquellos que, por falta de providencias precautivas de la demasiada agregación de tierras en un solo sugeto, han podido,

In the years 1788–1790, Espejo lived in Santa Fe de Bogotá, the capital of the Viceroyalty of New Granada, working with selected members of the elite such as the *criollo* Juan Pío Montúfar, Marqués de Selva Alegre.[19] While Espejo was living in Santa Fe, General José de Ezpeleta de Galdeano became Viceroy of New Granada (1789–1797). His account of his tenure would bear the *leitmotivs* of Bourbon rule that we have seen in his predecessors' accounts. Though Caballero had glowed about the increase in over-all treasury revenues produced by Quito, General Ezpeleta gingerly reported that the respective faculties of the Viceroy (especially his powers as general superintendent of the treasury) and of the President of Quito had not been clearly stipulated in the Archbishop's times.[20] As a result, 'se introduxeron varios desordenes y abusos, se causó bastante atraso en la formación, presentación y examen de las cuentas de la Real Hacienda, y aun se dificultó saber su verdadero estado, que no era en realidad el que se informó al Señor Arzobispo Virrey al tiempo de formar su relación' (*Relación*, II, f. 67). Ezpeleta quickly proposed to the Crown the suppression of the financial tribunal in Quito that had been created under Viceroy Guirior. This tribunal supervised all recorded income and expenditures of concern to the Royal Treasury (*Relación*, II, f. 202). The accounting division was headed by an interim chief with a little bit of salary and a lot of connections to those who ran the Royal Treasury and were dependents of the (financial) tribunal (*Relación*, II, f. 205). Ezpeleta complained that nearly every official had embezzled monies or accepted bribes to defraud the royal treasury (*Relación*, II, ff. 207–08).

a viles precios, adquirir inmensos terrenos, en que por lo regular tienen como feudatarios a los de inferior fortuna. Los primeros perseveran más arraigados a sus posesiones, por la ganancia que reciben de sus esparcidos domésticos; pero éstos, que forman el mayor número de habitantes libres, hacen propiamente una población vaga y volante, que obligados de la tiranía de los propietarios, transmigran con la facilidad que les conceden el poco peso de sus muebles, la corta pérdida de su rancho y el ningún amor a la pila en que fueron bautizados' (Caballero y Góngora, *Relación,* 328–29).

19 Minchom details Eugenio's friendship with the *criollo* revolutionary Juan Pío Montúfar, Marqués de Selva Alegre, during Espejo's banishment to Santa Fe (*The People of Quito, 1690–1810*, 235). The Marquis' father, Juan Pío de Montúfar y Frasco, was a Spaniard who served as governor and president of the high court in Quito and wrote a geographical report of the Kingdom in 1754 (see Ruth Hill, 'Arrate's *La Habana descripta* and the Modernization of the Geographical Report [*ca.* 1750–1769]', *Revista Hispánica Moderna*, 49:2 [1996], 329–40 [pp. 330–31]). Espejo himself indicates in Quito's first newspaper, *Primicias de la Cultura de Quito* (which he founded), that their friendship dates back to their childhood—i.e., when the senior Juan Pío was the governor of Quito—and he makes explicit that the young nobleman supported the exiled Espejo (*Primicias de la Cultura de Quito*, in *Escritos del Doctor Francisco Javier Eugenio Santa Cruz y Espejo*, I, 1–99 [pp. 96–97]).

20 José de Ezpeleta de Galdeano, *Relación del gobierno del Excelentísimo Señor D. José de Espeleta, Virrey, Gobernador y Capitán General que fue del Nuevo Reino de Granada*, Colección Ayala, t. II, MS 2896, ff. 62–261, Biblioteca del Palacio Real, Madrid, ff. 198. Further references to this *Relación* are given in my main text.

Moral and political corruption in Quito was rampant in Espejo's times, and in *Primer sermón panegírico* he calls on the entire continent to unite around St Rose, who exhibited the very traits that Crown officials ignore or abhor:

> Porción ilustrísima de la Iglesia! América meridional, corazón intacto del cristianismo! Quito, Lima, Perú, regiones dominadas de la sangre del Cordero Inmaculado! Ojalá que mejorada la faz de vuestras costumbres, podáis hacer nueva ostentación de que un ente americano compuesto de cuerpo y alma, en medio de su invecilidad, de sus pasiones, de sus flaquezas, de su afeminación y su temperamento mole, es racional, es espiritoso, es humano, capaz de ser el edificio augusto de la razón y la virtud [. . .]! (*Primer sermón panegírico*, II, 554).

At the very same time, Espejo waxes proleptic, reiterating the loyalty of the continent to Spain:

> La América bendiciendo mil y mil veces la dichosa suerte que le tocó ser esclava de la ley, que abraza con su dependencia voluntaria y meritoria; de ser sierva de su Rey, que adora con la humilde reunión de todo su cuerpo a su cabeza suprema [. . .] (*Primer sermón panegírico*, II, 563)

This toadiness contradicts Espejo's revolutionary activities in the 1790s as well as his pointed warnings to the Crown in the 1780s.

In his *Defensa de los curas de Riobamba*, for instance, he claimed that if nothing was done to reform the agricultural, manufacturing, and trading sectors, the King would be forced to send in troops because the lower orders were on the verge of revolt (III, 184–85). The Crown's reforms executed by local elites had failed the indigenous because Crown officials in Quito knew about Indians only what ignorant naturalists had written in their histories.[21] Bourbon reforms had failed all residents, in fact, because they had not been based on experience:

> Por lo que mira a las [reflexiones] de *críticos y políticos*, es preciso confesar que éllas no se deben recibir como quiera, sino con discernimiento y atención, a lo que pide, en primer lugar, la Religión Cristiana; lo segundo, la felicidad de los pueblos; y, lo tercero, la grandeza del Estado. [. . .] [C]omo un sabio inglés, verdadero político dice: 'De todas las especies de hombres no hay otra más perniciosa que la de los

21 'Querer suponer a los indios rústicos, salvajes y divorciados de la común luz natural, prontos por eso a hacer fiestas, sin discernimiento, elección ni gusto, acerca de ellas, es el error de gentes que no saben su idioma, sus usos y costumbres, y es un absurdo político, filosófico y aún teológico, el mayor que pueda escogitarse, y es un oprobio de la humanidad pensar así [. . .]. ¿Qué dirán los impíos, en contra de la Religión, cuando [los políticos] sólo quieren acumular sobre la faz de la tierra, lapones, iroqueces, hotentones, patagones, negros y sobre todo indios naturalistas? [. . .] Fuera, pues, de nuestros escritos y papeles, las palabras *instinto, rusticidad, imbecilidad, tontería y bobería de los indios*' (*Defensa*, III, 225–26).

> Proyectistas, cuando éllos tienen el poder en la mano, ni más ridícula cuando no lo tienen. Al contrario, (prosigue) un sabio político revestido de autoridad es el actor más útil que puede presentarse sobre el teatro de la vida humana'. (*Defensa*, III, 202–03)

Espejo's variegated ideology has received far less attention than his satirical novels, and it calls to mind the classic study by Ivy McClelland, *Ideological Hesitancy in Spain*: for at times Espejo plays the moderate, at times the radical reformer.[22] In the above passage he does not allude to a revolutionary figure; Espejo's 'English sage' and 'true statesman' was Scottish and an economist: Adam Smith. The above quote, I believe, is Espejo's translation of passages in Smith's *The Theory of Moral Sentiments* (1759)[23] on the *spirit of system* that envelops a state in disorder (232–34). The tenor of reform may lead to an improved state of affairs, Smith notes, or it may well destroy public spirit altogether by trying to fix the unbroken. Members of political schools ('proyectistas' in Espejo's rendering above) become the dupes of chimerical reform with which the worst leaders delude their followers (232–33). Among the sensible lobbyists and leaders, however, is that figure of genuinely public spirit who 'will accomodate, as well as he can, his public arrangements to the confirmed habits and prejudices of the people; and will remedy as well as he can, the inconveniences which may flow from the want of those regulations which the people are averse to submit to' (233). As Espejo re-states Smith, 'Es, pues, principio de política, que el mejor método de establecer ventajosamente una sociedad, es acomodarse al humor general de los hombres, y sacar de él el mejor partido' (*Defensa*, III, 196). One year before *Primer sermón panegírico*, he would again elaborate on Smith's axioms in a legal and economic brief commissioned by a high court minister.[24]

Proyectismo is synonymous with the Bourbons and Enlightenment Spain,[25] but Espejo seems to be suggesting in the 1780s that Bourbon

---

22 I. L. McClelland, *Ideological Hesitancy in Spain 1700–1750*, Publications of the *Bulletin of Hispanic Studies*, Textual Research and Criticism (Liverpool: Liverpool U. P., 1991).

23 Adam Smith, *The Theory of Moral Sentiments*, ed. D. D. Raphael and A. L. Macfie (Oxford: Clarendon Press, 1976), 232. All references are to this edition.

24 In *Voto de un ministro togado de la Audiencia de Quito* (1792), in *Escritos del Doctor Francisco Javier Eugenio Santa Cruz y Espejo*, I, 165–99, Espejo details the two political economies (the agricultural and the commercial) defined by Smith, and how the wealth of the King and the State depends upon the wealth and happiness of the vassal (181–82). It is not improbable that Espejo saw himself as a disciple of the foremost political economist of his day (Smith's works were republished over and over in the 1770s, '80s, and '90s).

25 José Muñoz Pérez, 'Los proyectos sobre España e Indias en el siglo XVIII. El proyectismo como género', *Revista de Estudios Políticos*, 81 (1955), 169–85; Francisco Sánchez-Blanco, *El absolutismo y las Luces en el reinado de Carlos III* (Madrid: Marcial Pons Historia, 2002); Ruth Hill, 'Bourbon Castile and Other "Antiquities": Memory, Conquest and Tradition in Luzán's Occasional Poetry', *Journal of Spanish Cultural Studies*, 4:1 (2003), 95–110.

reform projects could not reform the Bourbons themselves: they were *men of system*.[26] When he mentions 'las cortes corrompidas' in his *Primer sermon panegírico*, he is intimating that the very so-called reformers who promised to flush out corruption in fact expedited it. A case in point: Viceroy Guirior of New Granada accepted bribes from the Lima Consulate of Commerce and was truly at the beck and call of a handful of *criollos* who were his friends, relatives and advisers.[27] When Espejo's brother Juan Pablo delivered the *Segundo sermón panegírico de Santa Rosa de Lima* in 1794,[28] members of the high court and the Governor of Quito were present. Espejo's second heading of 'Charity', with its subtheme of trust or confidence in one's fellow man, would have lent itself to situational irony. Crown officials, Church officials, and town folk alike knew the hardships suffered by the Espejo family because of Eugenio's political and economic ideas and activities. Espejo contrasts Rose's charity toward her fellow citizens of Lima with the mistrust, ambition, and envy that his fellow citizens exhibit in Quito:

> Ahoga [Rosa] en las ondas del amor divino cualquiera intención y pensamiento del prójimo y no le juzga sino según el mar de su caridad, que es decir, según su corazón. Y es así que el hombre de estos tiempos modifica el uso de su discurso?; es así que pone en la caridad el éxito de su fortuna? No es así, que es agitado de un remolino de sospechas crueles, de desconfianzas y de juicios temerarios? No es así, que su corazón es un mar revuelto de los huracanes más furiosos de sus propios temores, con que á todos, ó trata de enemigos, ó recela competidores? No es su alma toda un mar turbulento, donde naufraga su paz, y donde se alternan las representaciones funestas de la iniquidad agena, en tanto que no hace más que pintar el carácter de su propia corrupción, de sus celos, de su envidia? Aprended de Rosa el espíritu de verdadera confianza [...].
>
> (*Segundo sermón panegírico*, II, 583 84)

---

26 Again, it is the Scottish economist who sheds light on Espejo's dreary allusion to Bourbon officials in Quito: 'The man of system [...] is apt to be very wise in his own conceit; and is often so enamoured with the supposed beauty of his own ideal plan of government, that he cannot suffer the smallest deviation from any part of it. He goes on to establish it completely and in all its parts, without any regard either to the great interests, or to the strong prejudices which may oppose it. He seems to imagine that he can arrange the different members of a great society with as much ease as the hand arranges the different pieces upon a chess-board. He does not consider that [...] in the great chess-board of human society, every single piece has a principle of motion of its own, altogether different from that which the legislature might chuse to impress upon it' (Smith, *The Theory of Moral Sentiments*, 234)

27 John L. Phelan, 'El auge y la caída de los criollos en la Audiencia de Nueva Granada, 1700–1781', *Boletín de Historia y Antigüedades*, 59 (1972), 597–618.

28 Francisco Javier Eugenio de Santa Cruz y Espejo, *Segundo sermón panegírico de Santa Rosa de Lima predicado en la Iglesia de los ex-Jesuitas, el día 31 de agosto de 1794,* in *Escritos del Doctor Francisco Javier Eugenio Santa Cruz y Espejo*, II, 565–88. All references to this work, hereafter *Segundo sermón panegírico*, are to this edition, and are given in my main text.

This rhetorical caginess does not address St Rose, but, rather, the Crown and Church officials in attendance. The abundant praise of Church and Crown aims equally to please and to persuade elites that they have nothing to fear. At the same time, Espejo again mentions corruption; this time, he argues that it ('su propia corrupción') motivates people to accuse others (like Espejo himself) of wrongdoing ('la iniquidad agena').

Trust of one's fellow man, rhetorically anchored in St Rose's exemplary charity, yields to the topic of public trust or security, which is threatened by the economic hardships and moral and political corruption signalled in Espejo's treatises from the 1780s:

> Señores, haced vuestro corazón el domicilio de una seguridad verdaderamente caritativa. Véis á esta ciudad, sumergida en un mar de miserias, de necesidades, de abatimientos, de pobrezas, de contradicciones, de enemistades, de vanidad, de lujo y de todo vicio? Pues, esperad quietamente y sin falso celo, de estos sabios Magistrados el ejemplo y la protección; de esos celosos Pastores, la doctrina y la edificación; de esas nobles Señoras, el honor y la limosna; de esos ilustres Patricios, la libertad y la racional emulación. De esas niñas, la docilidad y la inocencia; de esos jóvenes, la aplicación y la sabiduría. Del mismo cielo de Quito, la renovación de la faz de su Patria. A ella cooperá nuestra paisana con los ardores de su caridad [. . .]. Sí, porque la sabiduría y prudencia de un corazón abrasado del amor divino, no reconoce los impenetrables resortes del artificio; no camina por las ocultas y retiradas sendas de la duplicidad; no constituye su habilidad en la simulación y el engaño; no adelanta el mérito de sus alcances, por el disfraz, por la mala fe, por la falsedad, por las bajezas y por el perpetuo halago formado en el seno de una eterna alevosía. (*Segundo sermón panegírico*, II, 584–85)

Espejo manages to usher the Crown in and out by appealing to the audience's affection for their *paisana*, St Rose of Lima. Rhetorically this passage illustrates the 'artificio,' 'duplicidad' and 'engaño' that it condemns.

Espejo continues in the *Segundo sermón panegírico* to manipulate his tropes and figures with the intention of securing the third, emotive link between the Viceroyalties of Nueva Granada, Peru, and the Riverplate. The very arrangement of his *Segundo sermón panegírico* reveals this conjoining. Espejo reiterates the unity of the Continent throughout, and near the end this unstated proposition is amplified by repetition and clarification: he applies Augustine's words on fraternal charity to 'todo el Perú, y este mundo americano' (II, 587). Espejo's peroration moves out of the moderate or acute style appropriate to treating vices and virtues, as he adopts the sublime style suited to conversion. Again the unstated proposition of continental unity appears, now insinuated alongside the two headings of 'Prudence in the sublimity of faith' and 'Charity':

Oh Rosa, cuyo corazón fue hoguera inmensa de amor á Dios y al prójimo! *Mare vitreum mistum igne*. Tú quisiste por tus semejantes ser condenada á penas más exquisitas, que las que fabricó tu ingeniosa penitencia, y por tu Dios sacramentado, tú quisiste sacrificar la última gota de sangre y ser mártir de un nuevo amor! Enciende, pues, nuestros corazones con los verdaderos sentimientos de la caridad. Pero vos, Dios de eterna luz y eterno incendio, haced útil mi lengua á la santificación de mi Patria. Haced que nuestra prudencia sea divina y permanente. Que nuestra fe sea viva y luminosa. Que nuestra caridad sea ardiente y universal. Que Rosa sea una antorcha de ejemplo, que nos obligue á ser sabios y prudentes para la gloria eterna.—*Amen*.

(*Segundo sermón panegírico*, II, 588)

In October 1794, just over a month after Juan Pablo preached Eugenio's second sermon on St Rose, Quito's town councilmen expressed concern about an increase in unruliness and disrespect for the law among the lower orders. In 1795, Espejo contributed to *pasquinadas*, or the posting of *pasquines*, in Cuenca, Guayaquil and Quito. The *pasquines* posted in Quito explicitly referred to rebellion in the Viceroyalty of New Granada, while those appearing in Cuenca mentioned the upheaval against the Crown in the Viceroyalty of Peru as an example to be imitated.[29] These regions were like beads on a necklace, according to my understanding of Espejo's revolutionary thought and activity; in a continental uprising each had to be joined to its neighbour, in spirit and in action. Espejo's choice of St Rose, then, reveals his understanding of how female sainthood might affectively unite peoples in a revolt against the Crown and the Church that linked them administratively to one another. The roots of that revolt are to be found in his economic and political treatises from the 1780s. Plotting that revolt landed Espejo in prison for the last time in 1795.

29 Minchom, *The People of Quito, 1690–1810*, 238.

The Authorship of *Portrait of a Young Woman with a Rose*, Formerly Ascribed to Goya

NIGEL GLENDINNING

Queen Mary, University of London

In the Albright Knox sale held by Sotheby's in New York on 8 June 2008, Lot 270 was *Portrait of a Young Woman Holding Two Roses,* assigned by the auctioneers to Agustín Esteve y Marqués, following the conclusions drawn by Martin S. Soria in a book published in 1957.[1] Before that book was written, the portrait had been generally considered to be by Goya, and since Soria had admitted that he had never seen the painting itself and only knew it from photographs, his view was clearly open to challenge. I had the good fortune to be able to see the picture in person and study it in detail in 2005, when the then owners had the portrait unhung so that it could be viewed in a variety of lights, close to, and at leisure. It looked to me more like Goya's work than Esteve's, and since I had been given a full dossier of the history of the picture and several excellent photographs on the occasion of my visit, I wrote up my conclusions for the owners in imperfect French, adding several references to the standard literature, from published and manuscript sources not previously used by Goya specialists. In the wake of the recent auction, whose conclusions about authorship seem questionable to me, I have revised and reworked my arguments in English, as a tribute to the memory of Professor Ivy McClelland, a great pioneer of the study of eighteenth-century Spanish culture, with the hope that more attention might be paid, in the future, to this extraordinarily attractive and ingenious painting, so that it can perhaps be restored to the Goya canon.

The *Portrait of a Young Woman with a Rose* first appeared in the Goya literature in April 1867, when Charles Yriarte's book on Goya was published in Paris. Amongst the private collections in Madrid which Yriarte had visited when preparing his book in Spain, was that of the Patriarch of the Indies, and it was there that the French expert saw the Goya portrait he called

1 Martin. S. Soria, *Agustín Esteve y Goya, con un prólogo del Excmo. Sr. D. Enrique Lafuente Ferrari* (Valencia: Institución Alfonso el Magnánimo, 1957), 93, N° 22.

Francisco de Goya y Lucientes (1746–1828) (?)
Portrait of a Young Woman with a Rose
Oil on canvas. 105 × 84 cms.
Photograph from the Rothschild dossier.

Francisco de Goya y Lucientes (1746–1828) (?)
Detail of *Portrait of a Young Woman with a Rose*
Photograph from the Rothschild dossier.

La jeune Femme à la Rose.[2] Yriarte did not take too seriously the apparently commonly-held view that Goya had depicted the young French supporter of the Girondists and assassin of Marat, Charlotte Corday, in this painting, though he thought that Goya might indeed have been interested in her story. More surprising is the inaccuracy of his description of the young woman in the painting as 'une jeune fille très brune et d'un beau caractère, portant la jupe rayée et le bonnet blanc'. It is clearly not the sitter's skirt that is striped but her coat; and although her bonnet is indeed white, and in a style frequently associated with the name of Charlotte Corday, it is the coloured silk ribbons and flowers that decorate her head-dress that catch the eye most. In the years immediately following the appearance of Yriarte's book, Manuel Ossorio y Bernard's entry for Goya in his *Galería biográfica de artistas españoles del siglo XIX* (Madrid: Imprenta de Moreno y Rojas, 1868–69) recorded the portrait again,[3] now in the collection of the Marqués de Selva Alegre, in which Yriarte had seen a different Goya work. But it cannot have been with Selva Alegre long, for in July 1868 it was to be found in France, when it was listed in the stock of the great French dealer Durand-Ruel, who was active in purchasing from Spanish sources at the period.[4]

Given the political uncertainties in Spain in the 1860s, it is not surprising that paintings should have changed hands quite rapidly at that time. And since both the known owners of the *Portrait of a Young Woman* had important roles at the court of Isabel II, it is likely that they were in a particularly difficult position.

The Patriarch of the Indies in the 1860s was Tomás Iglesias y Barcones (1803–1874), who had been attached to the Court since 1851, when he moved from being Bishop of Mondoñedo to become the Patriarch responsible for the spiritual direction of the armed forces. The Chapel Royal was also in his charge, since he was Almoner to the Queen, and in addition he was a senator and president of several of the royal councils. The Marqués de Selva Alegre, for his part, was Juan Pío Montúfar, who was the official responsible for presenting foreign ambassadors and envoys at Court. Montúfar was descended from a family that had settled in Quito in the eighteenth century, whose antecedents had been ennobled for services to the Royal Chancellery of that province. Dividing their time between the New World and the Old, some members of the Montúfar clan played an important role in the Independence movement in Peru, while others remained loyal to the Spanish Crown. The Marquis who owned paintings by Goya was clearly one

2 Charles Yriarte, *Goya. Sa vie, son œuvre* (Paris: Plon, 1867), 136. I have respected Yriarte's title, with 'Rose' in the singular, throughout this article. There are, as the auctioneers correctly noted, two blooms visible, but they are both on the same stem.

3 Manuel Ossorio y Bernard, *Galería biográfica,* facsimile edition (Madrid; Librería Gaudí, 1975), p. 314 a.

4 Information provided in a letter from Durand-Ruel et Cie, dated 22 December 2005, in the dossier copied for my use and retained by me.

of the latter. According to Charles Yriarte he had owned a scene depicting Spanish country customs by Goya—*The Maypole*—before acquiring the *Young Woman with a Rose*.[5]

During the 1860s, both the Patriarch and the Marqués de Selva Alegre remained loyal to the Queen at a time when she was about to lose the support of the majority of her subjects, and wondering whether she would have to go into exile. After the establishment of a revolutionary council in Madrid in 1868, in the wake of earlier revolts and disturbances in the capital in June 1865 and later in Cádiz, the Court left for San Sebastián on 22 September 1868, and the Queen decided to take refuge in France on the 30 September, first in Biarritz and later in Pau, before moving definitively to Paris.[6] We know that the *Portrait of a Young Woman* went to France slightly before July 1868, but have not found any information about the movements of Selva Alegre and the Patriarch at that period. The later history of the painting is easy to follow. It was already on Durand-Ruel's books in 1868. Mr Edwards, a Levantine banker, seems to have had it in July that year, though payment was still outstanding, and a few months later it had passed to the Belgian artist Alfred Stevens, widely admired in France as a portrait painter, and a serious collector and connoisseur. Durand-Ruel bought it from him for 15,000 francs in December 1868, and in March 1870 it was offered for sale at the Hotel Drouot and reproduced in the catalogue. The sale in question was in the name of Mr Edwards, but he apparently had an agreement with Durand-Ruel to pay an annual advance of 10% of the price of paintings he liked, with the right to hang them in his house as if he already owned them, although the real owner was still, in fact, the dealer. Durand-Ruel 'purchased' the painting at the Edwards auction, where Théophile Gautier saw it and was able to declare that it was the finest Goya he had ever seen,[7] and Durand-Ruel then sold it in July 1872 to Baron Nathaniel Rothschild's agent, after which the painting descended through various branches of the Rothschild family until it was sold in 2008.

It is much harder to piece together the early history of the portrait, before it passed into the hands of the Patriarch of the Indies at an unknown date between 1851 and 1867. There has been no previous attempt to do this, so far as I am aware. But at least the date when the portrait was painted can be

5 Charles Yriarte, *Goya*, 136.

6 Marqués de Miraflores, *Continuación de las memorias políticas del reinado de Isabel II desde 1840 hasta el año de 1868*, 2 vols (Madrid: M. Rivadeneyra, 1873); edition consulted, *Memorias del reinado de Isabel II*, ed. Manuel Fernández Álvarez (Madrid: Atlas, 1964), BAE, continuación, vol. CLXXIV, pp. 259, 440–48 etc.

7 *Cf.* Ilse Hempel-Lipschutz, 'Théophile Gautier y su "quimera retrospectiva" captada en la obra pictórica de Goya', in *Goya. Nuevas visiones. Homenaje a Enrique Lafuente Ferrari*, ed. Isabel García de la Rasilla and Francisco Calvo Serraller (Madrid: Amigos del Museo del Prado, 1987), 207–25 (p. 223). Gautier's essay on paintings in the Edwards sale was published only two years before his death, at a time when his son and others sometimes wrote what he signed.

deduced with reasonable certainty from the dress worn by the young woman. The Conde de la Viñaza thought that the sitter might well have been a figure of the artist's imagination, and dressed in a fantastical style.[8] But Zeferino Araujo recognized that the girl was wearing the French fashion of the Republican period, immediately after the Revolution,[9] and this can be substantiated from the fashion magazines of the period. The girl is in fact wearing a coat known as a 'caraco'. There is a very similar jacket with comparable stripes in the *Journal de la Mode et Goût* for 1790 in France,[10] and also in *La colección de trajes y muebles decentes y de buen gusto* in Spain in 1791.[11] The long hair and bonnet decked with ribbons and flowers were also in fashion at the same period,[12] and it is also the case that the artist followed the common Spanish practice of the late eighteenth century in depicting young women with roses or other flowers (or also fans). The rose was also considered a traditional emblem of modesty, a natural virtue for fathers to want their daughters to have at that period, and others too. Both the portrait conventions and, above all, the style of the sitter's clothing, date the picture almost certainly between 1790 and 1795.

So far as the early provenance is concerned, a document published for the first time in 1950 enables us to put forward a new hypothesis about this work. A previously overlooked mention of a painting by Goya with virtually the same title as the *Portrait of a Young Woman with a Rose* occurs in an inventory of property in the artist's *Quinta*, drawn up probably in 1823 with the assistance of the young artist Antonio Brugada, one of Goya's companions during his years in Bordeaux. A fragmentary version of this inventory remained in the hands of Brugada's widow, and she allowed Xavier Desparmet Fitz-Gerald to make his own copy of the document, when he was an art student between 1875 and 1880. Desparmet Fitz-Gerald's daughter, Xavière, edited and published her father's book on Goya in 1950, and the text of the inventory was given in a footnote.[13] The inventory itself was originally thought to have been drawn up after Goya's death in 1828, but Brugada is known to have been in France at that time and could not have helped with its transcription if it was made in Madrid then. The present

8 Conde de la Viñaza, *Goya. Su tiempo, su vida, sus obras* (Madrid: Manuel G. Hernández, 1887), 298, N° CXXXIV, under the category of History paintings and depictions of national customs rather than portraits.

9 Zeferino Araujo Sánchez, *Goya* (Madrid: La España Moderna, n.d.), 116–17, N° 238.

10 *Cf.* Aileen Ribeiro, *Fashion in the French Revolution* (London: Batsford, 1988), 56, fig. 27.

11 *Cf.* Álvaro Molina and Jesusa Vega, *Vestir la identidad, construir la apariencia. La cuestión del traje en la España del siglo XVIII* (Madrid: Ayuntamiento de Madrid, 2004), 135, fig. 48.

12 Ribeiro, *Fashion in the French Revolution,* 76–77, figs 46 and 47 (1792–93); Molina and Vega, *Vestir la identidad,* 137–39, figs 50–55.

13 Xavier Desparmet Fitz-Gerald, *L'Œuvre peint de Goya. Catalogue raisonné illustré de 447 reproductions suivies de 34 dessins inédits*, 2 vols (Paris: F. de Nobele, 1950), I, 54.

theory is that it was made in 1823, before either Brugada or Goya went to Bordeaux. The change in ownership of the *Quinta* at that period makes the need for just such an inventory highly probable. In 1823, Goya decided to give the *Quinta*, lock, stock and barrel, to his grandson Mariano, and the deed of gift was duly notarized on 17 September 1823.[14] Although the deed does not refer specifically to the furnishings, the inventory includes what are now called the 'Black Paintings', which formed an integral part of the buildings themselves, other paintings and some pieces of furniture. Among the female portraits in the inventory there is listed a *Portrait of a Lady with a Rose. Half length* ('Retrato de señora con una rosa. Medio cuerpo').

Neither Desparmet Fitz-Gerald's daughter Xavière, when she drew up the catalogue entry for the Rothschilds' picture, when it was exhibited as a portrait by Goya at the Jacqmart-André Museum in Paris in 1961–62, nor Martin Soria, when preparing his book *Agustín Esteve y Goya*, in which he attributed the *Young Woman with a Rose* to Esteve on the basis of photographs rather than direct knowledge, remembered the reference to a painting with almost the same title in the inventory of the contents of Goya's *Quinta* drawn up in the 1820s. Yet its presence in the *Quinta* at that period suggests that a new hypothetical provenance can be drawn up for the work, running as follows: 1. The family of the young lady depicted, from 1790–95 when it was painted, to an unknown date; 2. Francisco Goya; 3. Javier or Mariano Goya from 1823 to an unknown date; 4. The Patriarch of the Indies, perhaps from after Javier Goya's death in 1854 to the mid 1860s; 5. Marqués de Selva Alegre, perhaps between 1865 and 1867; 6. Durand-Ruel, Paris, before July 1868; 7. Alfred Stevens, Paris, briefly, until December 1868; 8. The Levantine banker Edwards, Paris, until 1872; 9. Family of Baron Nathaniel Rothschild and his descendants, from 1872 to 2008; 10. the present owner in the United States.

It is possible to add further references to this provenance line if the painting can be identified with an apparently lost Goya portrait of a lady. Most of Goya's female portraits whose sitters have not been identified depict 'señoras' or 'damas' rather than girls or young adolescents. Lost or unidentified Goya portraits of women are also mostly of married ladies, but one of these is particularly interesting since it is also listed in the Brugada inventory, immediately before the entry for *Portrait of a Lady with a Rose*. The painting in question is the *Portrait of Doña Catalina Viola with a Fan*, usually identified with the *Lady with a Fan* by Goya, in the Louvre. Could the young woman with the rose, perhaps be related to this lady with the fan?

---

14 *Escritura de donación de una Casa, y de 14 fanegas y 10 Celem.*[s] *de tierras situadas al otro lado del Camino del Puente Segovia, con las mejoras hechas en ellas, otorgada por D. Franco. Goya, Pintor de Camara de S.M. a favor de su Nieto D. Mariano Goya. En 17 de Setiembre de 1823*, Archivo Histórico de Protocolos, Madrid (AHPM), Protocolos de Antonio López de Salazar, 1823, *ff.* 93–96.

Catalina Viola was the younger of the two surviving daughters of Goya's patron and friend, Sebastián Martínez, whose portrait, now in the Metropolitan Museum of Art, New York, was painted by Goya in Madrid in 1792. Catalina married a Cádiz merchant called Francisco Viola, whose relatives had trading roots in Buenos Aires, in 1804, when she was about to acquire great wealth and half the immense art collection of her father, who had died a few years earlier in 1800. Interestingly, a painting by Goya of Catalina before her marriage also seems to have existed, since it was listed in the 'famous collection' of Fernando Casado de Torres, her brother-in-law, married to Catalina's sister Josefa.[15] In an undated manuscript list of Fernando Casado's collection of paintings drawn up by the artist Juan de Rivera (or Ribera) probably after the death of Casado in 1829, we find 'Retrato de Doña Catalina Martínez, de Goya, alto cinco cuartas, ancho tres [¿cuartas?]'.[16] If Goya in fact painted two portraits of Catalina, could the earlier of the two perhaps be the portrait of a 'señora con una rosa. Medio cuerpo' which preceded it in the Brugada inventory?

The potential family link between the sitter of the *Portrait of a Young Woman with a Rose* and Sebastián Martínez is extremely suggestive. If they were father and daughter and they were painted at the same time, that would explain the obvious similarities in the paintings. Both the subjects wear striped jackets following fashions dating from the early 1790s; both sit in the same chair, to judge from the top of one of the uprights visible in both portraits; and both are painted against a dark greenish background. So far as their dimensions are concerned, the Casado inventory makes the portraits both the same height (the equivalent of 104 cms). And if the figure given for the width of the portrait of the young woman listed by Casado is taken to be

15 For a brief biography and bibliography of Sebastián Martínez, *cf. Comerciantes, artistas y coleccionistas riojanos del siglo XVIII (XI Jornadas de arte y patrimonio regional, 6, 7 y 8 de Noviembre de 2008)*, ed. Ignacio Gil-Díez Usandizaga (Logroño: Imprenta Vidal, 2008), 8–12.

16 *Catálogo y tasación de la famosa colección de D. Francisco Casado de Torres, original de la misma letra de D. Juan de Ribera*, Biblioteca Nacional, Madrid, MSS 18.630/40, N° 649. (Francisco seems to be a misreading of Fernando in abbreviated form, taking 'Fdo' to be 'Fco'). The importance of the Casado de Torres collection in relation to paintings by Goya was first noted by Jeannine Baticle in her article 'Les amis "norteños" de Goya en Andalousie. Ceán Bermúdez. Sebastián Martínez', in *Actes du Congrès Internationale d'Histoire de l'Art: Granada, 1973, VI. La Peinture aux XVIIe et XVIIIe siècles* (Granada: Depto de Historia del Arte, Univ. de Granada, 1978), 15–30 (p. 22), where she listed the most significant Goya paintings owned by this marine engineer, who had also been, like Goya, a friend of Jovellanos. I am grateful to my friend Dr Jesusa Vega for checking the MS for me and making some additional notes of paintings of interest, apart from those by Goya. The compiler of the catalogue, Juan de Rivera or Ribera, was a well known Spanish painter of the period (see Ossorio y Bernard, *Galería biográfica* in note 3, above, pp. 574b–575b, under 'Ribera y Fernández, Juan Antonio'). The same artist was also one of the experts called upon to evaluate the 'Black Paintings' of Goya after the death of Javier Goya (*cf.* 'Protocolos del notario Juan Manuel Aguado, 1859', AHPM, P° 26525, 1859, *ff* 421^{v}–422^{r}).

tercias rather than *cuartas*, the dimensions of *Catalina Martínez* (if it is the *Portrait of a Young Woman with a Rose)* would be the same as they are now (105 x 84 cms). The discrepancy in the height of Sebastián Martínez requires explanation. In the Casado inventory it was 104 cms high, but it is now 93, a difference of 11 cms. However, recent investigations at the Metropolitan Museum of Art in New York suggest that the portrait may indeed have been cut down at some point in the past, so the original pairing of the two portraits may still be possible.[17] Past measurements of *Sebastián Martínez,* furthermore, are distinctly confused. Desparmet Fitz-Gerald and Gudiol both give 110 cms x 90 cms as the dimensions of the portrait, and if the French expert obtained his figures from the painting itself or from the Galerie Trotti which owned the portrait before it was bought by the Metropolitan, it might indeed have been larger in the late nineteenth century than it is now.

The dimensions of the *Portrait of a Young Woman with a Rose* are, at all events, in line with a number of Goya portraits, and this clearly strengthens the case for his authorship of the picture. The width of 84 cms, for instance, coincides with that of *Bernardo de Iriarte*, *The Duke of Osuna* (in the Frick Collection), the seated portrait of *General Ricardos*, the Prado's *Francisco Bayeu*, *Gil de Tejada* (in a private collection) and the *Man in a Brown Jacket* (in the Museum of Fine Arts, Boston). A height of 104 cms and a width not far from 84 are to be found in *Josefa Castilla y Portugal de Garcini* (New York, Metropolitan Museum), and *María Vicenta Baruso Valdés* and *Leonora Valdés de Baruso* (private collections). Stylistic arguments are naturally much more conclusive, yet despite the fact that Soria admitted he had not seen the painting, his judgment has been very little questioned subsequently. The portrait was not included in the *catalogue raisonné* of Goya's Work by Pierre Gassier and Juliet Wilson (1971), nor had it been in that of José Gudiol (1970).[18] Ilse Hempel Lipschutz reported that Xavier de Salas had also not been convinced that Goya had painted the portrait, although he apparently did not think it was by Esteve.[19] Gassier, on the other hand, changed his mind and reproduced the portrait in his book on Goya's paintings in 1980.[20] Only Jeannine Baticle, in an unpublished essay on the

17 Response given verbally to me by Juliet Wilson Bareau, reporting the conclusions of the Department of European Paintings of the Metropolitan Museum of Art, in response to my letter of 10 January 2006.

18 *Cf.* Pierre Gassier and Juliet Wilson, *Goya. His Life and Work with a catalogue raisonné of the paintings drawings and engravings,* ed. François Lachenal (London: Thames and Hudson, 1971) (text revised from the original French edition published in 1970); José Gudiol Ricart, *Goya, 1746–1828: biografía, estudio analítico y catálogo de sus pinturas, con mil doscientas noventa y cinco láminas presentadas en los volúmenes II, III y IV*, 4 vols (Barcelona: Polígrafa, 1970).

19 Hempel-Lipschutz, 'Théophile Gautier y su "quimera retrospectiva"', 223.

20 Pierre Gassier, *Goya. Das Gesamtwerk. Die grossen Meister der Malerei*, 2 vols (Frankfurt/Berlin/Wein: Ullstein Verlag, 1980), II, 38, N° 438, with illustrations facing p. 36.

painting written for its owners' dossier, has so far argued strongly for Goya's authorship on stylistic grounds.

It seems sensible to start any stylistic analysis of the *Portrait of a Young Woman with a Rose* by recapitulating the main conclusions reached by Lafuente Ferrari and Soria about the respective styles of Goya and Esteve.[21] They argued that Esteve was more preoccupied with neat draughtsmanship than Goya, defining more sharply the profiles and physical features of his sitters, and reproducing carefully the details of every kind of ornamentation: jewellery, rich materials, medals and the silk sashes of the Military Orders; the gold braid of court dress and military uniforms; and decorative patterns on furniture. Goya, on the other hand, followed Velázquez more closely, particularly from the 1780s onwards, and knew how to create a strong impression of secondary details without attempting an exact copy of their reality. Goya is skilful at suggesting space and background atmosphere, whereas Esteve usually places clearly defined objects in the middle distance or the background. So far as the handling of the face of the sitter is concerned, there is a considerable distance between them. Goya was able to convey the vitality and the character of the persons he depicted. The eyes of his subjects are full of life and extremely expressive, fixing their gaze on the spectator, who views them sometimes head-on and sometimes at an angle. The gaze of Esteve's sitters, on the other hand, rarely expresses much animation, and their large eyes—frequently with a small white spot in them to suggest the iris or the reflection of light—are more inclined to convey melancholy than vivacity or vitality. When painting the face, Goya often used bold touches, merging the colours on the canvas, wet on wet, or using dark glazes to add shadow to skin colour. Esteve tended to simplify contrasts and accentuate the outlines, and his works do not have to be viewed at a distance, as do Goya's.

The *Portrait of a Young Woman with a Rose* has few of the characteristics of Esteve. The treatment of the sitter's eyes is more complex, and small touches of a paler shade of brown in their corners, give a greater sense of life than Esteve achieves with his more usual white spots. There is a greater sense of life in the young lady's face, furthermore, than Esteve was capable of creating, less stiffness in the body, and a strong sense of its contours that is rare in Esteve. From a technical point of view, there is a subtler sense of colour and contrast, less hardness of line than is typical of Esteve, and an extraordinarily bold suggestion of the pattern on the white or creamy shawl. The painter of this portrait, in addition, does not hesitate to use the reddish tone of the ground to mark the borders between the stripes of the sitter's jacket, more particularly below the waist, a typically Goya touch of artistic sleight of hand. The pendants in the young woman's ears are not carefully

21 *Cf.* Lafuente's 'Prólogo' to Soria's *Agustín Esteve y Goya*, 15–28, and Soria's section on Esteve's *œuvre*, 47–80.

delineated as they would be in an Esteve portrait, but hinted at, each in a different way, with magical touches. Adjacent to the left ear, a circle of white dots suggest a pendant decorated with small diamonds; the right ear, on the other hand, is covered by the tresses of the sitter's long hair, and the artist merely hints at the luminosity of the pendant indirectly with two small touches of the brush, that are paler than the surrounding hair, and so hint at the hidden brightness of a jewel. Most magical of all is the depiction of the black lace which veils the cuffs of the jacket, forms a borderline under the fringe of the shawl from the left shoulder to the other side of the chest, and then crosses the upper part of the body from the right side to the waist. The transparent effect of the delicate black lace over the grey-blue stripes is largely achieved by delicately brushing black touches and glazes over the pattern of the stripes.

There is nothing to suggest that Esteve had the finesse, audacity, imagination, delicacy of touch and ability to capture the character of the sitter, that is shown in this portrait. Can it be by anyone other than Goya? And may it not indeed be the lost portrait of Sebastián Martínez's daughter, Catalina Martínez, who was baptized in Cádiz on 21 October 1777 and would have been fourteen, or, just possibly, fifteen years old in 1792, if her portrait had been painted at the same time or in the same year as that of her father? Should the provenance line for the portrait, suggested earlier, be modified to include the purchase of the painting by Fernando Casado de Torres from Javier or Mariano Goya between 1823 and 1829 (when Casado died), and can we now suggest that the Patriarch of the Indies acquired the work from Casado's and Josefa Martínez's heirs in the middle of the century? Other Goya scholars will no doubt have views on these things.

PART III

The London Merchant y sus relaciones con la experimentación dramática en la España del siglo XVIII

I. L. McCLELLAND†
University of Glasgow

ed. Fernando Huerta Viñas
Universidad Autónoma de Barcelona

The London Merchant y sus relaciones con la experimentación dramática en la España del siglo XVIII*

I. L. McCLELLAND†
University of Glasgow

ed. Fernando Huerta Viñas
Universidad Autónoma de Barcelona

La obra de George Lillo, *The London Merchant* constituyó un gran éxito en el Londres teatral de 1731,[1] aunque su calidad artística no fuera unánimamente aclamada. Los principales defectos que se le imputaban eran el que sus personajes fueran de humilde condición, condición supuestamente inadecuada para la escena, y el que su *pathos* dramático causara con frecuencia un excesivo derramamiento de lágrimas en el público de la época. Sea como fuera, los sucesivos ataques a la obra y las correspondientes defensas, tan vehementes los unos como las otras, se sucedieron a lo largo de dos siglos, lo cual es una buena prueba de que constituyó un importante impacto en la sensibilidad dramáticoteatral a partir de la fecha de su estreno. De ahí que su influencia en el teatro francés de la época fuera tan importante y que los dramas de autores como Diderot, Mercier, etc. reflejaran el nuevo espíritu dramático introducido en la escena dieciochesca por el inglés Lillo. Pero no es de esto de lo que nos

* Este texto consiste en una recopilación de las notas que Ivy McClelland redactó para una conferencia impartida en la Universidad Autónoma de Barcelona en la primavera de 1982 ante profesores y alumnos de la Facultad de Letras. He procurado ser lo más fiel posible al original, pero redactándolo en forma articulada, ya que sus apuntes eran notas no destinadas originalmente a su publicación. F.H.V.

1 Ver George Lillo, *The London Merchant or The History of George Barnwell*, 2 vols (London: printed for J. Gray, 1731), 5 actos en prosa.

interesa hablar aquí ahora, sino de cómo la influencia de Lillo en Francia se dejó sentir en el teatro español de la segunda mitad del siglo.[2]

Debemos recordar, ante todo, que el ambiente cultural de la España de la época se debía al nuevo desarrollo científico, el cual produjo un nuevo espíritu de experimentación e inquietud de pensamiento que afectó profundamente a las artes y las letras. El nuevo ambiente de cambio bien lo reflejaron escritores y pensadores como Feijoo, quien aconsejaba 'suspender el juicio' a la vista de las nuevas dudosas verdades introducidas por la ciencia, siempre y cuando ello no conllevara un cuestionamiento de la fe religiosa, naturalmente. El cuestionamiento de los valores aceptados anteriormente fue infiltrándose en las esferas sociales, políticas y, también, artístico-literarias. Y también la aparición de los primeros indicios de la revolución industrial en Inglaterra, que luego se manifestaron asimismo en Francia, hizo que una obra de tesis social como *The London Merchant*, posiblemente la primera de este género en el teatro del siglo, calara muy hondo en los dramaturgos contemporáneos.

Las obras dramáticas francesas que siguieron la línea del texto de Lillo consiguieron, sin embargo, una calidad artística muy superior a la del drama inglés. Y es comprensible que así fuera, si tenemos en cuenta las diferencias históricas en la evolución literaria de ambas naciones. Recordemos que Francia había llegado a su 'Siglo de Oro' y que contaba con algunos de los mejores escritores de la Europa de entonces, mientras que Inglaterra—al igual que España—había tenido el suyo en el siglo anterior. De hecho había existido más afinidad en el espíritu literario de estos dos países que con respecto al del país francés, poseedor de un intelectualismo razonador más frío, teórico y mecánico que el inglés o el español. En éstos se da por un igual un mismo sentido del humor, mucho más realista a la vez que satírico y burlón, llegándose a consolidar la forma caricaturesca que encontraremos tanto en Shakespeare como en un Don Quijote. No hay más que pensar en cómo Fielding en su *Tom Thumb* ridiculiza la tragedia por su heroísmo de altos vuelos, y en cómo un Ramón de la Cruz, en su *Manolo* (1769), que subtitula '*Tragedia para reír, o sainete para llorar*', acumula todo tipo de truculencias sensacionalistas tales como suicidios, muertes, alaridos, etc., para acabar haciendo que dos personajes, contemplando tanta mortandad, cierren la escena del siguiente modo:

---

2 Las relaciones entre los dramas franceses y españoles están ampliamente estudiadas en el segundo volumen del capital estudio de I. L. McClelland *Spanish Drama of Pathos 1750–1808*. I. *High Tragedy*; II. *Low Tragedy*, 2 vols (Liverpool: Liverpool U. P.; Toronto: Univ. of Toronto Press, 1970), traducido al español por Fernando Huerta Viñas y Guillermina Cenoz del Águila como *'Pathos' dramático en el teatro español de 1750 a 1808*. I. *La alta tragedia*; II. *La tragedia menor*, Hispanic Studies TRAC (Textual Research and Criticism) 7, 2 vols (Liverpool: Liverpool U. P., 1998).

Sabastián. Nosotros ¿nos morimos o qué hacemos?
Mediodiente. Amigo ¿es tragedia o no es tragedia?
Es preciso morir;[3]

En esta escena final de la obra, repleta de cadáveres, se hace patente el espíritu burlón con que el humor español ha mirado tradicionalmente de forma irónica a la fórmula trágica máxima. Y es esta tendencia a equilibrar lo trágico con lo cómico lo que caracteriza fuertemente la creación de tensión dramática en el teatro hispano. No es de extrañar, por consiguiente, que el drama de tesis social, con una propaganda explicitada mediante fríos razonamientos, con poca acción y con muchos diálogos llenos de ideas, encontrara difícil acomodo en la estética teatral española. Y sin embargo, el cambio de clima europeo acabó por imponer este nuevo teatro de crítica ideológica también en España, a pesar de que en sus principios los logros artísticos fueran mediocres. La experimentación era de mayor importancia en la historia del teatro europeo. Es gracias a esta experimentación inicial, recordémoslo, que más tarde el teatro europeo llegaría a tener dramaturgos del calado ideológico de un Ibsen, un Shaw o, también, de un Benavente.

Quizá lo más digno de ser resaltado en *The London Merchant* no sea su argumento, sino las ideas manifestadas a lo largo de las escenas incidentales de esta obra en prosa. Es la exaltación de la nobleza y honradez del comercio, frente a la tradicional exaltación de la aristocracia del género trágico, lo que resulta enormemente innovador en el drama. El comercio se mira como una ciencia que necesita habilidad intelectual. En las escenas de esta tragedia burguesa en que se dialoga largamente sobre aspectos técnicos del comercio, como los problemas del transporte—ahí están los navíos españoles dificultándoselo—, o la organización del comercio moderno, etc., puede apreciarse la importancia que ha cobrado de repente esta temática en un género que todavía es melodramático. Recordemos que el protagonista, George Barnwell, trabaja en un comercio londinense y que su amigo Trueman es también un aprendiz; el dueño del comercio, Thorowgood, tío del protagonista, tiene una hija, María, que está enamorada de George. El drama sobreviene cuando una mala mujer, Millwood, convence a George para que robe el dinero de su tío y poder así ella apoderarse de él, para después despreciar y abandonar al desgraciado aprendiz. El *pathos* del drama llega a su momento culminante con los personajes derramando abundantes lágrimas, en la escena de la cárcel, con el sonido de la campana que anuncia la inminente ejecución del reo en la horca y, finalmente, con el arrepentimiento del bueno de George. Toda esta fábula moralizante tiene el soporte de afirmaciones tales como 'El nombre de comerciante nunca deshonra el nombre de caballero', dicha por uno de los personajes, o la de 'Yo soy el que se ha hecho

3 Ver la edición de *Manolo* en Ramón de la Cruz, *Doce sainetes*, ed. José-Francisco Gatti (Barcelona: Labor, 1997), 103–21 (p. 121).

a sí mismo', etc. Los artesanos y comerciantes—que en Shakespeare, y en el Siglo de Oro español, solían ser humildes o cómicos—aspiran a una dignidad que pudiera compararse con la dignidad de caballero. Tienen su código de honor—su pundonor. Hablan de la dignidad de todo ser humano. De modo que se han convertido aquí en portavoces de lo que puede considerarse una verdadera propaganda social.

No hay que olvidar, además, que aparece en la obra inglesa un tipo de crítica que apunta hacia las injusticias sociales cometidas, por ejemplo, para con la mujer. Son frecuentes las alusiones a injusticias cometidas por magistrados, sacerdotes, etc. No eran estas críticas inusuales ya en los teatros inglés y español de los Siglos de Oro, aunque en aquellas obras las críticas se hacían de forma más sutil: la costumbre era alabar a los príncipes y gobernantes por cualidades y virtudes que realmente no tenían, esperando animarles de esta manera a mejorar su conducta. Así que solían alabarlos por todo lo que habían hecho por los necesitados, o por España en general, cuando la realidad más evidente era que habían hecho todo lo contrario. Y esto se vuelve a encontrar también en los dramas de finales del XVIII, como por ejemplo en el texto de Luciano Francisco Comella de 1795, *El hombre singular, o Isabel Primera de Rusia*, en donde, hablando de los reyes en general, la misma reina Isabel dice con una falsa ingenuidad:

> Sus almas son grandes,
> hay pocos [príncipes] que no la [beneficencia] sepan.
> [. . .]
> unos promulgando leyes
> que la justicia sostengan,
> otros aliviando al pobre
> los tributos y gabelas.
> Éstos haciendo dichosos
> prodigando sus riquezas,
> aquéllos dando fomento
> a las artes y las ciencias . . .[4]

En el momento histórico en que esto fue escrito, reinando el Borbón Carlos IV, uno de los monarcas más ineficaces y menos merecedores de respeto, no es extraño que el Censor se viera obligado a eliminar este pasaje. Esta clase de crítica existía en el teatro tradicional español e inglés, pero en el siglo XVIII la crítica del gobierno, la sociedad etc., se va introduciendo en el teatro

4 Hay un manuscrito de *El hombre singular, o Isabel Primera de Rusia*, en dos actos, de Comella en la Biblioteca Municipal, Madrid, con censura de 1795. Se representó esta obra en Madrid el 4 de noviembre de 1795 (ver Jerónimo Herrera Navarro, *Catálogo de autores teatrales del siglo XVIII* [Madrid: Fundación Universitaria Española, 1993], 115). Según Coe, este drama volvió a representarse en 1797, 1802, 1810 y 1815 (ver Ada M. Coe, *Catálogo bibliográfico y crítico de las comedias anunciadas en los periódicos de Madrid desde 1661 hasta 1819* [Baltimore: The Johns Hopkins Press, 1935], 118–19).

más abiertamente, como tesis—en obras de tesis social. El ambiente experimentador de la época, al que hacíamos alusión al principio, da a esta crítica social una carga moralizante de tipo 'tesis científica' o de 'ideología racionalista', que acabará convirtiendo al teatro de la segunda mitad del siglo en un arma propagandística. Tenía la misma importancia pública que tiene hoy en día la televisión.

Antes de referirnos a las traducciones de *The London Merchant*, conviene hacer referencia a alguna de las peculiaridades temáticas de esta tragedia burguesa, las cuales influyeron a nivel internacional. En primer lugar está la importancia de la amistad entre dos hombres, los dos aprendices protagonistas de la obra. Muy corriente en el teatro de Shakespeare, en que contribuye mucho a la fuerza de la caracterización shakesperiana, la presencia y desarrollo de esta amistad, honrada y madura, en el drama de Lillo refuerzan de modo realista la situación humana. Por otra parte, conviene apreciar cómo los toques de un humor irónico y realista acercan el drama de Lillo al estilo de obras como *La Celestina* o de algunas tragedias inglesas clásicas, alejándolo del estilo de las del teatro clásico francés. Es el caso, por ejemplo, del relato que hace Millwood de sus aventuras amorosas, escandalosamente cómicas. Escenas y elementos de este tipo producen ese efecto de inmoralidad realista e irónica a un tiempo, que, contribuyendo a un ambiente de tensión nerviosa, tanto gusta a ingleses y españoles por un igual.

Las traducciones francesas de la obra de Lillo aparecieron ya a mediados de siglo, mientras que en España no las realizaron antes de finales y cuando las hicieron fue por medio del francés y de la mano de dramaturgos menos dotados y de carácter popular. En Francia Louis Sébastien Mercier publicó en 1769 una refundición, escrita en prosa y en cinco actos como la obra original, titulada *Jenneval, ou le Barnevelt Français*, que situaba la acción en París y que incluía las alabanzas a la dignidad del comercio, así como los elementos melodramáticos. En 1770 Pierre-Augustin Caron de Beaumarchais adapta el texto inglés en su obra *Les Deux Amis, ou le Négociant de Lyon*, y en 1771 lo hace Charles-Georges Fenouillot de Falbaire de Quingey en su *Le Fabricant de Londres* ('Drame en cinq actes et en prose'). La influencia que ejercieron estas obras, combinada con la proclamación que hizo Carlos III de España sobre la dignidad del comercio y del trabajo manual y con el desarrollo de la prensa en el país, que contribuyó a difundir temas internacionales de carácter social, hizo que en el último cuarto de siglo fueran apareciendo en España traducciones o adaptaciones de las obras francesas las cuales incluían los temas comerciales.

Éste es el caso, por ejemplo, de la obra *Las ceguedades del vicio y peligros del rigor. El joven Carlos* de Manuel de Ascargorta, fechada en 1776, que adapta, también en cinco actos, la obra de Mercier, pero convirtiéndola en verso, y situando la acción en España; en ella se pone gran énfasis en lo emocional del drama.[5] En 1782 Antonio Valladares publica en verso y tres actos su *Los perfectos comerciantes* y en 1783, también en verso, pero en cuatro actos, su *El fabricante de paños, o el comerciante inglés*; ambas obras son bastante distantes del original inglés, y la segunda de ellas adapta directamente el texto de Fenouillot de Falbaire.[6] En *Los perfectos comerciantes*, de argumento bastante pueril, aparecen sin embargo importantes referencias a una ética moderna del comercio. Uno de los personajes, un mercante, negándose a vender el honor del comercio, dice, en alusión a las bancarrotas artificialmente provocadas:

Lorenzo. . . . eso sería
perdernos más.
[. . .]
El que quiebra por desgracia,
es digno de compasión;
mas quebrar con depravada
intención, es un delito
capital,
[. . .]; pues quebranta
la ley del comercio; y burla
a las ajenas confianzas.

Y comenta un amigo:

Patricio. ¡Qué honradez! Ah, si así todos
los comerciantes pensaran,
¡qué feliz fuera el comercio!

5 Hay un manuscrito de *Las ceguedades del vicio y peligros del rigor. El joven Carlos* de Manuel Ascargorta en la Biblioteca Nacional, Madrid, con fecha de 1776. Hay otro manuscrito (titulado *El joven Carlos*) en la Biblioteca Municipal, Madrid, con fechas de 1803 y 1804. Fue representada en 1803 y 1804 en el Teatro de los Caños (ver Herrera Navarro, *Catálogo de autores teatrales del siglo XVIII*, 34; René Andioc y Mireille Coulon, *Cartelera teatral madrileña del siglo XVIII (1708–1808)*, 2 vols [Toulouse: Presses Universitaires du Mirail, Univ. de Toulouse-Le Mirail, 1996], II, 748).

6 La Biblioteca Municipal de Madrid tiene un manuscrito de *Los perfectos comerciantes* de Antonio Valladares de Sotomayor, con censura de 1782, y otro de *El fabricante de paños, o el comerciante inglés*, con censura de 1783. *Los perfectos comerciantes* se representó en los teatros de Madrid en 1782, 1783, 1785 y 1787 (ver Andioc y Coulon, *Cartelera teatral madrileña*, II, 810). *El fabricante de paños, o el comerciante inglés* fue representada en los teatros de Madrid en 1783, 1784, 1785, 1787, 1794 etc.; y fue impresa sin lugar, impresor ni año (ver Herrera Navarro, *Catálogo de autores teatrales del siglo XVIII*, 454, 457; Coe, *Catálogo bibliográfico y crítico*, 94; Andioc y Coulon, *Cartelera teatral madrileña*, II, 717). Lafarga menciona otra versión de la traducción de Valladares titulada *El comerciante inglés*, 'comedia nueva en prosa', y 'en cinco actos', impresa en Barcelona: Carlos Gibért y Tutó, s.a. (ver Francisco Lafarga, *Las traducciones españolas del teatro francés (1700–1835)* [Barcelona: Ediciones de la Universidad de Barcelona, 1983], 75).

En una edición barcelonesa no fechada apareció la traducción de la obra de Beaumarchais titulada *Los dos amigos, o sea el negociante de León.*[7] Importa notar que el autor de esta obra, Domingo Botti, no la convirtió en verso sino que optó por seguir el ejemplo de Beaumarchais escribiendo su traducción en prosa, además de acentuar sobre todo el tema de la amistad. Pero quizá la obra que más se aproximó al texto de Lillo fue el drama escrito por Gaspar Zavala y Zamora titulado *El triunfo del amor y la amistad, Jenwal y Faustina*, que se representó en 1793 y se imprimió en 1804 y que derivaba directamente de Mercier;[8] en ella se llega a incluir alusiones a los derechos de la mujer, especialmente en lo que se refiere a los asuntos matrimoniales. Hubo muchas otras obras influidas por *The London Merchant*, pero que están más alejadas del texto de Lillo, aunque sí incluían diálogos de tono realista en torno a problemas comerciales y que también experimentaban con la presentación de recursos melodramáticos y elementos de excesiva sensibilidad, inspirados en las escenas incidentales del drama inglés. Entre las menos exageradas de ellas podríamos citar la de José Concha *El buen criado*, de 1775,[9] y una anónima titulada *El comerciante de Burdeos*,[10] derivada de la obra de Falbaire, que insiste en que no es humillante para la clase aristocrática unirse en matrimonio con alguien perteneciente al mundo del comercio, revistiendo así a éste de una dignidad no reconocida en épocas anteriores.

Está claro, por consiguiente, que *The London Merchant* fue fuente innegable de inspiración ideológica para el teatro de la Ilustración con temas sociales. Sin embargo, tanto el público inglés como sobre todo el español acabaron cansándose, e incluso riéndose, de tanto sentimentalismo en tantos dramas de asuntos domésticos, los cuales razonaban de forma tan poco artística y tan prosaica acerca de los temas citados. Entre los autores españoles más prolíficos de tales tragedias domésticas o burguesas se encuentran los ya citados Comella, Valladares y Zavala y Zamora. Comella,

---

7 *Los dos amigos, o sea el negociante de León* de Domingo Botti, comedia en cinco actos y en prosa, se representó en el Teatro de la Cruz el 14 de octubre de 1807; fue impresa en Barcelona: Librería de Juan Francisco Piferrer s.a. (ver Herrera Navarro, *Catálogo de autores teatrales del siglo XVIII*, 55; Coe, *Catálogo bibliográfico y crítico*, 48–49).

8 En la Biblioteca Nacional, Madrid hay un manuscrito de *El triunfo del amor y la amistad, Jenwal y Faustina* de Zavala y Zamora, descrita como 'comedia original en tres actos en prosa', con 'licencia para la impresión de Madrid, 24 de enero de 1804'. Según Herrera Navarro, fue representada en el Teatro de la Cruz, el 25 de agosto de 1793 (*Catálogo de autores teatrales del siglo XVIII*, 497); y hubo otras representaciones en 1803, 1804, 1805, 1807 y 1813 (ver Coe, *Catálogo bibliográfico y crítico*, 126; Andioc y Coulon, *Cartelera teatral madrileña*, II, 868; Emilio Cotarelo y Mori, *Isidoro Máiquez y el teatro de su tiempo* [Madrid: Imprenta de José Perales y Martínez, 1902], 756).

9 Hay dos manuscritos de *El buen criado* de José Concha, 'pequeña pieza seria moral', en la Biblioteca Nacional, Madrid, fechados en Cádiz en 1775. Se representó esta pieza, en un acto y en prosa, en el Teatro del Príncipe entre el 28 y 30 de junio de 1793 (ver Herrera Navarro, *Catálogo de autores teatrales del siglo XVIII*, 126).

10 Hay un manuscrito incompleto y sin fecha de *El comerciante de Burdeos* en la Biblioteca Nacional.

hombre de orígenes artesanales, tuvo siempre un cierto resentimiento contra las clases altas y en sus obras aprovechó para prodigarse en incluir ideas extranjerizantes y modernas, tanto si venían de Lillo como de Richardson—sobre todo de la novela de éste *Clarissa*. Comella no supo moderarse en la inclusión de escenas excesivamente lacrimógenas, con demasiados inocentes oprimidos injustamente o pobres exageradamente desgraciados, con lo cual su teatro fue ampliamente criticado. Un ejemplo parecido a este tipo de drama lo encontramos en la obra de Francisco Durán *La industriosa madrileña, y el Fabricante de Olot, o los efectos de la aplicación*, comedia en tres actos, la cual fue estrenada en el Teatro del Príncipe de Madrid en 1790;[11] en ella se ven reflejados los esfuerzos de las autoridades ilustradas de la época por introducir en España métodos y maquinaria extranjeros con el fin de modernizar el comercio. Su protagonista, disfrazada de hombre, ha aprendido a copiar los tejidos de algodón extranjeros, y el fabricante de paños con el que ella se hospeda acaba recibiendo la Cruz de Carlos III por su ejemplaridad industrial. El fracaso de la obra al estrenarse no resulta extraño ante tanto didactismo. Y lo mismo sucedió con una obra similar de Comella, *El pueblo feliz*;[12] eran obras demasiado 'ejemplares', faltas de sutileza y del sentido de moderación.

Ahora bien, los fracasos pueden a veces tener una influencia indirecta y tanto Comella como otros dramaturgos—especialmente Valladares y Zavala y Zamora—acabaron por aprender a dar más vida a la propaganda de la Ilustración y a mejorar su técnica de debatir sobre problemas cotidianos en dramas de otro género y de envergadura más recia. Aprendieron, en efecto, a modernizar el drama heroico—un teatro que en el Siglo de Oro gozó de gran éxito gracias a su acción viva, a su sentido de lo aventuresco, a su ambiente positivo etc.—, introduciendo en él temas y tesis sociales. De aquí que utilizaran con gran frecuencia argumentos y escenas militares, con especial énfasis en los episodios de batallas, creando así aparatosos espectáculos bélicos mediante el uso de moderna maquinaria escénica, rasgo no totalmente ajeno al fenómeno del auge de la ópera italiana. Sus protagonistas históricos solían ser relativamente modernos y extranjeros: Federico II de Prusia, María Teresa de Austria, Gustavo Adolfo de Suecia, etc., personajes todos ellos portadores de ideas modernas respecto a la educación, a la tolerancia ante las nuevas ideas científicas, a las nuevas técnicas militares, a la reforma de las cárceles, a la justicia en el gobierno de los pueblos, etc. Eran personajes que pertenecían a una especie de utopía extranjera y que propagaban sus ideas de forma menos directa o tosca o

11 Ver Herrera Navarro, *Catálogo de autores teatrales del siglo XVIII*, 153.

12 Hay un manuscrito (incompleto) de *El pueblo feliz* de Comella, comedia en cuatro actos, en la Biblioteca Municipal, Madrid. La obra se estrenó el 9 de septiembre de 1789. Volvió a representarse en 1790, 1791, 1793 y 1800 (ver Herrera Navarro, *Catálogo de autores teatrales del siglo XVIII*, 117–18; Coe, *Catálogo bibliográfico y crítico*, 189; Andioc y Coulon, *Cartelera teatral madrileña*, II, 826).

emocionada que los aprendices, comerciantes o fabricantes, típicos de las tragedias burguesas femeninamente lacrimosas.

Estos protagonistas heroicos poseían una profundidad de carácter mejor dibujada que la de los pobres aprendices; tampoco eran inverosímilmente valientes—como los antiguos del drama áureo—, sino que tenían sus momentos de dudas y miedo, los cuales exteriorizaban de forma indirecta mediante reacciones nerviosas: procuraban, en fin, ser más humanos y modernos que sus antecesores, los monarcas del teatro de Siglo de Oro, aunque frecuentamente resultaran algo excéntricos. Se trataba de dotarlos de una inseguridad interior, en vez de revestirlos de confianza ciega; su fin era el de demostrar la dificultad e importancia de conseguir el autodominio, a pesar de su nerviosidad, en situaciones de graves conflictos y dificultades.

Comella cultivó con frecuencia este género, como por ejemplo en la obra *Federico II, rey de Prusia*, de 1768, o en *El fénix de los criados, o María Teresa de Austria*, de 1791,[13] obra ésta en la que la emperatriz elogia propagandísticamente el descubrimiento médico de la vacunación, tema que había provocado en España polémicas acerca de sus implicaciones morales y que Comella defiende aquí vigorosamente haciendo que María Teresa someta a sus propios hijos al experimento médico de la vacuna.

No tenemos, por consiguiente, en este teatro militar o heroico un sucesor digno del teatro heroico del Siglo de Oro, pero sí hay en él un experimento temático de la mayor importancia, ya que servía para acostumbrar a los dramaturgos a adaptarse al clima del Siglo de las Luces y a preparar el camino para nuevas formas de expresión artística más maduras y más logradas. Sería injusto despreciar a los Comellas, Valladares y Zabalas, ya que fueron ellos los que llevaron a cabo la parte más difícil de la transición, y merecen, por consiguiente—desde el punto de vista teórico—, un justo respeto.

13 Ver el manuscrito de *Federico II, rey de Prusia* de Comella, con censuras de 1788 y 1789, en la Biblioteca Municipal, Madrid. Este drama se representó en el Teatro del Príncipe en 1789 (ver Coe, *Catálogo bibliográfico y crítico*, 96–97). Volvió a representarse en 1795, 1798, 1802, 1804 y 1805 (ver Andioc y Coulon, *Cartelera teatral madrileña*, II, 720). Cotarelo se refiere a una representación en 1815 'en el Príncipe, durante varios días, [de] la antigua comedia de Comella, *Federico II*, representada por Máiquez y vista el día 7 de febrero por el propio Fernando VII que fue al teatro' (*Isidoro Máiquez y el teatro de su tiempo*, 377). La Biblioteca Municipal, Madrid también tiene un manuscrito de *El fénix de los criados, o María Teresa de Austria*, con censura de 1791. Esta obra se representó en el Teatro del Príncipe del 11 al 20 de junio de 1791. Volvió a representarse en 1793, 1794, 1797, 1798, 1802, 1804, 1810, 1812 y 1819 (ver Herrera Navarro, *Catálogo de autores teatrales del siglo XVIII*, 114; Coe, *Catálogo bibliográfico y crítico*, 98; Andioc y Coulon, *Cartelera teatral madrileña*, II, 720).

Quintana's *Pelayo* Revisited

DONALD L. SHAW
University of Virginia

Inspired by seven years working alongside Ivy McClelland in Glasgow, I have ventured to publish some trifling articles on pre-Romantic drama in Spain[1] (1986, 1988, 1991, 1993, 1997) with the object of adding a few pebbles to the massive cairn erected by Ivy in her definitive *Spanish Drama of Pathos*.[2] I now embrace with nostalgic pleasure the opportunity of contributing a further item to this well-deserved commemorative number of the *Bulletin of Spanish Studies*. Having glanced successively at García de la Huerta and Montiano as tragic playwrights, before passing on to the early theatre of Rivas, I should now like to revisit Quintana's *Pelayo* (1805) which Ivy plainly regarded as the most accomplished tragic drama in the Spain of its day and to examine its technique in more detail than she had space for.[3]

Tragedy in its most familiar, classical form, derived from the Greek tragedians and Aristotle's ideas, points to an intrinsic disharmony in the way things are. It is exploratory of the stresses and strains attendant on the human condition, rather than prescriptive about how to deal with them. With hindsight, we can see that a tragic vision of life in this sense has never taken strong root in Spanish theatre, and that in particular the

1 Donald L. Shaw, 'Dramatic Technique and Tragic Effect in García de la Huerta's *Raquel*', in *Studies for I. L. McClelland*, ed., with an Introduction, by David T. Gies, Special Issue of *Dieciocho: Hispanic Enlightenment, Aesthetics, and Literary Theory*, 9:1–2 (1986), 249–58; '*Ataulfo*: Rivas's First Drama', *HR*, 56:2 (1988), 231–42; 'Montiano's *Athaulpho*', in *The Eighteenth Century in Spain. Essays in Honour of I. L. McClelland*, edited, with an introduction, by Ann L. Mackenzie, *BHS*, LXVIII:1 (1991), 153–61; 'Acerca de *Aliatar* del duque de Rivas', *Entresiglos*, 2 (1993), 237–45; and 'Rivas and Tragedy: The Cases of *El Duque de Aquitania* and *Malek-Adhel*', in *Spain and its Literature. Essays in Memory of E. Allison Peers*, ed., with an Introduction, by Ann L. Mackenzie, TRAC (Textual Research and Criticism) 15 (Liverpool: Liverpool U. P./London: MHRA, 1997), 253–67.

2 I. L. McClelland, *Spanish Drama of Pathos 1750–1808*. I. *High Tragedy*; II. *Low Tragedy*, 2 vols (Liverpool: Liverpool U. P./Toronto: Univ. of Toronto Press, 1970); I. L. McClelland, *'Pathos' dramático en el teatro español de 1750 a 1808*. I. *La alta tragedia*; II. *La tragedia menor*, traducción a cargo de Fernando Huerta Viñas y Guillermina Cenoz del Águila, Hispanic Studies TRAC (Textual Research and Criticism) 7, 2 vols (Liverpool: Liverpool U. P., 1998).

3 McClelland, *Spanish Drama of Pathos 1750–1808*, I, 260–66 (p. 260).

mind-set of the neo-classical and pre-Romantic playwrights in Spain was to some extent inimical to it. Ivy was, as usual, entirely correct when she asserted that (in Spain) 'the Age of Reason, despite its ambitions, could not be an age of successful High Tragedy'.[4] My aim in what follows is, as it was in previous articles, to examine what happened instead. All good drama arises from suspense generated by conflict. In High Tragedy such conflict ideally takes place between equally justified forces, the paradigmatic example being Sophocles' *Antigone*, in which Antigone's moral compulsion to bury her dead brother's corpse is balanced by Creon's reasons of state, which compel him to forbid the interment. It is this kind of conflict which generates true pathos and distinguishes High Tragedies from plays which are merely concerned with an unhappy series of events. But such conflicts tend to be implicitly critical of the way life is and to be subversive of our comfortable presuppositions. Hence they were not congenial to Enlightenment dramatists, least of all in Spain. The result was a tendency either to veer towards a concept of moral tragedy in which, instead of dramatizing the effects of a tragic error which produces disproportionate suffering, the error is the outcome of lack of emotional restraint or an evil disposition on the part of one of the main characters; or towards a concept of heroic tragedy in which any tragic error is offset by noble self-sacrifice. In each case what is important is to discern how these tendencies affected the structure of the play in question and the degree to which the generation of genuine tragic pathos was compromised.

In one of the few really illuminating contributions to the small amount of Quintana criticism which has appeared since *Spanish Drama of Pathos*, Valero situates Quintana's early outlook at the intersection between two attitudes towards human behaviour. He writes:

> Veremos en su producción textual de este período una negociación y a veces confrontación entre dos orientaciones morales, una centrada en el ideal cívico republicano del patriota-guerrero, y otra centrada en conceptos como benevolencia, sensibilidad, y humanidad [...] cuando entran en tensión, ésta se resuelve en favor del 'curso' masculino, de la virtud cívica estoica.[5]

This outlook was to be modified later. But for the period of *Pelayo* there can be no doubt that this quotation accurately summarizes Quintana's views. These reveal, needless to say, that far from belonging to the Romantic movement, as Martínez Torrón attempts to argue,[6] following Sebold's mistaken postulate of a 'primer romanticismo' long before what we normally

4 McClelland, *Spanish Drama of Pathos 1750–1808*, I, 43.

5 José A. Valero, 'Manuel José Quintana y el sublime moral', *HR*, 71:4 (2003), 585–611 (pp. 587–88).

6 Diego Martínez Torrón, *El alba del romanticismo español* (Sevilla: Alfar, 1993), 92.

take to be the start of Romanticism in Spain,[7] Quintana's thought was deeply rooted in Enlightenment ideas and preoccupations. Valero shows convincingly that Quintana fully accepted a notion put into circulation by Edmund Burke in his *Philosophical Enquiry into the Origins of Our Ideas of the Beautiful and the Sublime* (1757) and, more relevantly to Spain, by Hugh Blair in his *Lectures on Rhetoric and Belles Lettres* (1783; Spanish translation 1798–1801). This was that we can distinguish between the sublimity of certain 'feminine' virtues (e.g. sociability, compassion, sympathy and love) and that of 'masculine' ones, such as fortitude, justice and wisdom. Quintana's own version of the latter, which Valero calls 'el sublime cívico', is, according to this critic, in no wise Romantic: 'Es, al contrario, un sublime plenamente clásico, producto de un mundo de significados relativamente estables'.[8]

The importance of Valero's article, for our purpose, lies in the fact that it offers a sound basis for examining the dramatic technique of Quintana's *Pelayo* considered as a tragic play. For, as we analyse its structure we cannot fail to notice that Quintana's whole approach is based on his decision to incorporate the two ideals identified by Valero separately into the characters of the heroine Hormesinda and her brother Pelayo. By this means he is able to exploit the genuine tragic pathos of Hormesinda's situation, while at the same time offsetting its intrinsic subversiveness with Pelayo's heroic call to arms against tyranny. In effect, this division of the play's interest, between Hormesinda's dilemma on the one hand and Pelayo's uncompromising patriotic ideal on the other, underlines what Ivy McClelland suggested: that the Enlightenment was not a period in which true tragedy was likely to flourish. As Antonio Mendoza Fillola puts it: 'puesto que, en opinión de los ilustrados, el signo cerrado de la forma y de la idea trágicas resumía la manifestación artística de una sociedad civilizada y floreciente, el discurso razonado de sus textos, más que plantear inquietudes, ofreció soluciones a los conflictos para *purificar* así al auditorio según la moralidad deseada'.[9]

This is far from being an acceptable formula for tragedy. How does it work in practice? I have suggested elsewhere that a different formula from the traditional one was required: one in which the tragic malignity of things was not denied, but was counterbalanced by heroic nobility of conduct in the individual.[10] This is exactly what happens in *Pelayo*. Let us start by considering Quintana's intentions in the exposition. The play begins with

7 Russell P. Sebold, 'El incesto, el suicidio y el primer romanticismo español', *HR*, 41:4 (1973), 669–92.

8 Valero, 'Manuel José Quintana', 593.

9 Antonio Mendoza Fillola, 'El compromiso colonial y el despotismo en la tragedia neoclásica', in *Coloquio internacional sobre el teatro español del siglo XVIII: Bolonia, 15–18 de octubre de 1985*, ed. Mario di Pinto, Maurizio Fabbri and Rinaldo Froldi, Centro di Studi sul Settecento Spagnolo 3 (Abano Terme: Piovan Editore, 1988), 267–88 (p. 273).

10 '*Ataulfo*: Rivas's First Drama', 235.

the expression by Alfonso of his despair at the pusillanimity of his fellow Spaniards after their defeats by the Moors. To this Veremundo replies with a eulogy of the warrior qualities of Pelayo, tempered by the fact that his presumed death will have saved him from the shame of seeing his sister marry the victorious Munuza, who is now in control of Gijón, where the action is taking place. In these speeches, Quintana is able with great speed and economy not only to provide the audience with the information necessary to understand the action of the play which follows, but also to introduce the three basic dramatic forces which will operate during that action, associated respectively with Hormesinda, Munuza and Pelayo. More importantly, however, we must note Quintana's priorities. Who is here the tragic victim? It is Hormesinda. But the play's opening words do not relate to her. First and foremost Quintana chooses to emphasize the heroism of Pelayo. In this way the opening scene not only prepares us for the suspense of the future conflict, as well as explaining the circumstances and presenting the major characters, but also, by emphasizing the primacy of heroism over tragic pathos, foreshadows the basic ideological thrust of the play.

Veremundo's speech in the middle of the first scene establishes the tragic position in which Hormesinda finds herself, and which justifies a description of the play as a tragedy. To understand the role of Hormesinda we must first understand the place of love in the Enlightenment's scheme of things. The representative writers of the Enlightenment distrusted passion. They saw it, especially in the case of highly-placed powerful figures who needed to act with restraint, as apt to break the bonds of reason and morality and threaten the stability of the community. Love, on the other hand, was seen as a softening, moderating and civilizing influence, ideally wedded to reason, benevolence and moral uplift. The ideal of the Enlightenment was harmony. Passion, associated with violent impulses and instinct, threatened social and domestic harmony. Love, by contrast, implied the victory of nobler emotion over baser nature. This is exactly the case with Hormesinda. Veremundo makes it clear that Munuza had sworn to destroy Gijón, and especially to ravage its Christian churches. Only the supplications of Hormesinda had saved the city. The tragedy of her situation lay in the fact that, in order to dissuade Munuza from razing the city, she was forced to renounce her patriotism, to abandon her brother's ideals and become a comitted collaborator with the hated Moors.

This, then, is the tragic element in the play. In essence, it takes the situation which occurs in García de la Huerta's *Raquel*, a play which seems to have exerted a fascination on some later Enlightenment dramatists, and stands it on its head. In *Raquel* it is the uncontrolled passion of King Alfonso for Raquel which threatens to plunge the kingdom into chaos. In *Pelayo*, it is the love of Hormesinda for Munuza, involving the sacrifice of her allegiance to her nation and submission to an arrogant enemy, which saves Gijón and its inhabitants. This is a genuinely tragic situation and one which in principle generates true pathos. The forces in play are appropriately balanced. On the one hand, devotion to Spain in its hour of need and to the ideals represented by Pelayo, who is, in addition, Hormesinda's brother and entitled to expect her total identification with his own stance. On the other, the safety of the people and the city of Gijón. There is no difficulty in identifying ourselves with both the conflicting influences and in recognizing that Hormesinda has to follow through on the tragic choice she has already been compelled to make. If Quintana had left it at that, the play would have gained in tragic intensity. But the mind-set of the Enlightenment, as in *Raquel*, intervened. The *Ilustrados* found difficulty in accepting tragic situations of this kind for the reason which I have already suggested. They imply an intrinsic malignity in things. What Quintana, like García de la Huerta, believed, or wished to believe, was something different. As I attempted to argue in relation to Montiano's *Ataulpho*,[11] tragedy is not intended to leave us simply with a sense of indignation because life is like it is. Tragedy does not completely contradict our acceptance of the human condition. What it does ideally is to deepen our insight; but residual confidence in some over-arching pattern of values remains. The writers of the Enlightenment, Quintana among them, were not content with this. They wished to believe that tragedy could be used to reconcile the audience to moral values. For that reason, as we see very clearly in both *Raquel* and *Pelayo*, they prefer to see tragedy arising, not from circumstances which, if we were to reflect on them seriously, would undermine our existential confidence, but from the intervention of irrational, human evil. This has the advantage of avoiding the subversiveness of true tragedy; but at the risk of contaminating genuine tragic emotion with mere moral reprobation. At all events, this explains the roles of Rubén and Audalla respectively in *Raquel* and *Pelayo*. These two characters serve as additional tragic agents by injecting evil counsels into a pre-existing unhappy situation. With the reference by Alfonso to Audalla's 'celo fanático y sangriento' at the end of Act I, scene i,[12] the establishment of the dramatic forces is complete and the exposition has fulfilled its purpose.

The rest of Act I reverses the priorities of the first scene; that is to say, in the body of the act Quintana develops Hormesinda's tragic dilemma in a dialogue with Veremundo and Alfonso. This is then followed by the play's first *coup de théâtre* when Pelayo suddenly appears and the tone shifts from pathos to patriotic exaltation, before he learns of what he regards as his sister's teachery. His frenzied reaction provides the climax of the act. In one sense these two sections of Act I reinforce each other: tragic pathos is intensified by tragic irony. The pathos is generated by the fact that

11 'Montiano's *Athaulpho*', 154.

12 Manuel José Quintana, *Obras completas del Excmo. Sr. D. Manuel José Quintana*, BAE XIX (Madrid: Rivadeneyra, 1852; reprinted Madrid: Ediciones Atlas, 1946), 59. All references are to this edition.

Hormesinda is deeply conscious and ashamed of having, in a sense, betrayed her brother's ideals. Although she has fallen in love with Munuza, there is no passionate defence of the rights of such love. On the contrary, Hormesinda's language is predicated on shame, fear, doubt and anguish. Only after enduring harsh criticism from Alfonso does Hormesinda attempt to justify her actions, primarily by presenting them as dictated by the need to save Gijón and its inhabitants, and only secondarily as involving her love for Munuza. At the end of Act I, scene iii she cries out against the cruel destiny which has condemned her to choose marriage to Munuza rather than fidelity to her brother's uncompromising patriotism. We endorse her distress and recognize in her unhappy situation one of those tragic circumstances in which opposing ideals clash and produce undeserved suffering. But now, added to this, Quintana introduces the *plazo*-motif, which Larra in *Macías* and Hartzenbusch in *Los amantes de Teruel* were later to exploit so memorably. Pelayo, that is, arrives just too late to dissuade his sister from marrying the Moor. The *plazo* owes its appearance in this and future plays to the way in which it symbolizes life's hostility; it implies the opportunity to head off a tragic outcome lost at the very last moment.

To this extent, then, Act I of *Pelayo* lays a sound basis for a tragic development of character in Hormesinda during the rest of the play. Her tragic error, if it is an error, is to have fallen in love with a tyrannical enemy of her nation. But otherwise she has acted from the highest of motives and stands high in the moral scale. In the interval between Acts I and II, Hormesinda and Munuza are married. But this does not mean that Hormesinda has come to terms with the necessity of placating her husband. She remains haunted by shame at that which circumstances have forced her to do. Although she insists to Munuza:

> no me arrepiento,
> Soy vuestra, lo seré ... (II, i) (62)

she nevertheless regards her marriage vows as 'fatales palabras'. Still, the two forces outlined in Act I sustain her. On the one hand, she declares, she is defending her defeated fellow countrymen. On the other she is surrendering to an 'afecto imperioso', a 'tierno y dulce amor' (62). The question which now arises is whether in the rest of the play she undergoes a development of character which increases her tragic stature and deepens her insight through suffering. Tragedy requires vacillation and inner struggle, with which the audience can identify. The traditional vehicle by means of which such psychological stress is manifested is the soliloquy. We notice that Hormesinda has no soliloquies. Such development of her personality as takes place occurs in the *escena madre* of Act II, when she is confronted by Pelayo and called to account by him for her actions. Initially Hormesinda is trapped in a tragic situation, surrounded by defeat and believing her brother to be dead.

But does she rise in tragic stature when he suddenly reappears and bitterly reproaches her? To a certain extent, she does. While at first in Act II, scene vi, in order to mollify her brother, she refers to her marriage as 'mi caída' (64) and as a detestable error, when he wildly demands that she should flee with him to organize resistance in the mountains, she sheds her submissiveness and proudly proclaims her love for Munuza. With this her characterization undoubtedly progresses. In her final speech, the climactic words of Act II:

> Mi suplicio está aquí dentro;
> No es posible mayor para Hormesinda (65)

stamp her as a genuine figure of tragic pathos.

But what happens next? In five-act plays in this period, Act III is commonly the pivotal act. This is clearly the case in *Pelayo*. Hitherto, as I have suggested, the stress has been on the 'feminine' virtues of love and self-sacrifice, rising to a climax as Hormesinda finds in the former the strength to defy her brother and maintain her bridal vow to remain faithful to Munuza whatever the cost to her relationship with Pelayo:

> PELAYO ¡Promesa impía!
> HORMESINDA Yo la dije, él la oyó, mi pecho nunca
> La negará. (II, vi) (65)

But now the emphasis shifts to the 'masculine' qualities of courage and honour. The essential feature of the technique of Act III is that both Hormesinda and Munuza are off-stage for the entire act. In other words, the tragic situation, having been clearly delineated in Act I and having been developed through the clash of personalities at the end of Act II, is suddenly abandoned and replaced by heroics. Let us clearly understand what this means. At the beginning of Act III, *Pelayo* abruptly changes course. Hitherto the first force in the play has been that associated with Hormesinda, ground between the upper and nether millstones of patriotism on the one hand and the safety of her fellow-citizens on the other, with love assisting her in her decision to marry Munuza. The counterforce has been Pelayo, defeated at every point, since the moral position of Hormesinda is unassailable. At this stage in the play Pelayo's only weapon is frantic rhetoric, which beats in vain against the *force majeur* of the threat to Gijón and Hormesinda's love for Munuza. Munuza, meanwhile, despite the urging of Audalla, has played a totally passive role. Now all of this changes. What it amounts to is that the two themes of the play are developed separately and contradict one another in their implications. The first theme, involving Hormesinda, implies man's subjection to adverse fate, underlined by Pelayo's arrival too late to affect the issue of his sister's marriage. The second theme, centring on Pelayo, conversely implies man's ability through heroic action to overcome adversity. This is the theme which is developed in Act III.

The immediate result is twofold. From the point of view of the play as a tragedy, the action is stopped in its tracks. With Hormesinda off stage no further development of her character during the act is possible. From the point of view of the play simply as a dramatic artefact, what happens is that there is a rearrangement of the dramatic forces in conflict. In Acts I and II the opposing forces were those associated with Hormesinda and Pelayo. In Act III, however, this conflict is alluded to only insofar as it adds an extra dimension to Pelayo's resolve to head an insurrection against Munuza. When he attempts to decline the leadership of the rebellion because of his dishonour, Alfonso counters his reluctance with encouragement:

> No es dado a una mujer frívola y débil
> Manchar la gloria y trasladar su afrenta
> A aquel que sin cesar sus pasos guía
> Del honor y virtud por la ardua senda.
> Ese escándalo torpe que te ofende,
> En lugar de apocarte, te engrandezca. (III, iii) (67)

The tragic pathos built up in the first two acts is now brushed aside and a quite different issue is debated during most of this act. This is the question of whether prudent submission to what may be God's punishment of the Spanish for the 'ocio y molicie' of their rulers is preferable to an insurrection which may turn out to be a forlorn hope. This is the part of the play which brings to the fore what Valero calls Quintana's 'sublime cívico'. With its obvious relevance to the contemporary threat to Spain from Napoleonic France, it clearly explains *Pelayo*'s popularity. But it brings the action of the play down from the universal to the national level. What is gained in patriotic appeal is lost in terms of tragic pathos. At this point, Pelayo could have risen to acquire a tragic stature rivalling that of his sister. That is: he could have been presented as torn between the desire for Hormesinda's happiness and for the safety of Gijón on the one hand, and his role as leader of the Spanish resistance to Moorish domination on the other. But this is not what interests Quintana. Pelayo never really vacillates and is never shown as having to make a tragic choice. There is a conflict: that between Vermundo as the voice of caution, and the bellicosity of Alfonso and the other warriors on the stage. But it is not a tragic conflict. In any case Quintana at the end of the act tips the scales by introducing the announcement that the inhabitants of Gijón will either have to accept Islamization or be enslaved. Thereafter no more deliberation is necessary. In essence the function of Act III is to substitute the communal conflict for the private one which has involved Hormesinda in the first two acts. Thereby a new counterforce is built up, collective instead of individual, and directed against Munuza and the Moorish invaders. The attention of the audience is orientated in a fresh direction and Hormesinda's situation fades into the background.

That is where it remains. In Act IV the play begins to progress on its new course. When at the beginning of the act Hormesinda reappears on stage followed by Munuza, we might be forgiven for expecting that the action will swing back into the tragic mode with a big scene between the newly-weds in which the fate of the citizens of Gijón will once more be in the balance. Instead, Hormesinda merely repeats to her companion, Alvida the justification for her marriage and laments the fact that Pelayo's return has largely nullified her efforts on behalf of the city and its people. It has undermined the 'templanza y quietud' of the now subject-people with the result that Munuza has turned against her, so that she is now

> ... odiosa a un tiempo
> a mi hermano, a mi amante. (IV, i) (68)

Her despair is at its peak; but it finds no outlet in a verbal exchange with Munuza, who merely sends her away. At the same time we observe that his affectionateness in Act II has suddenly given place to vengeful suspiciousness, in which he is encouraged by Audalla. The play has in fact gone round a corner. Hormesinda has been momentarily pushed aside, and the conflict is now between Pelayo and Munuza. Quintana's problem at this point is to figure out how to integrate action on the part of Hormesinda into the new alignment of forces. So far, these have not clashed directly, since Pelayo has not yet confronted Munuza. Now the confrontation takes place as Munuza, suspecting collusion between Hormesinda and the two young Spanish warriors who pretend that they have simply come to announce Pelayo's death to her, decides to interrogate them. This is the weakest part of the plot. Pelayo and his companion-in-arms Leandro, having decided on rebellion, have inexplicably made no attempt to conceal themselves from Munuza, and are now discovered by him in Veremundo's house. Instead of continuing to play the role of a stranger passing through the city on his way to exile, Pelayo arrogantly defies Munuza with irreponsible temerity, and thereby forfeits his leadership of the insurrection which is about to break out. Why does Quintana place him in this unlikely position? The function of Act IV, scene iv is to ratchet up the dramatic intensity when Pelayo, in return for his temerity, is condemned to death by Munuza, egged on my Audalla, while the same fate awaits the other rebellious Spanish nobles in the city. This is the signal, now that all appears to have been lost, for Hormesinda to reveal Pelayo's identity and attempt to assume the blame for everything that has been happening. As she declares that she has failed in her duty both to Munuza and to Pelayo, calling on the former to kill her rather than her brother, we see that this scene is in effect the lowest point in the play's dramatic parabola and is intentionally designed to contrast with the successful outcome of the uprising in the last act.

Once more we see the relevance of Valero's distinction, previously mentioned. Pelayo's noble defiance of the all-powerful Munuza illustrates Quintana's notion of the 'civic sublime', with its 'masculine' virtues of courage and patriotic pride. By contrast Hormesinda's behaviour expresses the 'feminine' sublime, via submission and self-sacrifice on the altar of love. However, we have left tragedy behind and are coming perilously close to melodrama. In Acts I and II Hormesinda faced a true tragic dilemma and her situation evoked true tragic pathos. But in Act IV her situation, which earlier had been characterized by an internal struggle of allegiances, has been replaced by an external threat as Pelayo is condemned to execution. This produces a despairing gesture by Hormesinda, but it is not one which involves an authentic tragic choice. Her death would solve nothing. For this scene to produce more pathos it would be necessary for Hormesinda to accept death at the hands of her husband as the price of Pelayo's freedom. But this is not at issue. Munuza simply ignores her gesture and consigns both his wife and the two young warriors to captivity.

In addition, Act IV of *Pelayo* illustrates afresh the Enlightenment dramatists' tendency to try to replace the malignity of things as the source of tragedy by errors of judgment, uncontrolled passion or hearkening to evil counsels. Where we see this tendency at work is in the change which takes place in Munuza between Act II and Act IV. In Act II he is a caring and considerate husband. In Act IV, encouraged by the fanatical Audalla, he has abandoned love and reason, jumping to the conclusion that his newly-wedded wife is probably complicitous with his enemies. At the same time his mild treatment of Gijón and its inhabitants under the softening influence of Hormesinda's love has been replaced by his decision to convert the citizens by force or condemn them to slavery. This unmotivated change in Munuza's outlook and behaviour is a key-element in the play as a whole because of the way in which it reveals Quintana's determination to connect tragic events to moral lapses, rather than to the sheer injustice of life. What precipitates the tragic outcome in *Pelayo* is not something intrinsic to the human condition, but fanaticism and vengefulness.

The climax of the play in Act V brings a further twist of tragic irony when Hormesinda takes advantage of the insurrection which has broken out to liberate Pelayo from his dungeon. Here, if anywhere in the play, we might have expected vacillation and soliloquy as Hormesinda debated with herself how to make her decision. Foreseeably it would set her brother against her husband. But now Pelayo has seized centre stage from his sister. There is no time for vacillation on her part. Unwisely hoping that he will simply flee, she releases him only to see him plunge into the armed struggle against Munuza and the Moorish garrison. The outcome is a foregone conclusion: Munuza, defeated, takes refuge in the Alcázar, where he comes upon his wife. Now the situation is symmetrically reversed. Having saved Pelayo from execution, Hormesinda now prepares to save her husband from her brother and his men. There is the potential for harmony to be reestablished, with the 'feminine' sublime operating successfully alongside the 'masculine' civic sublime. But the possibility is destroyed by an act of irrational and uncontrolled passion as Munuza kills first Hormesinda and then himself. In this last act pathos and heroism go hand in hand: Hormesinda, for the last time, in scene iii laments the tragic choice she has had to make between husband and brother, while Pelayo after his release vanquishes Moorish oppression. The tragic plot is complete when Munuza takes vengeance on Hormesinda, but by then his character has fallen in the moral scale. We understand his action, but it does not carry with it a sense of tragic inevitability: it is the vengeful act of a less than noble individual. It conveys, not the impression of the tearfulness of things, but the notion that moral failure is the root cause of suffering. Some of the Romantics were to go to the opposite extreme and show men struggling in vain against adverse fate. The results in both cases are flawed tragedies.

Power, Opposition and Enlightenment in Moratín's *El sí de las niñas*

SALLY-ANN KITTS
University of Bristol

When it comes to exploring women's experience of Enlightenment in Spain, the Neo-classic theatre seems a useful place to focus attention. For not only were women involved with the theatre on every level—as consumers, actors, subjects and, increasingly, as playwrights—but the central tenet of Neo-classical thought, 'enseñar deleitando' meant that the theatre was one of the key methods through which Enlightenment discourse was disseminated.[1] These key notions of women and Enlightenment come together in what is arguably the most successful example of Spanish Neo-classic theatre, Leandro Fernández de Moratín's *El sí de las niñas*, a play about women's experience of society, family, education, love and marriage, first performed in 1806. It is also a play that is very much a product of Enlightenment discourse, both exploring the position of women in relation to it and using the controlling power of discourse to bring about modifications to the behaviour and attitudes of men and women from within its boundaries which delimit what is to be considered normal and acceptable.

In this article, I offer a new reading of the play based on a re-examination of the interactions of the central characters, comparing in particular the relationship between, on the one hand doña Irene and her daughter doña Francisca, and on the other don Diego and his nephew don Carlos.

---

1 Moratín's own formulation of Neo-classical dramatic theory can be found in the prologue to his *Obras dramáticas y líricas*:

> Imitación en diálogo (escrito en prosa o verso) de un suceso ocurrido en un lugar y en pocas horas, entre personas particulares: por medio del cual, y de la oportuna expresión de afectos y carácteres, resultan puestos en ridículo los vicios y errores comunes de la sociedad, y recomendadas, por consiguiente, la verdad y la virtud.

See Leandro Fernández de Moratín, *Obras dramáticas y líricas de D. Leandro Fernández de Moratín* (Paris: Imprenta de A. Coniam, 1826), xvii. All quotations from *El sí de las niñas* are taken from Leandro Fernández de Moratín, *'La comedia nueva' y 'El sí de las niñas'*, ed. John Dowling y René Andioc (Madrid: Castalia, 1968) with references in the text given by act- and scene-numbers.

Comparing and contrasting their various exchanges in the play, I will draw on a number of theoretical contexts to reveal the extent to which the play is composed around a central pole of oppositions that are designed to exalt the apparently reasonable behaviour of Diego in and through direct contrast with the supposedly unreasonable behaviour of Irene. Once this essentially gendered nature of the play's composition, and, indeed, of most readings of it so far, is revealed, I will then be in a position to offer an alternative reading of the play based on an analysis of the actions, behaviour and ideas of the four central characters. Drawing on the links established by Foucault between power and discourse, I will reassess the workings of gender within *El sí de las niñas* and endeavour to offer a better understanding of the relative positions of inclusion and exclusion of men and women in Enlightenment discourse.

Discourse is defined as 'ways of specifying particular "truths" or bodies of knowledge at particular times in history. [...] The ideas embodied in a discourse are generated by the socio-political interests of a group, which defines what is "normal" [...] and what is "abnormal"'.[2] As regards Enlightenment discourse, this involves 'a shared currency of images and idioms' expressed through keywords such as reason, nature, self-control, and moderation.[3] In exploring its workings in *El sí de las niñas*, my aim is to throw some light on how the language of Enlightenment discourse is constituted, disseminated and controlled by those with the power to employ it, since 'posing for discourse the question of power means basically to ask whom does discourse serve'.[4] In terms of Spanish Enlightenment discourse, the answer is men like Moratín or his literary counterpart don Diego. Yet what I hope to show is that while women did not have direct access to this power, they could make successful attempts to manipulate it and work it to their advantage. This situation is revealed in *El sí de las niñas* once the key gendered construction of the pole of oppositions that places Diego on the positive and Irene on the negative is revealed to be tainted and its authority thereby undermined.

2 Teresa Fuentes Peris, 'Drink and Social Stability: Discourses of Power in Galdós's *Fortunata y Jacinta*', *BHS* (Liverpool), LXXIII (1996), 63–77 (p. 64). My use of the term 'discourse' has also been informed by Caroline Ramazanoglu, 'Introduction', in *Up against Foucault: Explorations of Some of the Tensions between Foucault and Feminism*, ed. Caroline Ramazanoglu (London: Routledge, 1993), 1–24 (pp. 18–24), and by Paul A. Bové, 'Discourse', in *Critical Terms for Literary Study*, ed. Frank Lentricchia and Thomas McLaughlin (Chicago: Univ. of Chicago Press, 1995), 50–65.

3 Roy Porter, *Enlightenment: Britain and the Creation of the Modern World* (London: Penguin, 2001), 48.

4 Alessandro Fontana and Pasquale Pasquino interviewing Foucault on 'Truth and Power', in *The Foucault Reader*, ed. Paul Rabinow (Harmondsworth: Penguin, 1991), 51–75 (p. 57).

Moratín's *El sí de las niñas* has pride of place in the literary canon of Spanish Neo-classicism and has been seen over the years as a prime exponent of the philosophical tradition of the Spanish Enlightenment. Earlier views that saw the play as an affirmation of women's rights to freedom of expression and choice of social status have been replaced by more measured opinions of it as a prime example of Moratín's 'school for wives', an affirmation of the patriarchal ideology of the Enlightenment that sought to bring a measure of freedom to women's lives, in terms of a limited education and the choice of whether and whom to marry, while at the same time reinforcing the limitations of their subordinate position both in society and in the home.[5] Yet criticism has remained unswayed in seeing Diego as the Enlightened hero, the exemplary modern man who exercises self-control and moderation in all things, bringing his reason to bear on an emotionally charged situation that was truthfully reflective of contemporary society.[6] Through his wise and paternal intervention, disaster is avoided and a happy conclusion brought about. Some even see him as a reflection of Moratín himself.[7]

In these interpretations, Diego's position as man of reason and moderation, advocating and employing a discreet and persuasive authority, is reinforced and highlighted through the presence of the negative figure of Irene.[8] She is seen as the obstacle that stands in the

5 See, for example, Sylvia Vollmar, 'The Position of Woman in Spain As Seen in Spanish Literature', *Hispania* (USA), 8 (1925), 370–71; María del Pilar Oñate, *El feminismo en la literatura española* (Madrid: Espasa-Calpe, 1938); Kathleen Kish, 'A School for Wives: Women in Eighteenth-Century Spanish Theater', in *Women in Hispanic Literature. Icons and Fallen Idols*, ed. Beth Miller (Berkeley: Univ. of California Press, 1983), 184–200; Bernardita M. Llanos, 'Integración de la mujer al proyecto de la ilustración en España', *Ideologies and Literature,* 4 (1989), 199–223.

6 See, for example, John A. Cook, *Neo-classic Drama in Spain: Theory and Practice* (Dallas: Southern Methodist U. P., 1959), 101; Loreto Busquets, 'Iluminismo e ideal burgués en *El sí de las niñas*', <http://www.cervantesvirtual.com/FichaObra.html?Ref=10155> (consulted 15 November 2007) (also available in *Segismundo,* 37–38 [1983], 61–88); René Andioc, *Teatro y sociedad en el Madrid del siglo XVIII* (Madrid: Castalia, 1987 [1st ed. Madrid: Fundación Juan March/Editorial Castalia, 1976]), 487–88; Llanos, 'Integración de la mujer', 217–19; Leandro Fernández de Moratín, *La comedia nueva. El sí de las niñas*, ed., prólogo y notas de Jesús Pérez-Magallón; estudio preliminar de Fernando Lázaro Carreter (Barcelona: Crítica, 1994), 71; Philip Deacon, 'Introduction', in Leandro Fernández de Moratín, *El sí de las niñas,* ed. Philip Deacon (Bristol: Bristol Classical Press, 1995), xxix; Julio Prieto Martínez, 'El sí de los súbditos: Leandro Fernández de Moratín y la escenografía neoclásica del poder', *Hispania* (USA), 81 (1998), 490–500 (p. 496).

7 Russell P. Sebold, 'Autobiografía y realismo en *El sí de las niñas* de Moratín', in *Coloquio internacional sobre Leandro Fernández de Moratín, Bolonia, 27–29 de octubre 1978*, ed. Mario di Pinto, Maurizio Fabbri y Rinaldo Froldi (Abano Terme: Piovan Editore, 1980), 213–27 (p. 220).

8 Andioc, *Teatro y sociedad,* 468; Prieto Martínez, 'El sí de los súbditos', 492; Emilio Martínez Mata, 'Introducción', in Leandro Fernández de Moratín, *El sí de las niñas,* ed. Emilio Martínez Mata (Madrid: Cátedra, 2005 [1st ed. 2002]), 50.

way of the true path of enlightenment, as a representative of a stagnant and excessively oppressive tradition of upbringing. She is portrayed time and again as a self-seeking, uneducated, irrational woman, silly, scheming and fickle.[9] She represents the voice of unreason in the would-be forward-looking world of the late eighteenth and early nineteenth centuries, demonstrating the abuse of parental authority as she forces her daughter into a socially and financially advantageous but loveless marriage against her will. As Prieto Martínez notes: 'La estructura argumentativa de *El sí de las niñas* está, así pues, construida en torno a esta dicotomía que opone las figuras de Diego e Irene y, con ellas, dos concepciones antagónicas de la autoridad'.[10]

In setting out the case for seeing Diego as a model of persuasive authority, Prieto Martínez offers a highly convincing interpretation of the play that identifies Moratín's aim in the work as the presentation of 'una concepción flexible y económica del poder—una concepción "ilustrada"—que tiende a invisibilizarlo, a disminuir su intensidad, a fin de multiplicar su extensión y eficacia'.[11] His view of Moratín as a man above all of order, stability and moderation, is based on his reading of Moratin's experience specifically of the early 1790s, following the French Revolution, and concurs with that of Maravall who also describes Moratín as having 'una mentalidad moderada' as a result of his experience of the turbulent decades following the events of 1789.[12] Using the Foucauldian idea of the 'punitive city' as the site of 'hundreds of tiny theatres of punishment', Prieto Martínez explores the idea of Neo-classic theatre as 'otra forma de "disciplina espèctacular" ' and makes a strong case for seeing Moratín as expounding 'una concepción ilustrada del poder, que ahora se pone a la altura del súbdito para "educarlo": se hace (engañosamente) legible, accesible; se aproxima al súbdito para mejor dominarlo'.[13] This is a strategy found in many writings in eighteenth-century Spain, a particularly notable example being in the debates on woman's social role in the Periodical Press of the 1760s, where authors

9 See, for example, Sebold, 'Autobiografía y realismo', 217; Alberto Lista, 'Teatros. *El sí de las niñas*: comedia en tres actos en prosa', *El Censor*, 11 [1821], 339, quoted in Philip Deacon, 'La comicidad de Doña Irene en *El sí de las niñas* de Leandro Fernández de Moratín', in *Risas y sonrisas en el teatro de los siglos XVIII y XIX*, ed. Josep María Sala Valldaura, *Scriptura* (Lleida) 15 (1999), 145–58 (p. 150); *El sí de las niñas*, ed Pérez-Magallón, 77–78; Antonietta Calderone and Fernando Doménech, 'La comedia neoclásica. Moratín', in *Historia del teatro español*, ed. Javier Huerta Calvo, 2 vols (Madrid: Gredos, 2003), II. *Del siglo XVIII a la época actual*, 1603–51 (p. 1645).

10 Prieto Martínez, 'El sí de los súbditos', 494.

11 Prieto Martínez, 'El sí de los súbditos', 490.

12 José Antonio Maravall, 'Del despotismo ilustrado a una ideología de clases medias: significación de Moratín', in *Coloquio internacional sobre Leandro Fernández de Moratín,* 163–92, (p. 174); *El sí de las niñas*, ed. Pérez-Magallón, 70.

13 Prieto Martínez, 'El sí de los súbditos', 493.

employ 'subtle reactionary arguments', deceptive, manipulative forms of expression that appear to appreciate, understand and support the social groups to whom they are addressed while actually aiming at a reinforcement of the *status quo*.[14] Prieto Martínez illustrates this concept with the well-known speech by Diego: '¡Mandar, hija mía! ... En estas materias tan delicadas los padres que tienen juicio no mandan. Insinúan, proponen, aconsejan; eso, sí, todo eso sí; ¡pero mandar! ...' (Act 2, sc. 5) arguing that 'lo que propone Moratín a través de Diego es la sujeción del súbdito/hijo a través del poder de la razón: una autoridad racional que se opone diametralmente a la autoridad insensata de doña Irene, que sólo puede acarrear "resultas funestas"'.[15]

Yet Prieto Martínez's otherwise lucid and thoughtful article remains bound up in the very dichotomy it identifies and even extends it to the younger characters of Francisca and Carlos, declaring that 'Así como la autoridad insensata de doña Irene se subordina a la autoridad "juiciosa" de don Diego [...] así mismo, el constante disimulo de doña Francisca se opone, desde el principio, al "valor" y honestidad de don Carlos'.[16] This is a strange judgment to make of a young man whose actual interventions in the play, in contrast to the descriptions of him given by Simón in the opening scene, are characterized above all by falsehood and deception: throughout his entire relationship with Francisca he goes under the false name of don Félix de Toledo; he stays in Guadalajara for three months while deliberately misleading his uncle into believing he is with his unit in Zaragoza; he lies to his uncle about why he is in Alcalá and again in saying he will leave immediately; he leads Francisca to believe that he would rather lose his life than her love only immediately to give up all pretensions to her on discovering that his rival is his uncle.

These aspects of his character have not gone unnoticed. Andioc notes that some of Moratín's contemporaries saw an 'aparente contradicción' in the description of Carlos' bravery in the battlefield and his 'suma timidez' in front of his uncle, but argues that this is nothing more than 'un error de enfoque [...] pues no es posible que un dramaturgo entonces en plena posesión de su

14 Sally-Ann Kitts, *The Debate on the Nature, Role and Influence of Woman in Eighteenth-Century Spain* (Lewiston/Queenston/Lampeter: The Edwin Mellen Press, 1995), 133. The subject of women in Enlightenment Spain has received increasing scholarly attention in the last few years: see in particular Mónica Bolufer Peruga, *Mujeres e Ilustración. La construcción de la feminidad en la España del siglo XVIII* (València: Diputació de València, Institució Alfons el Magnànim, 1998); and, most recently, the excellent study by Theresa Ann Smith, *The Emerging Female Citizen: Gender and Enlightenment in Spain* (Berkeley/Los Angeles: Univ. of California Press, 2006).

15 Prieto Martínez, 'El sí de los súbditos', 493. Llanos, 'Integración de la mujer', 211, makes a similar argument: 'El objetivo real es que la mujer respete las jerarquías y la autoridad por propio convencimiento, sin que necesite de una autoridad represora que la someta'.

16 Prieto Martínez, 'El sí de los súbditos', 497.

arte haya cometido involuntariamente lo que viene considerándose como una torpeza'.[17] If Andioc is correct, and given Moratín's credentials at the forefront of Spanish Neo-classic theatre, he may well be, then we still need to explain this behaviour. Andioc argues that, in the character of Carlos, Moratín is presenting an Enlightenment alternative to the traditional 'galán':

> el ejemplo de un joven capaz de *dominar sus pasiones*, en vez de ser dominado por ellas (no es cobardía, sino, como se ve, valor), para salvaguardar unos principios tan esenciales como la autoridad del cabeza de familia y la del gobierno al que éste representa en su casa.[18]

Although a persuasive argument, this line of thought nevertheless seems insufficient when speaking of such a capable playwright as Moratín since it fails to address the inevitable inverisimilitude that this brings to the play.[19] And while Andioc notes that, 'Merece la pena advertir que, todo bien mirado, doña Irene no es más autoritaria con su hija que don Diego con su sobrino', this interesting line is also explored no further except to say that their attitudes only differ when it comes to marriage.[20] So how can these peculiarities and 'apparent contradictions' in Carlos' character be explained?

Prieto Martínez has argued that Moratín's aim in opposing the 'autoridad racional' of Diego with the 'autoridad insensata' of Irene is to expound a new Enlightenment concept of power. In offering a new reading of *El sí de las niñas*, I take Prieto Martínez's interpretation as the most persuasive of the many readings of authorial intention based on the polar opposition of these two characters. However, instead of seeing the text's series of binary oppositions as part of its successful pedagogic remit to present a morally and socially desirable outcome to its audience, dependent on a clear distinction between reasonable and unreasonable behaviour, I will explore,

17 René Andioc, 'Estudio sobre *El sí de las niñas*', in *'La comedia nueva' y 'El sí de las niñas'*, ed. Dowling y Andioc, 133–57 (p. 148).

18 Andioc, *Teatro y sociedad*, 445–46. See also *El sí de las niñas*, ed. Pérez-Magallón, 74–77.

19 Calderone and Doménech also note how the portrayal of Don Carlos stretches verisimilitude, while ultimately considering him both an 'amante fiel y constante ... [y] un héroe admirable porque sabe dominarse' ('La comedia neoclásica. Moratín', 1646).

20 Andioc, "Estudio sobre *El sí de las niñas*', 156. See also José Manuel González Herrán, 'La teatralidad de *El sí de las niñas*', *Segismundo*, 18:1–2 (1984), 145–71 (p. 170). In *Teatro y sociedad*, while Andioc writes that don Carlos' exclamation of 'Pero no el corazón' (Act 3, sc. 10) indicates that don Diego has indeed exceeded his authority, he paints this as 'una indudable afectación' in don Diego, who can be seen to 'abusar conscientemente de su autoridad' since he had already given up any idea of marrying Francisca before this scene even began. For Andioc, 'como se trata ante todo de salvaguardar la dignidad de [los cabezas de familia], el autor ha tomado varias precauciones para atenuar en lo posible la responsabilidad de don Diego y la gravedad del desacato de don Carlos, pues cada uno debe conservar su ejemplaridad en su esfera propia' (459).

to quote Terry Eagleton, 'how such oppositions, in order to hold themselves in place, are sometimes betrayed into inverting or collapsing themselves, or need to banish to the text's margins certain details which can be made to return and plague them'.[21] This in turn will reveal the *aporia*, or 'gap between authorial intention and textual meaning', the 'textual self-contradiction which is the essence of the deconstructive project' of Jacques Derrida.[22] In the case of *El sí de las niñas*, these 'details' are found in the relationship between Diego and Carlos and it is through a comparison of this relationship with that of Irene and Francisca that the *aporia* will be revealed and the gendered nature of the play's structure brought to the fore.

Diego's position as a man of reason and moderation is based on his repeated efforts to arrive at an understanding of Francisca's true feelings, constantly thwarted by Irene, and on his actions of self-sacrifice at the end of the play when he renounces any claim he might have had to Francisca's hand and enables her marriage to Carlos. It is also supported by three key speeches in which he decries what he sees as an authoritarian approach to the raising of children, girls in particular. The first is in Act 2, beginning '¡Mandar, hija mía! ...', and is cited above. The second is in Act 3, scene 8:

> Ve aquí los frutos de la educación. Esto es lo que se llama criar bien a una niña: enseñarla a que desmienta y oculte las pasiones más inocentes con una pérfida disimulación. Las juzgan honestas luego que las ven instruidas en el arte de callar y mentir. Se obstinan en que el temperamento, la edad ni el genio no han de tener influencia alguna en sus inclinaciones, o en que su voluntad ha de torcerse al capricho de quien las gobierna. Todo se las permite, menos la sinceridad. Con tal que no digan lo que sienten, con tal que finjan aborrecer lo que más desean, con tal que se presten a pronunciar, cuando se lo manden, un sí perjuro, sacrílego, origen de tantos escándalos, ya están bien criadas, y se llama excelente educación la que inspira en ellas el temor, la astucia y el silencio de un esclavo.

The third is in the final scene: 'Esto resulta del abuso de autoridad, de la opresión que la juventud padece; éstas son las seguridades que dan los padres y los tutores, y esto es lo que se debe fiar en el sí de las niñas. ...' (Act 3, sc. 13).

Similarly, Irene is characterized as oppressive and autocratic in the way she expects complete obedience from her daughter, by her actions in always answering for her and in the pressures she places upon her to agree to the marriage with Diego. This view is supported with reference to her repeated use of words meaning 'obey' and 'obedient', such as 'Es hija obediente, y no se

21 Terry Eagleton, *Literary Theory. An Introduction* (Oxford: Basil Blackwell, 1983), 133.

22 Christina Howells, *Derrida: Deconstruction from Phenomenology to Ethics* (Cambridge: Polity Press, 1999), 3.

apartará jamás de lo que determine su madre' (Act 1, sc. 3) and that she should 'pensar sólo en dar gusto a su madre y obedecerla' (Act 2, sc. 5). Her negative portrayal is further emphasized by suggestions that she is not, as she claims, wanting the best for her daughter but rather is motivated by self-interest, a position that is backed up by her references to how her family 'ha venido tan a menos ...' (Act 1, sc. 3) and to Diego as 'el bien que nos ha entrado por las puertas ...', which then continues with a complaint about the cost of her medicines and 'lo atrasada que me coge, que yo no sé lo que hubiera sido de tu pobre madre ...' (Act 2, sc. 2). That she inspires fear in her daughter is apparent from Francisca's comments to both Rita and Carlos and from Francisca's persistent deception and hiding of her true feelings.

As the so-called 'fruto' of a faulty education, Francisca exemplifies the effects of Irene's inappropriate upbringing. However, if we expect to find a similar illustration by example, this time of the right way to bring up a child, and of Diego's 'persuasive authority', in the character of Carlos, we will be disappointed, since in the three key scenes where Diego and Carlos interact, Diego is every bit as autocratic and demanding as Irene is with Francisca. Diego's effect on Carlos is immediate and startling: having said to Francisca only a few moments earlier that he could count on the assistance of 'un anciano respetable y virtuoso, a quien más que tío debo llamar amigo y padre' (Act 2, sc. 7), Carlos' first words on seeing his uncle and realizing that he is the rival suitor are '¡Todo se ha perdido!' and '¡Yo estoy muerto!' (Act 2, sc. 11). Why this sudden, extremely negative reaction? His first words to his uncle in this scene are also revealing: 'Si usted se altera y ...' as his uncle brusquely pulls back the hand that Carlos was about to kiss and then approaches him angrily. Carlos' fear of Diego's anger is very apparent and his immediate abandonment of his initial plans to seek his uncle's help suggests a very different sort of relationship to that which we have been led to expect. This is confirmed as the scene progresses and Carlos lies about the reasons for his presence in the inn, in spite of his uncle's questioning him and offering him an opportunity to come clean:

D. DIEGO ¿No hay más?
D. CARLOS No, señor.
D. DIEGO Míralo bien.
D. CARLOS No, señor ... A eso venía. No hay nada más.
(Act 2, sc. 11)

Carlos' refusal to speak up about his real intentions is very reminiscent of Francisca's similar denial of her true feelings:

D. DIEGO ¿Será posible que usted no conozca otro más amable que yo, que la quiera bien, y que la corresponda como usted merece?

Dª FRANCISCA	No, señor; no, señor.
D. DIEGO	Mírelo usted bien.
Dª FRANCISCA	¿No le digo a usted que no? (Act 3, sc. 8)

This exchange continues with Francisca declaring, 'Haré lo que mi madre me manda' and leads to Diego's key speech, arguably the most significant of the play, on 'los frutos de la educación' cited above. The similarity of the two exchanges is striking, in particular Diego's repetition of 'Míralo bien', a suggestion that both young people are too fearful to heed. His moralizing speech claims that the faulty upbringing delivered by such as Irene teaches a young woman to deny and hide 'las pasiones más inocentes con una pérfida disimulación'. Yet isn't this exactly what Carlos is also doing? Even as Diego speaks of the wrong sort of upbringing leading to deceit and the silence of a slave, yet he is deceived by Carlos who is frightened into silence by his uncle's mere presence in the inn. Carlos describes his own behaviour as 'una falta de sumisión a usted . . .' (Act 2, sc. 11) and Diego is clear in his expectations of Carlos: 'Lo que quiere su tío de usted no es verle cada ocho días, sino saber que es hombre de juicio, y que cumple con sus obligaciones' (Act 2, sc. 11), a requirement on Carlos very similar to that placed on Francisca to be 'hija obediente' and 'conducirse en todas ocasiones como es conveniente y debido' (Act 1, sc. 3).

Diego's admonition of Carlos is couched in terms of endearment:

> ¿No conoces que es todo por tu bien, y que ha sido un desatino el que acabas de hacer? . . . Y no hay que afligirse por eso, ni creas que es falta de cariño . . . Y sabes lo que te he querido siempre; y en obrando tú según corresponde, seré tu amigo como lo he sido hasta aquí. (Act 2, sc. 12)

It is an approach that has striking parallels with Irene's earlier exchange with Francisca:

Dª IRENE	Ven aquí, ven . . . Ven aquí, Paquita.
Dª FRANCISCA	¡Mamá! (*Levántase, abraza a su madre y se acarician mutuamente.*)
Dª IRENE	¿Ves lo que te quiero?
Dª FRANCISCA	Sí, señora.
Dª IRENE	¿Y cuánto procuro tu bien, que no tengo otro pío sino el de verte colocada antes que yo falte?
Dª FRANCISCA	Bien lo conozco.
Dª IRENE	¡Hija de mi vida! ¿Has de ser buena?
Dª FRANCISCA	Sí, señora. (Act 2, sc. 5)

Diego's speech also recalls Irene's similar requirement of Francisca to 'proceder con el honor que la corresponde' (Act 1, sc. 3), and his demand that Carlos 'obedece lo que te mando' (Act 2, sc. 12), repeated as 'Porque yo lo quiero y lo mando. ¡Oiga!' (Act 3, sc. 10), recalls similar statements by Irene,

'Cuando yo se lo mande' (Act 2, sc. 5) and Diego's criticism of parents who 'mandar' in the same scene. Just as Francisca says to Diego of her mother that 'en todo lo que mande la obedeceré' (Act 2, sc. 5), so Carlos declares to Diego, 'Lo haré sin falta' and 'haré lo que usted manda' (Act 2, sc. 12). The following two exchanges also have striking similarities of tone, approach and subject-matter:

D. CARLOS	¿Queda usted enojado conmigo?
D. DIEGO	No, no por cierto ... Me disgusté bastante, pero ya se acabó ... No me des que sentir. (*Poniéndole ambas manos sobre los hombros.*) Portarse como hombre de bien.
D. CARLOS	No lo dude usted.
D. DIEGO	Como oficial de honor.
D. CARLOS	Así lo prometo. (Act 2, sc. 12)

Dª FRANCISCA	No, señora. Créame usted. La Paquita nunca se apartará de su madre, ni la dará disgustos.
Dª IRENE	Mira si es cierto lo que dices.
Dª FRANCISCA	Sí, señora; que yo no sé mentir.
Dª IRENE	Pues, hija, ya sabes lo que te he dicho. Ya ves lo que pierdes, y la pesadumbre que me darás si no te portas en un todo como corresponde ... Cuidado con ello. (Act 2, sc. 4)

Neither is Diego above the sort of emotional blackmail used by Irene, as is clear from a comparison of Irene's speech 'yo no sé lo que hubiera sido de tu pobre madre ...' (Act 2, sc. 2) with Diego's 'alguna locura has hecho que le habrá de costar la vida a tu pobre tío' (Act 2, sc. 11). He demands an act of submission from his nephew (having rejected it in anger when it was first offered)—'¿Sin besar la mano a su tío, eh?' (Act 2, sc. 12)—that leads to a moment of reconciliation and tenderness, with expressions of concern for Carlos' welfare that can be seen to echo that of Irene and Francisca (Act 2, sc. 5). Even his comments to Simón calling Carlos 'un pícaro' (Act 3, sc. 9) find an echo three scenes later when Irene calls Francisca 'grandísima picarona' (Act 3, sc. 12).

The changes in Carlos' demeanour and behaviour are visible for all to see: Francisca herself says of him in front of Rita, '¡Ay, D. Félix! Nunca le he visto a usted tan tímido ...' (Act 3, sc. 2) and later declares 'Pero ¿sabes tú con qué temor que habló, qué agitación mostraba?' (Act 3, sc. 6). The effects of his uncle's authority over him are visible in Carlos' transformation from gallant army officer to fearful miscreant child, no more able than is Francisca to speak out about his true feelings. Carlos' response to his uncle's demand that he forget his pretensions to marry Francisca is a 'Sí, señor' (Act 3, sc. 10) that is a perfect example of the 'sí perjuro' that Diego inveighed against only a few moments earlier in his famous speech on the 'frutos de la educación' (Act 3, sc. 8). Is Diego's anger and threatened violence towards Carlos, '¿Qué temeridad es ésta? (*Se levanta con mucho enojo, encaminándose hacia don Carlos, que se va retirando.*)' (Act 3, sc. 10), any different from Irene's 'Te has de acordar de mí. (*Se encamina hacia doña Francisca, muy colérica y en ademán de querer maltratarla. [. . .]*)' (Act 3, sc. 12)? Or is his 'Haz lo que te mando' (Act 3, sc. 10) any less authoritarian or demanding than Irene's 'Respóndele' (Act 2, sc. 5)?

His interactions with Carlos reveal to us the wide gap between what Diego says in his moralizing speeches to Irene and Francisca and what he actually does and has done in the past in his relationship with his nephew. They undermine his characterization as a man of reason and moderation, and reveal hypocrisy in his pontificating speeches that condemn Irene's attitudes and behaviour. His relationship with Carlos exposes the extent to which the opposition between Diego and Irene is far from clear-cut, with Diego revealing a number of the characteristics—authoritarianism, lack of self-control, lack of judgment or reason, lack of responsibility—that supposedly define Irene. Similarly Irene's actions can be seen to be far less irrational and lacking in judgment than they have traditionally been presented. Indeed, seen in the light of the social expectations of the day, what Irene wants for her daughter is both sensible and reasonable.

Irene subscribes to the very commonly-held opinion that elders know better, one that Diego appears to share, as indicated both by his response to her comment regarding marriages where both parties are very young (Act 1, sc. 4) and, most tellingly, by his behaviour with Carlos. Certainly the match with Diego is socially excellent—he is, as Rita tells us, 'un caballero rico, honrado, bien quisto, en suma, cabal y perfecto, que no había más que apetecer' (Act 1, sc. 8), and as Irene notes, 'un sujeto de bienes y de posibles . . .' (Act 2, sc. 4). While the age difference is excessive and exaggerated, it was far from unheard of in the eighteenth century for there to be a significant difference between the man and the woman: the *Ilustrada* Josefa Amar y Borbón recommends that a husband be at least twelve years older than his wife, 'porque importa mucho que el hombre tenga algunos años más que la mujer, respecto de que ésta envejece antes y está expuesta a sufrir la frialdad de su marido'.[23] Marriage was still a social contract first and foremost at this

23 Josefa Amar y Borbón, *Discurso sobre la educación física y moral de las mujeres* (Madrid: Benito Cano, 1790), 266–67. Andioc, *Teatro y sociedad*, 436, has used Madrid census data from 1787 to show that there were three times as many widows as widowers, and similarly high numbers of married men over fifty and low numbers of married women in the fifty plus age group. It was still far from unusual in many societies throughout the nineteenth century: 'Taking his soldiering seriously, [Sir John] decided that he would not marry until he ceased to be actively employed. Accordingly at the age of sixty-eight he married Ellen Mayhew, by whom he had a son and two daughters' (*An Ensign in the Peninsular War: The Letters of John Aitchison*, ed. W. F. K. Thompson [London: Michael Joseph, 1981], 12).

time and young people hoped but did not expect to marry for love. A woman looked to gain social position, financial security and a man of good character who would provide a comfortable home.[24] Diego offers all this in good measure and so, judged against these parameters, Irene is acting reasonably in expecting Francisca to recognize the value and common sense of what she has arranged for her.[25]

Similarly, although ridiculed and undermined as a character throughout the play in order to demonstrate her lack of sense, Irene can be seen to act with extreme common sense in the context of a society that values money in a marriage (as noted by Carlos in Act 2, sc. 9 and Act 3, sc. 10), and social position, and where the fate of the unmarried woman is clearly exemplified by Francisca's two aunts who are nuns. In this context, Irene's quick acceptance of Carlos in place of Diego at the end of the play is not so much an indication of her shallow character as of her ability to judge by society's standards. Indeed, Irene's aims and motivations are no different from those that motivate other well-known literary figures at this time: as Tony Tanner notes of Charlotte Lucas' acceptance of the hand of Mr Collins in *Pride and Prejudice*: 'In such a society, the need for an "establishment" is a very real one, and in putting prudence before passion, Charlotte is only doing what the economic realities of her society—as Jane Austen makes abundantly clear—all but force her to do'.[26] We have seen that Irene's interactions with Francisca are no more authoritarian than those of Diego with Carlos. In her forceful persuasions to make her daughter appreciate the good marriage she has arranged for her it could be argued that she is, in fact, acting just as Diego suggests when he notes that wise parents 'insinúan, proponen, aconsejan' (Act 2, sc. 5), a trio of approaches that could surely be as forceful, demanding and difficult to resist as any direct order. As she tells Francisca herself: 'No es esto reñirte, hija mía; esto es aconsejarte. Porque como tú no tienes conocimiento para considerar el bien que nos ha entrado por las puertas ...' (Act 2, sc. 2).

Yet critics are uniform in their condemnation of Irene, with one even suggesting she may deliberately be deceiving Diego, stopping him from talking to Francisca just long enough for the wedding to take place.[27] This

24 Indeed Jane Austen's character, Charlotte Lucas, gives these very reasons for her acceptance of the hand of the foolish Mr Collins. As she says to Elizabeth: 'When you have had time to think it all over, I hope you will be satisfied with what I have done. I am not romantic, you know. I never was. I ask only a comfortable home; and considering Mr Collins's character, connections, and situation in life, I am convinced that my chance of happiness with him is as fair as most people can boast on entering the marriage state' (Jane Austen, *Pride and Prejudice*, ed. Tony Tanner [Penguin: Harmondsworth, 1985], 166–67).

25 Amar y Borbón also considers in her *Discurso* that 'it is up to her mother to ascertain the qualities of the husband-to-be for her daughter' (Kitts, *The Debate on the Nature, Role and Influence of Woman*, 191).

26 Tony Tanner, 'Introduction' to *Pride and Prejudice*, ed. Tanner, 37–38.

27 Deacon, 'La comicidad de Doña Irene', 151.

fails, however, to take account of the consistency of her position and of the vehemence with which she defends it. Contrary to what Diego says in the last scene in his rather petulant recrimination that she and her sisters deceived him—'Él y su hija de usted estaban locos de amor, mientras que usted y las tías fundaban castillos en el aire, y me llenaban la cabeza de ilusiones, que han desaparecido como un sueño ...' (Act 3, sc. 13)—she has always been very open with him about her role in bringing about this marriage. In fact his attempts at shifting responsibility for the situation at the end of the play further undermine his characterization as a man of honour and integrity, since Irene's earliest exchange in the play with Diego makes her position as the decision-maker with regard to her daughter's future abundantly clear:

D. DIEGO	Es verdad. Sólo falta que la parte interesada tenga la misma satisfacción que manifiestan cuantos la quieren bien.
Dª IRENE	Es hija obediente, y no se apartará jamás de lo que determine su madre.
D. DIEGO	Todo eso es cierto; pero ...
Dª IRENE	Es de buena sangre, y ha de pensar bien, y ha de proceder con el honor que la corresponde.
D. DIEGO	Sí, ya estoy; pero ¿no pudiera, sin faltar a su honor ni a su sangre ...?
Dª FRANCISCA	¿Me voy, mamá? (*Se levanta y vuelve a sentarse.*)
Dª IRENE	No pudiera, no, señor. Una niña bien educada, hija de buenos padres, no puede menos de conducirse en todas ocasiones como es conveniente y debido.

(Act 1, sc. 3)

This statement of her position is further emphasized when her indignation at the insults she perceives in Diego's persistent questioning of Francisca, to reveal any possible prior attachments, is such that she comes close to cancelling the match altogether rather than see her daughter's good name dishonoured (Act 2, sc. 5).[28]

The fact that Irene carries most of the comedy in the play may also be a reason for the persistence of this view. The exaggerations of her character in terms of the numbers of children she has had and lost, her loquaciousness and inability to remain focused on the matters in hand, all add to the humour

28 Deacon thinks that Diego is referring to Christ in the phrase 'otro sujeto más digno' (Act 2, sc. 5) ('La comicidad de Doña Irene', 155). However, the sentence construction is such that this cannot be the case: Diego recognizes how Francisca might well have been influenced by the experience she has had of 'las santas costumbres que ha visto practicar en aquel inocente asilo de la devoción y la virtud', but continues that '*a pesar de todo esto*' he does not rule out that 'la imaginación acalorada, las circunstancias imprevistas' might have led her to find someone else. Irene is not therefore showing 'su ignorancia', as Deacon suggests, or 'imaginando' that Diego means another suitor.

of the play and act as a marked contrast to the seriousness of Diego's character. However these aspects can also distract from a full and balanced interpretation of these characters and lead to inaccuracies and misreadings of the play as critics seek to reinforce the positive aspects of the enlightened Diego and ignore the negative side revealed in his relationship with Carlos, by emphasizing instead the negative characteristics of his supposedly irrational counterpart Irene.[29] In focusing on the ridiculous only in Irene's character, for example, the obviously ridiculous aspects of Diego's pretensions towards Francisca are ignored: can we really take seriously his request to know if she holds him in special esteem after two days of acquaintance (Act 1, sc. 4 and Act 3, sc. 8) or believe that he can truly think that a sixteen-year-old girl would be in any way attracted to him as a husband for any reason other than his money (Act 2, sc. 5)? The breakdown of these gendered poles of opposition offers an opportunity to re-examine Irene's character, actions and motivations in the play. Just as the scenes with Carlos betray the inconsistencies of the 'enlightened man' and reveal Diego's lack of moderation, so a revision of Irene's behaviour in the context of the social expectations of the period highlights Irene's social awareness. They also help to reveal, as we shall go on to see, the problems she faces as a woman both defined and controlled by Enlightenment discourse and the attempts she makes to counter it and empower both herself and her daughter.

Diego, rich, male, middle-class, mature, a member of the social elite, dominates the play and uses his power in the form of access to the statements of Enlightenment discourse to undermine and relegate to outside the system the statements of non-members, such as Irene and Carlos. This is achieved through the 'privileging of one pole of the series of oppositions above the other'.[30] The ideological nature of this action to establish a series of unassailable 'first principles' is revealed when they are deconstructed and thereby 'shown to be products of a particular system of meaning, rather than what props it up from outside'.[31] In *El sí de las niñas*, the key Enlightenment concepts of reason, self-control and moderation are used to define the

29 Deacon's article ('La comicidad de Doña Irene') is a good example of this. In his eagerness to emphasize the comic in Irene's character, he also seeks to establish that Irene could easily be well into her sixties, making a number of her speeches, such as her implied desire for a fourth husband, seem particularly ridiculous. However, to do so he reads Irene's complaint (Act 3, sc. 11) that her health has never been the same since 'el último mal parto que tuve' as meaning that 'su último parto tuvo lugar hacía 19 ó 20 años' (148), an obvious error (also found in Deacon, 'Introduction', *El sí de las niñas*, ed. Deacon, xxxii) underlined by the presence in the play of the sixteen-year-old Francisca. Similarly his view that 'Doña Irene has apparently squandered much of her wealth' ('Introduction', *El sí de las niñas*, ed. Deacon, xxvi) has no textual evidence to support it—where her problematic financial situation is mentioned (Act 1, sc. 3 and Act 2, sc. 2) no reason is given for it other than the cost of medicines.

30 Howells, *Derrida*, 33.

31 Eagleton, *Literary Theory*, 132.

character of the mature man Diego. They are not only essential to the communication of the message that his character is designed to put forward—about the right way to exercise power, for example—but are also part and parcel of that message. That is, they are prized as the positive characteristics exhibited by the Enlightened man in contrast to the supposed irrationality, lack of control and immoderate behaviour of women like Irene. Indeed, they require the alignment of the opposite characteristics to his in his antithesis, in the mature female character Irene: 'Man is the founding principle and woman the excluded opposite of this; and as long as such a distinction is tightly held in place the whole system can function effectively'.[32] The power of this system is such that once established in a text it takes control and sets the rules for participation. The principles it is founded on are presented as the only acceptable way of viewing the world and any actions that differ from those prescribed, any attempt to question or alter them, are defined as unacceptable and thereby rejected.

Irene is denied any credibility in any of her speeches since as a woman she is defined by the series of characteristics that adhere to the negative pole of oppositions. Through her loquaciousness, her inability to stick to the point and frequent digressions into anecdotes, her heightened emotions, her interest in money, her complaints about her ill-health, and her rigid and inflexible approach to her daughter's upbringing, she is presented to the audience as the antithesis of Diego: she is irrational, uneducated, disordered, self-seeking, poor, lacking in self-control, extreme and authoritarian. All these negative characteristics adhering to Irene serve, in turn, to endow Diego with their positive opposites: he is reasonable, educated, orderly, self-sacrificing, rich, self-controlled, moderate. Even the staging of the play reinforces this dichotomy with the symbolic darkening and lightening of the stage, a metaphor for the enlightenment that Diego will bring to the play (Act 3, sc. 8), while the arrival of darkness is linked to the actions of Irene (Act 1, sc. 9).

Part of the message of Enlightenment discourse is the definition of what constitutes good and bad behaviour in women's acts and attitudes. Diego is able to articulate his values from a position of privilege and authority. Because of his position on the positive side of the pole, as the Enlightened man, endowed with and defined by reason, what he says takes on validity and is given the status of truth. Similarly, what Irene says is undermined and dismissed because she is aligned to the negative. Diego is looking for certain characteristics and, within this 'currency of images', these are given positive status and define a 'good' woman: pretty, graceful, humble, guileless, innocent, accomplished, industrious, hardworking, a good housekeeper, thrifty, all are mentioned in the play.[33] Similarly he tells us what makes a

32 Eagleton, *Literary Theory*, 132.

33 For a discussion of the meaning of these and other terms in eighteenth-century Spain, see Carmen Martín Gaite, *Usos amorosos del dieciocho en España* (Barcelona: Lumen, 1981).

bad woman, in his speech about housekeepers, which lists characteristics several of which Irene is to go on to demonstrate in abundance—pampered, meddlesome, talkative, hysterical, old, ugly. He also does so through other comments, such as those in his key speeches that condemn Irene's intelligence and approach to bringing up children, and in such lines as 'Esto le sucede a quien se fía de la prudencia de una mujer' (Act 3, sc. 11).

In this context, *El sí de las niñas* can be seen as a play about power and who controls it. Moratín's access, as a middle-class man, to Enlightenment discourse and, very importantly, to its means of dissemination, the Neo-classical theatre, allows him to express the values of that discourse through the character of Diego. As we have seen, these key values are reason, self-control and moderation and, as Maravall and Prieto Martínez have shown, Moratín is very much a man of moderation. It is an example of what Foucault termed 'disciplinary power' and draws support from a 'fixed conception of a population that reproduces itself in the proper way, composed of people who marry in the proper way and behave in the proper way, according to precisely determined norms'.[34] This is surely a phrase that could be used with some accuracy to describe Moratín's entire theatrical output, his 'proyecto de teatro disciplinario' as Prieto Martínez so aptly describes it.[35] In the case of *El sí de las niñas*, Diego exercises power over all other characters in the play by drawing on his access to the discourse of the social elite that seeks to control the behaviour of others. Neither Diego nor his creator Moratín are seeking to break or even seriously question this power structure, rather Diego's very actions both before and after his so-called enlightenment serve to confirm and reinforce it (the planned/arranged marriage, his control of Carlos, both financial and authoritarian, his ritualistic role at the end).[36] Similarly, Irene is powerless to act in any other way but to set her daughter up as worthy within the confines of acceptability as set out by the patriarchy. In doing this, she has sought to create the commodity that those with the power desire.[37] Her education of Francisca was clearly astute and successful since it attracted a prime example of the group in the form of Diego and, had Francisca not come into contact with Carlos, it is very likely that Irene would have succeeded without complications. As it is, Irene can still count Francisca's upbringing as a success; her acceptance of Carlos as her son-in-law at the end indicates this and again exemplifies her common sense, since she recognizes that Carlos has many of the qualities she appreciated in Diego and that his position as a rich male will soon afford him access to the elite.

34 Fontana and Pasquino, 'Truth and Power', in *The Foucault Reader*, 66.

35 Prieto Martínez, 'El sí de los súbditos', 491. He later notes: 'la poética neoclásica es, notoriamente, una poética disciplinaria, policial' (496).

36 On the ritual of the endings in Moratín's plays, see Nigel Glendinning, 'Rito y verdad en el teatro de Moratín', *Ínsula*, 161 (1960), 6.

37 See, for example, Diego's description of Francisca to Simón (Act 1, sc. 1) and Carlos' account of their relationship (Act 3, sc. 10).

It is vital for those with access to Enlightenment discourse such as Moratín to affirm it in this dichotomous form, since it provides both the rationale and the means for enabling the maintenance of the *status quo* through defining those who do not have power and keeping them from gaining access to it. As well as women, these include the lower classes—note the way in which Diego immediately quashes Simón's claim to have slept like an Emperor: '¡Mala comparación!... Di que has dormido como un pobre hombre [. . .]' (Act 3, sc. 1), suggesting that Simón's is an enviable social state since, in spite of his poverty, he can sleep free of the worries or regrets that accompany those who are unfortunate enough to be born rich, but also firmly keeping him in his subordinate social place. Given its tremendous popularity across class divides, the theatre forms a perfect location for this discourse to be articulated. As Foucault has observed: 'In the seventeenth and eighteenth centuries, a form of power comes into being that begins to exercise itself through social production and social service. It becomes a matter of obtaining productive service from individuals in their concrete lives. And, in consequence, a real and effective "incorporation" of power was necessary, in the sense that power had to be able to gain access to the bodies of individuals, to their acts, attitudes, and modes of everyday behaviour'.[38] Those able to employ Enlightenment discourse—men like Moratín—use the power that it gives them to put across this message. Neo-classic theatre is a good example of how this access could be achieved, with its emphasis on presenting a moral message and its support of the social *status quo*.

In revealing how power relations between the central characters are constructed through language and how power is used by those with access to it to control and repress, we can see 'how European men of reason and benevolence could inscribe a rationale of oppression and exploitation within their very discourse of Enlightenment'.[39] While it may well be the case, as many critics have argued, that Moratín's intention in *El sí de las niñas* was indeed to expound the Enlightenment rhetoric of reason, benevolence and moderation, in fact his play succeeds only to show how these very concepts form part of a powerful discourse that seeks to maintain the *status quo* through this seductive, deceptive approach to power relations that Prieto Martínez identifies. It is a tactic that masks the reaffirmation of traditional values in a language of comprehension and understanding, but one that ultimately fails to convince since the *aporia* that is revealed through an

38 Michel Foucault, 'Truth and Power', in *The Foucault Reader*, 66–67. This focus on 'obtaining productive service from individuals' underpins much of the debate on the social role of women in the Periodical Press of the 1780s and the discussions surrounding their admission to and subsequent role within the newly-formed Economic Societies. See Kitts, *The Debate on the Nature, Role and Influence of Woman*, Chapters 5 and 6, and Smith, *The Emerging Female Citizen*.

39 Barbara Johnson, 'Writing', in *Critical Terms for Literary Study*, ed. Lentricchia and McLaughlin, 39–49 (p. 47).

analysis of the interrelationship of Diego and Carlos exposes how even those set up as champions of Enlightenment are unable to free themselves from the very acts and behaviour they condemn in others. While Diego presents himself as believing in the need for 'un poder negociador' he is in fact unable to carry this out.[40] He does not allow Carlos any share in the power, instead claiming it all for himself, as he reinforces with his statement in the last scene: 'Yo pude separarlos para siempre y gozar tranquilamente la posesión de esta niña amable', and the fact that he does not allow Carlos or anyone else any active part at all, instead treating them as an Enlightened despot, prepared at this moment of triumph to have them kneeling before his majestic figure even as he denied the attempt of Francisca to kneel before him previously. At the end of the play, he is still deceiving himself and trying to shift responsibility for his actions. He talks about Irene and her sisters building castles in the sky and filling his head with illusions, yet it is quite clear from his exchanges with Francisca at the beginning of the play that he has a picture of her that is built entirely on his own projected desires of what he believes attractive in a woman. This is clear from his comments at the end, too, which project a view of marriage to this teenager as a salvation from emptiness in his old age.

The revelation of an apparent gap between authorial intention and textual meaning has given us the opportunity to reassess the workings of power within *El sí de las niñas*, revealing both the authoritarianism of Diego and the rationality of Irene. Yet is this really an *aporia* in Moratín's text? Does a deconstructive analysis of the play reveal it crumbling away to display its own inadequacies, or is it, perhaps, a revelation of the literary and philosophical complexities and subtleties of the author? Thinking back to Andioc's comments and of Moratín's lifelong commitment to the tenets of Neo-classical theory, is it more likely that, rather than examples of the way that the text betrays itself into an inevitable *aporia*, the complexities of characters in Irene and Diego are in fact part and parcel of the Neo-classic principles that guided Moratín so firmly in his writing of theatre? Are Diego's and Irene's apparent contradictions in character actually deliberate creative acts by the author? It could be argued that the fact that Diego should have some very human faults, even to the extent of not practising what he preaches, rather than detracting from his portrayal as a man of Enlightenment, in fact reveal the contradictions inherent within Enlightenment discourse, and add to the verisimilitude of his character. Similarly, Irene is made more believable as a character by the fact that, in spite of her lack of education, authoritarianism and verbosity, she displays common sense and can be seen, within the context of the time, to act

40 Prieto Martínez, 'El sí de los súbditos', 498. It is here that I disagree with Julio Prieto Martínez's otherwise excellent analysis. While I believe he is right in his presentation of the type of power Moratín is advocating through the character of Diego, I hope I have shown how this is not, in fact, what this character actually exercises.

rationally, sensibly and out of maternal love and duty in seeking a good match for her only surviving daughter. Indeed, the language used by Diego with Carlos seems so careful and deliberate in its positioning, in its careful structure and in its echoing of the approaches and vocabulary used by Irene with Francisca, as to support a view that Moratín is encouraging us to compare them and note their similarities. Are Diego's authoritarianism and Irene's practical reason there to make them all the more human, less stereotypical, more convincing as individuals, caught up in a very human and therefore understandable self-deception? Are these complexities indeed revelatory of the complexities of Spanish Enlightenment discourse at the end of the eighteenth and beginning of the nineteenth centuries, when enlightened thinkers were desirous of change but fearful of the consequences of it, of the extremes that could result when control was lost? Perhaps Sebold is correct in his identification of Moratín with his character Diego, and the contradictions in Diego's character reflect those that Maravall identifies in Moratín.

Whether this is a deliberate act by the author or an example of the inevitability of textual self-contradiction, a reconsideration of the interactions and relationship between Diego and Carlos has opened up the possible need for a review of the motivations and behaviour of Irene and of her position in relation to Enlightenment discourse. If we think of the word 'Enlightenment' as signifying learning, gaining knowledge from experience of the world and, from that, acquiring the ability to act within it, we could argue that Irene is indeed a woman of the Enlightenment. Deplorable as her actions may be in terms of modern views on the freedom of the individual that are beginning to be articulated in this period, we can see how, condemned to a series of arranged marriages from the age of nineteen, doubtless given scant intellectual education and taught only to please men and obey her elders, she has nevertheless used her experience of life within a patriarchal society to inform her decisions on the upbringing of her daughter, manipulating social conventions and strictures to both her own and her daughter's advantage so as to create of Francisca a commodity that will assure both of them their continued existence within that society. Diego himself confirms the common sense and rationality of Irene's actions: he has searched out 'una muchacha de juicio y bien criada' and he has deliberately gone for the product of a restricted convent education—'para conseguirlo no he ido a buscar ninguna hija de familia de estas que viven en una decente libertad' (Act 2, sc. 5). He reinforces this view in the shock he displays as Francisca's attachment to Carlos is revealed: '¿Qué amante es éste? . . . ¡Y dieciséis años y criada en un convento! Acabó ya toda mi ilusión' (Act 3, sc. 3). He is perfectly cognizant of the financial nature of their arrangements: 'yo no he buscado dinero, que dineros tengo' (Act 1, sc. 1), and in response to her self-description as 'una huérfana, pobre, desvalida', his response is 'pero de prendas tan estimables que la hacen a usted digna todavía de mayor fortuna' (Act 2, sc. 5). Francisca herself tells Carlos of Diego that 'él insta por su parte, me ofrece tantas cosas, me . . . ' (Act 2, sc. 6).

Foucault observed that power is 'a form of warlike domination' and asked: 'Shouldn't one therefore conceive all problems of power in terms of relations of war?'[41] The relevance of this notion to the relationship between Diego and Irene is striking. Their exchanges have an energy and aggression to them that befits a war metaphor: just as she perceives him to make assaults on her and her daughter's honour, so he perceives her to be deploying defensive strategies to avoid engagement with what he sees as the real issue of Francisca's true feelings. At the end of the play, Diego uses the power of his language and his position of knowledge to establish his dominance over Irene just long enough to bring about a peace. Neither he nor Irene loses the war: both achieve the resolution of the concerns that originally brought them into conflict, with Irene succeeding in establishing her daughter and thereby herself in a position of social and economic security, and Diego embracing his role at the head of a family that will grow to fill the loneliness he had feared in his old age. What does not change, however, are the relative positions of power of Diego and Irene. Diego is still the one with the power and the negotiated peace comes about through his benevolence, his continuing authority confirmed by the displays of obeisance by Carlos and Francisca at the end. Had he chosen a different path, such as the abandonment of all relations with Irene and Francisca, for example, Irene would have been powerless to resist. Yet, to continue with the war metaphor, we should not forget that the actual outcome does indeed represent a triumph for Irene, as Francisca has captured a prize every bit as valuable as the one Irene originally aimed for, and that this has come about through Irene's ability to present her daughter to the world as the essence of desirability in a wife, in accordance with Diego's definition. Despite her apparently powerless position, Irene has managed to win the battle that is the marriage-stakes through her understanding of the terms of engagement. Whatever Diego—or the audience—may think of her techniques, her upbringing of Francisca has yielded a positive result and both Francisca's and Irene's futures are assured. The manner in which she has brought up her daughter and the fact that she clearly understands the best way to present her to society reveal Irene's ability to work from a position of exclusion outside Enlightenment discourse through a subtle self-empowerment that leads to a form of inclusion—at least in terms of social position and financial stability—for her and her daughter. Perhaps before we judge her behaviour, we would do well to refer to the old adage that all is fair in love and war!

41 Foucault, 'Truth and Power', in *The Foucault Reader*, 65.

Equívocos, engaños y error en *El sí de las niñas* de Leandro Fernández de Moratín

PHILIP DEACON

University of Sheffield

En la primera escena de *El sí de las niñas* (1805) una conversación entre el protagonista don Diego y su criado Simón lleva a una situación en que el primero, un hombre adinerado de 59 años, revela por fin su intención de casarse con doña Francisca, una joven de 16 años que él ha llegado a conocer en persona solo dos o tres días antes. La falta de franqueza de don Diego, que solamente aclara sus intenciones cuando el secreto ya le resulta difícil de mantener, había hecho imaginar a Simón durante una parte considerable del diálogo que el futuro esposo de Francisca sería el sobrino de don Diego, el joven militar don Carlos.[1] El equívoco empleado por Moratín pone en primer plano la irracionalidad del hombre mayor que ha imaginado una vejez feliz casándose con una joven atractiva, inocente y simpática a quien acaba de conocer y de cuyos sentimientos e inclinaciones solo tiene noticia indirectamente, a través de la madre de la joven, doña Irene.[2] Si don Diego no ha sido sincero anteriormente con su criado, el espectador de la obra pronto descubre que la razón por la que se ha empeñado en su objetivo es porque doña Irene ha insistido en que la joven acepta la propuesta. Sin embargo, a medida que se desarrolla la obra el espectador ve claramente que el proyectado matrimonio se debe más bien a la voluntad de doña Irene, que piensa que el enlace de su hija con un hombre mayor con fortuna ofrece una solución a su propia condición económica empobrecida y permitirá rescatar a Francisca de una vida recluida en un convento.[3] Don Diego,

1 Jesús Pérez-Magallón, en su edición de la obra—Leandro Fernández de Moratín, *La comedia nueva. El sí de las niñas* (Barcelona: Crítica, 1994), 169, n. 19—señala equívocos parecidos en dos comedias de Molière, *L'Avare* y *L'École des femmes*, y en dos obras españolas, *La discreta enamorada* de Lope de Vega y *Marta la piadosa* de Tirso de Molina.

2 Loreto Busquets hace unos comentarios pertinentes sobre el significado de este equívoco en 'Iluminismo e ideal burgués en "El sí de las niñas" ', *Segismundo*, 17 (1983), 61–88 (pp. 79–80).

3 Hago un análisis del personaje de doña Irene en 'La comicidad de Doña Irene en *El sí de las niñas* de Leandro Fernández de Moratín', en *Risas y sonrisas en el teatro de los siglos XVIII y XIX*, ed. Josep Maria Sala Valldaura, *Scriptura* (Lleida) 15 (1999), 145–58.

por su parte, sin duda sería consciente de que la posibilidad de que una joven de clase media sin dote se librara de una vida conventual era limitada, e incluso habría imaginado que la oferta sería bien recibida por la joven, que en los días transcurridos desde que se conocieron no ha dado ninguna señal de oponerse a la idea del matrimonio propuesto por su madre.

Sin embargo, la voz de la razón en esa primera escena es la de Simón, que respalda el plan de su amo si se cumplen tres condiciones: 'Si está usted [don Diego] bien seguro de que ella le quiere, si no la asusta la diferencia de edad, si su elección es libre. . .'.[4] Las conversaciones previas mantenidas en Madrid con la madre de Francisca le han hecho creer a don Diego que ninguno de estos impedimentos supone un obstáculo, pero hasta el tercer y último acto de la obra no sabemos hasta qué punto doña Irene le ha engañado. Sólo cuando analizamos en detalle *El sí de las niñas* nos damos cuenta de cómo Moratín se sirve del engaño empleado en mayor o menor grado por todos los personajes principales para construir la armazón de su comedia. Mediante engaños, de duración variable y de distintos grados de seriedad, cada personaje intenta lograr sus objetivos en una sociedad en que un soltero con dinero ejerce mucho poder, los jóvenes obedecen a los mayores y las personas que carecen de recursos económicos se ven obligadas a disimular y a fingir para poder mejorar su situación.

Hasta ahora los análisis de los personajes principales de *El sí de las niñas* se han concentrado en destacar los aspectos negativos de doña Irene por ser ella el origen del plan de matrimonio de su hija, tan mal concebido, y que tiene las dolorosas consecuencias de que se ocupa el argumento de la comedia. Sin embargo, nadie parece haberse fijado en los engaños, quizás más leves y justificables, pero también determinantes en el curso de los acontecimientos, perpetrados por el propio don Diego, por don Carlos y por doña Francisca. La tendencia a idealizar los motivos de los personajes creados por Moratín puede hacer olvidar su declaración de que 'la comedia pinta a los hombres como son'.[5] Este naturalismo moral supone que los personajes, tomados de las clases medias de la España de finales del siglo XVIII, son una mezcla de buenas y malas cualidades, capaces de equivocarse y de mezclar vicios y virtudes en sus acciones cotidianas. Moratín, por tanto, concibe a los espectadores de su obra como personas deseosas de 'ver descubiertos vicios y errores, tan funestos a la sociedad como favorables a sus privados intereses'.[6] Este trabajo pretenderá, entonces, localizar y analizar los múltiples intentos de engañar de los personajes principales, demostrando cómo el engaño sirve al fin dramático de complicar el argumento, frustrando los intentos de los protagonistas de conseguir

4 Cito la obra por acto y escena según la edición siguiente: Leandro Fernández de Moratín, *El sí de las niñas,* ed. Philip Deacon (London: Duckworth, 2001).

5 Leandro Fernández de Moratín, 'Prólogo', en *Obras dramáticas y líricas*, 3 vols (Paris: Imprenta de Augusto Bobée, 1825), I, xi–xlii (p. xxiii).

6 Fernández de Moratín, 'Advertencia', *El sí de las niñas*, ed. Deacon, 1.

objetivos fundamentalmente naturales y razonables, pero objetivos que encuentran estorbos en las relaciones de poder existentes, en las prácticas sociales de la época y en los conflictos de deseos habituales en la vida humana.

Antes de pasar a analizar la obra, conviene recordar algunos de los principios de la poética de la comedia enunciados por Moratín en el 'Prólogo' doctrinal redactado para acompañar la edición definitiva de sus obras. El autor maduro reflexiona a dos décadas de distancia, en 1825, sobre el género dramático cómico, intentando situar sus propias obras dentro de la tradición clasicista, pero a la vez resaltando el desarrollo de las prácticas teatrales de su época. Su definición de la comedia, no obstante, muestra grandes semejanzas con la descripción aristotélica de la tragedia.[7] La imitación de la realidad que persigue Moratín intenta poner 'en ridículo los vicios y errores comunes en la sociedad' y recomendar 'por consiguiente la verdad y la virtud'.[8] Con tales términos de hondas resonancias filosóficas y éticas el autor eleva el nivel de seriedad de la comedia, distanciándola de la farsa, e incita al espectador a buscar valores morales universales en las acciones de los grupos sociales que representa. Los ecos de la teorización aristotélica resuenan a lo largo de *El sí de las niñas* y Moratín recurre a técnicas estructurales como el descubrimiento y el cambio de dirección identificados por Aristóteles como recursos prácticos y eficaces para articular el argumento de una obra dramática. Una característica humana que identifica Aristóteles como eje clave para resaltar el fin moral y didáctico de una obra de teatro es el error o yerro (*hamartia*) que comete el protagonista y que funciona como resorte fundamental del argumento, como espero quede claro abajo, al final del análisis de la comedia de Moratín.[9]

Un aspecto destacado de la maestría técnica del autor en *El sí de las niñas* es cómo ciertos elementos básicos para la interpretación más completa de la obra no revelan su significado hasta que el argumento está plenamente desarrollado.[10] Lo que a primera vista parece tener un significado o carecer

7 Utilizo la traducción inglesa y notas al texto de *La Poética* de Aristóteles en *Ancient Literary Criticism. The Principal Texts in New Translations*, ed. D. A. Russell y M. Winterbottom (Oxford: Oxford U. P., 1972), 85–132, y la traducción española en *Poética de Aristóteles*, ed. trilingüe de Valentín García Yebra (Madrid: Gredos, 1974).

8 Fernández de Moratín, 'Prólogo', en *Obras dramáticas y líricas*, I, xxi.

9 García Yebra comenta en sus notas a la *Poética* de Aristóteles que 'yerro no implica aquí maldad, sino ignorancia, pero ignorancia nociva para el que la sufre' (284).

10 Existe, a mi parecer, una tendencia extendida entre la crítica de *El sí de las niñas* a extraer frases sueltas pronunciadas por un personaje en una situación concreta y a considerarlas verdades absolutas o, lo que es igualmente peligroso, atribuirlas al mismo Moratín. A veces tales expresiones sólo reflejan las reacciones pasajeras del personaje que las pronuncia. Estas afirmaciones, a menudo tajantes y logradas en su formulación, deben considerarse siempre en el contexto total de la obra dramática, un producto literario cuya ideología tiene que buscarse en el significado final después de concluida la acción y cuando todas las posibles contradicciones se hayan resuelto.

de él asume una importancia distinta a la luz de acciones o revelaciones posteriores. Una característica de doña Francisca en que se fija don Diego como resultado de su primeros contactos con ella es su candor o inocencia (Acto I, escena i), facetas de su personalidad que él probablemente asocia con su juventud y su reclusión durante cuatro años en un convento. El espectador ve confirmada esta opinión en las primeras escenas en que aparece la joven (Acto I, escenas ii y iii). Sin embargo, cuando Francisca está a solas con su criada Rita en la última escena del acto, ella confirma la falsedad de su comportamiento delante de don Diego, que obedecía a una intención de no revelar sus sentimientos reales, y confiesa que procuraba 'reírme y hablar niñerías', por un deseo de no ofender a su madre, que '[e]mpeñada está en que he de querer mucho a ese hombre'.[11] Y a continuación desvela claramente la intención de su madre de que engañe a don Diego no mostrando ninguna oposición al matrimonio concertado, al revelar cuánto le cuesta hacerlo tanto con sus palabras como con sus acciones: 'Porque no miento ni sé fingir, por eso me llaman picarona'. Llama la atención la forma plural del verbo que parece dar a entender que la tía monja en Guadalajara ha añadido su presión a la de Irene para que la joven no eche por tierra el plan de matrimonio.

En efecto, Francisca es la víctima que más sufre a lo largo de la historia que narra y representa la llamada comedia de Moratín. El espectador supone que la joven se enteró del proyectado matrimonio a través de su tía monja que vive en el mismo convento. Esos planes, que parecen absolutamente firmes y definitivos, suponen el abandono de su propio objetivo de casarse con don Carlos. Aunque Francisca ha podido escribir al hombre que ama, pidiéndole que actúe para impedir la próxima boda a la que ella habrá tenido que asentir sin conocer en persona a su futuro esposo, no sabe hasta el final del primer acto que don Carlos ha respondido a su petición. Desde su posición de hija obediente y virtuosa, doña Francisca no ha tenido más remedio delante de don Diego que hablar lo menos posible, comportamiento que su madre ha criticado duramente ya, y que seguirá siendo—ya sabemos por qué motivo—la actitud que mantiene en las escenas ii y iv del segundo acto.[12]

El malestar de Francisca, desde que conoció el plan de matrimonio de doña Irene, es explicado con todos los detalles lastimeros por la criada Rita a Calamocha, asistente de don Carlos, cuando se encuentran de nuevo a la llegada del joven militar a Alcalá (Acto I, escena viii). Rita relata el sufrimiento

11 Su conducta tiene semejanzas con la de doña Clara en la comedia anterior de Moratín, *La Mojigata*. Véase mi análisis en ' "Efectos de la crianza": *La Mojigata* de Leandro Fernández de Moratín', *Dieciocho*, 27:1 (2004), 87–100.

12 Los magistrales análisis de René Andioc del comportamiento de doña Francisca y don Carlos han subrayado el hecho de la sumisión de los dos jóvenes en la obra; véase René Andioc, *Teatro y sociedad en el Madrid del siglo XVIII* (Madrid: Castalia, 1987 [1ª ed. Madrid: Fundación Juan March/Editorial Castalia, 1976]), 444–60, 469–88. Véase también René Andioc, '*El sí de las niñas,* segundo centenario', en *Cambio social y ficción literaria en la España de Moratín*, ed. Teresa Nava Rodríguez, *Cuadernos de Historia Moderna*, Anejos VI (Madrid: Univ. Complutense, 2007), 19–36 (especialmente pp. 29–33).

de Francisca, que tenía que defenderse en el convento de una tía que secundaba los planes de su hermana, dejando a Francisca 'angustiada incesantemente con los sermones de aquella bendita monja'. Observemos que es la criada, no la propia interesada, quien subraya la necesidad que tiene Francisca de ocultar su estado de ánimo real, pues tiene que acatar los planes de su madre aunque ella ama y echa de menos a don Carlos: 'Y al mismo tiempo era preciso disimular, para que su tía no sospechara la verdad del caso'.[13]

El temor de Francisca de revelar ante su madre lo que siente de verdad crea otro equívoco (Acto II, escena iv) cuando Irene sigue insistiendo en las ventajas del matrimonio e interpreta el silencio de su hija como el deseo de ser monja. Dado que doña Irene no aclara inmediatamente lo que sospecha, y que el sentido de sus palabras—'¿Me quieres engañar a mí, eh?'—parece dar a entender que ha descubierto la táctica de Francisca de fingir, la joven cree que su madre se ha enterado de su relación con don Carlos durante su supuesta reclusión en el convento. Afortunadamente la conversación de doña Irene vuelve a ser autocompasiva y su hija intenta consolarla ('La Paquita nunca se apartará de su madre, ni la dará disgustos'), a lo que doña Irene responde con un 'Mira si es cierto lo que dices'. De nuevo Francisca responde haciendo hincapié en su ausencia de falsedad, o lo que es lo mismo, enfatizando su sinceridad: 'que yo no sé mentir'.

El equívoco sobre la posible ambición de ser monja de Francisca es transmitido a don Diego cuando vuelve a aparecer (Acto II, escena v), novedad que, teniendo en cuenta su carácter generalmente impasible, le provoca a reaccionar con cierta preocupación ('¡Qué diantre!'). Cuando procura saber la verdad de la propia Francisca, ella le reitera a su madre su deseo de no darle que sentir, lo que lleva a don Diego a la convicción de que Francisca no dice nada que 'se oponga a lo que su madre quiere que diga. . .'. En dos parlamentos más extensos expone cómo deben comportarse los padres al tratar el matrimonio de sus hijos, y plantea con detalle cómo concibe una vida de casado con Francisca, una relación que más se parece a la amistad que a la pasión compartida de dos amantes. Sin embargo, don Diego pregunta lo que opina Francisca del matrimonio planeado porque 'la menor disimulación en esto nos daría a todos muchísimo que sentir'. Justo antes había pedido sinceridad: 'Yo soy ingenuo: mi corazón y mi lengua no se contradicen jamás. Esto la pido a usted, Paquita: sinceridad'.[14] Pese a la

13 Fray Rafael Muñoz, uno de los calificadores inquisitoriales encargados de examinar y pronunciarse sobre la obra en 1819, se refiere a Francisca como 'una joven de 16 años disimulada, sumamente artificiosa, q[u]e con una naturalidad encantadora encubre sus verdaderos sentimientos'. El texto ha sido transcrito por Manuel Fernández Nieto en ' "El sí de las niñas" de Moratín y la Inquisición', *Revista de Literatura*, 37 (1970), 15–54 (p. 42).

14 Monroe Hafter ha analizado con gran erudición el cambio de significado de la palabra 'sinceridad' desde el siglo XVII al XVIII: Monroe Z. Hafter, 'La sinceridad en la España del siglo XVIII', *Nueva Revista de Filología Hispánica*, 36 (1988), 1131–47. Encabeza su artículo con los consejos de don Diego (1131).

firmeza con que don Diego reclama una contestación clara y sincera, las intervenciones subsiguientes de doña Irene, que sin duda teme las consecuencias de una respuesta negativa, impiden una resolución a la incógnita que ha querido aclarar don Diego desde el momento del equívoco con Simón al principio de la comedia. Mientras soporta y teme los intentos de don Diego de obligarla a aclarar sus deseos, Francisca estará esperando la intervención de su amante, algo que no ocurre hasta que se hayan retirado don Diego y doña Irene al cuarto de ésta.

Poco después (Acto II, escena x) se produce una escena de múltiples engaños en que don Carlos y Calamocha ven llegar a Simón, y Carlos incita a su asistente a mentir, a decir 'lo que quieras'. Don Carlos y Calamocha están extrañados ante la presencia de Simón pero éste igualmente está intrigado por la presencia en la posada de don Carlos, y sólo algunas de las dudas se han disipado cuando sale don Diego. Aunque se da plena cuenta de que la presencia de su tío le identifica como su rival, don Carlos ha de someterse en seguida a las preguntas insistentes de don Diego, convirtiendo la escena xi en un interrogatorio no carente de dureza en algunos momentos. Don Carlos acepta su deber de adoptar una postura de sumisión al tío, pero el saber que éste piensa robarle su amante le impide contestar con tranquilidad ya que la relación entre los dos hombres ha cambiado totalmente. Las respuestas de don Carlos revelan ambigüedades y evasivas que a veces significan una cosa para él y otra para el tío, como cuando confiesa que 'Mi desgracia me ha traído'. Cuando don Diego quiere saber detalles precisos, su sobrino no tiene más remedio que mentir:

DON DIEGO. ¿Y qué otra cosa hay?
DON CARLOS. Nada más, señor.

Como resultado de esta escena tensa aunque poco reveladora, Don Diego no tenía realmente necesidad de mandar que don Carlos y Calamocha se trasladaran al 'mesón de afuera' (Acto II, escena xii), pero interpretamos sus actos como consecuencia de la vergüenza que siente con respecto a su matrimonio con Francisca. La sinceridad que había reclamado de ésta unos minutos antes no está presente en las palabras de don Diego ante su sobrino. No hay explicación de por qué pide acciones tan extremas, incluyendo la extraordinaria prohibición de que don Carlos vuelva a entrar en la ciudad 'por ningún pretexto'. Sin embargo, la subordinación de don Carlos a lo que manda su tío parece absoluta y el comportamiento del joven oficial subraya su capacidad para obedecerle sin cuestionar las razones. Y antes de despedirse, don Diego le recuerda a su sobrino que está enterado de su conducta anterior cuando debía volver a Zaragoza y le engañó sobre la fecha de su llegada a la capital aragonesa mientras en realidad estaba en Guadalajara, donde, sin que lo supiera don Diego, se enamoró de doña Francisca. Si la decepción que siente don Diego por el ocultamiento y las mentiras de su sobrino ocupa la última parte de la conversación, una vez que el militar ha desaparecido el espectador sabe que lo que está dando vueltas en la mente de don Diego es su propia falta de sinceridad con el joven sobre su proyecto de matrimonio con Francisca ('Luego lo sabrá enhorabuena...').

El segundo acto termina con un engaño más, que entienden mejor los espectadores (o lectores) de la obra que la persona engañada, Francisca, que imagina que su amante la ha abandonado sin explicación alguna:

> ¡Qué bien supo fingir!... ¿Y con quién? Conmigo... ¿Pues yo merecí ser engañada tan alevosamente?...
>
> (Acto II, escena xvi)

En efecto, el segundo acto termina con una situación en que la intriga ha llegado a su mayor grado de complicación debido al hecho de que todos los personajes principales han continuado con su táctica de no revelar lo que realmente sienten por temor a las consecuencias. Su afán de no descubrir la verdad de sus sentimientos les induce a ocultar y engañar, fingiendo en sus acciones y mintiendo en sus palabras. Y el enredo sigue complicándose hasta que la vuelta de don Carlos durante la noche desencadene la serie de sucesos que llevan a una resolución. Esta vez el deseo de desengañar a Francisca sobre sus motivos y acciones aclara para don Diego, sin que don Carlos tenga la intención de hacerlo, el comportamiento de Francisca con respecto a su amor por don Carlos.

La vuelta del joven militar a la posada a altas horas de la madrugada, en un gesto de flagrante desobediencia a su tío, tiene el objetivo de que don Carlos se sincere ante su amante, aunque la aceptación del derecho de su tío a casarse con Francisca supone su propia renuncia a convertirse en su esposo. La primera escena del acto III repite el mismo esquema que la del acto I entre Simón y su amo; esta vez, sin embargo, don Diego es incapaz de confesar su vergüenza de que su sobrino sepa de su plan de matrimonio. La inesperada llegada de don Carlos y su conversación con Francisca a través de la ventana le informa a don Diego de la existencia de un amante de la joven, pero sólo la carta tirada por la ventana, interceptada y leída por don Diego, deja clara la identidad de ese rival. En paralelo, el hecho de haber hablado sólo brevemente con don Carlos y de no haber podido recoger su carta, supone para Francisca la cumbre de su desgracia, por la clara conciencia que adquiere en ese instante de haber sido traicionada por su amante: 'Todo engaños, Rita, de un hombre aleve, que prometió lo que no pensaba cumplir' (Acto III, escena vi).

La escena siguiente (Acto III, escena vii), en que don Diego, después de haber leído la carta de su sobrino para Francisca, ordena a Simón volver con don Carlos, encierra cierto misterio para un espectador que no espere un final feliz. El diálogo subsiguiente entre don Diego y Francisca (Acto III, escena viii) podría interpretarse como casi cruel, dado el estado anímico en que se supone que ella se encuentra. De nuevo la sumisión de la joven a la voluntad de la persona mayor explica la falta de protestas de parte de Francisca, que es sometida a un interrogatorio llevado a cabo por el hombre que hasta entonces no había logrado que manifestara claramente su sentimientos hacia él. La ironía que emplea aquí Moratín agudiza la sensación de incomodidad que sentiría cualquier espectador que se identificara con Francisca en esos momentos. Don Diego sabe algo (que don Carlos la quiere) que ella no sabe que él sabe; y el espectador sabe que ella cree que don Carlos no va a volver, mientras que en realidad Simón le ha ido a buscar a instancias de don Diego. El humor agridulce con que se desarrolla el diálogo, en que don Diego afirma lo que cree verdad, esperando que Francisca lo confirme, mientras ella responde dando por terminada su relación con don Carlos por imaginar que la ha abandonado para siempre, produce un enfrentamiento de gran dramatismo y tensión. Don Diego empieza reiterando el deseo de franqueza que le ha ocupado desde que ha conocido a la joven: 'Hablemos siquiera una vez sin rodeos ni disimulación'. Sin embargo, lo que contesta Francisca es la verdad para ella, aunque no toda la verdad. Su reticencia ahora se explica por no querer ofender a don Diego; no menciona el amor que desde hace tiempo siente por don Carlos, pero no es capaz de mentir para decir que quiere a don Diego. Lo que supone el último escollo para ella, y un momento de gran dramatismo para el espectador, es el rechazo a revelar por qué no puede ser dichosa con él.

La negativa desencadena el parlamento más célebre de la obra, en boca de don Diego:

> Ve aquí los frutos de la educación. Esto es lo que se llama criar bien a una niña: *enseñarla a que desmienta y oculte las pasiones más inocentes con una pérfida disimulación. Las juzgan honestas luego que las ven instruidas en el arte de callar y mentir.* [...] *Todo se las permite, menos la sinceridad.* Con tal que no digan lo que sienten, con tal que finjan aborrecer lo que más desean, con tal que se presten a pronunciar, cuando se lo manden, un sí, perjuro, sacrílego, origen de tantos escándalos, ya están bien criadas, y se llama excelente educación la que inspira en ellas el temor, la astucia y el silencio de un esclavo. (El subrayado es mío).

El hecho de que don Diego no parece dirigirse a Francisca en concreto, al equiparar su conducta con la de otras muchas jóvenes, les da a sus palabras un aire de declaración absoluta, para ser interpretada de esa manera por los espectadores.[15] Aunque las frases finales se dirigen a la extendida práctica del engaño en casos de matrimonio, las primeras palabras abogan por una

15 Un crítico contemporáneo anónimo calificó el parlamento, sin embargo, de sermón. Véase la 'Carta crítica sobre *El sí de las niñas*', Biblioteca Nacional, Madrid, MS. 12963, núm. 3. Los censores inquisitoriales en 1818, Juan José Tolrá y Francisco Xavier Bouzar, se refieren a las palabras de don Diego como 'una escandalosa invectiva, contra la educacion de las niñas en Conventos', a lo que añaden: 'la calumnia [...] que la educacion tenida por buena, qual es la de los Conventos, consiste en el arte de mentir; que todo lo permite, menos la sinceridad, hasta el perjurio sacrilego. Omitimos las monstruosas consequencias, que derivan de esta paradoja, en ofensa de la Religion y del Estado' (Fernández Nieto, ' "El sí de las niñas" de Moratín', 33).

sinceridad explícita al hablar de los sentimientos, poniendo así de relieve el gran cambio en las prácticas sociales de la época al dar preferencia a los sentimientos de afecto mutuo a expensas de razones familiares de índole económica.

El esquema del interrogatorio presenciado entre Francisca y don Diego se repite poco después entre don Diego y su sobrino (Acto III, escena x). El joven militar, sin muchos preámbulos, confiesa todo, una vez que se da cuenta que su tío ha leído la carta destinada a Francisca. Don Diego mantiene cierta dureza de trato y no da indicios al principio de anunciar lo que después sabemos estaba decidido ya. Don Carlos revela detalladamente cómo se enamoraron él y Francisca, admitiendo la necesidad de engañar al tío para poder proseguir la relación mientras ella vivía en el convento. Y por fin explica cómo desde muy pronto también había practicado cierto engaño con su amada, haciéndole creer que se llamaba don Félix, y ofreciendo una explicación que demuestra su cautela para no caer en los lazos de una mujer interesada por su riqueza. Sin embargo, durante toda la escena don Diego finge todavía querer casarse con Francisca y termina mandándole a esperar en su cuarto.

La voluntad de engañar de don Diego se convierte en jocosa en el episodio siguiente (Acto III, escenas xi y xii) en que doña Irene sale de su cuarto sin haberse enterado de nada de lo que ha ocurrido durante la noche y aún menos de lo que acaba de pasar con Francisca y Carlos. El golpe teatral de su aparición produce risas entre los espectadores por la fingida indignación de don Diego al declararse engañado sobre los amores de Francisca.[16] La ingenua doña Irene lo toma todo en serio, y de nuevo el espectador goza de la ironía a expensas del personaje más cómico de la obra que no entiende lo que está ocurriendo a su alrededor, sorda, como tiene que serlo cualquier actor cómico, a la reacción del público que presencia su posible humillación. Sólo cuando doña Irene amenaza con golpear a su hija, sale en su defensa don Carlos, que no puede refrenar su impulso de proteger a la mujer que quiere, ofreciendo así a doña Irene la primera oportunidad de ver al hombre que ama su hija (Acto III, escena xiii).

A la vez que don Diego resuelve el argumento de la obra ofreciendo a Francisca como mujer a su sobrino, saca las conclusiones oportunas sobre por qué se había producido una situación aparentemente insoluble. Echa la culpa en parte a doña Irene y sus hermanas monjas que le 'llenaban la cabeza de ilusiones que han desaparecido como un sueño'. Las palabras que emplea son moderadas y de esta manera renuncia definitivamente a la idea de casarse con un 'niña', aunque algún crítico de la época sugirió que tales renuncias eran escasas en la vida real.[17]

16 Baso el comentario en la reacción del público madrileño a este momento de la obra cuando la dirigió Miguel Narros para la Compañía Nacional de Teatro Clásico en la temporada teatral de 1996–1997.

17 '[L]os viejos enamorados no son tan generosos' (Anón., 'Crítica de *El sí de las niñas*', Biblioteca Nacional, Madrid, MS. 18.666, núm. 2).

El sí de las niñas pretende enseñar a la vez que divertir, y Moratín no se olvida de la doctrina aristotélica cuando la obra llega a su escena final. Don Diego se había dejado engañar por los argumentos de doña Irene; sin embargo, una serie de sucesos le ha revelado la verdad pese a todos los engaños practicados por las personas implicadas, él incluido: 'Por una casualidad he sabido a tiempo el error en que estaba... ¡Ay de aquellos que lo saben tarde!'.[18] Aunque la obra tiene otras características propias de la tragedia de tipo aristotélico, las palabras que se acaban de citar traen a la mente el concepto de error o yerro que identifica el filósofo griego como motivo de la acción trágica. El personaje creado por Moratín pasa por varios estadios de duda sobre el plan de matrimonio con Francisca antes de la renuncia final que constituye el reconocimiento de su autoengaño o error (*hamartia*). Incitado por doña Irene, es capaz de imaginar una vida sexual con Francisca después de la boda (Acto I, escena iv), y más adelante prevé una relación que 'se parece a la amistad' (Acto II, escena v), pero para la segunda mitad del acto III está claro, aunque mucho más en retrospectiva, que don Diego ha renunciado el plan de casarse.

En el enfrentamiento crucial con su sobrino (Acto III, escena x), don Diego finge todavía tener esa ambición, pero el tesón con que don Carlos defiende su propia relación con Francisca provoca a su tío a responder con argumentos aparentemente convincentes: 'me ha dicho que está pronta a obedecer a su madre y darme la mano, así que...', frase que provoca la interrupción de su interlocutor con una negación definitiva: 'Pero no el corazón'. Con aquella frase don Carlos sintetiza el significado de la obra, que el matrimonio tiene que basarse en lo que pide el corazón, si no las 'resultas funestas' son como las que don Diego había afirmado antes: 'matrimonios infelices, uniones monstruosas' (Acto II, escena v). El yerro aristotélico de don Diego era creer en lo que parecía ofrecer doña Irene y olvidar lo que le había recordado con tanta precisión Simón. La naturaleza de la falta que comete se aclara a medida que avanza la comedia, y el público se da cuenta en paralelo de cómo un hombre aparentemente sensato y equilibrado puede equivocarse, y cómo una equivocación puede tener consecuencias de gran trascendencia no sólo para el protagonista sino también para las demás personas implicadas.

La comedia de Moratín confronta ciertas prácticas matrimoniales de las clases medias de su época con las demandas de los jóvenes de basar esas relaciones en los sentimientos del individuo. El no hacer caso a la importancia de los sentimientos, que pueden tener un componente moral que guía al individuo a actuar bien, parece inducir a las partes implicadas a engañar y a mentir. La artimaña de doña Irene lleva a don Diego, un hombre

18 La frase final recuerda la obra anterior de Moratín, *El viejo y la niña*. En ese caso el matrimonio sin amor entre un viejo y una joven lleva a una situación que sólo se resuelve cuando la niña del título, Isabel, abandona la casa matrimonial, con el permiso del marido don Roque, para pasar el resto de sus días en un convento. Isabel había aceptado el matrimonio con don Roque después de haber sido engañada por su tutor.

fundamentalmente bueno, al autoengaño, un estado antinatural que a su vez repercute en todos los demás personajes de la obra, produciendo en consecuencia la serie de engaños que da forma al argumento. La maestría de Moratín se revela en la sutileza con que construye *El sí de las niñas* para que el significado de los componentes a pequeña escala reflejen fielmente el sentido global de la comedia resultante.

Playing the Enlightenment: Eighteenth-Century Spain on the Nineteenth-Century Stage

DAVID T. GIES
University of Virginia

Well before the middle of the nineteenth century, the figure of the 'clásico' had become a stock character in Spanish literature. Satires of the (normally rigid and rule-bound) type—particularly when counterpoised against the more 'natural' and free-spirited 'romántico'—grew increasingly more frequent as the debates over Ancient *vs* Modern literature heated up once again. Espronceda's contribution to the discussion, 'El pastor Clasiquino', appeared in the first issue of *El Artista* in 1835,[1] where he captured with brilliant satirical flourish the dubiously-educated simple shepherd ('"Nada como las reglas de Aristóteles", solía también decir Clasiquino a veces, que aunque pastor, había leído más de una vez las reglas del esagirita') who spent his time 'recordando los amores de su ingrata Clori, en un valle pacífico, al margen de un arroyuelo cristalino'. Six years later, when Antonio de Iza Zamacola published his one-act comedy, *El clásico y el romántico* (1841),[2] the author's note concerning the protagonists' sartorial choices suggests that the 'clásico' and the 'romántico' had already taken shape as fixed types in the popular mind: 'Los trages de Gervasio y Federico deben exagerarse algún tanto, para caracterizar con más perfección sus diversas inclinaciones', the implication being, of course, that those 'inclinaciones' would be well-known to the audience. Gervesio, the 'clásico', is portrayed as boring, not only in his dress, but also in his writing and his habits:

> Escribe en pedestre prosa,
> Viste como te he pintado,
> charla más que un abogado,
> es cantárida, venturosa,

1 José de Espronceda, 'El pastor Clasiquino', *El Artista*, I (1835), 251–52.

2 Antonio de Iza Zamacola, *El clásico y el romántico. Comedia en un acto original y en verso* (Madrid: Boix, 1841).

y es, en fin, un avestruz
que en casándose promete
trocarse en buey. (10)

The classical type has been already clearly set. References to eighteenth-century authors abound in the play (Iriarte, Cadalso, 'el pueril Moratín'), and in a nod to the anacreontic poetry that had been so in vogue during the previous century, Elisa tells Teresa that Gervasio's poetry—like Clasiquino's mind—is crammed with 'praderas esmaltadas de flores', 'arroyuelos', 'pajarillos', 'el dulce ambiente del aura', 'ameno(s) valle(s)' and a 'casto harem de las zagalas'. Naturally, she favours the more exciting Federico, whose lugubrious but passionate poetry suggests a danger and darkness that she finds attractive. Yet in an interesting turn, while Iza Zamacola marries Elisa off to Federico and Margarita (Federico's sister) to Gervasio, it is the servant woman Teresa's equanimity that wins out in the end. As she states about Roque, her future husband: 'Sí, que Roque con ardor / sin visos de nigromántico, / de clásico, ni romántico, / supo inspirarme el amor' (38). *Ni chicha ni limonada*, neither Classic nor Romantic, wins the day.

Yet not all plays on this theme demonstrated such balance. The eighteenth century provided diverting fodder for playwrights in the nineteenth century who turned their eyes back to earlier times with a look at literary conventions, political activities, general customs or theatre history. The Duque de Rivas' famous *Don Álvaro o la fuerza del sino* (1835) takes place in the eighteenth century (he specifically alludes to the Battle of Velletri, which dates from 10 August 1744),[3] but uses none of the expected conventions—apart, perhaps, from a generalized respect for verisimilitude in the temporal structure—from that time period; in fact, the very purpose of his new play seemed to be to break or avoid Enlightened and Neo-classical conventions. Even a cursory look at the thousands of plays written and performed during the nineteenth century in Spain produces dozens of titles situated in the eighteenth century, plays representing different genres and different styles, written by a wide array of fondly remembered and long-forgotten individuals. These plays flooded Spanish stages and left in their wake a constructed memory of the eighteenth century that often differed sharply from the historical reality. Plays or adaptations by well-known Spanish writers (Larra, Bretón, Ventura de la Vega, Martínez de la Rosa, Rodríguez Rubí, Gil y Zárate, García Gutiérrez) or European dramatists (Dumas) alternated with works staged by now unfamiliar names (Nicolás Lombía, Cipriano López-Salgado,

3 John Dowling, 'Time in Don Álvaro', *Romance Notes*, 18 (1978), 355–61.

Felipe Luna, Enrique Zumel).[4] The locales ranged from Madrid and Spanish provincial towns to the capitals of Europe (England, France, Italy, Russia, Scotland) and North America, and the time periods encompassed everything from the initial years of the Bourbon monarchy to the death throes of the Ancien Régime. Some, naturally, dealt with specific historical moments (the British siege of the Puerto de Santa María in 1702, the War of the Spanish Succession, the expulsion of the Jesuits in 1767), while others viewed the eighteenth century as a rather generic time of 'enlightenment' or 'reason', populated by *ilustrados*, *petimetres* and *majas*. A rough tally suggests that about one per cent of the plays staged in the nineteenth century in Spain (which number in the thousands) dealt in some way or other with the eighteenth century.[5]

It would be impossible to discuss all of these plays in the space provided here; for that reason, I shall focus on seven original titles, plays from which we might be able to extract some tentative conclusions about the use of the eighteenth century as a dramatic space and theme in the Spanish nineteenth century. I shall look at Carlos García Doncel's and Luis Valladares y Garriga's *Sobresaltos y congojas* (1841),[6] Eusebio Asquerino's *Españoles sobre todo* (1844),[7] Tomás Rodríguez Rubí's *Alberoni* (1846),[8] Juan de Alba's *Escenas del Siglo de las Luces* (1853);[9] Luis Mariano de Larra's *Chorizos y Polacos* (1876);[10] Tomás Luceño's *El corral de las comedias* (1885);[11] and, just after the turn of the twentieth century, Deusdedit Criado's *La Tirana* (1905).[12] All draw on the eighteenth century as a source of inspiration, a place of reference, or a well-spring of satire, although in very different ways. In this article I propose to look at these plays in order to determine in what ways, if any, they incorporate tropes from the eighteenth century into their ideological base, their rhetorical expression, or their thematic or aesthetic concerns. I will signal my conclusions here: what we find is a surprising lack of serious engagement with the previous century's political, ideological, historic and aesthetic concerns.

4 For more on Zumel, see my '*In re magica veritas*: Enrique Zumel y la comedia de magia en la segunda mitad del siglo XIX', in *La comedia de magia y de santos,* ed. F. J. Blasco, E. Caldera, J. Álvarez Barrientos and R. de la Fuente (Madrid: Júcar, 1992), 433–61.

5 I am grateful to my friend and colleague José Luis González Subías for much of the information provided in this section of my study.

6 Carlos García Doncel and Luis Valladares y Garriga, *Sobresaltos y congojas* (Madrid: Vicente de Lalama, 1841).

7 Eusebio Asquerino, *Españoles sobre todo* (Madrid: José Repullés, 1844).

8 Tomás Rodríguez Rubí, *Alberoni* (Madrid: Antonio Yenes, 1846).

9 Juan de Alba, *Escenas del Siglo de las Luces* (Madrid: José María Repullés, 1853).

10 Luis Mariano de Larra, *Chorizos y Polacos* (Madrid: José Rodríguez, 1876).

11 Tomás Luceño, *El corral de las comedias* (No place of publication or publisher, 1885). See also in *Teatro breve*, ed. J. Vidanes, doctoral thesis (Madrid: Univ. Complutense, 2003).

12 Deusdedit Criado, *La Tirana* (Madrid: R. Velasco, 1905).

The best known of the works mentioned above is Luis Mariano de Larra's *zarzuela* (with music by Barbieri), *Chorizos y Polacos*, written in the spring of 1876 and first performed at the Teatro del Príncipe Alfonso in Madrid on 24 May of that year.[13] Larra had already located two plays in the eighteenth century: his successful *La flor del valle* was first staged in Madrid in 1856 (the action takes place during the initial years of Fernando VI's reign) and his even more successful *La oración de la tarde* appeared in 1858 (it takes place six leagues from Madrid in the year 1718). *Chorizos y Polacos* is billed as dealing with 'costumbres teatrales del siglo XVIII', and, true to its word, it incorporates references to numerous authors, actors and works from the period.[14] Larra himself is one of the most fascinating playwrights of mid nineteenth-century Spain, a man deservedly overshadowed by his brilliant father but unjustly forgotten by theatre historians.[15] We hardly need to rehearse here the famous tension between the so-called *Chorizos* and *Polacos*, and Larra takes as a given his audience's familiarity with the conflict, although he does pause to explain the putative origins of the names:

Como desde que el gracioso
Rafael de Oros, el bueno,
faltándole unos chorizos
en un sainete, hizo de ello
tal chacota y rompió en chistes
tantos y tales, que el pueblo
dio en llamarnos los Chorizos
a los de la Cruz; quisieron
los del Príncipe mofarnos
por el apodo, y como ellos
iban siempre con un fraile,
a quien los de su convento
llamaban Padre Polaco,

13 According to a letter he wrote to Barbieri in mid-March, he was in the process of revising the first act ('Hoy paso el día reluciente arreglando el 1° acto de los *Chorizos* y no salgo por la noche. No te digo esto para comprometerte a venir por estos barrios, si no lo has pensado, pero si por acaso vinieras, serías recibido con alma y vida. Mi familia estará de teatro, yo de butaca. ¡Abajo los fueros y las fiestas!' (Francisco Asenjo Barbieri, *Biografías y documentos sobre música y músicos españoles. Documentos sobre música española y epistolario [Legado Barbieri]*, ed. Emilio Casares, 2 vols [Madrid: Fundación Banco Exterior, 1988], II, 680–81).

14 As might be expected, mention is made of Iriarte, Ramón de la Cruz, Moratín (*La comedia nueva*), and Comella. There is even mention of *Paca la salada*, a *sainete* that, according to Andioc and Coulon, was performed at the Teatro del Príncipe on 29 January 1790. See René Andioc y Mireille Coulon, *Cartelera teatral madrileña del siglo XVIII (1708–1808)*, 2 vols (Toulouse: Presses Universitaires du Mirail, Univ. de Toulouse-Le Mirail, 1996), II, 801.

15 For more on Larra *hijo*, see my 'El otro Larra: Luis Mariano de Larra y Wetoret, dramaturgo "desconocido" de la segunda mitad del siglo XIX (con Apéndice de títulos)', *Anales de Literatura Española*, 20 (2008), 241–57.

juzgando el apodo bueno,
los Polacos los pusimos;
y estos dos bandos opuestos
como no anden siempre a palos
no pueden estar contentos. (I.3)[16]

The list of players is taken straight out of theatre history (indeed, this is the most historically-grounded of the plays discussed here): José Espejo,[17] María Antonia Fernández *la Caramba*,[18] and Josefa Figueras *la Figueras*[19] were all well-known players on the stages of Madrid in the second half of the eighteenth century. The place is real, as well: the first act opens in the Plaza de San Juan, at the intersection of the Calle de San Juan and the Calle de Santa María (today Huertas and Moratín), in front of Moratín *hijo*'s birthplace. But Larra is a creative writer, not an historian, and he slips up on his chronology: he

16 In his 'Advertencia importante' he attempts to clarify the names for the readers of his play. Correcting Nicolás Fernández de Moratín's comments, and basing his arguments on Leandro's clarification in the *Obras póstumas* of Nicolás (full reference at note 17), he states: '*Chorizos* eran los apasionados que sostenían a la compañía de que era autor (*o empresario como hoy se dice*), Manuel Martínez; y *Polacos* los intransigentes defensores de la de Eusebio Rivera. Y como quiera que ambas compañías solían mudar con frecuencia de teatro, y los *Polacos* y *Chorizos* no defendían el teatro, sino la compañía que en él actuaba, dicho se está que unas veces los *Chorizos* eran los del Príncipe y otras los de la Cruz [...] yo he debido ceñirme a lo que los autores de aquella época dan por seguro y cierto.'

17 Espejo first appears in Cotarelo's *Estudios sobre la historia del arte escénico en España* as a *tercer galán* in the company of José Parra at the Teatro de la Cruz in 1759–1760. I will cite from Álvarez Barrientos' new edition of Cotarelo's work: *Actrices españolas en el siglo XVIII. María Ladvenant y Quirante y María del Rosario Fernández 'La Tirana'*, ed. Joaquín Álvarez Barrientos (Madrid: Publicaciones de la Asociación de Directores de Escena de España, 2007), repr. of Emilio Cotarelo y Mori, *Estudios sobre la historia del arte escénico en España. María Ladvenant y Quirante. Primera dama de los teatros de la corte* (Madrid: Est. Tipográfico 'Sucesores de Rivadeneyra', 1896), and *Estudios sobre la historia del arte escénico en España. María del Rosario Fernández, 'La Tirana'. Primera dama de los teatros de la corte* (Madrid: Est. Tipográfico 'Sucesores de Rivadeneyra', 1897). Moratín recounts an amusing anecdote about his father and Espejo: when the senior Moratín solicited the actor's opinion about his drama *Hormesinda*, the following dialogue took place: ' "La tragedia es excelente, señor Moratín, y digna de su buen ingenio de usted. Yo, por mi parte, haré lo que pueda; pero, dígame usted la verdad, ¿a qué viene ese empeño de componer a la francesa? Yo no digo que se quite de la pieza ni siquiera un verso; pero ¿qué trabajo podía costarle a usted añadirla un par de graciosos?" Moratín le apretó la mano, llorando de risa, y le dijo: "Usted es un buen hombre, tío Espejo. Estudie usted su papel, bien estudiadito; que lo demás sobre mi conciencia lo tomo" '. See Leandro Fernández de Moratín, 'Vida del autor', in Nicolás Fernández de Moratín, *Obras póstumas*, ed. L. Fernández de Moratín (Barcelona: Viuda de Roca, 1821), i–liv.

18 *La Caramba* retired from the stage in 1785 and died on 10 June 1787 (Cotarelo, *Actrices españolas*, ed. Álvarez Barrientos, 252).

19 Josefa Figueras, who had been in Madrid since 1770, was the *primera dama* in the company of Manuel Martínez in 1780; she had previously been in the company of José Ponce, but moved to Martínez's group because of a conflict with an actor called Ildefonso Coque de Llano (Cotarelo, *Actrices españolas*, ed. Álvarez Barrientos, 187, 190).

mentions Moratín's *La comedia nueva, o el café* (17), which was premièred in 1792, without remembering that one of his main characters, *la Caramba*, had died in 1787; a similar anachronistic allusion is made to Comella's *El mayor rival de Roma*, not performed in Madrid until 1799.[20] Other references to theatrical works such as *Troya abrasada (por el astuto Sinón)*[21] lend seeming authenticity to the internal workings of the play. But what the audience might have expected (and had been hoping) to see on stage—raucous squabbles between the defenders of each theatre group[22]—is delayed until the end of the first act, when the tensions finally erupt:

> Se pegan unos a otros. Por los aposentos y por la puerta de las localidades asoman unos cuantos soldados con fulsiles. Chillidos de las mujeres, y en medio de este escándalo y con un fuertísimo de orquesta, cae el telón. (90)

Mainly, Larra focuses on a love story set among the petty rivalries of the two groups. There is talk of disruption ('Tosecitas y risas / son lo primero, / y tirar avellanas / al alojero' [14]), but it is all talk. Still, the talk is lively, animated, and fun, and interspersed with melodies. Will the groups reconcile? Will they fight? For the second act, Larra takes us into the dressing room of the Teatro del Príncipe and, allows us to hear echoes of his father's famous article, 'Yo quiero ser cómico' (1833),[23] as Espejo finds out that the sets, wigs, costumes and props for the plays are all inappropriate, anachronistic, or downright silly. For example:

ESPEJO: ¡Virgen santa de la O!
¡Estos *griegos* han venido
de las Ventas de Alcorcón!
Esos cascos son terribles!
Esos péplum dan horror!
COMPS: ¿Pues qué griegos quiere este hombre
por dos reales de vellón?

In Act III, scene 3, D. Preciso harks back to Larra's article when he states:

¡Mientras exista el tío Tusa
y otros como él, no hay escape,

20 See Andioc y Coulon, *Cartelera teatral madrileña*, II, 773.

21 See Andioc y Coulon, *Cartelera teatral madrileña*, II, 868.

22 Larra explains in his 'Advertencia importante' (citing Moratín *hijo*): 'Como estos partidos usurpaban frecuentemente los derechos del público, y lo que a ellos no era agradable caía sin remedio a fuerza de silbidos crueles, entre las oleadas del patio que hacían crujir y tal vez rompían el *degolladero* (viga robusta que dividía a los mosqueteros de la luneta pacífica), los cómicos procuraban aumentar el número de sus parciales y tenerlos muy en su favor, a lo menos para evitar su cólera, ya que no les mereciesen su aplauso'.

23 Mariano José de Larra, 'Yo quiero ser cómico' (1833), in *Artículos varios*, ed. E. Correa Calderón (Madrid: Castalia, 1976), 354–61.

y mientras que la Figueras
persista en equivocarse,
y por *chocolate*, diga
cocholate y *cholocate*,
será en esta compañía
cada función un desastre! (95)[24]

The satire is quick, witty and hilarious as Espejo learns more and more about that day's performance.

Not unexpectedly, Leandro Fernández de Moratín is viewed as the model of order and good taste. In the third act, as the characters squabble about appropriate conduct in the theatre, D. Preciso asks Espejo (with some surprise): '¿Se ha hecho usté *Moratiniano*?' (94), to which the actor replies:

Yo siempre, y como él nos salve
de este caos, y haga que cesen
todas las parcialidades;
y dé decoro al teatro,
y haya órden terminante
de prohibir que penetre
entre bastidores nadie,
¡bendito sea mil veces
Moratín y sus secuaces! (94–95)

While much of the play is dominated by the gossip and complications of the company, the characters also express concern for the future of the theatre ('a estas horas se decide / en una junta de Alcaldes / el porvenir del teatro' [100]), which speaks to the fate of live theatre in the capital. Larra allows us to overhear the concerns that dominated theatre administration at the end of the century, accurately reflecting the instability of ownership, finances, and performance that had been major areas of complaint and concern for years. When the theatres close for reform, Tusa proclaims:

Que el Gobierno al fin ha dado
Un reglamento o pramática,
Por la cual, desde hoy, él mismo
De los teatros se encarga,
Reforma ajustes, comedias,
Cómicos, público, salas,
En fin, destroza y destruye
Costumbres inveteradas,

24 'No jure usted. ¿Sabe usted pronunciar con afectación todas las letras de una palabra, y decir unas voces por otras, *actitud* por *aptitud*, y *aptitud* por *actitud*, *diferiencia* por *diferencia*, *háyamos* por *hayamos*, *dracmático* por *dramático*, y otras semejantes?' See 'Yo quiero ser cómico', 357.

Y a Chorizos y Polacos
Con su proyecto nos mata! (119)

To which Espejo shouts, '¡Viva Moratín!' While we glean more costumbristic ambience than depth from Larra's play, at least we get that—a witty window into acting companies in Madrid at the end of the eighteenth century.

Clearly, the most controversial of all the plays situated in the eighteenth century was Eusebio Asquerino's *Españoles sobre todo*, a rabble-rousing political screed that drew protests and provoked closures all over Spain.[25] Rodríguez Rubí's follow-up play on the same subject, *Alberoni*, generated such nervousness on the part of the authorities (in spite of—or perhaps because of—its enthusiastic public reception) that it was banned after just a few performances. This is hardly surprising. Both plays were openly political (*Alberoni*'s subtitle was *La astucia contra el poder*), and both linked eighteenth-century court politics with a contemporary monarchy that had recently fought a bitter civil war. In fact, the War of the Spanish Succession plays a prominent role in several of the plays under discussion here, primarily because it reminded contemporary playwrights and the theatre-going public of current politics.

Set in the nineteenth century rather than in the eighteenth, *Escenas del Siglo de las Luces* (1853) draws on the trope of Enlightenment in an ironic (and, one must confess, cursory) manner, since for Juan de Alba, the nineteenth, not the eighteenth, is the 'siglo iluminado'. The irony in his case flows from his adoption of the word 'iluminado' to castigate his century for its excess of bad family relations, rocky marriages and corrupt business ventures. Woven into his text are numerous references to the past century that reflect the nineteenth-century's ill-defined memory of previous times. For example, for the Vizconde, this 'siglo de las luces' is one that values 'foreignness', a clear echo of the debates that raged in the eighteenth century about the excess of French influence in the Peninsula: 'Lo estrangero es lo que vale / en el siglo de las luces' (5), but the references to playwrights, when they appear, are not to the Moratíns (as remembered by Larra) but rather to contemporary playwrights such as Antonio García Gutiérrez and Eusebio Asquerino (6). Remembering Espronceda's El pastor Clasiquino (or any number of the clichéd shepherds of Spanish literature), Marcelo brushes Alberto off with the question, '¿Por qué no te vas al campo / a cuidar cabras?' (13), when he wants to dispatch him. Alba peppers his text with vague and superficial references to the past, hoping his audience will fill in the necessary information and make the connections. That is, for him, the spillover from the eighteenth century is complete: all that is bad, or shady, or in need of reform is summed up in his Larra-like exclamation, '¡Oh, siglo, siglo ilustrado!'

25 I have dealt with this play in 'Rebeldía y drama en 1844: *Españoles sobre todo*, de Eusebio Asquerino', in *De místicos y mágicos, clásicos y románticos. Homenaje a Ermanno Caldera*, ed. Antonietta Calderone (Messina: Armando Siciliano Editore, 1993), 315–32.

(28) or in his conclusion that 'Siempre habrá quien marche a oscuras / en el siglo de las luces' (71).

Only slightly more substantive is the earlier *Sobresaltos y congojas* (1841) by García Doncel and Valladares y Garriga, which looks at the early eighteenth century through the prism of history. The War of the Spanish Succession and the actions of the controversial Princesa de los Ursinos are highlighted in a play that inserts the convoluted political machinations of the period into a highly-charged romantic structure. Historical dramas were much in vogue during the Romantic period, but not much is made here of the real history of the time and how it intersects with the troubled period in which García Doncel and Valladares y Garriga wrote their work. Students of Spanish history might be expected to know some of the major players, but the general theatre-going public would focus instead on the twists and turns of the plot. Madrid, 1715. Conspiracies against Felipe V, divisions between the competing factions for control of the throne, and tension between ministerial and ecclesiastical power lead the characters through betrayal, fear, mistaken identities, terror, bad luck, insanity and ... on to a happy ending! Indeed, as the action progresses, the history recedes and the plot itself takes centre stage. When the uprising finally comes it feels like an afterthought, not central to the concerns being laid out in the preceding acts, although it does reflect the confusion lived by *madrileños*:

> Gritando muera el ministro,
> Y viva ... yo no sé quién ...
> No, al revés, viva el ministro,
> Y mueran ... el Cardenal
> Y la princesa de Ursinos:
> Eso es, eso ... mas no ... en fin,
> Yo no entiendo cómo ha sido.
> ¡Figúrate tú qué infamia! (III, iv)

All of this, however, might be moot since, while the title-page of the published edition claims that it was performed on 1 September 1841 in Madrid (no theatre is given, owing to the standard practice of stating the theatre in which the play was first seen), no notice at all can be found in newspapers of the day, suggesting its rapid disappearance (or suppression) from the stage and from the public's mind.

Tomás Luceño's 1885 play, *El corral de las comedias*, a one-act *sainete* that brings Moratín, Ramón de la Cruz, Comella and others back onto the stage, likewise received no notice in the press.[26] Luceño (b.1844, the year of Zorrilla's

26 *Veinticuatro diarios. Madrid, 1830–1900*, ed. José Simón Díaz, 4 vols (Madrid: CSIC, 1968–1975). See also Heinrich Richard Falk, 'Actors, Audiences, and Theatrical *sainetes*: A Formula for Success on the Eighteenth-Century Spanish Stage', *Educational Theatre Journal*, 28:3 (1976), 299–311.

Don Juan Tenorio), now forgotten,[27] belonged to a new generation of writers—Ricardo de la Vega, Vital Aza, Carlos Arniches, Julián Romea, Celso Lucio, and Joaquín Dicenta, among them—working alone or in tandem with the great composers of the day to produce material for the ever-expanding market for theatre in Spain.[28] Luceño did have success in the 'género chico', where he excelled as an exponent of local customs and types in the style of the great eighteenth-century models Ramón de la Cruz or Juan Ignacio González del Castillo. In this play, he returns to Larra *hijo*'s theme—Chorizos *versus* Polacos—and places the action in a specific setting (in front of the façade of the Teatro del Príncipe in Madrid) on a specific date (7 February 1792). A poster hung up beside the entrance to the theatre announces Moratín's *La comedia nueva, o el café* in conjunction with a *sainete* by Ramón de la Cruz. As the action begins, Nicolás, a poor actor sentenced to selling tickets for today's performance, overhears three failed actresses badmouthing Moratín:

> No puede tener talento . . .
> y voy a darte una prueba.
> Cuando llevó a tu teatro
> su detestable comedia
> *El viejo y la niña*, y quise
> hacer yo, por ser muy cuerda,
> la dama joven, me dijo
> manifestando sorpresa:
> ¿Cómo pretende usté hacer
> un papel que representa
> una niña candorosa,
> inocente, pura y bella
> de quince años? Eso es
> bien claro llamarme vieja. (I, 3)

They complain that Moratín's slow pace of writing ('tarda dos años / en hacer una comedia') is prejudicial to the theatre. By comparison, Lucía brags about her father—the playwright Comella—who 'en cuatro noches / compone cinco tragedias' (I, 3). When Comella himself makes an appearance, it is to accuse Moratín of arrogance: 'Lo que yo no le perdono / y no olvidaré jamás / es que ha llegado a creerse / (¡si no lo quiero pensar!) / ¡que es superior su talento / al mío!' (I, 4). As the characters comment on the play—the play that was indeed performed in 1792, the play that the audience in 1885 would have known, and

27 'Es Tomás Luceño en la actualidad un escritor olvidado?', asks José Montero Padilla in 'Acercamiento a Tomás Luceño', *Anales del Instituto de Estudios Madrileños*, 33 (1993), 601–16 (p. 601).

28 Emilio Casares Rodicio, 'El teatro musical en España (1800–1939)', in *Historia del teatro español*, ed. Javier Huerta Calvo, 2 vols (Madrid: Gredos, 2003), II. *Del siglo XVIII a la época actual*, 2051–84 (p. 2063).

the play we know today—the metatheatricality of the endeavour produces nods of recognition and agreement. Agapito tells us:

> ¡Qué don Hermógenes! ¡Vamos,
> si hace reír a las piedras
> con aquellos latinajos
> que a cada momento suelta.
> Don Eleuterio, no hay duda,
> es don Luciano Comella,
> con sus dramas terroríficos
> y espeluznantes tragedias. (I, 5)

At this point, Moratín chimes in to defend not only his work but also his position on theatrical reform:

> Bien sabe Dios que trabajo
> por ennoblecer el arte,
> lleno de fe y entusiasmo;
> y si algún día consigo
> que se levante el teatro
> de la postración en que
> Comella y sus partidarios
> le tienen, no habrá en el mundo
> hombre más afortunado
> que yo. (I, 7)

There is much more of this back and forth between the rival parties, but the point is that Luceño captures the debate as it raged in the 1790s and as it was remembered throughout the nineteenth century. Full of description of theatrical activity as well as criticism of the abuses perceived by Moratín (and by Luceño), this play is in itself a kind of *Comedia nueva* for the end of the nineteenth century, as they look back at the Romantic and Neoromantic plays being produced at the time. '¡Ya se acabaron / las tremebundas tragedias / de princesas deshonradas, de muertos, de sangre y guerra!' (I, 10):

> Moratín, con su talento
> señala una nueva senda,
> y desde hoy el teatro
> será imagen verdadera
> y exacta de las costumbres
> de la sociedad moderna;
> y criticará sus vicios
> y ensalzará sus grandezas. (I, 10)

Luceño's cleverness shines in scene 13, where he has Comella protest about the play's denouement and suggest an alternative, more melodramatic (i.e., crowd-pleasing and perhaps romantic) ending:

> No me llama
> lo de que don Eleuterio
> de ser autor se arrepienta.
> Debe dispararse un tiro
> y morir.
> [. . .]
> La hermanita, envenenarse,
> y la mujer del poeta,
> meterse monja. . . (I, 13)

He keeps the spirited debate over theatre alive a century later by bringing Moratín and Comella comically to life on the stage. Moratín, naturally, resists changing his words to suit popular whim, and indeed it is he who gets the last word: 'cumple[n] siempre / la misión de la comedia, / que es deleitar enseñando' (I, 15).

One final look at the eighteenth century on stage takes us into the first years of the twentieth century. Deusdedit Criado published his comedy, *La Tirana*, in Madrid in 1905, and it draws on the same tropes and clichés that by now were standard fare in Spanish theatre. That the Spanish *zarzuela* never transformed itself into a broadly-accepted (by the elite) European musical phenomenon seemed to be of little interest to writers like Criado, who looked at the protagonists of such plays as heroes of an autochthonous tradition worth remembering and even foregrounding.[29] María del Rosario Fernández (1755–1803), known popularly as *La Tirana,* gained notoriety as the best *tonadillera* of her day, sat for a Goya portrait in 1799 and excelled at performing the solo ditties regularly sung in conjunction with short theatre pieces. She had already been turned into a theatre personage by José Picón and Francisco Asenjo Barbieri in their highly acclaimed *zarzuela* called *Pan y toros* in 1864 (Goya himself makes an appearance in the work), and Criado drew on that characterization for his recreation of the popular singer. Criado sets his play simply in the 'época de Carlos III' and populates it with several dozen characters drawn from history and culture. Although the play is basically a domestic comedy, a love story (whom will Rosaura, *La Tirana*'s niece, marry?), the author adds a note of the class discrimination that actors suffered in the eighteenth century (and, indeed, in his own). The main character says to Rosaura's suitor, a rich nobleman (we know he is rich because she tells him:

29 Rafael Lamas takes a refreshing new look at the *zarzuela* in 'Zarzuela and Anti-Musical Prejudice of the Spanish Enlightenment', *HR*,74:1 (2006), 39-58, where he discusses the rejection of musical hybridity that inhibited the development of a broad-based modern national opera.

'Vos poséeis riquezas y blasones / y ella es pobre y plebeya' [19]) that 'Conozco demasiado el mundo / y conozco, además, vuestro abolengo' (19).

As much as one might have thought that the immediacy of the Enlightenment project and its seeming relevance to the Spanish nineteenth century would have been reflected on stage (which voraciously absorbed all of the most hotly debated topics being played out across the century), the absence of any sustained thought about or analysis of the eighteenth century surprises. Perhaps it was too early, but while the eighteenth century makes itself felt with some frequency in the theatre of the century to follow, the incursions into that distant terrain remain superficial and cliché-driven. Little real engagement with the deeper issues of Enlightened and Neo-classic Spain become woven into the fabric of these entertainments, even if they did serve the purpose of reinforcing certain issues that modern Spanish dramatists wished to convey to their theatre-going public (theatrical reform, foreignness *versus* Spanishness, nods to the great dramatists of the past). There existed no perceived need to revisit the aspirations and accomplishments of the past century; these works are not historical dramas in their traditional mode since they refused to engage with the 'intellectual systems' of the past.[30] Some internalization inevitably took place, particularly when the themes dealt with the theatre itself or with theatrical history, and there was an awareness on the part of some dramatists of the usefulness of drawing on the past to make comments on the present. Still, most 'dieciochismo' on the nineteenth-century stage rarely rose above ambience, *costumbrismo*, or plot-detail when plays dealt with that now-past 'Siglo de las Luces'.

30 Herbert Lindenberger, *Historical Drama. The Relation of Literature and Reality* (Chicago: Univ. of Chicago Press, 1975), xii.

A Propaganda Play of 1808 F. Enciso Castrillón's *La defensa de Valencia y castigo de traidores*

I. L. McCLELLAND[†]
University of Glasgow
ed. Ann L. Mackenzie
University of Glasgow

Introductory Note to I. L. McClelland†, A Propaganda Play of 1808 F. Enciso Castrillón's *La defensa de Valencia y castigo de traidores*

The date when Ivy McClelland wrote this previously unpublished article is uncertain. The typescript was found, after her death, among her papers,[1] in an envelope on which she had written the information that it was: 'unused' and that it dealt with 'propaganda drama'. No doubt she had first read Enciso's play about *La defensa de Valencia y castigo de traidores* in the 1950s and early 1960s, when conducting the extensive researches into eighteenth-century Spanish theatre which culminated in her two-volume *magnum opus*.[2] *Spanish Drama of Pathos 1750–1808*, however, contains only brief, passing references to Enciso Castrillón.[3] In the late 1970s her friend, and former colleague at Glasgow University, Fernando Huerta, Universidad Autónoma, Barcelona, had discussions with her about undertaking a joint study of Encisco Castrillón, and at this time, Dr Huerta tells me, she sent him a draft of her essay on *La defensa de Valencia*. It seems likely that Ivy revised and completed this article in the early 1980s,[4] but chose to delay publication, intending it to form part of her projected collaborative work with Dr Huerta on Enciso Castrillón which, unfortunately, was never realized. Nevertheless, Dr Huerta and his wife, Guillermina Cenoz del Águila, **did** collaborate with her in another enterprise, when, to the enduring benefit

1 So, too, was an earlier draft of this article, together with handwritten notes on the same topic and play.

2 See *Spanish Drama of Pathos 1750–1808*. I. *High Tragedy*; II. *Low Tragedy*, 2 vols (Liverpool: Liverpool U. P., 1970) (simultaneously published Toronto: Univ. of Toronto Press). This monumental study was completed and sent to press in 1963, but Liverpool University Press took seven years to effect its publication. In a letter to Geoffrey Ribbans, then Gilmour Professor of Spanish at Liverpool University, the author, despite her customary forbearance, was moved to complain: 'I feel depressedly outraged about the delay of my drama book. The Liverpool Press have had it in hand for seven years, and whenever I write to protest I am told that authors need to be patient' (letter dated 9 December 1969; McClelland Papers, Archives, University of Glasgow).

3 See McClelland, *Spanish Drama of Pathos 1750–1808*, I. *High Tragedy*, pp. 63, 239; II. *Low Tragedy,* 396n., 463, 531n., 546, 567n.

4 In editing this article I have altered only minimally its main text, to conform to the *Bulletin*'s stylistic norms. To assist readers, I have added some notes derived mostly from the author's own papers about the play concerned. Her original article carried only two footnotes, which have been renumbered here, but are identified by asterisks (notes 8* and 11*).

of non-English-speaking scholars of the Spanish Enlightenment, they published, in the year of the author's ninetieth birthday, their outstanding translation of *Spanish Drama of Pathos 1750–1808*.[5]

Ann L. Mackenzie

University of Glasgow.

5 I. L. McClelland, *'Pathos' dramático en el teatro español de 1750 a 1808*. I. *La alta tragedia*; II. *La tragedia menor*, traducción a cargo de Fernando Huerta Viñas y Guillermina Cenoz del Águila, con prólogos de Ann L. Mackenzie y Francisco Aguilar Piñal, Hispanic Studies TRAC (Textual Research and Criticism) 7, 2 vols (Liverpool: Liverpool U. P., 1998).

A Propaganda Play of 1808 F. Enciso Castrillón's *La defensa de Valencia y castigo de traidores*

I. L. McCLELLAND†

University of Glasgow

ed. Ann L. Mackenzie

University of Glasgow

For fifty or sixty years before the outbreak of the Spanish War of Independence, Peninsular dramatists, philosophic in unsuccess, had been conducting ideological experiments. Estranged from their national tradition, unprofessed as yet in the cultures of Enlightenment, they found themselves at their most perceptive in a limbo of awareness. Confusedly, they had begun to recognize the need for re-setting dramatic theme and conversation in a mental background proper to their own times. More clearly they had been aware of foreign debate on aesthetic form: an aspect of drama more easily comprehended, systematized and imitated than the abstract ideas of which it was a vehicle. Golden-Age achievement had predisposed eighteenth-century dramatists to an anachronistic orientation of reasoning and emotion even where the form of expressing these was changing. So that in 1808 Spanish playwrights still had nearly everything to learn about the primary thought-values of modern European drama which, in secondary ways of shape and pattern, they were already imitating. To understand constructively how the thought of the age could be subtly used to inform stage conflicts in that age—new thought crossed creatively with new thought, new thought crossed ironically with old thought—and be presented, by new techniques, in new relief, required perhaps a penetratingly philosophical outlook, unjaded imagination and surging new vitality: qualities which German dramatists were now demonstrating with startling distinction.

Nevertheless Spanish playwrights had acquired a fecund receptivity. They had grown self-conscious and self-critical. They had read, translated and imitated dramas French, Italian, English and German, in that order of popularity or accessibility. Under such influence they had begun to domesticate their open-air enthusiasms, to restrain their oratorical fluency, to examine seriously the disciplines needed for communicating artistically their epoch's scientific logic. Moreover, they had made some attempt, if not on the highest artistic level, to present modern characters, in modern conditions, beset with modern preoccupations, and suffering the anxieties created by a European revolution in thought and behaviour. By 1808 they darkly knew that even historical characters in fancy dress, who legitimately might follow ancient codes of reasoning, must, to make an impression anything like so profound as Schiller's *Maria Stuart*, be presented illuminatively rather than with luminousness. Spain's artistic weakness in the Age of Reason ought not to obscure for us the historical importance of her gathering understanding.

The War of Independence which produced a crop of popular, patriotic dramas cannot be held altogether responsible for delaying dramatic recovery, but it impeded development of thought at a critical juncture by diverting attention from difficult intricacies of reasoning to those easy ways of enthusiasm which led back to an old, uncritical formula of heroics and loyalties. Therefore, inspiring as they were to the national cause, popular, patriotic dramas were largely retrogressive. Lyrical poets may write creatively of the turmoil of their own experience of war, perhaps because its force as a direct, personal shock, fertilizes their imagination. But it seems less common at times of active warfare for dramatists to write with such distinction. They cannot convey vicariously the full immediacy of their own experiences, and, if they are Spaniards, their emotions under these conditions tend artificially to dissipate themselves in rhetoric.

Nevertheless dramas of war usually contain an element more interesting to posterity than the patriotism of exclamation, invocation and lamentation. They may betray, incidentally, some deliberately directed concern with practical, day-to-day problems of war-effort, thus foreshadowing the 'documentary' material of modern times and showing that a national war-cause does not consist only of outward, spontaneous heroism, but is held together by what would now be thought of as propaganda. Certainly the patriot-dramatists of 1808–14 contributed their plays as war-work and took upon themselves a certain responsibility for the cautionary encouragement which now is provided by more mechanical means. In some of the Spanish war-dramas, therefore, we may find, beneath official attitudes, beneath historical facts, certain indications of shifting public moods, qualities, and methods of understanding to which leaders needed to address themselves. The mass-mind may spontaneously quicken to resist an enemy, but the mass-mind has to be discreetly and persuasively instructed in the art of knowing what, in military terms, the enemy really consists of: discreetly, because the public must be flattered into supposing that it is more perceptive, or even right-minded, than it really is; persuasively, because the public is an impatient subject for direct methods of tuition. Literary dramatists, scarce in wartime, might have wanted provocatively and subjectively to subtilize the experience they shared with all their compatriots. Popular dramatists, of whom there were many in Spain, dealt with what, at any given moment, the man-in-the-street was taking for granted, and therefore, by implication, with what in wartime was ordinary, obvious and topical. For historical purposes, then, the popular dramatists may sometimes be more informative than their literary superiors.

Spanish war-plays also throw light on popular artistic history. By taking the form of the traditional heroic drama they show that this was still a natural, if degenerated, vehicle for conveying a national sense of crisis and excitement. By divergences in detail from Spanish tradition, particularly as this was depicted in servile, eighteenth-century imitations of the masters which had been among the most acceptable forms of popular entertainment, they show how certain foreign influences had become so completely assimilated into the national system that they could contribute in naturalness to Spain's patriotic enthusiasm. They illustrate the contemporary conception in the average mind of tragedy and comedy. They indicate the degree of humanity or realism popularly required of national characters, and, of course, explain what sort of dramatic people could live between 1808 and 1814 on the stage at all. In some ways they also reflect, however badly, the kind of influences operating on higher literary levels.

Within their popular category the war-dramatists vary both in kind and in ability. One type is represented by the volcanic Zavala y Zamora,[1] purveyor of large-scale sensation, and enjoying, with the same degree of justification, such popular fame as is acquired by sensational script-writers for modern films or radio.[2] Representative of a comparatively cultured group is Enciso Castrillón,[3] a man of quieter aspirations than Zavala, who had been busily translating modern pieces from the French and recasting Montalbán and other

1 Gaspar Zavala y Zamora (born 1762—died ?). Popular in the late eighteenth and early nineteenth centuries, he wrote both military-heroic and sentimental dramas and some patriotic pieces, and also *sainetes* and *loas*. For information on his career and for a list of his plays see Jerónimo Herrera Navarro, *Catálogo de autores teatrales del siglo XVIII* (Madrid: Fundación Universitaria Española, 1993), 492–99. Herrera Navarro observes that Zavala y Zamora 'destacó por sus comedias heroico-militares y por las sentimentales, aproximándose en éstas a una estética que anuncia el romanticismo' (493). See also McClelland, *Spanish Drama of Pathos 1750–1808*, II, 481–87, 551–65. Her unpublished article on 'La contribución que hizo Gaspar Zavala y Zamora al desarrollo del Ilustrismo español', unfortunately, appears to be no longer in existence (see above, 'Preface', 3–4; Ceri Byrne, 'I. L. McClelland (1908–2006). Bibliography (1930–1999)', 48.

2 It should not be thought surprising that Ivy makes no reference here to television, for she had little time for it, but was always an avid listener to the radio.

3 For information on the career of Félix Enciso Castrillón (born 1750s?–died 1840s?) and a list of his works see Herrera Navarro, *Catálogo de autores teatrales del siglo XVIII*, 156–64. For a thought-provoking study, see Joaquín Álvarez Barrientos, 'Acercamiento a Félix Enciso Castrillón', in *II Seminario de Historia de la Real Sociedad Bascongada de Amigos del País: ponencias y comunicaciones, días 1, 2 y 3 de diciembre de 1988* (San Sebastián: Caja de Guipúzcoa, 1989), 57–84.

Golden-Age authors into partially disciplined shapes.[4] Presumably Enciso in the relatively cultured character he normally assumed when writing for the Caños del Peral, a more experimental theatre than the Cruz or Príncipe,[5] considered himself rather a reformer than a common member of the theatre-rabble with which Zavala, somewhat unfairly, had been identified. At all events Enciso's *Defensa de Valencia* almost gives the impression of issuing officially from some national ministry of propaganda. It is a document valuable for its indirect revelation of the public moods with which civic and military leaders were just then having to contend, and, on the literary side, for the coordination of foreign and Spanish traditions on which automatically it draws, and for sporadic hints of a modern dramatic mentality proving that, under traditional and foreign influences, Spain's dramatic consciousness had been developing.[6]

La defensa de Valencia, a dramatization of the historic defence against Moncey in June, 1808, is one of a number of war-dramas and sketches rapidly created by Enciso Castrillón,[7] in urgent competition with Zavala y Zamora,[8*] during the autumn of 1808. This was the season of short-lived elation in Madrid when, with the withdrawal of the French and the triumphal entry, in

4 Enciso Castrillón was a prolific dramatist and translator and adapter of plays. His translations and adaptations from the French included: *El distraído*, *El español y la francesa* and the tragedy in three acts called *Ester* (translated from Racine). Among the Golden-Age plays he revised were Pérez de Montalbán's *La doncella de labor*, Rojas Zorrilla's *Abrir el ojo* and Cubillo's *Las muñecas de Marcela*.

5 Enciso Castrillón was, says Cotarelo, 'el poeta oficial de los Caños' (see Emilio Cotarelo y Mori, *Isidoro Máiquez y el teatro de su tiempo* (Madrid: Imprenta de José Perales y Martínez, 1902), 206.

6 For the text of Enciso's *La defensa de Valencia y castigo de traidores* (sometimes known as *El escarmiento a los traidores o defensa de Valencia*) see the (anonymous) manuscript in the Biblioteca Municipal, Madrid, written in verse in four acts (Shelf No. 105-3). All references are to this text.

7 Enciso also wrote, for instance, the propaganda play, *Una fineza de Inglaterra, o sea la libertad de las tropas españolas que entraban en el norte*, which was performed in Cádiz in 1809. And he composed *El sermón sin fruto, o sea Josef Botellas en el Ayuntamiento de Logroño*, which was performed in the Teatro de la Cruz on 14 November 1808. See Herrera Navarro, *Catálogo de autores teatrales del siglo XVIII*, 159, 162. About this 'pieza jocosa', in one act, Cotarelo comments: 'Es muy graciosa, especialmente por el lenguaje chapurrado de italiano, que pone en boca del intruso, quien busca su inspiración en las botellas' (*Isidoro Máiquez y el teatro de su tiempo*, 293). For an instructive article on 'propaganda' drama at this period, and on this piece in particular, see Hans-Joachim Lope, 'La imagen de los franceses en el teatro español de propaganda durante La Guerra de la Independencia (1808–1813)', in *The Eighteenth Century in Spain. Essays in Honour of I. L. McClelland*, ed., with an introduction, by Ann L. Mackenzie, *BHS*, LXVIII:1 (1991), 219–29 (pp. 222–24).

8* See, for instance, Zavala's *Los patriotas*, also known as *Los patriotas de Aragón*, in three acts, of which there is a manuscript, with *censuras* of 1808, in the Biblioteca Municipal, Madrid (Shelf No. 55-2). It is a more melodramatic play than Enciso's *Defensa* but deals with similar material. It was performed at the Príncipe at the end of September, 1808 and a second part in four acts also by Zavala y Zamora was evidently performed in the same theatre in late November of that year (see Cotarelo, *Isidoro Máiquez y el teatro de su tiempo*, 291–92, 693).

August, of General Castaños, strengthened by his victory at Bailén, the Villa's tongue was loosed, only to be curbed again by the return of French troops at the end of November. The play was performed on the 29th October at the Cruz, and, with other war-dramas, was revived when national circumstances permitted in 1813.[9]

It records on its more superficial plane not only the heartening stamina of the Valencians earlier in the summer, but the enthusiasm injected into all the negative business of defence throughout the country by the inspiring positiveness of that Bailén victory. It ends on trumpet-calls of hope, with rousing strains of national intent, and with glorification of the name of Ferdinand the Desired, and of the Catholic religion which to Spanish minds had disappeared from France in 1789, if not earlier. At the same time it summons urgently to battle, and the rhetoric of the last lines, which now read like the end of any of the mass-produced heroic dramas of the eighteenth century, must, in their hackneyed phraseology, have acquired an enkindled meaning.

The first sign of social disturbance at deeper levels than that indicated by the enthusiasm, the victory-shouts with which the action culminates, appears when the play is quietly proceeding through preliminary formalities. The scene is a Valencian tavern conveniently acting as an off-duty meeting-place and news-market for soldiery and civilians, and providing opportunities for some of the most spontaneous dialogue of this relatively undistinguished drama: talk, with natural reference to serious political and military events, set, for its ulterior momentousness, in the nervous immediacy of day-to-day trivialities. This is the kind of conversation on which dramatists sensitive to atmosphere of ironic contrast have eagerly seized, and which, being drawn from life in the midst of life-like anxieties, is nearly always convincing. Enciso, who could hear or take part in such talk at any tavern where the national militia was free to come and go, would have been a much worse playwright than in fact he was if he had been unable to use it effectively. Conspicuous in the rough exchange of common topics here is a consciousness of inter-regional cooperation, that rare feat which Spain, for all its tendency to think and react within narrowly regionalistic limits, had, in 1808, been able to achieve. But awareness of regional peculiarity is never lost. It is inherent for instance in Valencian accents and forms of speech thrown into relief by the speech of non-Valencian customers of the tavern. The urgent coming and going of soldiers and civilians from different parts of Spain must have been to the provinces, even to the Northern and

9 Enciso's *La defensa de Valencia* was performed at the Cruz on 22 July 1813 (see Cotarelo, *Isidoro Máiquez y el teatro de su tiempo*, 758). For information on performances of Zavala y Zamora's *Los patriotas de Aragón* in 1812 (Príncipe) and 1818, see Ada M. Coe, *Catálogo bibliográfico y crítico de las comedias anunciadas en los periódicos de Madrid desde 1661 hasta 1819* (Baltimore: The Johns Hopkins Press, 1935), 177.

Eastern ports, a fairly uncommon experience, and the unusual cooperation it signified in 1808 was therefore noteworthy.

Later in the same act, references to war-activities, 'documentary' contributions, as it were, like radio talks on civil defence in the Second World War, are more business-like means than a tavernful of assorted accents of attracting interest and conveying practical suggestions. Carlos—an enemy collaborator—explains disingenuously to Antonio, a like-minded companion, that their task of undermining Peninsular resistance is made difficult by the fact that Valencia as a whole is sturdily committed to the national cause; that all its sons incapable of fighting, together with all its daughters, have taken up some kind of war-work. Spectators have already been conducted to the home of a patriot Count (I, viii) whose wife and daughters sat tirelessly employed in making cartridge-bags. Now Carlos complainingly enumerates to his friend all sorts of other delaying activities engaging non-fighting Valencians and so provides patriot-audiences in Madrid with constructive suggestions:

Carlos: Aquí se ven
los jóvenes empleados
en aprender el manejo
del fusil . . . otros cavando
fosos [. . .]
los inútiles y ancianos
hacen tacos y cartuchos;
otros con harto trabajo
por ser muy cortas sus fuerzas
a los puertos van llevando
las balas y municiones
que el inglés con franca mano
da a este reino.

A more abstract, though an even more realistic representation of wartime, is expressed in a general atmosphere of insecurity. Talk of distant operations, and of an approaching French contingent; avidity for news; the temporary nature of the soldiers' circumstances and therefore the artificial pitch of a present merriment in the context-possibility of 'for tomorrow we may die'; the rapid circulation of confused and confusing rumours; the acceptance of an unpredictable future, all fix the rate of dramatic tension and remind the audience that, despite recent successes, the war goes critically on. An instinctive distrust felt by Manuela, who keeps the inn, towards Don Antonio, alleged to be a Spanish patriot newly escaped from French persecution, becomes not only a dramatic device but an emphatic warning against trusting strangers whose credentials cannot be proved. For, as the dramatist insists throughout the play, it is the friendly enemy agent within the gate, mixing comfortably with all classes, sympathizing with grievances, advising in perplexities, who can do more harm than recognizably hostile troops. Since Spaniards, as a race, are not unfriendly to friendly strangers, or given to mercenary treachery and treason, it must have been difficult to make the man-in-the-street, who found it as natural to 'desire' the reign of Ferdinand as to 'desire' the reign of God, to understand that any of his own countrymen could desert to the French, could, least of all, act as a secret-service agent for the enemy.

Yet the political crisis to the less simple-minded was not such a clear conflict of national right and foreign wrong, of uncritical desire for Ferdinand and of single-minded hatred of France; and the Gallic-indoctrinated intellectuals, nearly all of whom had been opposed to the court-figureheads of the last régime, and who probably knew something of Ferdinand's perilously limited outlook, might wonder, or doubt, might evade the issue in passivity, or even, in a few cases, might desert to what they believed to be enlightenment. So to the national command the problem of treachery, or more likely of a treacherous *manía* for thinking in wartime, must have been a sufficiently serious one, all the more difficult of solution in that so much of Spain's territory was occupied, and that the Spaniard was impatient of organized coordination. This play does not leave the problem to be merely implied. Some of the most urgent speeches openly discuss it. Don Antonio, emerging in his true colours towards the end of Act I in his aforementioned conversation with Don Carlos, remarks that, in view of Valencia's enthusiasm for the cause of Ferdinand and of its valour and determination, only intrigue remains as a practical means of undermining resistance and that, in this respect, even Ferdinand realizes that individual collaborators exist among the patriots. In Act II, the Spanish General himself comments on the fact that there are many traitors about, and, in Act III, Don Antonio's corpse is exhibited, for all to see, in the very *plaza*, admittedly in accordance with Spanish stage-tradition and with poetic justice, but partly, one may also assume, as a warning to potential traitors in the audience and as a deterrent to fraternization with occupying forces. Delivered in this atmosphere and in these circumstances, the final rhetorical speeches of Act IV must have had the value of slogans like 'Your country needs you':

Y tú, gloriosa nación,
pelea por tu Fernando,
guerra eterna declarando
al cruel Napoleón.
Defiende tu religión,
tu Rey y tu patria amada,
y la cadena pesada
que te destinó el cruel,
trueca en glorioso laurel
con que quedas coronada.

[. . .]
A la lid, a las armas, al triunfo,
españoles, mostrad el valor.
Viva siempre el augusto Fernando,
Tiemble el trono de Napoleón.

Rhetoric in wartime is obviously essential as mass-encouragement to mass-endeavour. Politically considered, it was convenient in the circumstances of 1808 that Spain's traditional eloquence made that country susceptible to oratorical influence. Artistically considered, rhetoric was an inconvenient quality of modern drama because it petrified thought. But more historically interesting and dramatically constructive than brave speeches and actions is a political preoccupation set into this play with poignant implicitness and naturalness. Only the rare Spaniard would knowingly and actively turn traitor. If he did, he would certainly constitute a danger and the masses must be put on their guard. But commoner and much graver hazards to success were provided by the Spaniard's emotional temperament: his dislike of bodies of government, organized systems, and prolonged deliberations, and so, most pressingly and immediately, the uncertainty of his loyalty on everyday issues to any local or central Junta. It is easy to assume that the Spaniard's valiant spirit of nationalism and consequently his resistance to the invader in the War of Independence meant that he spontaneously cooperated with the democratic or semi-democratic Juntas set up or re-organized locally to provide for his food supplies and for the coordination of his war-effort with that of his fellow countrymen. Indeed, despite some open opposition to the Junta Central, the individual Spaniard must generally have been stimulated by emergency to cooperate with these self-governing bodies, if in a manner most foreign to his disposition. Even so, vulnerable as they were to local criticism, the local Juntas, at tedious times when little seemed to be happening, must have had difficulty in establishing their self-made rights to lead, govern and command in large as well as in small matters. Popular patriotic plays.contemporary with the events they dramatize, make unsound historical documents. But the public attitudes they indirectly take for granted are likely to be attitudes which their audiences took for granted also. For which reason Enciso's *Defensa de Valencia* is not historically unrevealing.

One of the problems it poses about wartime Spain concerns public unfamiliarity with those Juntas which differed from municipal councils in having a scope more national than local, often, perhaps, to the sacrifice of merely local needs, and which, in any case, may have seemed to ultraconservative minds disquietingly similar in principle to the democratic committees of Revolutionary France. To lose patience with these relatively impersonal bodies, as the Spaniard might be expected to do, to try to upset their management of affairs, would provoke local revolutions and constitute the greatest war-hazard. Cases of mutiny are undoubtedly exaggerated in the play for dramatic effect, but the tendencies they represent correspond so closely to Spain's instinctive tendencies towards political disintegration, recorded not only by modern historians but by such creative witnesses of modern history as Sr Gironella,[10] that they give to drama a quality of realism.

The local Junta is first mentioned, at the end of Act I, by Don Antonio when, searching for the most likely means of undermining Valencia's resistance, he conceives the idea of discrediting the Junta before the populace. In the next act the Spanish General, entrusted with defence, and finding himself under the necessity of quelling a street-disturbance engineered by enemy agents, is careful to explain to the mutineers the form and function of the Junta. Its members, he tells them, are citizens known for their wisdom, men who work in the interests of the common good. Why therefore disturb their critical deliberations on the successful results of which must depend the happiness of the whole community? He calls to the mutineers—and the call, continuing to stress a practical requirement, sounds more urgent than rhetorical—to place their trust in the zeal and loyalty of those whose business it is to organize the nation's resistance movement:

> Valencianos, confiad
> en el patriotismo y celo
> de los que a su cargo toman
> oponerse a los intentos
> del enemigo de España.

Valencia's leaders, he goes on, know well where danger lies, they are trying to devise a means of combating it. But to this end order must be secured:

> [. . .]
> no os precipitéis vosotros
> en el abismo tremendo
> de la funesta anarquía.

He even says, in so many words, that heroism is not enough, that loyalty to the government is equally necessary. The plain words with which he drives home this point, and the fact that it is a point which has to be stressed wherever and whenever Spaniards are governed by supreme bodies rather than by supreme individuals, bring sections of this speech to life. Stimulated and convinced by him, the mob is eventually persuaded to take up the loyal call for King and Junta; that is, to adopt the idea that these two institutions, at least for the time being, are interdependent.

10 A reference, of course, to the Civil War novels of José María Gironella (*Los cipreses creen en Dios*, *Un millón de muertos* and *Ha estallado la paz*) of which the author was a profoundly interested and admiring reader.

Enciso's deliberate presentation of the problem posed for the local government by mob-hysteria is, historically and artistically, one of the best features of his drama. Where a mob is not composed of cowardly material this problem, as Spanish leaders have often discovered, is more difficult than ever. Here, it is emphasized, the Valencian General has to contend not merely with the enemy, but with popular impatience at prosaic, untraditional systems, and with the insidiousness in such circumstances of rumour. Let idle tongues but suggest that that newly exalted body, the Junta, is inept, criminally inactive, or in any way impeachable, and the General ironically may have to fight a patriot-mob. To undermine the Valencian Command enemy agents merely have to encourage the growth of popular impatience. Only a little later in the same act the General is to be found answering charges against the innocent Junta:

> *General*: Señor Doctor, conteneós.
> Los vocales de la Junta
> son muy dignos de respeto,
> [. . .]

and the urgently repeated attempt to recommend it—for instance a guard on duty at the citadel, defends it, to the mob, in similar terms: '¿Quién con crimen tan horrendo / calumnia así a los vocales / de la noble Junta?'—may seem to be addressed to the Spaniard's reluctance to identify essentially and thoroughly the whole national cause with so small, tedious and local a part.

Meanwhile Antonio himself, taking the Spanish line of cutting through reason with action and in anticipation of more than a century of shock solutions, shouts his pronouncement that government (i.e. Junta) and General have been overthrown, and, with the demand for a new Junta, he leads the misguided patriots into anarchist protest against deliberation.

Throughout the rest of the play the Junta continues to occupy the centre of interest. In Act III the General, who by now is in possession of the facts of Antonio's machinations but cannot seize him publicly for fear of precipitating a civil war, is arranging with the Junta to have him arrested when he arrives to assert his claim to membership at the next meeting. It is true that the angry exchanges shortly to ensue there, will have a value more dramatic than historical, but the scene begins with certain formalities of Junta-procedure taken, however crudely and inaccurately, from real life, and acquires thereby a double importance. First, at this stage of Spain's dramatic development, artistry gains potentially from any reproduction of life-like circumstances conducive to life-like orientation of mind. Secondly, this scene has all the appearance of performing a 'documentary' function of familiarizing the general public with an unknown or partially unknown institution constituted for its good. Enciso goes to some trouble to give to the Junta-concept a practical significance and to underline the Junta's respectability. By the time the audience has heard of the swearing-in ceremony for a new member, and has discovered that any new member, before being admitted, will be required to prove his allegiance to the national cause and satisfy the Board on any charge of collaboration with the enemy, the responsible nature of the Junta has become a dominant idea. The setting for this meeting: a room 'adorned with all possible magnificence', may have had little to do with real conditions in wartime, but the dramatist's desire to give to this institution all the prestige in his power would seem to reflect the need in real life for bolstering the Junta's importance.

Later in the third act, the arrival of a French aide-de-camp bearing Napoleon's conciliatory wishes for Spain's peaceful prosperity, and only half concealing in these word-flowers the dagger-edge of coercion, anticipates the kind of inducement likely to be made by the enemy. The letter of an enemy General to Jovellanos in 1809 more subtly presents the same argument for negotiating an ignoble peace, and Enciso's General, in his melodramatic way, as decisively rejects Napoleon's terms as does the stately Jovellanos.[11*] It was a wise move to counter tempting offers by rejecting them in advance, and a play was as good a medium as any for acquainting as large a public as possible with the dangers of insidious diplomacy and with model-methods of combating it. For similar reasons Antonio's corpse, later to be seen languishing in the *plaza*, anticipates the parallel hazard of fraternization. The General's harangue before this corpse may not be in the best literary taste, but it must have brought home to Madrid audiences the peril of muddled emotionalism, for they already knew enough about the complications of living, while not collaborating, with an occupying enemy to take such words as fearfully instructive:

Gen. (to the *edecán*) Considerad esta escena
y decid a vuestro jefe
que de este modo en Valencia
se escucha la voz de aquellos
que persuadirnos intentan
a sufrir un yugo infame.

As Enciso and the Valencian General knew, the average honest citizen was too single- or simple-minded to be cautious. Propaganda drama, therefore, like any other existing form of propaganda, could instruct him in ways and means, direct his intention, vividly warn him of danger, revive or refresh his spirits, and, perhaps most needful of all, organize his enthusiasms.

11* See Gaspar Melchor de Jovellanos, *Obras publicadas e inéditas*, ed. C. Nocedal, BAE XLVI & L, 2 vols (Madrid: Rivadeneyra, 1858–59), I, BAE XLVI, xxxvii.

Certain artistic qualities in the *Defensa* exist in spite rather than because of its patriotic topicality, but they are not completely independent of its propaganda. The fact that Spanish playwrights of the eighteenth century had been searching for themes compatible with modern understanding and ways of life made any urgent treatment of any genuinely contemporary problem potentially inspiring. A realistic consideration of current problems might cause a playwright to observe how, in the world about him, the leaders and the led became humanly aware of their own problems and how, collectively and individually, they behaved in this process of discovery. An orderly demonstration of living problems and of life-like ways of speaking and behaving expressed, moreover, Spain's slowly emerging empiricism. Fifty years earlier the serious playwright had kept drama so rigorously separated from modern life that dramatic conversation, instead of developing under the force of interest inherent in the subject, had been artificially arranged as a series of informative statements punctuated by reminiscence or exclamation. But now, violent experience produced the conscious need to discuss that experience. 'Just now', as one character remarks in Act I, 'there is no lack of things to talk about'.

> Ahora cabalmente estamos
> en tiempo que nunca falta
> de qué hablar.

What is new in the thought-content of the *Defensa,* though it is by no means original to Enciso, is his examination of realistic cause and effect as the stuff of which problems are made. His idea of analysing—however inept his analysis may become—the reasons why a loyal people could be led into anarchy, gives an apparent thought-density to types of crises which, in most heroic dramas of the eighteenth century, would have relied archaically on Golden-Age watchwords, a Golden-Age assumption of Spanish superiority, and therefore a Golden-Age confidence in unreasoning enthusiasms. Spain in the eighteenth century had been learning to substitute common for the once inspiringly uncommon sense. Accordingly neither General nor enemy agent in Enciso's play assumes that men respond to poetic logic but, addressing himself to their tangled inner motives, he attempts to convince by practical, modern forms of reasoning.

For all its foreign arrangement in four acts and the omission of a love interest, the *Defensa* takes the form of national heroic drama, or rather of the eighteenth-century version of traditional heroic drama, and presents a complicated intrigue involving patriotic honour, a considerable amount of comic and serious action and a liveliness emphasized by shouting crowds (the 'pueblo' of the *dramatis personae*) and by fighting and manoeuvring soldiery. These features are treated less successfully by Enciso than by, for instance,

Comella or Zavala y Zamora.[12] Zavala's heroic plays of spying and counter-spying are more imaginative and ingenious than this drama and not much less topical. Enciso's diction may be more correct than Zavala's, but he has a more limited range of technical contrivances than any of the popular dramatists whom he would have considered his inferiors. Like most Spanish playwrights he was very uncomfortable in four acts. His last act, comprised largely of shooting, shouting and celebrating, could easily have been eliminated without detriment to the plot, and is directed almost exclusively to maintaining the pitch of victory-enthusiasm. Nevertheless at least a few scenes, particularly in the early part of Act I, have an intrinsic artistry worth examining.

These are scenes derived from a combination of national and foreign sources. The setting for much of Act I is the outside of a tavern in a popular quarter: a setting common enough in Spanish national plays old or new and not in itself worthy of comment. But it may be remembered that in the last decades of the eighteenth century, and before Moratín had written *El café*, the outside or inside of inn or café had been used for the special purpose of symbolizing psychological cross-roads in themes of political intrigue by authors of such international influence as Goldoni and Lessing. Inns, therefore, which, on or off stage, have always been obvious meeting-places, had become invested with the mystique of modern mental crossways.

Traditionally Spanish too and yet a striking modern feature of, for instance, Goldoni's *La bottega del caffè*,[13] is the method, so conducive to suspense, of leading up to the serious and elevated business of the play from a comic and apparently irrelevant level. The popular characters, familiar types with interests familiarly adjustable to the topics of any period, encourage a sense of relaxation and eventually enable the playwright to score a forceful point by taking the audience off its guard. At Enciso's inn the *clientèle* is composed of such popular types, comic enough in themselves to hold spectators' attention and yet destined to play the unconscious *rôle* of introducing or furthering catastrophic developments. One of them is Blas, an endearing fool of a servant, who, sent out to draw water, returns bearing, instead, the news of a traveller's escape to Valencia through the French lines, yet who is labouring so excitedly under the burden of his tale that his

---

12 For McClelland on Luciano Francisco Comella (1751–1812), see ' "Comellan Drama" and the Censor', *BHS*, XXX:117 (1953), 20–31 and 'The Comellan Conception of Stage-Realism', *Dieciocho*, 16:1–2 (1993), 111–17; also *Spanish Drama of Pathos 1750–1808*, II, 487–97, and especially 518–36. For an illuminating article on this playwright, see also Fernando Huerta, 'El comediógrafo mal-tratado: Luciano Comella y la Ilustración', in *The Eighteenth Century in Spain. Essays in Honour of I. L. McClelland*, 183–89. For McClelland on Zavala y Zamora see above, at note 1.

13 For McClelland on Goldoni see *Spanish Drama of Pathos 1750–1808*, II, 436–37, 483, 499, 517.

exasperated hearers have the utmost difficulty in persuading him to tell it coherently. As in the infinitely more artistic circumstances of Tirso de Molina's *Antona García*, which Enciso, a recaster of Golden-Age masterpieces,[14] probably knew, it is ironically the fool who, stuttering and stumbling, sets the chief machinery in action. Other popular characters who play parts more significant than they realize are the coarse soldiers, strumming their guitars, cracking hoary tavern jokes about watered wine, paying rude compliments, teasing the staff, and treating the war for the joke which, as the audience very well knows, it is not. Manuela, the mistress of the inn, an even-humoured, motherly woman, directing operations, parrying gallantry, and keeping her rough guests in their places, is a good comedy-character in her own right:

Cabo: Vamos
no me seas retrechera,
y cree que me has pasado
el corazón con tus ojos.
Manuel: ¡Ay! ¿mis ojos pinchan tanto
que atraviesan la camisa
y la casaca?

But, like many hostesses ancient and modern, Manuela it is, who, feeling that her customers are passing the bounds of propriety, redirects them in all naturalness to a less frivolous topic of conversation:

Voluntario 1°: Chic, qué bueno está el pescado.
Cabo: Está como a mí me gustan
las mujeres.
Manuela: ¿Qué? ¿os gustamos
bien fritas?
Cabo: No, hija, saladas,
por eso te quiero tanto,
porque eres ...
Manuela: Si habéis de hablar
sólo de amores, me marcho.
Cabo: Pues ¿de qué he de hablar?
Manuela: ¡Ay Dios!
ahora cabalmente estamos
en tiempo que nunca falta
de qué hablar ¿No sabéis algo
de ese ejército francés
que dicen que viene andando
hacia aquí? ...

14 Compare note 4 above.

And, when the approach of the stranger with the Spanish General and an escort of the curious of Valencia is announced, and the soldiers hastily take their arms and move towards the crowd, Manuela, ever practical, rapidly removes the remains of the meal, and, facilitating stage production, takes in her furniture lest, she says, in the flood of excitement her property should be swept to ruin:

> no sea que a río revuelto
> se haga mi hacienda pedazos

—a sentiment, which while characterizing her humble, domestic plane prepares us for the rush and tumult about to break out on socially superior levels.

For all his failings, Enciso had a native sense of the dramatic and could deal easily, even excitingly, with stage irony and suspense. One of his most useful agents in this respect is the clownish company of Blas and his friends who, in Elizabethan and Golden-Age fashion, return at intervals to the major plot for the purpose of intensifying the dramatic atmosphere by a false appearance of relieving it. And one should remember that Enciso had not inherited a famous tradition at a vague eighteenth-century remove, but, as a student and recaster of Golden-Age drama, he had a first-hand knowledge of Golden-Age methods. Clownish remarks at delicate moments, forced jokes of soldiers going into battle, inane comments of civilians under siege or bombardment, or of anybody, anywhere, under the necessity of keeping his mind off present danger, have far less to do with relief than with purgative terror. If well contrived they may imply suppressed hysteria. Spain's ironic sense of humour has probably supplied Peninsular dramatists with a natural talent for dealing with such situations. At any rate, Blas and his companions, scurrying along a Valencian street during a bout of sniping, contribute to the general suspense by making the breathless, half-comic and yet frightening remarks which only partially reveal the true state of affairs and therefore nervously tease and tantalize. Later, this same company, like a flock of poor starlings valiantly imitating the blackbird-fools of the Golden Age, chatter ludicrously about their own experiences and leave the objective spectator to assess the latent gravity of this whole incident from their ironically disproportionate view of it.

Various other traditional ingredients of Spain's dramatic atmosphere are also effectively present. The impression of crisis produced by gathering crowds, by urgent speeches addressed to the crowd become mob, and by talk about difficulties of controlling it; the doubts and worries of individuals: of the Count's wife and daughters who fearfully calculate his chances of survival in the event of his falling into the hands of the French, or the humble doubts of Manuela who took an irrational dislike of some 'no sé qué' in the face of Don Antonio; the dilemma of the High Command anxious to avoid bloodshed; the cries, the confusion, the danger for all the officials involved; the changing items of news, reports of the arming of the populace, even the *flambeaux* carried through the dark crisis-ridden streets in Act II, are inherited dramatic devices. They are also sufficiently up to date in detail to illustrate realistic circumstances of the wartime year of 1808, and to anticipate the atmosphere of political emergency, to be expertly reconstructed from life by Gironella in his Civil War trilogy,[15] where, in homeliness, tragicomedy and cumulative alarm, a man through normal processes may suddenly discover that his closest neighbour is mentally unknown to him. Enciso was not qualified to experiment in abstractions. Still, by means of the play's atmosphere, a dramatic quality he thoroughly understood, he managed to create an effect of public crisis which, because it was real in his own experience, makes an artistic and a convincingly modern impression. The Spanish masters had also been deft and ingenious in their use of incident and action, but here Enciso showed his artistic inferiority. Mob-movements, battle-scenes, speeches calling to action with inflammatory words like:

Valencianos ... España ... enemigo ...

may be justified in strategic places, but they are used artificially also to pad out the empty corners of this awkwardly shaped play of four acts, to extend urgent addresses for longer than is artistically desirable, and to supply in physical activity what is lacking in thought.[16]

Altogether, 'propaganda' drama of the War of Independence might be said to make a minor contribution to the history of literature in so far as it injected actuality into the exhausted heroic genre and helped to restore a national balance. So many of the ideologically interesting heroic plays of the late eighteenth century were foreign-inspired works about foreign personages and foreign social circumstances, and although related to Spain's awareness of foreign Enlightenment were not fully identifiable in thought-content with the Spaniards' processes of absorbing Enlightenment. As an over-all criticism of serious eighteenth-century drama one might say that where it was not decayed it was either too sensational or too discreet. For the Spaniards, usually willing enough by then to experiment in new ideas and techniques, were impeded, by censorship, or by their commitments with tradition, from representing modern mental processes, and the effect on themselves, as Spaniards, of the eighteenth-century revolution in thinking. Consequently any modern

15 Compare note 10 above.

16 Enciso's *Defensa de Valencia* has not previously been analysed in any detail. There is only a very brief discussion of it, for instance, in Jorge Campos, *Teatro y sociedad en España (1780–1820)* (Madrid: Editorial Moneda y Crédito, 1969); see ch. III, 'La Guerra de la Independencia y el teatro', 152–53.

problem—like that of combating Napoleon's methods of mental infiltration—, and any modern form of discussion—like arguments on ways and means of establishing the Junta-image in the mentality of the common people—, would tend to loosen the playwright's ideological engagement with the past and the fixed scheme of rhetoric connected with that past. Later in the nineteenth century it would not matter, in the interests of actuality, whether dramatists were dealing with an ancient or a modern theme. They would have learnt to interpret problems of a Macías or a Don Juan Tenorio through what they themselves, as distinct from their Golden-Age models, could understand as problems. And one of their most vital modern problems would consist in the knowledge, slowly acquired by their rationalist predecessors, that black could no longer be regarded as simply black, or white as simply white; that plays could no longer continue to be peopled with uncomplicated heroes and villains. Any eighteenth- or early nineteenth-century serious drama not reflecting this disturbing discovery, which only universal masters had discovered in the past, was a work devoid of life. Propaganda dramatists might, in absolute terms, produce inartistic creations, but they conspicuously presented their own experiences of actuality, and therefore they were likely to goad their artistic superiors into expressing their understanding of actual problems and so into reconstituting the popular heroic play on less anachronistic lines. In this sense and in these peculiar Spanish circumstances, therefore, propaganda drama had a potential literary value.

INDEX